Animal-Assisted School Counseling

Animal-Assisted School Counseling (AASC) is a hands-on resource that provides invaluable information for school counselors interested in partnering with a therapy animal on campus to help students meet social and emotional goals.

This book presents a wealth of resources for school counselors and school-based mental health practitioners to incorporate animal partners on school campuses with individual students and groups and in classroom and schoolwide settings. Using the American School Counselor Association (ASCA) National Model framework, this book presents AASC interventions that can be implemented as part of the multitiered system of support to address students' mental health needs. The text also meets the important demand for accountability in school counseling by providing resources for assessing the effectiveness of AASC interventions for meeting student and school outcome goals. Addressing such issues as getting school district buy-in, choosing an animal partner, preparing the school for an animal partner, theoretical applications of AASC, and student-affirming AASC services, the book is organized such that each chapter builds upon the next so school counselors understand what steps to take to become an effective AASC team.

Ideal for the school counselor, social worker, or psychologist who may not have specific training in AASC, this book will encourage school mental health practitioners to seek out training programs to become an AASC team.

Elizabeth Kjellstrand Hartwig, PhD, LMFT-S, LPC-S, RPT-S, is a Professor at Texas State University. She is the founder and director of the Texas State University Animal-Assisted Counseling Academy.

Animal-Assisted School Counseling

Edited by Elizabeth Kjellstrand Hartwig

Routledge
Taylor & Francis Group

NEW YORK AND LONDON

Designed cover image: Cover collage by Elizabeth Kjellstrand Hartwig

First published 2024
by Routledge
605 Third Avenue, New York, NY 10158

and by Routledge
4 Park Square, Milton Park, Abingdon, Oxon, OX14 4RN

Routledge is an imprint of the Taylor & Francis Group, an informa business

Library of Congress Cataloguing-in-Publication Data
Names: Hartwig, Elizabeth Kjellstrand, editor.
Title: Animal-assisted school counseling / edited by Elizabeth Kjellstrand Hartwig.
Identifiers: LCCN 2024001232 (print) | LCCN 2024001233 (ebook) | ISBN 9781032491646 (hardback) | ISBN 9781032491639 (paperback) | ISBN 9781003392415 (ebook)
Subjects: LCSH: Student assistance programs. | Students–Mental health. | Children and animals. | Animals–Therapeutic use.
Classification: LCC LB3430.5 .A65 2024 (print) | LCC LB3430.5 (ebook) | DDC 371.1–dc23/eng/20240207
LC record available at https://lccn.loc.gov/2024001232
LC ebook record available at https://lccn.loc.gov/2024001233

ISBN: 978-1-032-49164-6 (hbk)
ISBN: 978-1-032-49163-9 (pbk)
ISBN: 978-1-003-39241-5 (ebk)

DOI: 10.4324/9781003392415

Typeset in Times New Roman
by MPS Limited, Dehradun

To my sister, Katie Kjellstrand Burns,

for making a difference in children's lives as a teacher for 26 years

Contents

List of Contributors   *xiii*
Editor   *xiv*

1 An Introduction to Animal-Assisted School Counseling   **1**
ELIZABETH KJELLSTRAND HARTWIG

  Who Should Read This Book? 1
  Why Should This Book Be Read? 3
  AASC Terminology 4
  AASC Book Overview 4
  AASC Chapter Structure 7
  Bringing It All Together 8

2 Getting School and District Approval for an AASC Program   **10**
NICOLE LOZO

  Literature Review 11
    School Staff Perceptions of AASC 13
    Student Perceptions of AASC 13
  Linkage to ASCA Standards 14
    ASCA Professional Standards and Competencies 14
    ASCA Ethical Standards 15
  School and District Considerations 15
    AASC Training 16
    Policies for Promoting Safety and Preventing Harm 17
    Animal Welfare 18
    Seeking Approval Before Starting AASC Training 18
    Professional Liability Insurance 19
    AASC Informed Consent 19
    Other Considerations 20
  Getting AASC Program Approval 20
  Trauma-Informed and Diversity Considerations 22
  Bringing It All Together 23

3 Choosing an AASC Animal Partner   **26**

MELISSA E. TREVATHAN-MINNIS AND KIMBERLY SCOTT

Literature Review: Canine Partners 27
   Qualities of a Canine Partner in AASC 27
   Canine Welfare in AASC 28
Literature Review: Critter Counselors 29
   Rabbits 31
   Guinea Pigs 33
   Cats 34
Linkage to ASCA Standards 37
AASC Interventions for Primary-Level Schools 37
   Practical Applications for Elementary Counseling 38
AASC Interventions for Secondary-Level Schools 39
   Special Education 40
Trauma-Informed and Diversity Considerations 41
Bringing It All Together 43

4 AASC Competencies   **47**

JORDAN JALEN EVANS

Literature Review 48
AAC Competencies 49
Linkage of ASCA Standards 50
   Knowledge 50
   Skills 51
   Attitudes 51
AASC Competencies 51
Applying AASC Competencies to Primary-Level Schools 56
Applying AASC Competencies to Secondary-Level Schools 58
Trauma-Informed and Diversity Considerations 58
Bringing It All Together 59

5 Training in AASC   **61**

KIM SULLIVAN AND AMY BLASINGAME

Literature Review 62
Promoting Student and Animal Welfare 63
Linkage to ASCA Standards 64
Integrating AASC Competencies 64
Current Training in AASC 66
Recommended AASC Training Protocol 68
   Prerequisite Training – Introduction and Mastery of Basic Skills 68
   AASC Knowledge – New Learning for Human and Animal Team Members 70
   AASC Skills – Transforming Knowledge into Skills 71
   AASC Attitudes – Discovering Your Professional Identity 73
   AASC Supervision – Application in a Real World 74
Applying AASC Training to Primary-Level Schools 75

Applying AASC Training to Secondary-Level Schools 76

Applying AASC Training to Students with Special Needs 77

Trauma-Informed and Diversity Considerations 78

Bringing It All Together 79

6 Preparing the School for an Animal Partner   **82**
KRISTINA KERN

Literature Review 83

Linkage to ASCA Standards 84

Steps to Preparing Schools for an Animal Partner on Campus 85
  AASC Family Survey 85
  Welcome Letter 86
  Frequently Asked Questions Page 86
  Signs 86
  Informed Consent 89
  Space and Supplies for Animal Partner 90
  Acclimating the Animal Partner 90
  Apparel 91
  To Leash or Not to Leash 91
  Introducing the Animal Partner Presentation 92
  Program Schedule 93
  Swag 95

Trauma-Informed and Diversity Considerations 96

Bringing It All Together 96

7 Assessment in AASC   **98**
KRISTA K. SCHULTZE

Literature Review: AASC Assessment Cycle 99

Creating Data-Driven AASC Lesson Plans 102

Linkage to ASCA Standards 105

Assessment in Primary-Level Schools 108
  Individual Session Assessment 108
  Classroom Guidance Intervention 109

Assessment in Secondary-Level Schools 109
  Classroom Guidance Intervention 110
  Small Group Intervention 111

Trauma-Informed and Diversity Considerations 111

Bringing It All Together 113

8 Theoretical Applications of AASC   **115**
HEIDI SCHILLING AND JOY CANNON

Literature Review 116

Cognitive-Behavioral Therapy 116
  Applying CBT to AASC 119

Solution-Focused Therapy 120

Applying SFT to AASC 122
Person-Centered Therapy 123
  Applying PCT to AASC 125
Linkage to ASCA Standards 125
  ASCA Professional Standards and Competencies 126
  ASCA Ethical Standards 126
Applying Theories in Primary-Level Schools 127
Applying Theories in Secondary-Level Schools 128
Trauma-Informed and Diversity Considerations 130
Bringing It All Together 131

9 AASC Classroom and Schoolwide Interventions   **135**
MELISSA WHITSETT AND HEATHER C. TRUPIA

Literature Review 137
Linkage to ASCA Standards 138
  ASCA Professional Standards and Competencies 138
  ASCA Ethical Standards 139
AASC Schoolwide and Classroom Lessons for Primary Schools 139
  Schoolwide Lessons 141
  Classroom Lessons 142
AASC Schoolwide and Classroom Lessons for Secondary Schools 143
  Schoolwide Lessons 144
  Classroom Lessons 145
Trauma-Informed and Diversity Considerations 146
Bringing It All Together 147

10 AASC Individual and Small-Group Interventions   **149**
AMANDA ARRIOLA, KRISTEN TURPIN, AND CRYSTAL REESE

Literature Review 150
Linkage to ASCA Standards 153
  ASCA Professional Standards and Competencies 153
  ASCA Ethical Standards 154
AASC Individual and Group Interventions in Primary-Level Schools 154
AASC Individual and Group Interventions in Secondary-Level Schools 157
Trauma-Informed and Diversity Considerations 158
Bringing It All Together 161

11 Student-Affirming AASC   **163**
JENNIFER H. GREENE-ROOKS AND WANDA MONTEMAYOR

Literature Review 164
Linkage to ASCA Standards 164
Using AASC to Support LGBTQIA+ Students in Schools 166
Student-Affirming AASC in Primary-Level Schools 167
Student-Affirming AASC in Secondary-Level Schools 168
  Considerations for Using Student-Affirming AASC in Individual Counseling 168

Considerations for Using Student-Affirming AASC in Small Groups 169

Trauma-Informed and Diversity Considerations 170

Bringing It All Together 171

12 Future Directions in AASC   **172**

ELIZABETH KJELLSTRAND HARTWIG

AASC Overview 172

Future Directions in Training 173

Future Directions in Research 174

Future Directions in Practice 175

Stories from the Field 175

    Sommer Bowers Hynes and Croix 175

    Lisa Klink and Thor 175

    Breanne Long and Mickey 178

    Cortnie Wise and Irie Grace 179

    Laura Wheeler and Winnie 180

What's Next for Future AASC Teams 181

Appendix A   **183**

AASC Program Request Form 184

AASC Training Verification Form 186

AASC Animal Health Screening Form 188

AASC Presentation Slides 189

AASC Competencies 196

AASC Skills Checklist 200

AASC Family Survey 203

Appendix B   **204**

AASC Lesson Plan 3.1 – Meet the AASC Team 205

AASC Lesson Plan 3.2 – Prickly Coping Strategies 208

AASC Lesson Plan 3.3 – Respect Agreement 211

AASC Lesson Plan 3.4 – Overcoming Obstacles 214

AASC Lesson Plan 4.1 – Waiting with Hank 217

AASC Lesson Plan 4.2 – Compassionate Thinking 220

AASC Lesson Plan 7.1 – Size of Your Problem 223

AASC Lesson Plan 7.2 – Exploring Careers for My Future 225

AASC Lesson Plan 7.3 – Caring for Animals and Our Bodies 228

AASC Lesson Plan 7.4 – Managing My Stress 231

AASC Lesson Plan 8.1 – Emotion Balls 234

AASC Lesson Plan 8.2 – Nondirective Play Session 237

AASC Lesson Plan 8.3 – Animal Obstacle Course Challenge 240

AASC Lesson Plan 8.4 – The Floor is Lava 243

AASC Lesson Plan 9.1 – Weekly Student Greeting 246

AASC Lesson Plan 9.2 – Get Caught Being Pawsitive 249

AASC Lesson Plan 9.3 – Exploring Identity 252

AASC Lesson Plan 9.4 – PAWs Down Against Bullying 256

AASC Lesson Plan 9.5 – Personal Space and Needs 263

AASC Lesson Plan 9.6 – Become a Dog Advocate 267

AASC Lesson Plan 10.1 – Emotions Hide and Seek 270

AASC Lesson Plan 10.2 – Many Feelings of Hank 274

AASC Lesson Plan 10.3 – Paws and Pals 276

AASC Lesson Plan 10.4 – Hula Challange 279

AASC Lesson Plan 10.5 – Mindful Moment 282

AASC Lesson Plan 11.1 – Our Families 285

AASC Lesson Plan 11.2 – Affirming Each Other 288

AASC Lesson Plan 11.3 – Bill of Rights 291

AASC Lesson Plan 11.4 – True Colors Group 294

AASC Lesson Plan 12.1 – Future AASC Team 297

Index   *299*

Contributors

Amanda Arriola, MA, LPC, RPT, School Counselor, New Braunfels Independent School District, New Braunfels, Texas

Amy Blasingame, MEd, NCC, LPC, School Counselor, Coppell Independent School District, Coppell, TX; Child & Adolescent Counselor, Emerald City Therapies, Waxahachie, Texas

Joy Cannon, MA, NCC, LPC, RPT, Counselor, Inkling Therapy, Austin, Texas

Jordan Jalen Evans, PhD, NCC, LPC, Counselor, Texas A&M University-Corpus Christi, Corpus Christi, Texas

Jennifer H. Greene-Rooks, PhD, Associate Professor, Texas State University, San Marcos, Texas

Elizabeth Kjellstrand Hartwig, PhD, LMFT-S, LPC-S, RPT-S, Professor, Texas State University, San Marcos, Texas; Director, Pawsitive Family Counseling, LLC, New Braunfels, Texas

Kristina Kern, MEd, LPC, Former School Counselor, Austin Independent School District, Austin, Texas

Nicole Lozo, MEd, NCC, LPC, RPT, SEP, School Counselor, Austin Independent School District & Therapist, Texas Taproot Counseling, PLLC in Austin, Texas

Wanda Montemayor, MA, LPC-S-AT, ATCS, ATR-BC, RPT-S, School Counselor, Austin Independent School District; Director, Community Arts LLC, Austin Texas

Crystal Reese, MEd, School Counselor, Manor Independent School District, Manor, Texas

Heidi Schilling, PsyD, Psychologist, Alpenglow Counseling, LLC, Austin, Texas

Krista Schultze, MEd, MS, School Counselor, Marion Independent School District, Marion, Texas

Kimberly Scott, MS, NCC, School Counselor, North East Independent School District, San Antonio, Texas

Kim Sullivan MA, NCC, LPC-S, RPT-S, Counselor, Heart and Soul Counseling, Round Rock, Texas; Trainer, Animal-Assisted Counseling Academy, Texas State University, San Marcos, Texas

Melissa Trevathan-Minnis, PhD, Professor, National University and Goddard College; Licensed Psychologist, Austin, Texas

Heather Trupia, MEd, CSC, School Counselor, Hays Consolidated Independent School District, Niederwald, Texas

Kristen Turpin, MEd, LMSW, School Counselor, Manor Independent School District, Manor, Texas

Melissa Whitsett, MA, LPC, School Mental Health Counselor, Liberty Hill Independent School District, Liberty Hill, Texas

Editor

Elizabeth Kjellstrand Hartwig, PhD, LMFT-S, LPC-S, RPT-S, is a Professor in the Professional Counseling Program at Texas State University where she teaches play therapy, animal-assisted counseling, and marriage and family therapy courses. She is the founder and director of the Texas State University Animal-Assisted Counseling Academy. She specializes in strengths-based approaches for working with children and families. Dr. Hartwig is the author of the book *Solution-Focused Play*

Therapy: A Strengths-Based Clinical Approach to Play Therapy and co-author of the book *Canine-Assisted Interventions: A Comprehensive Guide to Credentialing Therapy Dog Teams*. She is a Past President of the Texas Association for Play Therapy and has served on the Association for Play Therapy Board of Directors. Prior to her work at Texas State, she worked for 13 years at Communities In Schools of San Antonio, a school-based dropout prevention organization that empowers children to stay in school and achieve in life. Dr. Hartwig has a private practice in New Braunfels, TX called Pawsitive Family Counseling, LLC, where she works with her canine partner, Holly.

Chapter 1

An Introduction to Animal-Assisted School Counseling

Elizabeth Kjellstrand Hartwig
Texas State University

Welcome to the wonderful world of animal-assisted school counseling (AASC)! AASC is a goal-directed process in which a trained school-based practitioner and their animal partner work together as a team in schools to promote social and emotional wellness in students using the power of human-animal interactions. The inspiration for this book came from the many school-based practitioner-animal teams who have been trained in AASC and made a lasting impact on a multitude of students. Through the editor's teaching, research, and training in the field of animal-assisted counseling (AAC), she has come to understand that AASC teams need specialized knowledge, skills, and experience when working with their animal partner in school settings. Given that these settings are complex environments with hundreds of children, lots of sights, sounds, and smells, and many people not knowing how to interact or communicate effectively with animals, AASC teams need intensive training, supervision, and support to navigate various challenges that can arise.

Current training in animal-assisted interventions is often focused on training for volunteer therapy animal teams that do brief visits in schools with limited contact with students. AASC teams, however, are on campus for longer timeframes and have much more interaction with students, teachers, and staff. AASC practitioners are called to provide comprehensive school counseling programs that address the essential social and emotional needs of diverse students. Thus, AASC teams need a wealth of resources, training, assessment tools, and guidance to develop successful programs. This book seeks to provide a framework for designing and implementing effective AASC programs (Figure 1.1).

Who Should Read This Book?

This book was primarily written for potential and current AASC practitioners as a how-to guide for implementing their programs and advocating for their animal partners. This book can also be used by school and district administrators who are interested in developing an AASC program that can be accessed in one or several schools throughout the district. Furthermore, this text serves as a guide for AASC supervisors and trainers who want to enhance their curricula or training programs. This book can also be used in university settings to promote college-level learning about animals in school settings.

Throughout the world there are animal partners working in schools. For this text the editor chose to use school counseling practices and standards in the United States because the American School Counseling Association (ASCA) has set forth distinct professional, ethical, and student standards that ground AASC services. ASCA's multi-tiered system of support (MTSS) is an evidence-based framework that uses student data to provide tiered interventions to support academic growth, career

DOI: 10.4324/9781003392415-1

Figure 1.1 Adrianne Ortiz and her animal partner, Starlette.

development, and social-emotional learning (Sink, 2016). Goodman-Scott et al. (2020) described the tiered services as:

- Tier 1 – classroom instruction and schoolwide initiatives
- Tier 2 – individual and group counseling, collaboration with school personnel, families, and community stakeholders
- Tier 3 – indirect services for students, such as referrals to outside resources and consultation

AASC practitioners can plan their comprehensive school counseling program by developing lessons that address the various tiers and integrate the animal partner into those services. ASCA also provides position statements for working with diverse students in schools to ensure that all students are affirmed and supported.

While this book uses ASCA as a framework for school counseling programs, there are many different countries that integrate animals in schools. Studies cited throughout the book recognize animals working in schools in countries around the world. Practitioners who live and work outside the United States can look to school counseling guidelines in that country and see how they align with or differ from the ASCA standards noted in this text. Popov and Spasenović (2020) compared aspects of school counseling in 12 countries and found that school counselors were identified as the most multifunctional people in the school system. They found many similarities in the role of the school counselor but different functions depending on the needs of children in various communities.

International school-based practitioners can also look to organizations such as the International School Counselor Association (2021) for resources, professional development, and networking opportunities.

Why Should This Book Be Read?

One clear response to this is that if a practitioner is thinking about partnering with their animal in a school setting, or is already doing so and would like additional guidance, information, and intervention ideas, this book is an excellent resource. School and district administrators may need direction on information they need to address stakeholder concerns and provide approval to potential AASC practitioners. AASC training programs and supervisors can utilize this text to ensure that trainees develop the competencies needed to do AASC work with children in schools.

Another reason to read this book is the variability that currently exists in the AASC field. This text seeks to reduce variability by presenting a clear framework of competencies, training recommendations, assessment practices, theoretical approaches, and tiered interventions that best meet the social and emotional needs of students and uphold the welfare of animals. Integral to this text is the sequencing of chapters that see a potential AASC team traverse the process of becoming credentialed, developing an effective program, and delivering affirming and evidence-informed interventions (Figure 1.2).

Figure 1.2 AASC animal partner, Emma Rose, loves to read books with students in the school library.

Table 1.1 Types of AAIs in Schools

Term	Description	Example
Animal-assisted activities (AAA)	Informal visits that focus on broad wellness goals, such as comfort, social interaction, or stress reduction	A therapy dog team visiting the teacher's lounge for Teacher Appreciation Week
Animal-assisted education (AAE)	Structured interventions that focus on academic goals	A canine-assisted reading program
Animal-assisted counseling (AAC)	Goal-directed interventions that focus on mental health goals	An AAC team meeting with an individual counseling client in a school setting
Animal-assisted school counseling (AASC)	Goal-directed interventions in school settings that focus on social and emotional goals	An AASC team meeting with children in small groups or facilitating a bullying prevention program

AASC Terminology

There is ample variability in terms used in the AASC field. This section will explore terminology related to AASC. First and foremost, human-animal interaction (HAI) is the mutual and dynamic exchange between humans and animals (Griffin et al., 2011). AASC promotes positive HAIs by integrating an animal partner's authentic self, such as their affiliative traits, in a school setting. Animal-assisted intervention (AAI) is a broad term for a host of services provided by human-animal teams. An AAI is defined by the International Association for Human-Animal Interaction Organizations (IAHAIO, 2018) as a "goal oriented and structured intervention that intentionally includes or incorporates animals in health, education and human service for the purpose of therapeutic gains in humans" (p. 5). AAIs in school settings range from volunteer services, such as an animal-assisted reading program, to more targeted and counseling-based services, such as an animal-assisted small group for children who have experienced the death of a loved one. Table 1.1 presents definitions and examples of AAIs in schools.

In addition to AAI terms, this text will refer to the practitioner-animal team as an "AASC team." This human-animal team works together to promote and deliver AASC services. The human part of the team will be referred to as a school counselor or practitioner. These terms are used interchangeably, but it's important to acknowledge that there are other types of school-based practitioners who provide AASC services. These include school social workers, school psychologists, professional counselors, marriage and family therapists, and school-based site coordinators. Depending on their role in the AASC program, these practitioners may also provide AASC services in schools. For the animal part of the AASC team, the term "animal partner" will primarily be used. The terms "therapy dog" and "therapy animal" are commonly used terms; however, they are often used in relation to volunteer teams who don't necessarily provide actual therapy. The term "animal partner" was chosen to emphasize that the animal is partnering with the practitioner in the implementation of AASC services.

AASC Book Overview

This book takes readers on a journey from the foundations of AASC to future directions in AASC. This section will review the progression of chapters and describe how each one builds upon the other, such that practitioners can see each step of the process in implementing an AASC program. This scaffolding strategy helps prepare practitioners to have a successful learning experience by ensuring they have the foundational knowledge and resources for developing an AASC program. The book begins with an introduction to AASC and the basics of getting school and district approval and progresses through the process of choosing an animal partner, AASC training, assessment, theoretical applications, and tiered interventions with students. Throughout the book are AASC forms and resources that provide guidance as practitioners navigate the program approval and implementation process. Readers will also see a myriad of AASC lesson plans that offer creative and educational lessons to employ with an animal partner for schoolwide, classroom, small group, and individual interventions. This section will provide a brief overview of each chapter.

Chapter 1 – An Introduction to AASC

This first chapter is a primer to the dynamic field of AASC. This includes an introduction to human-animal interactions, defining AASC terms, and a rationale for this book. This chapter explores the need for quality training of AASC teams and alignment with the ASCA standards. After this chapter overview, a description of chapter highlights and organization are provided. This chapter concludes by providing guidance on how the book may best be used.

Chapter 2 – Getting School and District Buy-In for an AASC Program

One of the most important steps in developing an AASC program is to get approval and endorsement of the program before pursuing training or bringing an animal partner on campus. Chapter 2 provides guidance on what to consider and address before seeking program approval and how to present information about creating an AASC program to school administration and district personnel. The author will share ideas for addressing common questions related to training, liability, costs, and student and animal welfare. Appendix A includes four forms discussed in this chapter that can be used to secure approval for an AASC program. These include the AASC Program Request Form, AASC Training Verification, AASC Animal Health Screening Form, and sample AASC presentation slides.

Chapter 3 – Choosing an AASC Animal Partner

Chapter 3 explores the variety of animal partners who can work in schools. This chapter reviews the most common types of animal partners who work in schools, which include canines, rabbits, guinea pigs, and cats. For each type of animal, there is a discussion of the beneficial qualities of that species and welfare considerations. The authors provide recommendations for how to choose an AASC partner who is the best fit for the school counselor and different school levels. Appendix B includes four AASC lesson plans developed by these chapter authors that describe lessons that can be facilitated with different animal partner species.

Chapter 4 – AASC Competencies

It's crucial for school counselors to understand what competencies are needed to partner with an animal in a school setting. This chapter reviews current standards in the HAI field and how these standards are adapted for school settings. Chapter 4 presents AASC knowledge, skills, and attitudes competencies that school districts and administrators can use to ensure that AASC teams are sufficiently trained to provide services to children in schools. Appendix A includes a complete list of the AASC Competencies. In Appendix B, practitioners will find two AASC lesson plans that integrate the AASC competencies with different school levels.

Chapter 5 – Training in AASC

AASC training and supervision is an essential step in order to ethically practice AASC in schools. Chapter 5 explores the difference between volunteer and professional therapy animal training. Steps to training include prerequisite work with an animal partner, training in AASC knowledge and skills, and post-training supervision. The authors provide a framework for training that aligns with the AASC competencies and promotes positive HAIs in schools. Appendix A includes an AASC Skills Checklist discussed in this chapter that can be used by practitioners and supervisors to assess the acquisition of essential AASC skills.

Chapter 6 – Preparing the School for an Animal Partner

A lot of preparation goes into bringing an animal partner on campus. From preparing students and staff for the animal partner to identifying a place for the animal to rest, this chapter covers a lot of ground. Chapter 6 offers a host of ideas for introducing the animal partner, welcome letters, frequently asked questions, supplies needed, scheduling, and teaching others how to greet the animal. Additionally, the chapter discusses ways to prepare the school members and school environment for a successful AASC program. Appendix A includes an AASC Survey for Families to identify any questions or concerns that caregivers or students may have about having an animal partner on campus.

Chapter 7 – Assessment in AASC

Using assessment practices in an AASC program provides helpful data about the effectiveness of the program and interventions. As school counselors implement AASC, data collection can be used as a tool for planning, evaluating, and advocating for the AASC program. Assessment should take into consideration the diverse perspectives of students as that may influence the analysis component. Chapter 7 provides guidance on AASC assessment as a tool to advocate for goal-focused and outcome-based services for students. Appendix B includes four lesson plans from this chapter that provide examples of various assessment tools that can be implemented for AASC interventions.

Chapter 8 – Theoretical Applications of AASC

One of the most important concepts school counselors learn in graduate school is how to implement a primary counseling theory. This chapter will describe three counseling theories that have demonstrated efficacy and are frequently used in school settings: cognitive-behavioral therapy, solution-focused therapy, and person-centered therapy. The chapter explores parallels between key theoretical concepts and ASCA standards. Chapter 8 demonstrates the application of these theories with students through AASC interventions at primary and secondary schools. In Appendix B, practitioners will find four lesson plans that apply these different theories to play-based and expressive AASC interventions.

Chapter 9 – AASC Classroom and Schoolwide Interventions

School counselors create and deliver a range of services to meet the social and emotional needs of students. Through a three-tiered approach, school counselors provide direct and indirect services. Chapter 9 presents Tier 1 AASC interventions that support schoolwide and classroom initiatives. The authors share considerations for working with animals in large groups and how to modify services to support animal welfare. Appendix B contains six lesson plans created by the authors that describe AASC interventions for schoolwide and classroom services.

Chapter 10 – AASC Individual and Small Group Interventions

In addition to schoolwide and classroom initiatives, school counselors provide targeted services to address individual student goals. Chapter 10 presents Tier 2 AASC interventions that are delivered in individual and small group settings. The authors provide examples of individual lessons and small group curricula that support the involvement of an animal partner in meeting student goals. In Appendix B, practitioners will find five AASC lesson plans to employ for small group and individual counseling services.

Chapter 11 – Student-Affirming AASC

School counselors are called to create safe and supportive learning environments for children to thrive. This chapter reviews how animal partners can support student-affirming services by emphasizing student competence and embracing diversity, equity, and inclusion. The authors will present AASC practices that celebrate culture, gender identity, sexual orientation, and disabilities. Appendix B includes four student-affirming AASC lesson plans.

Chapter 12 – Future Directions in AASC

As this book comes to a close, this chapter reviews key points from each of the chapters. Chapter 12 presents stories and insights from AASC practitioners who have been in the field (Figure 1.3). Future directions in AASC training, supervision, and research will also be explored.

AASC Chapter Structure

Throughout this book, the chapters maintain a consistent structure so practitioners can know what to expect from each chapter. There are seven main sections in the book: scenario, introduction, literature review, linkage to standards, application to primary schools, application to secondary schools, and trauma-informed and diversity considerations. This section will describe each of these chapter sections. Each chapter begins with a scenario involving Rosalie, a school counselor, and her animal partner, Hank. Over the course of the various chapters, Rosalie and Hank navigate the journey of developing an AASC program. These illustrative scenarios provide context for the chapter and help readers consider why the topics of each chapter provide essential knowledge for partnering with an animal in a school. After the scenario is an introduction to the topic. Authors describe the essence of each topic and define AASC- or school-related words or concepts that are important to understand as the chapter progresses. The next section in the chapter is a literature review. This section presents research that has been conducted on the specific topic and offers evidence-based support for working with animals in schools.

Figure 1.3 Walking Ahsoka with a double-handle leash.

The following section provides linkage to ASCA professional and ethical standards. Effective school counseling programs are able to demonstrate how they meet professional competencies and underscore ethical principles that promote student success. This linkage section shows how each AASC topic is relevant to specific ASCA standards. The next two sections take the information that is already presented and apply it to different age groups of students. Primary and secondary level students have different social and emotional needs, so the authors describe how their topic is applied in developmentally appropriate ways to students. Many of the chapters also provide resources for lesson plans in Appendix B based on information from these two sections. The next section presented in each chapter is on trauma-informed and diversity considerations. It's important for practitioners to consider how diverse students with differing abilities, cultures, and experiences may respond to and interact with animal partners in schools. This section offers recommendations that can help practitioners use trauma-informed approaches and promote diversity in the AASC program. The final section in each chapter brings together the highlights from the chapter. This section reviews the main points and provides a conclusion to the chapter.

Bringing It All Together

This chapter provided an introduction to AASC, the rationale for this book, and a description of AASC-related terms. A review of each chapter was presented with highlights from chapter topics and information about additional resources that can be found in Appendices A and B. This chapter also includes a description of how each chapter is organized and the main sections that are addressed throughout the book. Practitioners can best use this book by exploring each chapter in the order they are presented. This will help readers to build upon foundational knowledge. For any questions that practitioners have along the way, look to additional resources found in the appendices and references provided at the end of each chapter for further reading.

As a professor, researcher, and AASC training director, the editor hopes to ensure that AASC programs are developed and implemented in the best interest of all stakeholders, including those at the heart of the counseling process – the animal partners. Dr. Hartwig offers this book as a framework for informing best practices in AASC program development, training, assessment, and service implementation. Her hope is to inspire school-based practitioners' work in this exciting and rewarding field of AASC.

References

Goodman-Scott, E., Betters-Bubon, J., Olsen, J., & Donohue, P. (2020). *Making MTSS work*. American School Counselor Association.

Griffin, J. A., McCune, S., Maholmes, V., & Hurley, K. (2011). Human-animal interaction research: An introduction to issues and topics. In P. McCardle, S. McCune, J. A. Griffin, & V. Maholmes (Eds.), *How animals affect us: Examining the influence of human-animal interaction on child development and human health* (pp. 3–9). American Psychological Association.

International Association of Human-Animal Interaction Organizations (IAHAIO). (2018). *IAHAIO white paper: The IAHAIO definitions for animal-assisted intervention and guidelines for wellness of animals involved.* http://iahaio.org/wp/wp-content/uploads/2018/04/iahaio_wp_updated-2018-final.pdf

International School Counselor Association. (2021). *Home page.* https://iscainfo.com/

Popov, N., & Spasenović, V. (2020). School counseling: A comparative study in 12 countries. *BCES Conference Books, 18*, 34–41.

Sink, C. A. (2016). Incorporating a multi-tiered system of supports into school counselor preparation. *The Professional School Counselor, 6*(3), 203–219. http://tpcjournal.nbcc.org/wp-content/uploads/2016/09/Pages203-219-Sink.pdf

Getting School and District Approval for an AASC Program

Nicole Lozo

Austin Independent School District & Texas Taproot Counseling, PLLC

Box 2.1

Chapter 2 Scenario

Rosalie is a school counselor and recently brought home a puppy named Hank a year ago. She would like to create an animal-assisted school counseling (AASC) program on her campus and thinks Hank is a great candidate. He has been excelling in his basic obedience training and interacting favorably with other animals. Rosalie has also noticed that he specifically enjoys being around children and adolescents. However, she's not familiar with best practices in this field and how to implement an AASC program. Rosalie begins researching different programs and finds one that provides the necessary training and supervision.

In order to bring Hank into the school setting, Rosalie recognizes that she needs to get approval from her school administrator and district. She's not sure what information she needs to provide or even how to address certain questions and concerns that they may have about having an animal on campus. Rosalie hopes that she can learn how to present information to her school and district personnel about the benefits of an AASC program and address common questions and concerns with regard to having an animal on campus.

School and district buy-in is important to establish, support, and create a comprehensive AASC program. The process of working with school and district stakeholders not only helps gain their approval but also provides an opportunity to teach and educate them on the imperative components of a quality AASC program. In return, this will help provide the best possible programming for students, teachers, staff, and the community.

Therefore, it's important for the school district and their schools to have consistent procedures and policies in place for any animal coming into a school. The district is ultimately held liable for the safety of the students and staff. With this said, not just anyone can bring an animal to school. There are many topics to consider and address by the district and school beforehand, such as:

- Who is allowed to bring an animal on campus (e.g., students, teachers, counselors, caregivers, volunteers, pet therapy organizations)?
- What are the important characteristics of quality preparation and training for an AASC program?
- Why is it important for an AASC team to get approval before starting a training program?
- Are resources available to help fund the training for an AASC team?

DOI: 10.4324/9781003392415-2

Figure 2.1 Emma Rose advocating for school therapy dogs in the district's board room.

- How can the district make sure the AASC team (i.e., school counselor and animal partner) has sufficient training to prevent liability?
- What health standards are expected with an AASC team?
- What policies are in place to protect the safety of the animals and humans on campus?
- How will the school counselor ensure everyone's safety, including the animal partner?
- How will staff and students know the safety measures when working with an animal partner?

These questions will be addressed throughout this chapter (Figure 2.1).

School counselors are ideal candidates for AASC teams because of their unique role in the school. They support the entire student body, as well as collaborate with administration, teachers, staff, students, and families to support student success. School counselors also have a vested interest in student safety, preventing mental health crises, providing mental health interventions, nurturing students' social-emotional learning, and assisting with academic goals. Having an additional counseling partner, such as a trained animal partner, helps school counselors increase their mental health services and support throughout the school.

Literature Review

The need for expanded and targeted school counseling services is essential due to the increasing number of children experiencing varied mental and behavioral health challenges. More than two-thirds of children have reported at least one traumatic event before they were 16 years old (Substance Abuse and Mental Health Services Administration; SAMHSA, 2017). The National Survey of Children's Health reports that children aged 3 to 17 diagnosed with anxiety grew by 29% and those with depression increased by 27% between 2016 and 2020. Children diagnosed with behavioral or conduct problems grew by 21% (Leos et al., 2022; SAMHSA, 2017). For U.S. youth aged 6 to 17, 1 in 6 are experiencing a mental health disorder each year, with suicide as the second leading cause of death among people aged 10 to 34 (Whitney & Peterson, 2019).

According to Hillis et al. (2021), the rates of psychological distress, such as anxiety, depression, and mental health disorders, have increased among children since the COVID-19 pandemic. These authors report that over 140,000 children in the United States experienced the death of a caregiver due to

COVID-19 by June 2021, with children of ethnic and racial minorities accounting for 65% of this number (Hillis et al., 2021). Before the pandemic, 1 in 14 children lost a caregiver before the age of 18 (Burns et al., 2020). The bereavement of a primary caregiver is considered an adverse childhood experience, which can increase the risk for future relational problems and earlier mortality, as well as behavioral health and academic issues (Burns et al., 2020). This increase of student mental health concerns requires more immediate attention and time from the school counselor's overall role and own individual capacity. As a result, more mental health services are critical in schools to adequately address these issues. It is no wonder adding an animal partner could very well enhance and better support the school counselor's capacity and range of essential services.

There are countless benefits to animal-assisted interventions (AAI). The presence of an animal partner can provide connection and rapport between the child and school counselor, release tension, and achieve physiological regulation when touching and petting (Ng, 2019). Playing with the animal partner can help lighten the mood and momentarily reduce the heaviness of a situation. Many studies have demonstrated that the presence of an animal partner can contribute positively to social and educational gains in children (Chandler, 2017). Identifying these students, and helping nurture the human-animal interaction, can provide that much-needed support to help make the academic and social gains they need to thrive (Figure 2.2).

Figure 2.2 Cleo works with a group of students in New Braunfels ISD.

School Staff Perceptions of AASC

Understanding how school staff perceive animal partners on campus may provide a foundation for current beliefs about them in school settings. Two research studies suggest that therapy dogs are well received in a school setting by staff for a multitude of reasons. These studies also note the efficacy of AASC teams and their positive outcomes within the school system (Leos et al., 2022; Zents et al., 2017).

The first qualitative study by Zents et al. (2017) evaluated student and faculty perceptions about having a therapy dog in their school while assessing their perception of a therapy dog's ability to increase students' well-being. The study was completed in four schools, ranging from elementary to the high school level, that had a therapy dog in the building two to three days per week. Most of the faculty were more receptive after receiving psychoeducation on the rationale for a therapy dog. Many responded positively to having a therapy dog and enjoyed its presence as much as the students. In fact, an improvement in the overall school climate was reported in the research survey.

Teachers' reasoning for referring students to spend time with the AASC team included the following: coping with anxiety, low self-esteem, depression, and specific social skills. Teachers viewed the therapy dog as showing unconditional affection to students that helped them open up more to communication, regulate quicker when they were upset, and foster a friendlier environment. One of the most notable pieces of the study was their recollection of student cases that were successful because of increased attendance, reduced meltdowns, and improved communication skills for children with autism and selective mutism.

The second qualitative study by Leos et al. (2022) was with school staff that served preschool and elementary school children. The focus was on the staff's perceptions of the efficacy of AAIs in addressing children's mental health and overall well-being. Many participants shared that the involvement of an animal partner was a less threatening approach when working with children, especially with those who had experienced trauma and struggled to feel safe or open up with an adult. They also felt that social-emotional skills were fostered by a therapy dog's presence in the school. The animal partner could create opportunities for teachers to build on numerous skills, such as relationship-building and self-regulation. The identified students would have a sense of responsibility for the animal's well-being, which would help them practice empathy and eventually apply this directly with their peers.

The majority of school staff reported positive effects on their own feelings and emotions from their personal experiences with animals. Those who were unsure or afraid of dogs had experienced past traumas involving an animal, unfamiliarity, or misinformation about certain breeds of animals, and allergic reactions. School staff even provided ideas on ways to work around allergies or animal fears. This included offering alternate activities without the animal partner, having established protocols and proper planning, and/or possibly partnering with another type of animal that may not cause allergies.

Student Perceptions of AASC

Students perceive therapy dogs, and animals overall, as non-judgmental and unconditionally accepting (Friesen, 2010; Leos et al., 2022; Weinbaum & Kimberly Pruitt, 2021; Zents et al., 2017). Their quiet presence and listening ears don't go unnoticed by their human counterparts. Animals in school may have different roles in providing services, such as teams who provide animal-assisted education services to increase academic skills. Children who struggle with reading often don't get enough practice because they feel uncomfortable reading aloud to their peers (Lane & Zavada, 2013). This isn't the case with therapy dogs. As a result, multiple studies with canine-assisted reading programs have significant gains in reading fluency, self-confidence, and overall motivation to read (Kropp & Shupp, 2017; Lane & Zavada, 2013) (Figure 2.3).

Figure 2.3 First grade boy reading to therapy dog, Emma Rose.

Research on AASC shows that therapy dogs have a positive social-emotional impact on children in counseling (Zents et al., 2017). Students often view therapy dogs as a way to connect, feel seen, heard, and accepted, as well as reduce their overall anxiety (Friesen, 2010; Weinbaum & Kimberly Pruitt, 2021; Zents et al., 2017). They often report that dogs understand them (Jenkins et al., 2014) and provide the compassion that they need (Weinbaum & Kimberly Pruitt, 2021). Oftentimes students see the animal partner as an ally and friend to the school counselor which creates a safer and more secure environment for them to disclose their feelings and talk about difficult issues (Walsh, 2009).

Linkage to ASCA Standards

The American School Counselor Association (ASCA) outlines the School Counselor Professional Standards and Competencies (ASCA, 2019) and Ethical Standards (ASCA, 2022 through specific mindsets and behaviors that school counselors need to meet the high demands of the school counseling profession and Pre-K through 12 students (ASCA, 2019). There are four specific standards that are integral to the development of an AASC program and in seeking district and school approval and support.

ASCA Professional Standards and Competencies

ASCA professional standard B-PA 7 states that school counselors "establish agreement with the principal and other administrators about the school counseling program" (ASCA, 2019, p. 7). A detailed proposal for the advocacy of an animal partner on campus needs to be developed by the school counselor that will clearly outline the desired AASC program. The proposal should be presented in a meeting with the principal and appropriate district personnel. It's important to present all the necessary policies and procedures that the school counselor should have in place beforehand. The school counselor also needs to discuss the training, evaluation, and supervision, including the financial commitment, that are necessary to implement the program.

Through this process it's important to consider the feedback of those stakeholders that will be directly affected by the program, such as teachers, nurses, and custodial staff. Their own understanding of an AASC program and input on having animals on campus will add to the chances of a program's success due to their direct buy-in and feeling included in the process. (Chandler, 2017). It also helps to correct any misunderstandings of the program and animal partner, including any concerns around risks and safety.

Another ASCA professional standard related to planning and assessment, B-PA 2, asserts that school counselors "identify gaps in achievement, attendance, discipline, opportunity, and resources" (ASCA, 2019, p. 6). As part of earning school and district endorsement, it's beneficial to collect and analyze data to identify areas of success or gaps between and among different groups of students (ASCA, 2019). These areas should include achievement, attendance, and discipline. Collaboration with the school administration on these data areas helps to create clear communication in addition to consistency and unity for the students' needs.

It also assists the school counselor in creating goals that can help close gaps with the implementation of an AASC program and its interventions. Goals may include improving socialization and communication skills, increasing student engagement and attendance, improving reading fluency, improving self-esteem, reducing general anxiety, and addressing grief and loss concerns. The AASC team, for example, can assist with social skills by having the student receive and give appropriate attention and acceptance with the animal partner, as well as discussing how it may feel in certain social situations (Chandler, 2017).

ASCA Ethical Standards

Two ethical standards are relevant to procuring school and district support for an AASC program. ASCA ethical standard B.3.e asserts that school counselors "engage in routine, content-applicable professional development to stay up to date on trends and needs of students and other stakeholders, and regularly attend training on current legal and ethical responsibilities" (ASCA, 2022, p. 8). The school counselor has an ethical obligation to safeguard participants in an AASC program and the only way to ensure this is through proper training. The school counselor should have specialized training, assessment, and supervision. Volunteer animal partner organization training is sufficient for volunteer work but doesn't meet competencies for professional AASC work (Hartwig, 2020; Chandler, 2017). Those AASC teams who are insufficiently trained can cause potential harm to students and animals.

Another ethical standard is relevant to getting school and district support. ASCA ethical standard A.5.e asserts that school counselors "act to eliminate and/or reduce the potential for harm to students and stakeholders in any relationships or interactions by using safeguards, such as informed consent, consultation, supervision, and documentation" (ASCA, 2022, p. 3). School counselors reduce the potential for harm to the school and the community by having the proper training and certification in AASC, which includes developing and being evaluated for skills in advocating for the animal's safety and welfare, as well as responding to the animal's stress signals. The school counselor also needs to collaborate with the nurse, caregivers, staff, and teachers about any fears and allergies to the animal.

School and District Considerations

The school and district are in a unique position to review and consider a comprehensive AASC program. The benefits for the students, staff, and community are well-documented, but the risks and liability can cause concern. How will the risks be addressed and prevented? What do the school and district need to look for when considering a proposal for an AASC program? Let's explore the considerations that schools and districts will need to review to build successful AASC programs across the district.

AASC Training

It is highly recommended that school counselors receive specialized training in AASC, are evaluated on their skills, and receive supervision for AASC services. The Animal-Assisted Therapy in Counseling (AATC) Competencies were endorsed by the American Counseling Association in 2016 (Stewart et al., 2016). As a result, this provided a framework for the specialized skills of proficient AAC professionals. Stewart et al. (2016) identified three domains of the AATC competencies: *knowledge, skills, and attitudes*. These domains can be applied to AASC practitioners. For the *knowledge* domain, practitioners should complete formal coursework, have specific comprehension of AASC interventions, and take part in professional practice under the supervision of a qualified AASC supervisor. For the *skills* domain, school counselors should be able to attend to the student and animal simultaneously, respond to animal behavior and responses, know how to address stress signals, provide for the animal's needs, and maintain compliance with registration and care. The *attitudes* domain emphasizes that the school counselor should be able to advocate for the animal's welfare, engage in professional development, have familiarity with the AASC literature, and demonstrate the professional values of AASC.

It's important to note that school counselors registered only through volunteer animal partner organizations do not receive the specialized training in the three AATC competency domains. The training for volunteer organizations often consists of a one-day or an online handler training course. Their training is specific to volunteer settings, such as hospitals and assisted living facilities, that are only allowed for two-hour visits for the day (Pet Partners, 2021).

Hartwig (2020) advised that practitioners who do not receive training, skills practice, and supervision in the field of AAC with their animal partner could cause harm in the following ways: (1) increase the risk of injury to an animal or child by bringing an animal that does not have adequate training or the appropriate temperament, (2) fail to assess student's willingness and interest to work with the animal, (3) ignore animal stress signals, which could lead to increased fear for the animal or injury, (4) increase the risk of animal-transmitted diseases by not requiring hand washing, as well as assessing the health of the student and animal, and (5) not know how to incorporate the animal into the process of goal setting and interventions. With proper training for both the school counselor and animal partner, the risks and harm to others are significantly reduced.

School professionals who engage in AASC should demonstrate knowledge and skills in the following areas (Chandler, 2017): (1) social skill development and obedience training for the animal, (2) therapy or activity skill training for the animal and handler, (3) establishing and maintaining a positive relationship with counseling and school staff, (4) assessing the appropriateness of AASC with a particular student, (5) the basics of zoonoses (transmittable diseases) and risk management, (6) establishing and applying counseling or educational goals and interventions, and (7) assessing therapeutic or educational progress. These skills promote positive human-animal interactions and increase the integrity of AASC programs and services.

Chapters 4 and 5 provide guidance and recommendations for AASC-specific competencies and training. The content covered in an AASC training program should align with the AASC competencies and require specific training hours toward skills practice with the animal. This includes an assessment of the animal and supervision of the school counselor's clinical skills (Hartwig, 2020). Ideally, the program has a practicum for the school counselor to practice working with their animal partner and different types of volunteer students to receive direct supervision and feedback.

Policies for Promoting Safety and Preventing Harm

The district and school should require that an AASC program has procedures and policies in place to reduce the potential for risks and injuries. The school counselor should have the following included in the development of their AASC program:

1 Obtaining informed consent to participate from caregivers and approval from students.
2 Procedures for keeping the environment clean: cleaning and removing any animal fur from the floor or furniture; having available safe, nontoxic cleaning items in case of accidents (e.g., animal vomits indoors; Chandler, 2017); identifying outside areas for animal potty breaks and keeping those areas clean.
3 Procedures for hand washing and sanitizing before and after contact with the animal partner.
4 Procedures for reporting and handling possible injuries to animal and human engaged in AASC.
5 Psychoeducational lessons to all students and staff on animal behavior and stress signals before the animal partner starts.
6 Collaboration with nurses and teachers on animal allergies, phobias, and cultural beliefs to have an alternative plan in place or location when the animal partner is present.
7 Procedures and expectations for how to approach and pet the animal safely and respectfully; when it is an appropriate and inappropriate time; limit setting around hugging and kissing animal partner.
8 Proper grooming and bathing expectations for when the animal partner attends school.
9 Designated space that is quiet and free from human interactions for the animal to rest, have water, and eat. Regular exercise breaks should also be scheduled.
10 Supervision and facilitation of all interactions between animal partner and staff and students.
11 The animal partner is always accompanied by the practitioner and is never left alone with a child.

The practitioner needs to consider the number of days and hours the animal partner is working in a school. A 40-hour work week is generally too much for any animal partner. The school counselor should prioritize the AASC team's hours, breaks, and downtime. When starting out, one suggestion is to increase the animal partner's schedule incrementally from a few hours once a week, to a half day, and then to a full day, depending on the animal partner's level of energy and engagement. The schedule can then begin to increase to two or three days per week slowly. If the animal partner is no longer voluntarily engaging with students or appears to have increased stress, the school counselor should remove the animal from the environment and consider reducing its workload and hours. Prioritizing and advocating for the animal partner helps decrease its stress level and prevents burnout. As a result, the AASC team's interactions are kept enjoyable for everyone involved.

It's also important to consider the safety of those participating in an AASC program, specifically children. Elementary-aged children tend to engage in more face-to-face interactions with dogs that include children wanting to kiss or hug an animal (Horswell & Chahine, 2011). Consequently, this puts them at a higher risk of bite injuries to the face, head, and neck area (Schalamon et al., 2006). It's important for the school counselor to recognize the animal partner's stress signals and supervise all interactions (Bidoli et al., 2022). Chandler (2017) recommends that animal partners should never be left alone with a child or client. Preventive steps to keep children and staff safe are lessons about how to approach, pet, and interact correctly with the animal partner, as well as an understanding of stress signs and behavior signals. (Breslford et al., 2017; Chandler, 2017; Glenk, 2017; Jalongo, 2006).

Also, proper hygiene is a significant factor when working with animals in a school setting that has the potential to introduce and spread diseases, such as zoonoses (Bidoli et al., 2022; Linder et al., 2017).

Much of this risk can be minimized through the pet owner staying up to date on vaccinations and ensuring the animal partner is free of parasites, such as ticks, worms, and fleas (Chandler, 2017; Linder et al., 2017). Staff and students should wash their hands before and after petting the animal partner since germs can spread from direct contact with the animal partner's fur (Chandler, 2017).

Animal Welfare

The animal welfare is in the hands and care of the handler (Ng, 2019), which in the case of AASC is the school counselor. The International Association of Human-Animal Interaction Organization (IAHAIO, 2018, pp. 8–9), provides this welfare guidance:

> Professionals must have an understanding of animal specific boundaries that are normal and respectful to them. Animals participating in AAI (animal-assisted interventions) should never be involved in such ways that their safety and comfort are jeopardized. Examples of such inappropriate activities and therapy exercises include, but are not limited to, recipients (children and adults) jumping or bending over animals, dressing up animals in human clothes or costumes, outfitting animals with uncomfortable accessories (dressing other that clothes such as bandanas, weather related jackets, booties designed specifically for animals), or asking an animal to perform physically challenging or stressful tasks (e.g., crawling, leaning/bending in unnatural positions, pulling heavy gear) or tricks and exercises that require such movements and postures. Recipients should be supervised at all times and in all settings (e.g., schools, therapy sites, nursing homes) to make sure that they are not teasing the animal (e.g., pulling tail/ears, sitting on or crawling under the animal) or otherwise treating the animal inappropriately, thereby putting themselves and the animal at risk.

The school counselor is solely responsible for providing the guidelines and expectations for safe interactions (Ng, 2019). Their skills and training are imperative to prevent, recognize, and manage behavior and stress signals of the animal partner to ensure the well-being of the animal and the human participants (Bidoli et al., 2022; Binfet & Hartwig, 2020; Ng, 2019).

Understanding animal stress signals accurately allows the school counselor to advocate for the animal's needs whether it needs to be reassured, removed from the stressful situation (Gammonley et al., 2003), or given a break (Chandler, 2017). There needs to be an adequate space that is quiet and comfortable for the animal to rest free from human interactions (Bidoli et al., 2022; Ng, 2019; Chandler 2017). Other important factors include regular exercise breaks, access to water, and availability of an outdoor area to urinate and defecate (Ng, 2019).

Seeking Approval Before Starting AASC Training

School counselors need to seek district and school approval before proceeding with any specialized training in an AASC program. It's a significant expense, commitment of time, and dedication to complete the required training, evaluations, and supervision. The school district needs proper planning time to make well-informed decisions, such as the required level of training, when considering a future AASC team. If a school counselor completes the training first, but doesn't seek approval, the district may feel overwhelmed to make a lot of decisions without the necessary planning.

The district should consider covering the cost of an AASC training program for school counselors. This can be very beneficial because an AASC program increases additional mental health services for students who may not initially be inclined to access them but would with the presence of an animal partner. It boosts morale for students and staff, creates humane education, and builds social-emotional skills. An AASC team can help facilitate goal-directed services for students at the Tier I, II, and III levels. Additionally, districts can implement specialized AASC crisis teams that help support the district's response to a school crisis. All the above is beneficial to a district's attention in the media.

Whether the cost is covered partially or in full, the district should consider having clear guidelines and conditions in place if the school counselor were to leave before or after training has been completed. The allotted resources and the school's expectations for an established AASC program need to be protected. One recommendation is asking the school counselor to stay for at least two more years after the training is completed or pay back the expenses that were covered by the district.

Professional Liability Insurance

Preventing liability concerns is an important consideration for school districts. Some public school districts may be covered by sovereign immunity, meaning that the district cannot be sued unless the government waives this immunity or identifies exceptions to this immunity (Gjelten, 2019). In order to protect themselves from potential lawsuits, school counselors should carry their own professional liability insurance that covers AASC. To find the right policy, they can contact different professional liability insurance carriers and ask if they cover animal-assisted services. This is an additional cost to the practitioner but is important to provide an extra layer of legal protection in the case of an accident or injury.

AASC Informed Consent

A school counselor should have procedures in place to obtain informed consent from caregivers for students to participate and assent from students themselves. Risk factors can be mitigated by having an informed consent for participants interacting with the animal partner at school. Two versions are recommended to help cover all the AASC services offered. One for students interacting with the AASC team for school-wide services, such as counselor-led classroom lessons. The other for students who interact more directly with the AASC team in individual and/or small group counseling.

Chandler (2017) recommended that informed consent should include these items:

1 Animal and food allergies
2 Animal fears or phobias
3 Positive and negative experiences with animals
4 Any history of aggression or abuse towards animals
5 Benefits and risks of AASC
6 Rules and procedures about proper handwashing and sanitation before and after petting.
7 Disclosure of zoonoses risk and prevention
8 Animal partner rights
9 Student behavior expectations (including proper ways to greet and pet the animal)
10 Limits to confidentiality

It's also important to provide caregivers and the community with information about the type of animal partner, current training and credentials, and the overall purpose of the AASC program. Examples of informed consent forms should be available in AASC training programs. AASC practitioners should be sufficiently trained in AASC and informed consent procedures before using an AASC informed consent form.

Other Considerations

School counselors should be able to provide a program mission statement and ways the animal partner will be engaged in the school setting. This includes the type of activities and interventions that will take place in the program. Goals and objectives should be identified to assess the progress of the AASC program. The outcome measures and results help provide any adjustments to the program services and goals. The overall benefits that an AASC program provides to the school, staff, student body, and community are important to consider.

Getting AASC Program Approval

School counselors help establish programs that promote student academics, physical health, and mental health (Yordy, 2022). AASC programs are gaining popularity for many reasons, such as the benefits they provide to a variety of student needs and how they enhance the ways school counselors provide interventions and resources (Anderson & Olson, 2006; Chandler, 2017; Zents et al., 2017). There is a variety of literature and data to support the successful outcomes of AASC. With all this valuable data and information, how can school counselors get approval to start an AASC program? This next section will provide ideas and recommendations for school counselors to consider when writing their proposal for an AASC program to get buy-in from their school and district. The AASC Program Request Form found in Appendix A can be used by practitioners to request approval for an AASC program. Practitioners should get this approval before beginning an AASC training program or making plans to have an animal partner on campus (Figure 2.4).

As part of the proposal process, school counselors need to find training programs in AASC that offer in-depth knowledge, practice, assessment, and supervision for the human-animal partnership. According to ASCA's professional competencies and ethical standards, it's the school counselor's responsibility to seek proper training and supervision. As a result, this will help reduce potential harm and increase the safety for all stakeholders participating in an AASC program. Chapter 5 provides an in-depth review of AASC training. After practitioners have received training in AASC, they can provide documentation to administrators that they have the necessary training to provide AASC services. In Appendix A, practitioners will find the AASC Training Verification Form and Animal Health Screening Form. These forms provide confirmation to school administrators and districts that AASC teams have the necessary training and animal health records in place prior to the implementation of an AASC Program.

Figure 2.4 Emma Rose with her school's Principal and Assistant Principal.

Another important step is finding your other half, an animal partner that is the right fit for therapy work. This can be a difficult task. It's common to consider family pets, but it's important to evaluate whether they are an appropriate fit for a school setting. Choosing an animal partner will be covered in further detail in Chapter 3.

School counselors need to clearly outline the program they wish to establish for their school and district *before* proceeding with any training. The AASC training is a substantial investment and a significant commitment of time. This can also be an opportunity for school counselors to take creative approaches to funding, such as applying for grants or engaging in special fundraising opportunities. The school may also have funds that can be allocated for professional development and training purposes.

As school counselors develop their AASC program proposal there are several items they should consider. Chandler (2017) recommends that it includes the following:

- A program mission statement.
- Animal partner's information (if available at the time of the proposal).
- Educational or therapeutic objectives.
- Risks of the program and how they will be prevented and managed.
- Adults who will participate in the AASC program.
- Students who will participate in the AASC program.
- Additional training, evaluations, and supervision needed to safely and effectively implement an AASC program.
- Who will be consulted with or has been consulted with about the development of an AASC program (e.g., school nurse, custodial staff, teachers, administration, and caregivers).
- Intent to develop policies and procedures for the AASC program that include consultation with appropriate school personnel.

Additional items the school counselor should also consider are as follows:

- Staff, teacher, and community perceptions about an animal partner in their school.
- The possible schedule of days and hours of animal partner.
- Designated bathroom and relaxation areas.
- Expected benefits of the program for students and staff.
- Ways the school counselor will advocate for the animal partner.
- How the counselor will provide education to the entire school about proper ways to approach, pet, and recognize the stress signals of the animal partner.
- Ways the school counselor will implement an animal partner into the school programs to help with meeting academic and social-emotional needs.
- How allergies, fears, and phobias will be addressed.
- Handwashing expectations and procedures.
- Cultural considerations.
- Informed consent procedures.
- How the program and plan align with ASCA's professional competencies and ethical standards.
- Funding considerations and requests.
- Desired timeline of implementation.

It's important to remember that many stakeholders are open to the idea of an AASC program but may be more hesitant due to concerns around safety and liability. Therefore, it will be necessary to

Figure 2.5 Jennifer Grant's animal partner, Tucker, learning about AASC.

emphasize the need for additional training and the ways it will greatly minimize the risks of injury. Presenting those details with the school counselor's evidence of intentional planning and consultation can help stakeholders see how the overall risks can be mitigated (Figure 2.5).

The format of the presentation can be done in a variety of ways. Some school counselors have used trifolds, PowerPoints, Canva, videos, and Google Docs/Slides. Handouts to help deliver and emphasize main points are valuable resources as well. It's a great way to divide up all the content that is being presented and leave the stakeholders with the information to review later. Also, sharing links to the presentation for them to review later can be helpful too. Refer to Appendix A for sample AASC Presentation slides. These slides provide guidance on topics to cover that are most relevant to seeking district support for an AASC program.

Last, but not least, it can be beneficial to explain the difference regarding the level of training offered through volunteer and professional therapy animal programs (VonLintel & Bruneau, 2021). Volunteer organizations may already visit schools for a variety of reasons, but their offerings are limited because of their scope in mental health training and limited AASC training. Professional programs have much more intensive training and support practitioners, such as school counselors, working in professional settings.

Trauma-Informed and Diversity Considerations

School counselors are a fundamental part of crisis response interventions in schools. They are called on to provide their expertise and make immediate connections with those in need. Many times, the school counselor is a familiar face to students, so the trust and rapport have already been established. However, this isn't always the case when the crisis response requires more mental health professionals. They often come from the district level or other school campuses to provide the additional support needed.

One way districts can bolster their crisis response services is to create AASC Crisis Teams. These teams would be specifically designated for this purpose across the school district and have the specialized training. The AASC Crisis Team would provide comfort, stress relief, emotional support, and immediate counseling services to those affected by crises and disasters. It's important to note that not all animal partners have the temperament to be crisis-response animals. They must be able to handle stressful and crowded situations that are often chaotic and emotionally charged.

Other considerations include cultural beliefs. In some cultures, such as the Middle East, dogs are seen to be 'unclean' and the interaction between children and dogs is strongly discouraged (Jalongo et al., 2004). Informed consent needs to be addressed before there is any interaction between the child and therapy dog. Conversations with specific families regarding expressed cultural concerns can be addressed by the school counselor to help establish a safe and respectful protocol moving forward.

Bringing It All Together

In summary, the current state of mental health shows the alarming need for more mental health services due to the increasing number of children experiencing a variety of mental and behavioral health challenges. School counselors can find more ways to expand their mental health services to meet these increasing demands. They can create robust AASC programs to help maximize their services. This type of programming requires school and district buy-in prior to implementation.

School counselors and districts were given recommendations for in-depth AASC training, animal welfare advocacy, establishing safety procedures, and the necessary protocols to help prevent injuries and harm during human-animal interactions. Staff and student perceptions were included as key voices to elicit feedback for the development of an AASC program. Districts were given specifics on information to expect from school counselor proposals. School counselors were then given discussion points and the must-have information to include in their proposals and presentations. All these resources can provide a strong foundation to assist the school system in developing a successful AASC program.

References

American School Counselor Association. (2019). *ASCA school counselor professional standards & competencies.* Author. https://www.schoolcounselor.org/getmedia/a8d59c2c-51de-4ec3-a565-a3235f3b93c3/SC-Competencies.pdf

American School Counselor Association. (2022). *ASCA ethical standards for school counselors.* https://www.schoolcounselor.org/getmedia/44f30280-ffe8-4b41-9ad8-f15909c3d164/EthicalStandards.pdf

Anderson, K. L., & Olson, M. R. (2006). The value of a dog in a classroom of children with severe emotional disorders. *Anthrozoös, 19*(1), 35–49. 10.2752/089279306785593919

Bidoli, E. M. Y., Firnkes, A., Bartels, A., Erhard, M. H., & Döring, D. (2022). Dogs working in schools – Safety awareness and animal welfare. *Journal of Veterinary Behavior, 57,* 35–48. 10.1016/j.jveb.2022.09.004

Binfet, J. T., & Hartwig, E. K. (2020). *Canine-assisted interventions: A comprehensive guide to credentialing therapy dog teams.* Routledge. 10.4324/9780429436055

Brelsford, V. L., Meints, K., Gee, N. R., & Pfeffer, K. (2017). Animal-assisted interventions in the classroom – A systematic review. *International Journal of Environmental Research and Public Health 14*(7), 669. 10.3390/ijerph14070669

Burns, M., Griese, B., King, S., & Talmi, A. (2020). Childhood bereavement: Understanding prevalence and related adversity in the United States. *The American Journal of Orthopsychiatry, 90*(4), 391–405. 10.1037/ort0000442

Chandler, C. K. (2017). *Animal assisted therapy in counseling* (3rd ed.). Routledge. 10.4324/9781315673042

Friesen, L. (2010). Exploring animal-assisted programs with children in school and therapeutic contexts. *Early Childhood Education Journal, 37*(4), 261–267. 10.1007/s10643-009-0349-5

Gammonley, J., Howie, A. R., Jackson, B., Kaufman, M., Kirwin, S., Morgan, L., et al. (2003). *AAT applications I: Student guide.* Delta Society.

Gjelten, E. A. (2019, February 5). *When are schools immune from lawsuits?* Lawyers.com. https://www.lawyers.com/legal-info/research/education-law/when-are-schools-immune-from-lawsuits.html

Glenk, L. M. (2017). Current perspectives on therapy dog welfare in animal-assisted interventions. *Animals*, *7*(2), 7. 10.3390/ani7020007

Hartwig, E. K. (2020). Advancing the practice of animal-assisted counseling through measurable standards. *Journal of Creativity in Mental Health*, *16*(4), 482–498. 10.1080/15401383.2020.1792382

Hillis, S. D., Blenkinsop, A., Villaveces, A., Annor, F. B., Liburd, L., Massetti, G. M., Demissie, Z., Mercy, J. A., Nelson, C. A., III, Cluver, L., Flaxman, S., Sherr, L., Donnelly, C. A., Ratmann, O., & Unwin, H. J. T. (2021). COVID-19-associated orphanhood and caregiver death in the United States. *Pediatrics*, *148*(6). 10.1542/peds.2021-053760

Horswell, B. B., & Chahine, C. J. (2011). Dog bites of the face, head, and neck in children. *The West Virginia Medical Journal*, *107*(6), 24–27.

International Association of Human-Animal Interaction Organizations (IAHAIO). (2018). *The IAHAIO definitions of animal assisted intervention and guidelines for wellness of animals involved in AAI.* https://iahaio.org/wp/wp-content/uploads/2018/04/iahaio_wp_updated-2018-final.pdf

Jalongo, M. R. (2006). On behalf of children: When teaching about pets, be certain to address safety issues. *Early Childhood Education Journal*, *33*(5), 289–292. 10.1007/s10643-006-0083-1

Jalongo, M. R., Astorino, T., & Bomboy, N. (2004). Canine visitors: The influence of therapy dogs on young children's learning and well-being in classrooms and hospitals. *Early Childhood Education Journal*, *32*(1), 9–16. 10.1023/B:ECEJ.0000039638.60714.5f

Jenkins, C. D., Laux, J. M., Ritchie, M. H., & Tucker-Gail, K. (2014). Animal-assisted therapy and Rogers' core components among middle school students receiving counseling services: A descriptive study. *Journal of Creativity in Mental Health*, *9*(2), 174–187. 10.1080/15401383.2014.899939

Kropp, J. J., & Shupp, M. M. (2017). Review of the research: Are therapy dogs in classrooms beneficial? *Forum on Public Policy Online*, *2017*(2). https://eric.ed.gov/?id=EJ1173578

Lane, H. B., & Zavada, S. D. W. (2013). When reading gets ruff: Canine-assisted reading programs. *The Reading Teacher*, *67*(2), 87–95. 10.1002/TRTR.1204

Leos, R. A., Cuccaro, P. M., Herbold, J. R., & Hernandez, B. F. (2022). Exploring school staff perceptions relating to animals and their involvement in interventions to support mental health. *International Journal of Environmental Research and Public Health*, *19*(12). 10.3390/ijerph19127126

Linder, D. E., Mueller, M. K., Gibbs, D. M., Siebens, H. C., & Freeman, L. M. (2017). The role of veterinary education in safety policies for animal-assisted therapy and activities in hospitals and nursing homes. *Journal of Veterinary Medical Education*, *44*(2), 229–233. 10.3138/jvme.0116-021

Ng, Z. (2019). Advocacy and rethinking our relationships with animals: Ethical responsibilities and competencies in animal-assisted interventions. In P. Tedeschi & M. Jenkins (Eds.), *Transforming trauma: Resilience and healing through our connections with animals.* Purdue University Press.

Pet Partners. (2021). *Pet Partners handler guide.* Author. https://petpartners.org/wp-content/uploads/2022/01/PetPartners_HandlerGuide_JULY2021.pdf

Schalamon, J., Ainoedhofer, H., Singer, G., Petnehazy, T., Mayr, J., Kiss, K., & Höllwarth, M. E. (2006). Analysis of dog bites in children who are younger than 17 years. *Pediatrics*, *117*(3), e374–e379. 10.1542/peds.2005-1451

Stewart, L. A., Chang, C. Y., Parker, L. K., & Grubbs, N. (2016). *Animal-assisted therapy in counseling competencies.* American Counseling Association, Animal-Assisted Therapy in Mental Health Interest Network. https://www.counseling.org/docs/default-source/competencies/animal-assisted-therapy-competencies-june-2016.pdf?sfvrsn=14.

Substance Abuse and Mental Health Services Administration (SAMHSA). (2017) *Understanding child trauma.* https://www.samhsa.gov/child-trauma/understanding-child-trauma.

VonLintel, J. & Bruneau, L. (2021). Pathways for implementing a school therapy dog program: Steps for success and best practice considerations. *Journal of School Counseling*, *19*(14). https://eric.ed.gov/?id=EJ1301291

Walsh, F. (2009). Human-animal Bonds I: The relational significance of companion animals. *Family Process*, *48*(4), 462–480.

Weinbaum, R. K., & Kimberly Pruitt, M. (2021). Perceptions of junior high students of animal-assisted interventions for school connectedness and school climate. *Journal of School Counseling*, *19*(54), 1–38. https://eric.ed.gov/?id=EJ1328898

Whitney, D. G., & Peterson, M. D. (2019). U. S. national and state-level prevalence of mental health disorders and disparities of mental health care use in children. *JAMA Pediatrics*, *173*(4), 389–391. 10.1001/jamapediatrics.2018.5399

Yordy, M., Tuttle, M., Meyer, J. M., & Kartovicky, L. (2022). What factors influence perceptions about animal-assisted therapy? *Journal of Creativity in Mental Health*, *17*(2), 230–245. 10.1080/15401383.2020.1848681

Zents, C. E., Fisk, A. K., & Lauback, C. W. (2017). Paws for intervention: Perceptions about the use of dogs in schools. *Journal of Creativity in Mental Health*, *12*(1), 82–98. 10.1080/15401383.2016.1189371

Choosing an AASC Animal Partner

Melissa E. Trevathan-Minnis[1] *and Kimberly Scott*[2]

[1]*National University; Goddard College;* [2]*North East Independent School District*

Box 3.1

Chapter 3 Scenario

Rosalie and Hank have been partners in the school for some time now and have progressively developed more comfort in their roles together. Hank loves children and looks forward to going to the school. Rosalie's colleague, Jan, who is a school psychologist, admires Rosalie's work with Hank and shares with Rosalie that she'd like to bring her dog, Bruno, to school with her. Rosalie and Hank have met up with Jan and Bruno previously, and Rosalie knows that Bruno seems to get anxious in crowds and often hides between Jan's legs when children come up to pet him. Jan acknowledges that Bruno prefers being at home with family and that he has not received any behavioral training or assessment, nor has she. Despite this, Jan really wants to have an animal partner and asks Rosalie for her advice on how to become certified. While Rosalie wants to support her colleague, she feels it is important to advocate for Bruno, who does not seem to enjoy the activities that would be required. Furthermore, Rosalie knows that a fearful dog not only suffers, but also poses a possible risk of injury to children.

As an AASC advocate, Rosalie decides to share her concerns with Jan. She points out some tell-tale signs of stress in Bruno's body language when he interacts with children, such as tucking his tail between his legs, hiding behind Jan, tension in his body, and how he often yawns and pants. Jan appreciates Rosalie's observations and begins to reconsider her options for an animal partner. After further research, Jan decides to enroll in a training program and begins to work with a local rabbit rescue to find a rabbit that enjoys regular activity and socialization. Jan now understands that ample training in AASC is a critical first step and that animal partners have to be carefully assessed for their fit in animal-assisted work in schools.

While there are a variety of animal partners who can work in schools, dogs are the most common. Other small animals such as rabbits, guinea pigs, and cats, called critter counselors, can also be animal partners in schools. There are examples of each of these species working well as animal partners, but not every animal will be an appropriate fit and not all animals will want to participate in AASC. As we saw in the case of Jan and Bruno, not all animals enjoy interacting with children or new people. This might create more stress than enjoyment for them, which is not a recipe for successful AASC services. Further, the school environment includes specific challenges that require careful consideration of animal partners in order to keep all parties safe and comfortable, such as loud noises and spontaneous

DOI: 10.4324/9781003392415-3

movements. As a result, choosing an animal partner requires careful thought and planning and it should not be assumed that any animal will be a good fit for the work.

When careful consideration is given to goodness of fit of an animal partner for AASC, as well as to whether or not the animal partner enjoys the work required, there are many benefits to the animal partner, the school counselor, and the school. However, when this step is rushed or an animal partner is thrown into the mix haphazardly, this introduces many potential risks. This chapter will review how to choose an AASC partner who is the best fit for the school counselor, as well as for the school and the animal partner. The authors will also review benefits and challenges about working with different species within the school setting.

Literature Review: Canine Partners

Research consistently finds that the presence of animals has a positive physiological impact on people across age groups, including children and young adults (Friedmann et al., 1983). The most common animal seen in animal-assisted activities and counseling are canines (De Santis et al., 2018). Besides humans, canines are the most domesticated of animals (Masson, 1998) so it may come as little surprise that they demonstrate such strong aptitude for therapeutic work that requires relational connection to humans. In fact, some authors suggest a survival of the friendliest theory regarding early dogs and domestication, whereby friendlier-looking dogs were more tolerated by early humans resulting in more acceptance by humans and increased survivability (Hare & Woods, 2013). As a result, dogs learned to read human body language, make eye contact with humans, and respond in more reciprocal ways which led to a strong symbiotic relationship that provided protection for humans and food for canines, and companionship for both species, which continued to evolve over time.

While dogs such as Sigmund Freud's Jofi have been included in the therapy room since the beginning of conventional therapy, a growing body of research points to the support that animals such as canines offer to the therapeutic process. This inclusion has demonstrated a powerful positive impact on the ability of children to develop attachment and social connection with providers as well as to increase engagement and retention and decrease disruptive behavior (Jones et al., 2019). Winnicott (1971) suggested that some clients are limited in their capacity for play but desperately need the integration of play into therapy. This may be especially true for children who often work through traumas and challenges via play, and dogs can often facilitate play in humans who struggle to engage in play naturally (Zilcha-Mano, 2011).

Dogs also demonstrate a desire to please and follow commands, coupled with intelligence that makes them trainable and cooperative. Dogs can be trained to potty outdoors and walk on a leash, and are often easy to train to ride in cars. Once a positive association is made between the car and outings, canines often enjoy car rides and visiting new places (Figure 3.1).

Qualities of a Canine Partner in AASC

Canines vary greatly in size, temperament, and breed. Bred for various purposes, some breeds may demonstrate more proclivity toward counseling activities, but no breed should be left out as a possible candidate for relational work. While socialization early on has a big impact on the personality and responses and stress tolerance of dogs throughout their life, there are many successful therapy dogs without early training or that have been rehabilitated from shelters and/or rescue groups. In fact, these stories of early challenges and rehabilitation can be powerful models for change for clients and for those who have experienced their own early life challenges. Dogs that enjoy interacting with people,

Figure 3.1 Therapy dog, Neo, is ready to work with a child.

namely children, can tolerate loud noises and quick movements, show tolerance of new people and places, and enjoy play and novelty, demonstrate some of the characteristics of a dog that may do well in AASC. Dogs that are a good fit for AASC need to be able to follow basic cues, ignore other assistance dogs while working, and demonstrate no signs of aggression.

School environments offer some unique conditions that therapy animals must be able to tolerate including large groups, small children, and loud noises such as fire alarms. Some assessments help flesh these characteristics out further such as the Canine Behavioral Assessment and Research Questionnaire (C-BARQ; Hsu & Serpell, 2003), which rates canines along the following categories: stranger-directed aggression, owner-directed aggression, dog-directed aggression/fear, trainability, chasing, stranger-directed fear, nonsocial fear, dog-directed fear, separation-related behavior, touch sensitivity, excitability, attachment/attention-seeking, and energy level. Another assessment tool that can be used to evaluate skills is the Canine Good Citizen test, which evaluates dogs along basic behavioral factors related to manners and training.

Canine Welfare in AASC

While some dogs demonstrate characteristics more aligned with therapeutic work, the goal should be for dogs to enjoy this work versus just tolerating it. A handler should look for signs of enjoyment such as a wagging tail, relaxed mouth and body, and moving toward people. A handler should also watch for

Figure 3.2 Athena receives a treat while she is brushed.

signs of stress such as a tense body, tail between legs, shaking, panting, hiding, growling, and whites of eyes exposed. When signs of stress are exhibited, canine partners should be removed from the situation to decrease their stress, and to remove any risk to the animal or children involved (Figure 3.2).

The canine partner's basic needs for food, water, shade, and a place to relieve themselves on a regular basis are critical to consider. A canine partner should also have regular breaks from work and interaction, and should be provided a safe place to retreat to during breaks or during interactions if they need to disengage from the activity. Dogs should not be forced to interact for longer than is comfortable and still need to be able to engage in typical canine behaviors such as running, playing, and resting. A canine partner should always be able to count on the advocacy of their human partner, which includes preparing and assessing children prior to visits, redirecting or removing children if they are engaging in unkind or rough ways, and helping educate the school as a whole on ways to engage in respectful ways toward the animal partner.

Literature Review: Critter Counselors

While dogs remain the most common therapy animal in schools, often exhibiting a strong instinct for relational connection, a number of other animals have served successfully as therapy partners, many of which are capable of similar relational connection. Even when an animal is not able to interact directly, or perhaps is less relational in nature, there can still be benefits to therapy. For example, studies suggest that children and adults feel that animals empathize with them and that this emotional projection can help to make a child feel validated in their experience (Hiestand et al., 2022). One study even demonstrated therapeutic gains when pediatric oncology patients interacted with animal pen pals via their human companion, which created an opportunity for these children to feel they were sharing the experience with a kindred spirit, which allowed them to process their experience (Gillespie & Neu, 2020).

Another benefit to partnering with critter counselors is that they are smaller, easier to transport or keep in an office, and generally require less skill training than canine partners. Critter counselors can be brought to campus on certain days or be kept in safe habitats on campus with proper and frequent attending, feeding, and care. Critter counselors should be assessed for temperament and behavior. However, they generally don't need to demonstrate a lot of specific skills like canines do, such as sit,

Figure 3.3 Torty, the sulcata tortoise, enjoying a treat.

stay, and come when called. Instead, critter counselors interact with students in ways that the animal chooses. Students learn important skills about approaching and touching the animal in ways that work for the animal rather than how the child may want to interact (Figure 3.3).

Further, partnership with these smaller animals can lead to significant therapeutic gains. The authors of this chapter in fact, have partnered with a sulcata tortoise (MTM) and a hedgehog (KS) in therapeutic spaces and can attest personally to the power of these less traditional therapy partners. However, it is not enough to lean on anecdotal evidence. In the section below we'll explore literature on partnering with critter counselors, specifically rabbits, guinea pigs, and cats. These animals are covered in this chapter in part because of the potential they demonstrate for effective therapeutic partnership within a school setting, but also because more research exists on these species than others.

As we saw with Jan and Bruno, not all pets are appropriate AASC partners in schools. Careful assessment of fit and desire to participate is critical to a successful partnership and this assessment should take place prior to an animal's involvement in any work. Hearn (2022) describes the benefits of partnering with cats through a program called Pets as Therapy (PAT) and shares some guiding questions one might ask to assess their cat's interest such as:

• Does my cat enjoy being stroked, held, approached, and befriended by strangers?
• Does my cat enjoy visiting new places?

Similar questions can and should be applied to any animal or species being considered for inclusion in AASC:

• Will they enjoy the work?
• Will it stress them out?
• What specific activities might lead to enjoyment versus stress?
• Will transportation between locations be tolerated?

These questions should be asked on an ongoing basis to protect the welfare and comfort of any animal involved in AASC.

While there are numerous benefits to including animals in schools for AASC, there are also risks and challenges that are important to consider. First and foremost, when the signs of stress as noted above are not addressed, these factors pose potential risks to the animal or people involved. A child may, at a minimum, interpret the animal's signs of stress as disinterest or rejection, or at worst the child may be bitten or scratched by the animal due to fear or distress. It is the responsibility of the school counselor to stay attuned to the signs of stress their animal partner may be exhibiting in order to avoid these potential risks, which jeopardize all parties involved.

Allergies and sanitation are perhaps the most commonly cited drawbacks that can rule out certain children from participation, as well as sensory challenges a child may experience toward an animal such as sensitivity to smells and sounds (Grové et al., 2021). Some schools will not allow reptiles in schools because of the risk of salmonella (Flom, 2005). While the risk of salmonella is actually quite low, washing hands before and after interacting and not kissing reptiles is an important step toward prevention.

Fear of the animal partner, or animals in general, can also pose a challenge. Or the opposite, where there is a desire to be close to the animal in a way that might overwhelm or stress the animal partner can also pose a challenge. In both cases some authors have noted this can serve as a teachable moment and a workable goal within therapy (Flynn et al., 2020) whereby the child can learn to develop mutual trust with the animal and school counselor, learn to establish boundaries that are appropriate for everyone involved and transferable to other settings and relationships, and regulate their bodies in a way that keeps the animal safe (Flom, 2005). This self-regulation is important with all animals, but perhaps most especially with critter counselors such as hamsters, guinea pigs, and hedgehogs, to name a few, that are most vulnerable to injury from rambunctious or quick movements or to being squeezed or shaken. Assessment and screening of any child that is allowed to interact directly or hold a critter counselor becomes a critical step to preventing injury to an animal partner, as well as never leaving a child unattended with the animal partner.

Each species exhibits unique signs of stress which are critical to understand and pay attention to throughout the process of assessing goodness of fit as well as after an animal is integrated into one's care. Understanding the stress signals of one species does very little toward one's understanding of the stress signals of another. While the domestication of animals tends to result in more physiological tolerance of stressful situations, each individual animal exhibits unique signs of stress and engagement and some react more intensely to stressful situations than others (Karaer et al., 2023). Individual personalities and baseline stress tolerance are critical to understand in an animal partner. With each critter counselor species listed below, we'll also explore topics of animal welfare, animal communication, and some ways to ameliorate stress when partnering with these animals in schools.

Rabbits

A number of studies demonstrate positive outcomes for clients working with rabbits. Rabbits are friendly, intelligent, and playful small animals (Loukaki & Koukoutsakis, 2014) who often initiate interaction with humans (Molnár et al., 2019), making them strong candidates for therapeutic work. Rabbit-keeping in general has been found to increase both empathy as well as a sense of responsibility (Sipos & Bodnar, 2020). One study found that students who kept rabbits spent less time playing computer games and on social media sites (Sipos & Bodnar, 2020), a result that the authors suggest could lead to improved communication and socialization.

Studies also demonstrate the ability of rabbits to decrease anxiety in students, thereby increasing the potential education efficiency of teachers with these same students (Suba-Bokodi et al., 2022).

When considering the role of rabbits on stress and anxiety, one study assessed the impact of six-week interventions on first-grade students. Results suggested a significant decrease in symptoms of anxiety and this finding was most pronounced for students with the highest levels of anxiety (Molnár et al., 2019).

Qualities of a Rabbit Partner for AASC

Foote (2020) points out that since rabbits are prey animals, they are quite susceptible to fear and stress, and that poor health and welfare standards, lack of companionship, poor handling techniques, and disruptions in routine are often catalysts for stress. As a result, some rabbits are not good candidates for partnering in AASC work if they exhibit low stress tolerance.

Conversely, rabbits that move toward human contact, enjoy physical touch, and are less deterred by loud noises and sudden movements are better candidates for working in schools. These traits are more likely in rabbits that enjoy regular contact and attention from caretakers, and positive socialization from a young age helps increase their tolerance for handling and petting (Suba-Bokodi et al., 2022). Since rabbits enjoy companionship and need consistent care, it is not ideal to leave a rabbit AASC partner on their own at school after hours or over the weekends without companionship and supervision. Thus, a rabbit that can tolerate travel between home and school is ideal (Figure 3.4).

Figure 3.4 Jalen Evans works with her rabbit partner, Loyal, using a hoop intervention.

Rabbit Welfare in AASC

Reducing rabbit stress in AASC can promote rabbit health and welfare. Lu and colleagues (2013) found that psychological stress in animals is associated with a systemic inflammatory response, and that in rabbits, even mild chronic psychological stress can induce vascular inflammation and cardiovascular disease. Mild chronic stress in rabbits also led to depression-like behaviors, decreased body weight gain and hypertension (p. 87).

Rabbits rarely communicate stress audibly, save for occasional grunts or teeth grinding or a fear scream in extreme cases, which makes it even more important to pay attention to the many signs in the body and posture of a rabbit that indicate stress or fear. These can include: crouching close to the ground and keeping head low and muscles tensed (Royal Society for the Prevention of Cruelty to Animals (RSPCA), 2023a), holding ears wide apart or laying ears flat against back, eyes opened wide with pupil dilation, and increased breathing with short, shallow breaths. A rabbit may thump their back legs to communicate stress, and in some cases, may bite as well. More subtle signs of stress can include hiding, changing activities, moving away from people, loss of appetite, and over-grooming (Foote, 2020).

Historically, it was thought that rabbits liked to be picked up and cuddled. Research suggests this type of handling is actually quite stressful since it emulates an attack from a predator and that keeping rabbits at ground level and allowing them to approach new people is much less stressful (Bradbury, 2016). Rabbits that have been socialized from a young age and engage in regular socialization from their caretaker respond more positively to being handled but one study found that stress increased after multiple interactions and recommended no more than two 20-minute sessions to avoid overarousal and stress (Suba-Bokodi et al., 2022). Finally, rabbits as a species, enjoy companionship and develop complex familial and social orders. Living in isolation as a pet or even as a therapy partner, can lead to depression in rabbits (Foote, 2020).

Guinea Pigs

Guinea pigs can be a great choice as an AASC partner due to their social and interactive nature. A handful of studies have found a positive impact on students when partnering with guinea pigs in schools. While one study found an overall increase in social functioning in students, an increase in social skills, and a decrease in behavioral challenges (O'Haire et al., 2013), another study found that animal-assisted activities with guinea pigs led to an increased sense of school belonging and emotional well-being (Miller, 2018) (Figure 3.5).

Qualities of a Guinea Pig Partner for AASC

Guinea pigs are herd animals, preferring to have company from other guinea pigs as well as humans (Sachser & Lick, 1991). Guinea pigs that are affectionate and seek out human contact and attention are good candidates for AASC, and these traits increase in likelihood when they are socialized regularly. It is important to note that some male guinea pigs will fight when housed together so it is important to assess their behavior and not force a cohabitation that will result in harm. Increasing the size of the space can help keep the peace among the group, and this can be a good option to avoid pairing male and female guinea pigs in order to avoid unwanted litters.

Figure 3.5 School counselor, Krista Schultze, partners with her guinea pig, Snickers, to help children succeed in school.

Guinea Pig Welfare in AASC

Guinea pigs are also known social creatures. They are at their happiest when with others of their species and developing stable, peaceful social structures (Sachser & Lick, 1991). Like other animals, stress can impact a guinea pig's health and has been connected to changes in cortisol levels (Zipser et al., 2013) and decreased body weight (Sachser & Lick, 1991), among other things.

Signs of stress in a guinea pig might include: hiding, chewing, turning in circles, overgrooming, sitting in a hunched position, changes in food and water intake, and reluctance to move (RSPCA, 2023b). Some studies suggest that handling and holding a guinea pig have not been found to increase stress levels but that breaks and the ability to retreat to a protected enclosure enhance a feeling of safety in guinea pigs as well as other animals that interface with the public (Anderson et al., 2002; Sachser & Lick, 1991).

Cats

With any animal, temperament, personality, and desire for activity with strangers is key. Though not yet a typical practice, animal-assisted interventions with felines are gaining in popularity. It is important to note that cats come with some special considerations which are described below. Allergies to cats are somewhat common and may preclude some students from engaging with the therapy cat. Despite these challenges, interventions with cats can produce similar benefits to children such as increased communication and decreased stress and anxiety, and cats also offer a good option for children who cannot work with large animals or are afraid of dogs (Tomaszewska, et al., 2017). Tomaszewska et al. (2017) additionally report that working with therapy cats "provides children with vital life skills, helps them overcome their fears, gives motivation, and builds a sense of self" (p. 286). Cats are useful partners in multiple settings. For instance, Purina and Pet Partners developed a partnership to provide support to senior citizens in nursing homes during the pandemic and demonstrated that even just seeing a cat virtually can lead to improved mood when an in-person visit is not possible or safe (PR Newswire, 2022).

Qualities of a Cat Partner for AASC

It is important to note that it takes a special cat with a particular temperament to want to engage in the work of AASC. Many cats prefer the quiet and relative ease and routine of staying at home and interacting with others on their terms. Some cats demonstrate an exceptional desire to interact with humans and have regular physical contact. Some breeds noted in the literature to have more of a proclivity for this work are Ragdolls, Maine Coons, and American Shorthairs (Tomaszewska, et al., 2017). A cat chosen for AASC work should enjoy human contact such as being stroked and cuddled (Kapustka & Budzyńska, 2020). Further, a cat compatible with AASC must be willing to adapt to their litter box in a new place, for example, in a school office versus at their home. Not all cats are adaptable in this way and some are not tolerant, or become distressed by travel between home and office. Using a backpack or stroller for transport to and from school as well as between locations in the school is important to prevent a cat from unsafely fleeing. The ease of use and preference of a backpack or stroller for a cat is dependent upon the cat (Figure 3.6).

Cat Welfare in AASC

Creating an environment in which cats have minimal stress is essential. Having an office where cats primarily stay during the school day can help to mitigate stress in cat partners. School counselors should consider how to set up an office that provides the cat ample opportunities to play, explore, use the litter box, and take a nap. It is also important to make sure the cat cannot escape through open doors and has a safe space to explore and relax freely but with supervision. Cats should not be

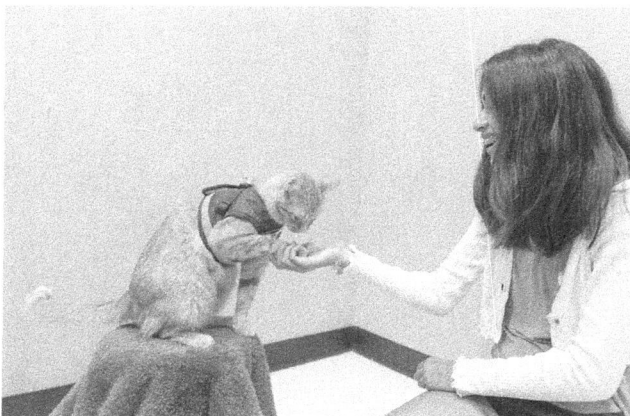

Figure 3.6 Zoe Dou learns how to greet cat partner, Texas Red.

allowed to roam the school halls on their own, as this puts the cat in danger of getting lost, distracting students and teachers, and exposing students with allergies to a potential allergic reaction. AASC teams with cats should have a primary office where they can offer services to students.

Cats exhibit a number of signs of stress including tense posture, shaking, quick and shallow breathing, dilated pupils, flattened ears, tail kept close to body, plaintive vocalization, fleeing, hiding, reduced exploration and activity, reduced eating and drinking, less socialization, reduced facial marking, uncharacteristic soiling, overgrooming, and aggression (Zhang et al., 2022). Stress in felines can lead to a number of behavioral and health changes such as loss of appetite and weight and increased susceptibility to disease (Tanaka et al., 2012). Like other animals, allowing felines to exhibit instinctual behaviors such as scratching to release their scent in their environment, helps to reduce stress (Ellis et al., 2021). Additionally, creating enriched environments and places to retreat to such as a hiding box or high shelf have also been found to reduce stress signals in cats (Ellis et al., 2021; Foreman-Worsley & Farnworth, 2019) (Figure 3.7).

Relational connection and proximity to a primary caretaker who can serve as a secure base, is thought to serve as a protective factor for cats even when in novel environments that might otherwise lead to a heightened stress response (Vitale et al., 2019). Thus, if a cat counselor enjoys a positive relationship with their human partner, this may in part mitigate any stress associated with the work so long as accommodations are made for the comfort and welfare of the feline counselor.

Figure 3.7 Claudia Ikonomopoulos works with youth with her cat partners, Nala and Simba.

Linkage to ASCA Standards

The American School Counseling Association (ASCA) charges school counselors to prepare students with mindsets and behaviors that will enable them to become lifelong learners, interpersonal skills that show self-respect and respect to others, and college and career readiness (Flom, 2005). The ASCA Ethical Standards for Counselors (2022) outlines specific mindsets and behaviors that school counselors should target to meet the needs of children in schools. Two standards are relevant to choosing an AASC animal partner.

ASCA ethical standard B.3.b asserts that school counselors "stay up to date on current research and to maintain professional competence in current school counseling issues and topics." (ASCA, 2022, p. 8). Developing competence in animal-assisted interventions (AAIs) requires training, skills practice, clinical experience, and supervision (Hartwig, 2020). School counselors wanting to partner with an animal in their school should know current literature on AASC and once trained in AASC, attend continuing education to maintain their competence in this specialization area.

ASCA ethical standard B.3.e asserts that school counselors "engage in routine, content-applicable professional development to stay up to date on trends and needs of students and other stakeholders, and regularly attend training on current legal and ethical responsibilities" (ASCA, 2022, p. 8). The school counselor has an ethical obligation to safeguard and advocate for children, staff, and animals in school settings. Given the varied qualities and needs of animal partners discussed in this chapter, it is imperative for school counselors to seek out specialized training, assessment, and supervision in AASC. Practitioners should be properly trained on the care and keeping of animal partners, animal communication, AASC treatment planning, and how to facilitate interventions with their animal partners. School counselors can find programs that provide training specifically for AASC.

AASC Interventions for Primary-Level Schools

The biophilia theory in the human-animal interaction field suggests that humans are naturally attracted to animals and form an innate connection to animals (Wilson, 1984). Because of the inherent connection between children and animals, the incorporation of animals into a classroom seems to be a natural way to also enhance the environment. Schools utilize programs that bring animals to school for reading and incorporate live animals in science lessons, which has been shown to increase motivation and attention (Knowles et al., 2021).

School counselors have a wide reach with their caseloads as well as cover a range of topics, including intrapersonal challenges, interpersonal conflict, coping skills, social/emotional distress, developmental issues, bullying, neglect/abuse, substance abuse, grief/loss, transitional family issues, witnessing traumatic events, and psychological conditions and distress (Jalongo & Guth, 2022). An animal partner is seen by students as non-judgmental and provides unconditional acceptance of the student, regardless of the distress that the student might be experiencing. Students are able to feel valued by the animal and this connection can transfer to caregiving skills outside of the counseling office (Flynn et al., 2020) (Figure 3.8).

O'Haire et al. (2013) found that having a guinea pig in the classroom was associated with increased social functioning compared to the control group, more socially skilled behaviors, improved psychological well-being, and fewer problem behaviors. Children often feel a sense of belonging, reduced anxiety, improved mood, reduced problem behaviors, and a strengthening in the psycho-therapeutic process when interacting with animals (Flom, 2005; Chandler, 2017). During therapy

Figure 3.8 Critter counselors should be handled carefully.

partnering with felines and children in schools, children demonstrated a reduction in stress and anxiety, improved communication with their peers, and were able to build a sense of self through discussing differences between felines, and relating these unique aspects back to themselves (Tomaszewska et al., 2017). With increasing demands in education and community stressors, children may be more willing to go to animals for comfort, companionship, and understanding (Suba-Bokodi et al., 2022). This can in turn bridge the gap between students and adults in the school setting.

From her own experience with working with a pocket pet in the school counseling program, Flom (2005) found that students learned about feelings, self-control, responsibility, and grief as a complementary part of the school counseling program. Students were able to identify with the animal and offer solutions for concerns/issues that might be happening for the animal partner, indirectly helping themselves through similar issues by developing strategies for handling challenging emotions. Exploring what the animal is feeling not only can create a deeper empathy for the animal, but also help the student understand more about their own responses.

Practical Applications for Elementary Counseling

To fully integrate AASC into the school setting requires forethought, planning, preparation, advocacy, and careful execution. Elementary students, especially younger and first year elementary students, are setting out on their school experience by learning social skills and general school expectations. Students are still developing impulse control, emotional regulation, and developing listening and sustained attention. There are several considerations for including animals in AASC with primary-level and younger children:

- Assess the compatibility between the student and the animal (Jalongo & Guth, 2022)
- Consider if the animal will be more disruptive than therapeutic (Jalongo & Guth, 2022)
- Explore the fit of the AASC intervention with the animal's personality/behaviors
- Acknowledge allergies and sensory issues related to the animal (e.g., smell, touch, sound (Flynn et al., 2020))
- Be prepared to respond to animal stress, aggression, or illness (Knowles et al., 2021)
- Make a plan for sanitation, including approved areas that the animal can use
- Be aware of and have a plan when the animal is experiencing stress

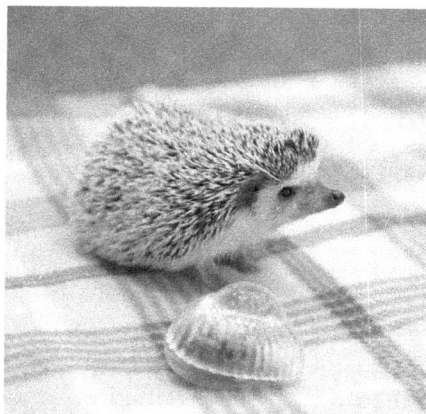

Figure 3.9 Mr. Pricklepants is a hedgehog partner who has worked in an elementary school for several years.

- Discuss expectations before the animal is present, including modeling and visuals for students
- Know how to facilitate therapeutic interventions with your animal partner as part of a goal-directed process

AASC interventions use the unique qualities of the animal to tailor interventions to meet the needs of the students. Working with animals can be unpredictable at times but can provide lessons on expected and unexpected behavior as well as what happens when there might be a challenging behavior.

The AASC team can provide services that meet the students' mental health needs in a unique way. AASC also gives the counselor a method to be more creative in meeting student needs as well as determining interventions that work with their animal partner's attributes. With support from school stakeholders and with proper training, the AASC team can provide creative and innovative interventions to the students.

Appendix B includes examples of two lesson plans of AASC interventions for primary students. AASC Lesson Plan 3.1 is called Meet the Counselor and Counseling Partner. This lesson involves introducing students to the role of the counselor, the counseling partner, and identifying positive qualities. AASC Lesson Plan 3.2 is called Prickly Coping Strategies. This intervention shows how to describe coping strategies with the help of a hedgehog partner for when children feel unsafe. Review the description of these lesson plans in the appendix (Figure 3.9).

AASC Interventions for Secondary-Level Schools

At the middle school and high school levels, AASC can be an advantageous intervention due to the animal partner providing unconditional positive regard to students (Flynn et al., 2020). The animals can reduce anxiety and provide physical comfort for students. Physical comfort is developmentally appropriate for younger students, but older students might feel uncomfortable seeking that comfort. Seeking physical touch/comfort from an animal has the potential to be viewed by those at the secondary level to be more acceptable, increasing their engagement.

One of the benefits found with working with animals at the secondary level is the transfer of skills. The animals provide a way for students to practice appropriate boundaries with positive engagement without the fear of confrontation and judgment (Flynn et al., 2020). By practicing the skills with the animals, students are able to transfer the skills to peer-based responses.

In a study by Grové et al. (2021) through the involvement of therapy dogs, students felt more of a sense of belonging at school and transitions from one grade level to the next improved. Sipos and Bodnar (2020) found that rabbits had a positive effect on the personality development of high school students. The students were able to learn empathy and responsibility through the opportunity to care for the rabbits.

At the secondary level, the considerations for the animal's welfare might be different than those at the primary level. The animal's stress level could be impacted by common daily occurrences such as the notifications between class periods (e.g., school bell or other noises), the number of students in the hallway transitioning between classes, and multiple buildings. The school counselor will need to make sure that the animal is able to take breaks and have scheduled down time throughout the day (Grové et al., 2021).

School counselors at the secondary level should consider the following when bringing an animal to school in secondary settings:

- Plan for breaks throughout the day
- Identify students and staff who may have allergies to the animals or their food (peanut butter treats) and negative past experiences with the selected animal (Knowles et al., 2021)
- Have a plan to obtain consent for students who will be interacting with the animal
- Have a plan for unexpected events, such as a fire drill, crisis, and school evacuation
- Review expectations for working with the animal
- Be aware of stress signs in the animal, and have a plan for noises and disturbances such as loud noises and large crowds of people
- Consider cultural differences that make interacting with the animal less desirable

Working with an animal partner in a secondary setting can provide a welcome outlet to students as a coping strategy and calming presence (Knowles et al., 2021). By adhering to the above considerations, the school counselor and animal partner will be able to more effectively and sustainably incorporate into the school. With adequate planning and training, an engaging AASC program can be developed that meets the needs of the students, and takes into account the safety and well-being of the animal partner (Figure 3.10).

The authors developed two lesson plans that can be used in secondary schools with critter counselors. AASC Lesson Plan 3.3 is called Respect Agreement. This lesson plan guides students through the creation of a Respect Agreement that helps students learn how they would like to have respect shown to them, how they show respect to the counselor, how the counselor would like to have respect shown by students, and how they will show respect to their community. AASC Lesson Plan 3.4 is called Overcoming Obstacles. This intervention involves creating an obstacle for the critter counselor. Students will discuss and explore what obstacles they face and how they navigate them. Both of these lesson plans can be found in Appendix B.

Special Education

In a study with special education students, Knowles et al. (2021) found that emotionally and behaviorally challenged students who interacted with an animal had reduced episodes of emotional crisis. The interactions with the animal helped with decreasing frustrations and promoting social

Figure 3.10 Gently stroking the shell growth patterns on a tortoise can serve as a grounding activity for clients.

opportunities. Knowles et al. (2021) noted that instructional time during class can be interrupted due to a behavioral crisis, which can be mitigated with the therapy animal. In this study, outcomes revealed that the therapy animal increased the motivation of students academically with reading.

When working with special education students, the counselor needs to be aware of their animal partner's well-being, especially their stress signs. When in a behavioral crisis, the student may cause the animal to experience stress. A plan for the counseling partner's safety should be made prior to working with students. Prior to introducing the animal to the students, the expectations of the students should be discussed without the animal present. When working with an animal, appropriate interactions should be discussed as well as providing visuals. The visuals should include modeling the behavior with a stuffed animal that looks like the counseling partner and posting the expectations where the students can see what is expected. The students will also need to know what will happen if the expectations are not being met. For example, if a student has a behavioral challenge in the classroom which makes it not safe for the animal partner, the animal will be removed. Practice and planning is necessary for the safety of the students and the animal partner.

Trauma-Informed and Diversity Considerations

AAIs with children who have suffered abuse or boundary violations of any kind can benefit tremendously in many cases from learning ways to enact healthy boundaries, safe touch, and consent (Faa-Thompson, 2012). AASC creates a useful way to practice these skills in a safe space with guidance from a proficient school counselor who is there to protect both the child and the animal. While relational violations are often the cause of trauma, relational therapy is often a pathway to healing. In fact, Ludy-Dobson and Perry (2010) refer to relational connection as the biological gift that heals. Parish-Plass (2021) discusses the positive impact that AAIs can have precisely because of the relational power of this work. Research supports the notion that AAIs can reduce PTSD and depressive symptoms in children and adults with a diagnosis of PTSD (Hediger et al., 2021).

Animals can also serve to lubricate the relational connection with the school counselor. Parish-Plass (2021) shares that when children observe a helper caring for and respecting an animal, they can begin to conceptualize the adult helper as someone who may provide this same care and respect to them. This can offer a corrective emotional experience whereby the child not only can begin to develop a healthy relationship with a safe adult, but also with a safe animal, and with themselves. Animals can create a strong physiological response in humans which can increase the capacity for relational connection and presence. Specifically, the presence of an animal can result in a decrease of cortisol and stress response, and an increase in oxytocin which can lead to increased socialization (Tedeschi, 2020; Knowles et al., 2021).

Children who exhibit fearfulness toward animals may especially benefit from working with critter counselors, given their quiet disposition and less-assuming physical presence. Interacting in this way may create an opening for AASC that a larger animal, such as a dog, may not allow. Additionally, critter counselors create an opportunity for teachable moments regarding safe handling and engagement. While these are critical skills to teach when engaging with any animal, this is perhaps doubly true given the vulnerability of small animals. Teaching children how to safely touch and interact with a small animal allows them space to practice using their own bodies in a safe and respectful manner, and opens the door to discuss ways in which they deserve that same care and consideration of boundaries.

Small animals also create direct feedback regarding the behaviors of children. Prey animals respond to quick, rough, and loud movement and their fear is often easy to recognize in their physical movements, postures, or behaviors. While some of these signs of stress and distress are immediately evident such as shaking or hiding, some signs are less immediately obvious and can be taught such as body posture, heart rate, and gaze. These fear responses not only serve as a learning opportunity about the animal, but also create a nice opening to discuss ways in which the child may experience fear and stress, and ways they may express feelings around difficult or scary experiences.

It is also important to consider that children in schools arrive with a wide variety of life experiences and cultural backgrounds that can impact their perceptions of, and gravity toward or against animals. Invariably, various cultural groups view animals differently, with some placing high value and devotion onto animals and some placing low value and regard onto animals. With this in mind, it is not unusual for a child to not want to interact with an animal or to exhibit a fear response. The clinical value of working to decrease this fear response will vary from case to case, but small animals and critter counselors may offer a safer entry into AASC. This is also true for children with physical limitations which might make interacting with a larger animal more challenging. On the other hand, it is important to assess any risk a child might pose to a small animal with regards to holding or petting them gently and using calm and slow movements around them. One way to asses this risk might be to allow them to practice petting a stuffed animal first to assess their ability to be gentle and control their movements and follow the directions given first, before letting them interact directly with an animal.

Some children may come from backgrounds where animals are viewed as objects. This can be true of all animals, but dogs can sometimes be associated with danger and small animals sometimes associated with being dirty or diseased. If a child is willing, working with animals in a safe space can result in undoing inaccurate or harmful messages or associations they have developed around animals, as well as provide an opportunity to explore these themes and messages as they may relate to other clinical content. Respect and careful handling that considers the animal's comfort and boundaries, alongside the child's, become especially important here. This serves to increase empathy toward animals and others (Thomas & Matusitz, 2016) and increases the likelihood of a safe interaction for everyone involved (Figure 3.11).

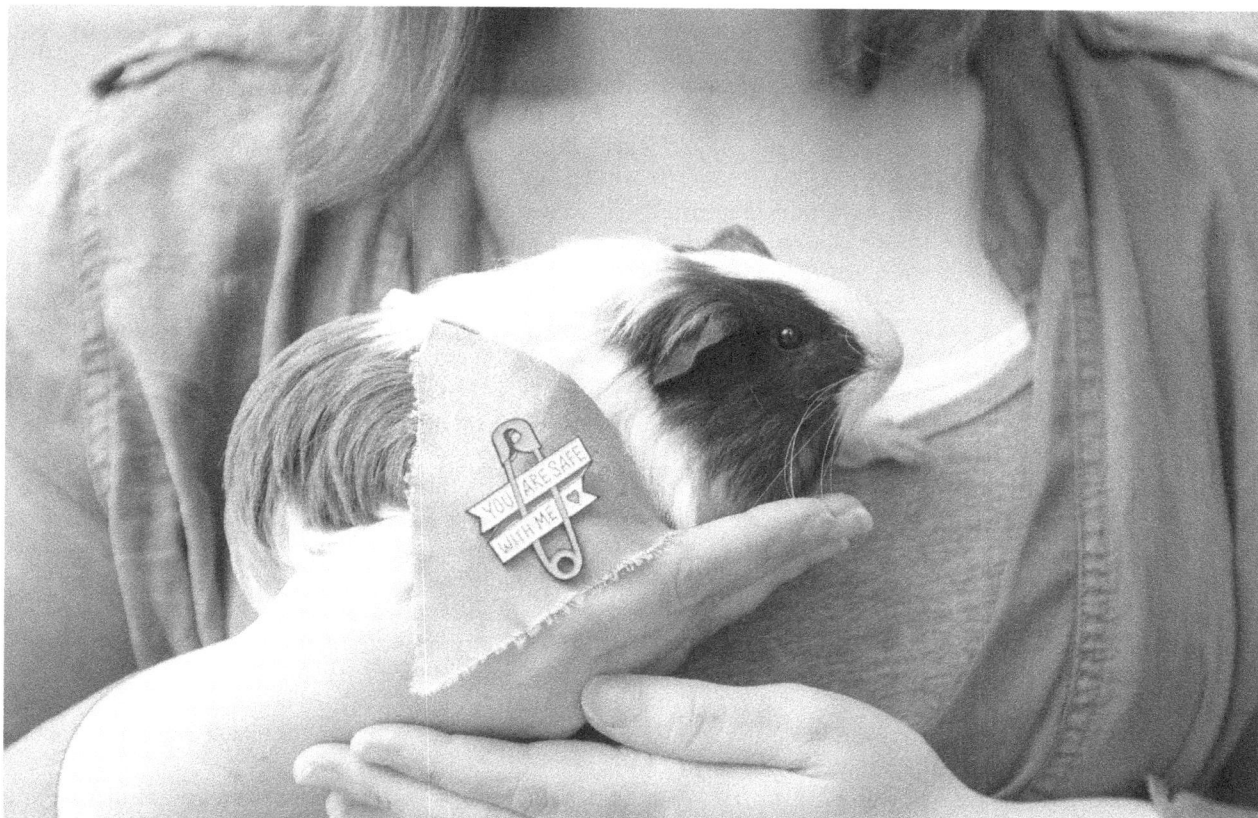

Figure 3.11 Counselor, Nicole Harris, holds her guinea pig partner, Goliath.

Bringing It All Together

When most individuals think of therapy animals, it is common to envision a canine. However, there are a variety of animals with whom one can partner within AASC which can include hamsters, guinea pigs, cats, and hedgehogs, among others. In choosing a partner, it is important to look at the population that the counselor will be working with as well as the temperament and overall welfare of the animal.

Increasingly, animals are becoming more commonplace to see in educational settings. These animals range from visiting reading partners to part of a counseling team. When considering the addition of an animal partner to the team, the temperament of the animal, as well as their desire for participation, must be considered as the animal will be working with a diverse population. Elementary schools provide an opportunity for students to learn social interactions, emotional regulation, and coping strategies which animals assist with through students gaining transferrable skills and with providing a calm and non-judgmental place for the students. Students at the secondary level are still learning social skills through conflict resolution and also finding ways to manage stress. Animal partners provide stress relief and a means for students to practice skills without feeling judged by peers and social groups.

By being deliberate in choosing an animal partner with a temperament that will work in the student population and tolerate the setting, the counselor is providing positive opportunities for students, while also taking into account the well-being of the animal partner. The ideal situation would be for the counselor and the animal partner to integrate into already existing counseling frameworks as a complement to enhance the supportive and safe environment for the students and community.

References

American School Counselor Association (ASCA). (2022). *ASCA ethical standards for school counselors.* https://www.schoolcounselor.org/getmedia/44f30280-ffe8-4b41-9ad8-f15909c3d164/EthicalStandards.pdf

Anderson, U. S., Benne, M., Bloomsmith, M. A., & Maple, T. L. (2002). Retreat space and human visitor density moderate undesirable behaviour in petting zoo animals. *Journal of Applied Animal Welfare Science, 5*(2), 125–137. 10.1207/S15327604JAWS0502_03

Bradbury, G. (2016). Getting to grips with correct rabbit handling. *Veterinary Times, 46.* https://www.vettimes.co.uk/app/uploads/wp-post-to-pdf-enhanced-cache/1/getting-to-grips-with-correct-rabbit-handling.pdf

Chandler, C. K. (2017). *Animal assisted therapy in counseling* (3rd ed.). Routledge. 10.4324/9781315673042

de Santis, M., Contalbrigo, L., Simonato, M., Ruzza, M., Toson, M., & Farina, L. (2018). Animal assisted interventions in practice: Mapping Italian providers. *Veterinaria Italiana, 54*(4), 323–332. https://www.izs.it/vet_italiana/2018/54_4/VetIt_1226_6831_1.pdf

Ellis, J. J., Stryhn, H., & Cockram, M. S. (2021). Effects of the provision of a hiding box or shelf on the behaviour and faecal glucocorticoid metabolites of bold and shy cats housed in single cages. *Applied Animal Behaviour Science, 236.* 10.1016/j.applanim.2021.105221

Faa-Thompson, T. (2012). Safe touch using horses to teach sexually abused clients to value their bodies and themselves. In K. S. Trotter (Ed.), *Harnessing the power of equine-assisted counseling: Adding animal assisted therapy to your practice* (pp. 53–58). Routledge. 10.4324/9780203802038

Flom, B. L. (2005). Counseling with pocket pets: Using small animals in elementary counseling programs. *Professional School Counseling, 8*(5), 469–471. https://www.jstor.org/stable/42732491

Flynn, E., Gandenberger, J., Mueller, M. K., & Morris, K. N. (2020). Animal-assisted interventions as an adjunct to therapy for youth: Clinician perspectives. *Child and Adolescent Social Work Journal, 37*(6), 631–642. 10.1007/s10560-020-00695-z

Foote, A. (2020). Evidence-based approach to recognising and reducing stress in pet rabbits. *Veterinary Nursing Journal, 35*(6), 167–170. 10.1080/17415349.2020.1790449

Foreman-Worsley, R., & Farnworth, M. J. (2019). A systematic review of social and environmental factors and their implications for indoor cat welfare. *Applied Animal Behaviour Science, 220,* 104841. 10.1016/j.applanim.2019.104841.

Friedmann, E., Katcher, A. H., Thomas, S. A., Lynch, J. J. & Messent, P. R. (1983). Social interaction and blood pressure: Influence of animal companions. *The Journal of Nervous and Mental Disease, 171*(8), 461–465.

Gillespie, A. I., & Neu, M. (2020). Youth and pet survivors: Exploring the experiences of pediatric oncology and bone marrow transplant patients in a virtual animal-assisted therapy pen pal program. *Journal of Pediatric Oncology Nursing, 37*(6), 368–376. 10.1177/1043454220944122

Grové, C., Henderson, L., Lee, F., & Wardlaw, P. (2021). Therapy dogs in educational settings: guidelines and recommendations for implementation. *Frontiers in Veterinary Science, 8.* https://www.frontiersin.org/articles/10.3389/fvets.2021.655104/full

Hare, B., & Woods, V. (2013). *The genius of dogs.* Penguin.

Hartwig, E. K. (2020). Advancing the practice of animal-assisted counseling through measurable standards. *Journal of Creativity in Mental Health, 16*(4), 482–498. 10.1080/15401383.2020.1792382

Hearn, K. (2022). Becoming a therapy cat. *Your Cat,* 12–14.

Hediger, K., Wagner, J., Künzi, P., Haefeli, A., Theis, F., Grob, C., Pauli, E., & Gerger, H. (2021). Effectiveness of animal-assisted interventions for children and adults with post-traumatic stress disorder symptoms: A systematic review and meta-analysis. *European Journal of Psychotraumatology, 12*(1), 1–21. 10.1080/20008198.2021.1879713

Hiestand, K. M., McComb, K., & Banerjee, R. (2022). "It almost makes her human": How female animal guardians construct experiences of cat and dog empathy. *Animals, 12*(23). 10.3390/ani12233434

Hsu, Y., & Serpell, J. A. (2003). Development and validation of a questionnaire for measuring behavior and temperament traits in pet dogs. *Journal of the American Veterinary Medical Association, 223,* 1293–1300. 10.2460/javma.2003.223.1293.

Jalongo, M. R., & Guth, L. J. (2022). Animal-assisted counseling for young children: Evidence base, best practices, and future prospects. *Early Childhood Education Journal,* 1–11. 10.1007/s10643-022-01368-5

Jones, M. G., Rice, S. M., & Cotton, S. M. (2019). Incorporating animal-assisted therapy in mental health treatments for adolescents: A systematic review of canine assisted psychotherapy. *PLoS ONE, 14*(1). 10.1371/journal.pone.0210761

Kapustka, J., & Budzyńska, M. (2020). The use of various animal species for therapeutic purposes in Poland: Current perspectives. *Acta Scientiarum Polonorum Zootechnica, 19*(2), 3–10. https://asp.zut.edu.pl/2020/19_2/asp-2020-19-2-01.pdf

Karaer, M. C., Čebulj-Kadunc, N., & Snoj, T. (2023). Stress in wildlife: comparison of the stress response among domestic, captive, and free-ranging animals. *Frontiers in Veterinary Science, 10*. 10.3389/fvets.2023.1167016.

Knowles, C., Shannon, E. N., & Lind, J. R. (2021). Animal-assisted activities in the classroom for students with emotional and behavioral disorders. *Children and Youth Services Review, 131*. 10.1016/j.childyouth.2021.106290

Loukaki, K., & Koukoutsakis, P. (2014). Rabbit-assisted interventions in a Greek kindergarten. *Journal of the Hellenic Veterinary Medical Society, 65*(1), 43–48. 10.12681/jhvms.15512

Lu, X. T., Liu, Y. F., Zhao, L., Li, W. J., Yang, R. X., Yan, F. F., Zhao, Y. X., & Jiang, F. (2013). Chronic psychological stress induces vascular inflammation in rabbits. *Stress: The International Journal on the Biology of Stress, 16*(1), 87–98. 10.3109/10253890.2012.676696

Ludy-Dobson, C. R., & Perry, B. D. (2010). The role of healthy relational interactions in buffering the impact of childhood trauma. In E. Gil (Ed.), *Working with children to heal interpersonal trauma: The power of play* (pp. 26–43). Guilford Press.

Masson, J. M. (1998). *Dogs never lie about love: Reflections on the emotional world of dogs*. Three Rivers Press.

Miller, L. (2018). *The power of the guinea pig: Exploring children's sense of school belonging through animal-assisted activities*. University of East London School of Psychology. 10.15123/uel.874wq

Molnár, M., Iváncsik, R., DiBlasio, B., & Nagy, I. (2019). Examining the effects of rabbit-assisted interventions in the classroom environment. *Animals, 10*(1). 10.3390/ani10010026

O'Haire, M. E., McKenzie, S. J., McCune, S., & Slaughter, V. (2013). Effects of animal-assisted activities with guinea pigs in the primary school classroom. *Anthrozoös, 26*(3), 445–458. 10.2752/175303713X13697429463835

Parish-Plass, N. (2021). Animal-assisted psychotherapy for developmental trauma through the lens of interpersonal neurobiology of trauma: Creating connection with self and others. *Journal of Psychotherapy Integration, 31*(3), 302–325. 10.1037/int0000253

PR Newswire (2022, May 2). *New virtual therapy cat visits for seniors available throughout May*. https://www.prnewswire.com/news-releases/new-virtual-therapy-cat-visits-for-seniors-available-throughout-may-301536872.html

Royal Society for the Prevention of Cruelty to Animals (RSPCA). (2023a, May 16). *Understanding rabbit behaviour*. https://www.rspca.org.uk/adviceandwelfare/pets/rabbits/behaviour

Royal Society for the Prevention of Cruelty to Animals (RSPCA). (2023b, May 16). *Guinea pig behaviour*. https://www.rspca.org.uk/adviceandwelfare/pets/rodents/guineapigs/behaviour

Sachser, N., & Lick, C. (1991). Social experience, behavior, and stress in guinea pigs. *Physiology & Behavior, 50*(1), 83–90. 10.1016/0031-9384(91)90502-f

Sipos, K, & Bodnar, K. (2020). The positive effects of pet rabbits on the study and school attitudes of high school students. *Agricultural Management, 22*(2), 159–163. https://lsma.ro/index.php/lsma/article/view/1783/pdf

Suba-Bokodi, É., Nagy, I., & Molnár, M. (2022). Changes in the stress tolerance of dwarf rabbits in animal-assisted interventions. *Applied Sciences, 12*. 10.3390/app12146979

Tanaka, A., Wagner, D. C., Kass, P. H., & Hurley, K. F. (2012). Associations among weight loss, stress, and upper respiratory tract infection in shelter cats. *Journal of the American Veterinary Medical Association, 240*(5), 570–576. 10.2460/javma.240.5.570

Tedeschi, P. (2020). *Transforming trauma resilience and healing through our connections with animals*. Purdue University Press.

Thomas, R., & Matusitz, J. (2016). Pet therapy in correctional institutions: A perspective from Relational-Cultural Theory. *Journal of Evidence-Informed Social Work, 13*(2), 228–235. 10.1080/23761407.2015.1029840

Tomaszewska, K., Bomert, I., & Wilkiewicz-Wawro, E. (2017). Feline-assisted therapy: Integrating contact with cats into treatment plans. *Polish Annals of Medicine, 24*(2), 283–286. 10.1016/j.poamed.2016.11.011

Vitale, K. R., Behnke, A. C., & Udell, M. A. R. (2019). Attachment bonds between domestic cats and humans. *Current Biology, 29*(18), R864–R865. https://www.sciencedirect.com/science/article/pii/S0960982219310863

Wilson, E. O. (1984). *Biophilia: The human bond with other species*. Harvard University Press.

Winnicott, D.W. 1971. *Playing and reality*. Tavistock Publications.

Zhang, L., Bian, Z., Liu, Q. & Deng, B. (2022). Dealing with stress in cats: What is new about the olfactory strategy? *Frontiers in Veterinary Science, 9*. 10.3389/fvets.2022.928943

Zilcha-Mano, S., Mikulincer, M., & Shaver, P. R. (2011). Pet in the therapy room: An attachment perspective on animal-assisted therapy. *Attachment & Human Development, 13*(6), 541–561. 10.1080/14616734.2011.608987

Zipser, B., Kaiser, S., & Sachser, N. (2013). Dimensions of animal personalities in guinea pigs. *Ethology, 119*(11), 970–982. 10.1111/eth.12140

Chapter 4

AASC Competencies

Jordan Jalen Evans
Texas A&M University-Corpus Christi

Box 4.1

Chapter 4 Scenario

Rosalie loves Hank and thinks that he would be a wonderful addition to her school counseling program. Through her counseling code of ethics, Rosalie knows that she needs to develop competencies in specialization areas. Being that AASC is a specialty area, she understands that she needs to get training and supervision in AASC. Rosalie is not sure what competencies she needs to develop for AASC specifically. She is also the first person at her school to incorporate AASC into their work and would like to be prepared to competently integrate AASC into her school. Rosalie wants to have a better understanding of what knowledge, skills, and attitudes she and Hank need to be able to work ethically in schools to promote student, staff, and animal welfare and well-being. She believes that bringing Hank to school without proper training and supervision can lead to potential ethical and legal issues for which she would be liable. Therefore, Rosalie is exploring what competencies she and Hank will need to integrate AASC effectively in her school.

The interest in animal-assisted counseling has grown throughout the years due to positive outcomes of involving animals in counseling settings (Trevathan-Minnis et al., 2021). Though various international organizations, such as the Animal Assisted Intervention International (AAII) and the International Association for Human-Animal Interaction Organizations (IAHAIO), have created guidelines and terminology specific to animal-assisted interventions (AAI), competencies have not been established for animal-assisted school counseling (AASC). In 2016 the American Counseling Association endorsed a set of competencies for animal-assisted therapy in counseling (Stewart et al., 2016). These will be referred to as animal-assisted counseling (AAC) competencies to be consistent with other literature on AAIs in the counseling field. The AAC competencies identified knowledge, skills, and attitudes that practitioners should be able to demonstrate for the ethical involvement of animals in mental health settings. The author will use the AAC competencies as a framework for recommending AASC competencies in this chapter. These competencies are important for the protection and well-being of students, animals, school staff, and practitioners.

In this chapter, the author will define AASC competencies and describe how they fit into a school setting and align with school counseling professional and ethical standards. Examples will be provided on ways to integrate AASC and school counseling standards to provide a safe and competent school counseling environment when utilizing AASC. First, literature related to school counseling ethical

DOI: 10.4324/9781003392415-4

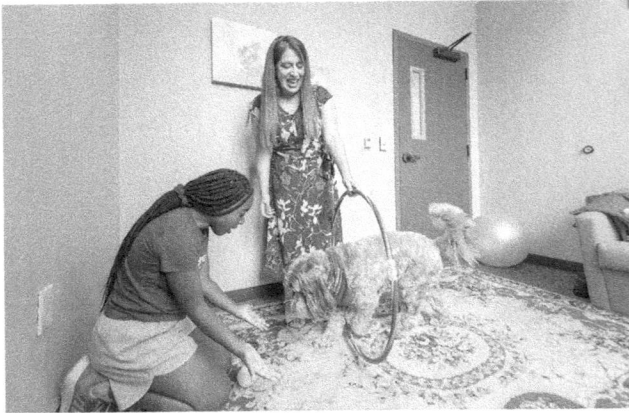

Figure 4.1 Maggie Dou and Dorothy facilitating the Hula Challenge with a teen client.

standards and animal-assisted competencies will be explored, followed by a discussion of the linkage of these documents to American School Counseling Association (ASCA) professional standards and competencies. Examples will be provided through two AASC lesson plans to assist school counselors in explaining AASC competencies to their students. The end of this chapter will delve into how AASC competencies can assist practitioners in integrating trauma-informed and diversity considerations in their work with students and their animal partners (Figure 4.1).

Literature Review

School counselors in the United States are required to uphold a set of ethical and professional standards and competencies set by ASCA (2019). Counselors, in general, also follow ethical codes to protect the welfare of clients. In order to practice specialized modalities of therapy, counselors are required to seek proper education that includes training and supervision (ACA, 2014). Fine et al. (2019) asserted that competencies and standards are needed to be in place and training should be thorough. These authors maintain that certification and possible credentialing processes are essential to ensure that AAC practitioners create a safe and competent therapeutic environment (Fine et al., 2019). Similarly, AASC competencies should address competencies in knowledge, skills, and attitudes that incorporate concepts of the human-animal bond, animal welfare, ethics, and multicultural considerations in AASC. Hartwig (2020) contended that a lack of practice, supervision, and training for both the practitioner and the animal partner could potentially lead to harm to a child or animal partner, inadequate assessment of clients, lack of knowledge related to animal stressors and stress signals, increased risk of transmission of animal diseases, and lack of skills that could impact the appropriate incorporation of AAC into counseling sessions. Practitioners who have a dearth of competencies in AASC can cause injury or harm to the students, the animal partner, and school staff. Relevant education, training, and supervision will help to ensure that AASC practitioners are competent and can provide the safest environment possible for all parties involved.

Consider the example of Rosalie and Hank. If Rosalie had no knowledge of Hank's canine communication, stress signals, and warning signs, then she would not have the skills necessary to protect Hank and students when Hank feels stressed. Hank may react to stressful events like students running up to him by running away, growling, or hiding behind Rosalie. Hank could grow fearful of and anxious about students and staff in the school. AASC animal partners should be able to enjoy their

Figure 4.2 Jalen Evans holding her rabbit partner, Loyal.

work in school, rather than tolerate or fear it. With Rosalie being properly trained for these situations and being aware of what Hank does not like, she can think of ways to prevent these scenarios. Rosalie developing competencies in AASC through training and supervision can help her to navigate various challenges in schools.

Consider another example with an AASC practitioner who has a rabbit partner. It's important to be properly trained on rabbit behaviors and communication as well as potential allergy issues, such as children with a hay allergy. If a student with a hay allergy were to interact with a rabbit partner who has been eating hay, the student could experience an allergic reaction. Critter counselors, such as rabbits, should not be left unattended, as students may want to pick up and play with them without recognizing how or when to hold and interact with an animal partner. AASC practitioners should be trained to prevent situations like these. Knowledge, skills, and attitudes relevant to this field can help to better prepare these practitioners to navigate these events and advocate for their animal partners and the AASC field (Figure 4.2).

AAC Competencies

In this chapter, the author will provide information on AAC competencies, ASCA professional standards, and ASCA ethical standards. Based on these professional guidelines, the author will then recommend a list of AASC competencies. This list is a set of competencies that the author encourages AASC teams to utilize to guide their practice in schools. Stewart (2014) completed a qualitative study with 20 practitioners with proficient experience in AAC. The purpose of this research was to create a set of competencies in the field of AAC, which derived from a lack of standards in the field and a need for a differentiated set of competencies in its practice. Stewart and a team of researchers took the competencies derived from this study and identified specific AAC competencies in three domains: knowledge, skills, and attitudes (Stewart et al., 2016). These competencies were endorsed by the American Counseling Association (ACA).

This section will provide an overview of the AAC competencies by Stewart et al. (2016) that were comprised of three domains: knowledge, skills, and attitudes. The knowledge domain identifies specific content areas of knowledge that are fundamental for AAC. This domain includes guidelines for formal AAC training, ethical obligations, and comprehension of skills and interventions in AAC. The skills domain identifies skills necessary for counselors to practice AAC. This domain advises that practitioners are able to demonstrate basic counseling skills, purposeful use of AAC, attention to client and animal partner (including animal communication/stressors), and integration of AAC into evidence-based treatment modalities and counseling theories. The attitudes domain provides foundational content related to advocacy and professional development when working in the AAC field. This domain outlines a set of attitudes related to advocacy for animals and the profession of AAC, the responsibility to participate in professional development, remaining up to date with current literature, participating in supervision, and upholding professional values related to AAC. These competencies contributed to a much-needed framework in AAC practice.

Linkage of ASCA Standards

ASCA outlined the School Counselor Professional Standards and Competencies (ASCA, 2019) and Ethical Standards (ASCA, 2022) through specific mindsets, behaviors, and ethical guidelines that school counselors need to promote and champion Pre-K through 12 students. In this section, the author will identify and describe an ASCA standard for each AAC competency domain and then explore what AAC competencies are relevant to each standard. This section will build the foundation for a list of recommended AASC competencies.

Knowledge

ASCA has several standards that identify specific knowledge content that school counselors should know to effectively serve in schools. One of these standards is ASCA standard B PF 1, which states that school counselors should "apply developmental, learning, counseling, and education theories" (ASCA, 2019, p. 2). This standard identified that school counselors should first have knowledge of foundational theories and then know how to apply those theories in their work with children. For example, understanding how child development impacts a child's physical, social, cognitive, and psychological development is imperative for assessing children's needs and planning AASC interventions and lessons to meet those needs. Similarly, school counselors must have knowledge of how to apply counseling theories in their work, since they need a framework for helping children reach goals. An example of this is a school counselor using solution-focused therapy by emphasizing a child's strengths and resources to help them create solutions to their challenges in class or in social situations.

There are three relevant AAC competencies (Stewart et al., 2016) for this ASCA standard. They are: 1) understand animal training techniques - applying positive, non-coercive training methods, ensuring animal is trained for counseling settings, ability to detect and facilitate animal's welfare during session, 2) integrate AAC into a personal model of counseling, and 3) recognize the experiential nature of AAC interventions and demonstrate these skills in spontaneous situations. All three of these competencies require an understanding of AAC learning and counseling theories and the ability to apply those with clients.

Skills

School counselors must develop a host of skills to support children in schools. One standard related to AASC skills is B-SS-3: "Provide short-term counseling in small-group and individual settings" (ASCA, 2019, p. 2). This standard underscores the need for counselors to provide services to students. These services include individual and group counseling. School counselors are required to be able to describe interventions and differences between long- and short-term therapy. They are called to assess student needs and determine the helpful strategies for working with individual students. For example, if a student has experienced a traumatic event such as a car accident, a school counselor may decide to provide short-term trauma-informed techniques to support the student, while also providing referrals for more long-term counseling in the community.

There are two relevant AAC Competencies (Stewart et al., 2016) for this ASCA standard. They are: 1) selection of appropriate interventions and strategies for each client based on treatment goals, and 2) ability to understand the experiential nature of AAC interventions and demonstrate skills in spontaneous situations. These competencies require that practitioners can choose and utilize appropriate interventions based on the needs of the client.

Attitudes

It's important for school counselors to have certain attitudes and dispositions for working in schools that focus on student wellness. One standard that is relevant to the practice of AASC is ethical standard A.1.a., which states, "Have a primary obligation to the students, who are to be treated with dignity and respect as unique individuals" (ASCA, 2022, p. 1). This standard identifies school counselors' responsibility to treat students with respect and support students through culturally responsive behaviors. For example, being aware of the needs of cultural practices, the importance of family, and other values within a student's culture, and the respect for their beliefs, sexual orientation, and gender identity/expression. School counselors are also called to recognize potential mental health, environmental, and systemic barriers that impact students. An example of displaying an attitude of respect for students may look like a school counselor advocating and modeling the proper use of inclusive language regarding sexual orientation and gender identity in all educational spaces and in school counseling curriculum.

There are two relevant AAC Competencies (Stewart et al., 2016) for this ASCA Standard. They are (1) understanding why animal welfare and advocacy are essential to the ethical practice of AAC and (2) recognizing that animals have a right to choose their level of participation in AAC. These competencies describe advocacy practices that should be displayed by practitioners along with recognizing the animal partner's needs and respecting their choice of participation in treatment.

AASC Competencies

In new areas of specialization, it's important to identify competencies needed to help practitioners develop and hone specific knowledge, skills, attitudes, and experience to effectively work with clients. The AAC competencies and the ASCA standards all provide fundamental guidance for the creation of

AASC competencies (ASCA, 2019, 2022; Stewart et al., 2016). Furthermore, these competencies reflect skills and dispositions represented in the AAC Skills Checklist (Binfet & Hartwig, 2020). This section offers a list of recommended AASC competencies based on current guidelines in the AAC and school counseling fields. Appendix A includes a full list of these competencies. The AASC Knowledge Competencies encompass specific knowledge needed for partnering with animals in school settings. Practitioners need to understand basic animal welfare and training knowledge, as well as more specific knowledge related to AASC literature, risk management, diversity awareness, and AASC interventions. Table 4.1 presents the AASC Knowledge Competencies (Figure 4.3).

Table 4.1 AASC Knowledge Competencies

Code	Competency	Description
K1	Training	School-based practitioners complete comprehensive training in AASC that includes AASC-specific knowledge, skills practice, attitudes, and clinical experience.
K2	Supervision	School-based practitioners participate in clinical supervision or consultation provided by an AASC supervisor to promote professional growth and learning. Practitioners understand how to self-assess AASC skills and integrate an assessment of skills provided by an AASC supervisor.
K3	History	School-based practitioners possess knowledge of the history of AAC, AASC, and teams working with children in schools.
K4	Literature	School-based practitioners read foundational and emerging literature and research related to AAC, AASC, and animals in school settings and are knowledgeable of current AASC language and terminology.
K5	Human-Animal Bond	School-based practitioners understand what the human-animal bond (HAB) is and the impact of HAB on children, family members, educators, administration, and school staff and on the AASC process.
K6	Animal Knowledge and Care	School-based practitioners understand species-specific information about their AASC animal partner including communication signals, physiology, behavior, and care. Practitioners are knowledgeable of their animal partner's strengths and limitations within AASC work.
K7	Animal Health and Wellness	School-based practitioners understand their animal partner's needs and provide access to water, rest time, and bathroom breaks. Practitioners attend to the wellness of the animal through regular veterinary care, vaccinations, nutrition, grooming, and exercise. Practitioners understand health implications of AASC and minimize the risks of animal- or human-transmitted diseases through handwashing and sanitation procedures.
K8	Positive, Non-Aversive Training	School-based practitioners possess knowledge of and use positive and non-aversive training techniques for animal partners working in school settings.
K9	Ethics	School-based practitioners understand ethical and legal implications of AASC. Practitioners seek consultation from AASC supervisors and peers to guide ethical decision making.
K10	Risk Management	School-based practitioners understand potential liability involved in practicing AASC and possess knowledge of risk-management strategies including limit setting, informed consent, and insurance coverage.

(Continued)

Table 4.1 (Continued)

Code	Competency	Description
K11	Diversity Awareness	School-based practitioners understand the implications of the use of AASC with students with respect to race, ethnicity, age, sex, religion, sexual orientation, gender identity, gender expression, disability, economic status, and other diverse backgrounds.
K12	Interventions	School-based practitioners have knowledge of AASC interventions and how they can be applied to specific clinical goals for students in the school setting.

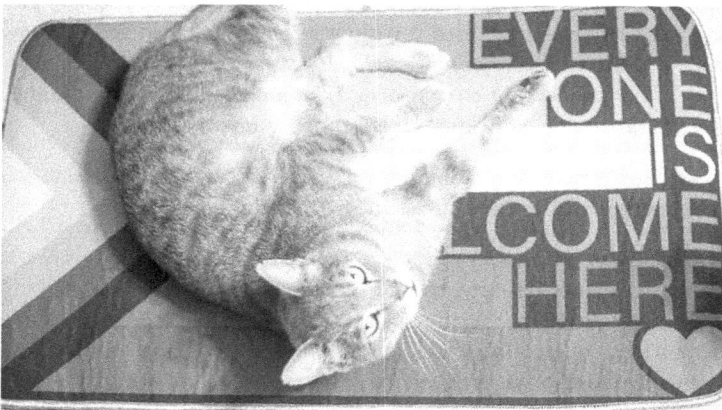

Figure 4.3 A cat partner letting children know that everyone is welcome in the school.

The AASC Skills Competencies cover skills needed to work with animals in school settings. Practitioners need to develop skills in AASC training programs and hone those skills during supervision. AASC skills range from applying clinical theory and goal setting methods with an animal partner to facilitating informed consent and AASC interventions. Table 4.2 presents the AASC Skills Competencies (Figure 4.4).

Table 4.2 AASC Skills Competencies

Code	Competency	Description
S1	Practitioner-Animal Relationship	School-based practitioners establish and maintain a strong working relationship with their animal partner. Practitioners advocate for the welfare of their animal partner in all AASC interactions. Practitioners demonstrate that they are not "using" an animal, but rather "partnering" with an animal.
S2	Animal Greeting	School-based practitioners show students, teachers, and staff how to greet their animal prior to the person interacting with the animal partner. Practitioners guide the greeting interaction between the person and animal.

(Continued)

Table 4.2 (Continued)

Code	Competency	Description
S3	Animal Communication	School-based practitioners recognize animal partner's communication signals, including positive and stress signals. School-based practitioners respond immediately to animal stress signals and implement strategies to ensure safety of the animal partner and students.
S4	Cultural Responsiveness	School-based practitioners evaluate and address their personal cultural influences, beliefs, values, and biases and avoid imposing these onto students. Practitioners make modifications to AASC interventions based on the needs, culture, values, and beliefs about animals that students, families, and staff may hold.
S5	Basic Counseling Skills	School-based practitioners exhibit proficiency in basic counseling skills within a school setting prior to the integration of AASC including showing empathy, respect, and unconditional positive regard toward the animal partner and students. Basic counseling skills include reflecting content and feeling, summarizing, and using open-ended questions.
S6	Student-Animal Relationship	School-based practitioners demonstrate facilitation of the student-animal relationship so that a working alliance is developed.
S7	Animal and Student Choice	School-based practitioners recognize and assess the animal partner and student's willingness, safety, and comfortability while participating in AASC interactions. Practitioners assert that both the animal partner and student have a choice in participating in interactions and interventions without judgment or consequences.
S8	Limit Setting	School-based practitioners demonstrate the ability to set limits when needed by using the RUF protocol: Recognize what the person wants, Underscore the limit, and Focus on an alternative. An example would be, "Jordan, I see you want to hug Hank, but he's not for hugging that way. You can pet him on the chest instead."
S9	Assessment of Students	School-based practitioners assess children's suitability to participate in AASC based on informed consent information, student behavior, and student interest.
S10	Assessment of Animal Partner	School-based practitioners continuously assess the animal partner's strengths, limitations, and appropriateness for AASC, regardless of the bond between the animal partner and practitioner. The practitioner can identify when it is appropriate to remove the animal partner from a particular session or retire them from the AASC program.
S11	Confidence	School-based practitioners demonstrate appropriate levels of self-assurance and trust in own ability and animal partner's ability to facilitate AASC interactions and interventions.
S12	Informed Consent	School-based practitioners facilitate and obtain AASC-specific informed consent.
S13	Clinical Theory	School-based practitioners apply a primary clinical theory in their AASC program (e.g., solution-focused, cognitive-behavioral, Adlerian). Through this theory they use key concepts, therapist role, and techniques to

(Continued)

Table 4.2 (Continued)

Code	Competency	Description
		provide AASC services and assess progress. School-based practitioners have knowledge of the difference between indirect and direct modalities and benefits and limitations of each in the school setting.
S14	Goal Setting	School-based practitioners establish appropriate goals with students and connect AASC interventions to students' goals.
S15	Facilitating Interventions	School-based practitioners select and facilitate appropriate AASC interventions for each student based on student goals and provide a rationale for activities and strategies utilized.
S16	Termination	School-based practitioners demonstrate the ability to end AASC services well through positive counseling termination strategies. Practitioners seek out consultation from AASC professionals and stakeholders if an adverse event and/or animal partner sudden death or illness is the cause of termination.

Figure 4.4 Kate Halinski and her canine partner, Moose, doing animal-assisted counseling with a young child.

Table 4.3 AASC Attitudes Competencies

Code	Competency	Description
A1	Professional Identity	School-based practitioners demonstrate AASC professional identity in their work in schools and in professional settings. This includes knowledge of their role as both a practitioner and advocate for their animal partner and developing, maintaining, and continuously improving AASC knowledge, skills, and attitudes.
A2	Values	School-based practitioners support, advocate for, and endorse AASC professional values and respect animal autonomy and welfare. Practitioners demonstrate enthusiasm related to their work with students and animal partners.
A3	Advocacy	School-based practitioners advocate for their animal partner's welfare and wellness. Practitioners understand the potential for animal exploitation in a school setting and realize their responsibility to the animal partner.
A4	Research	School-based practitioners support and contribute to literature and research in AASC through participation in research, writing, and presenting in local, regional, national, and international trainings or conferences.
A5	Professional Development	School-based practitioners participate in opportunities to enhance and hone their AASC skills through continuing education, consultation, and professional development activities.

Figure 4.5 Counselor Jalen Evans laughing with a client, while her rabbit partner takes a food break.

The AASC Attitudes Competencies focus on attitudes and dispositions that AASC practitioners should communicate in their role on campus. AASC attitudes include professional identity, values, and advocacy for the field. Table 4.3 presents the AASC Attitudes Competencies (Figure 4.5).

Applying AASC Competencies to Primary-Level Schools

Clients in this age group are usually between 5 and 11 years old. The emotional and social health of children has been a growing concern over the past couple of decades (Tahan et al., 2022). Research utilizing AAC with preschool-aged children showed that their symptoms of anxiety decreased. Various studies have shown the effectiveness of AAC on children and adults' emotional and social states (Tahan et al., 2022). Therefore, we know that AAC can be a reliable treatment when working in primary school.

Though there are benefits, counselors should keep in mind safety and welfare. A study in 2009, stated that in one year, 4.5 million people in the United States are bitten each year (Meints & de Keuster, 2009). The Centers for Disease Control and Prevention (CDC) suggests that children are at the highest risk for dog bits even with animals that are familiar with them (CDC, 2021). Just as AASC competencies recommend, the CDC suggests that owners learn the signs and communication of their animals to best prevent bites. They also recommend supervision of children and pets while also educating children on how to interact with animals (CDC, 2021) (Figure 4.6).

Primary-level students, especially the younger children, may need more explanation and education on animal welfare, infection control, and animal communication. Younger children may have issues with recognizing the animal partner's body language and may misinterpret what an animal is signaling to them (Schuck et al., 2019). If school counselors are unsure of whether an activity is age appropriate, to protect both the students and the animal, they should seek supervision from another animal-assisted counselor and/or someone with a background in both school counseling and AAC.

AASC practitioners should also identify how their interventions are aligning with the objectives and goals of ASCA. Practitioners should demonstrate strong school counseling skills prior to involving their animal partner in counseling. ASCA competency B-PF 1 states that school counselors are required to apply developmental theories as well as evidence-based counseling theories into their

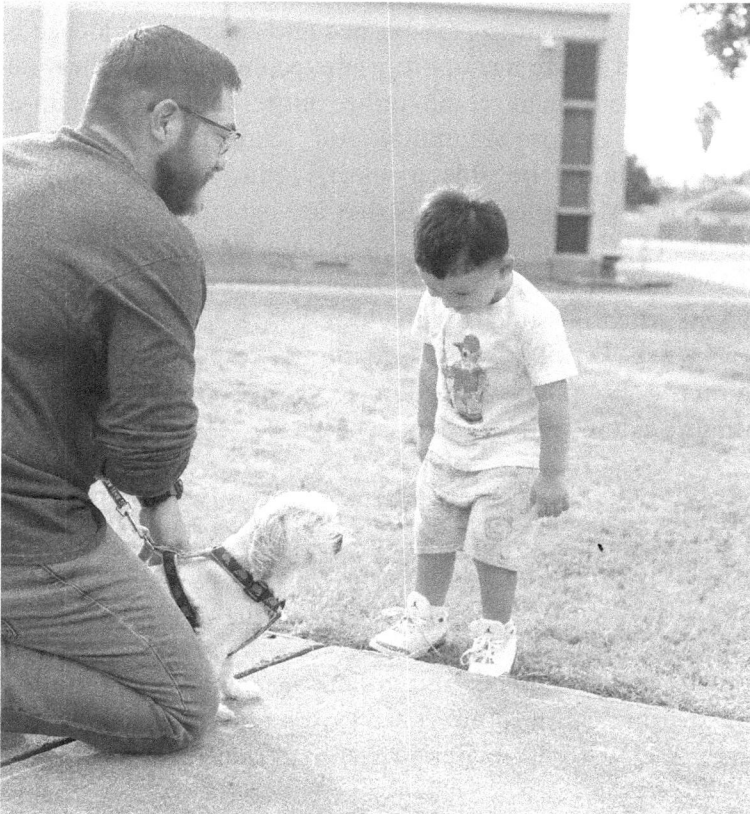

Figure 4.6 School counselor introducing a therapy dog to a young child.

practice (ASCA, 2019, p. 3). Therefore, AASC practitioners are required to navigate skills based on the developmental stage of their clients, their theoretical orientation, and their AAC training. ASCA competency B-PF 8 requires school counselors to advocate for their profession and their students' success (ASCA, 2019, p. 4). These practitioners are also required to understand the benefits of school counseling and be able to explain this to stakeholders. ASCA competency B-PF 8 states that they are also required to provide a reasoning for activities that they want to provide for students. AASC practitioners are also encouraged to advocate for animal welfare. AAC attitude competencies encourage practitioners to demonstrate empathy for humans and animals. Therefore, AASC practitioners would be able to explain the benefits of AAC and how it could support student success while also demonstrating the ability to protect the animal and the student.

AASC practitioners can become creative with interventions to help younger students in this age group learn about animal welfare and AASC competencies. Lesson Plan 4.1 in Appendix B describes an intervention that would assist students in learning about animal welfare.

Applying AASC Competencies to Secondary-Level Schools

Adolescents in secondary-level schools are usually about 12 to 18 years old. These students can complete more complex activities than youth in primary school. AAC has been found effective when working with both children and adolescents (Jones et al., 2019). In adolescence, youth are experiencing developmental changes in emotions, relationships, and identity development. The impact of mental health concerns at this age begins to affect youth's academic and social functioning which can result in high levels of distress (Jones et al., 2019).

ASCA standards assert that school counselors are to utilize established and emerging evidence-based counseling theories. Therefore, counselors should utilize age-appropriate techniques and interventions of their primary theoretical model. AASC practitioners could utilize more complex and in-depth animal-assisted techniques with students who are in secondary-level schools. In working with secondary-level students AASC practitioners should be able to clearly educate students on their animal partner's boundaries, plan intentional AASC interventions that are age appropriate and meet the standards of ASCA, and participate in AASC trainings and supervision when needed to address changes in the field. More specifically, AASC practitioners are encouraged to seek continuing education from school counselors who practice AASC when possible (Figure 4.7).

Lesson Plan 4.2 (Appendix B) is an example of how an AASC practitioner could teach a secondary-level school student about animal welfare and the animal's freedom to choose whether they want to participate in treatment while also relating it to the student's experiences.

Trauma-Informed and Diversity Considerations

AASC can provide students with a sense of safety and be beneficial when working with children who have experienced trauma (Tedeschi et al., 2019). AASC teams can model behaviors in real time. This may look like showing a student appropriate touch, setting boundaries, helping the student learn to communicate emotions, demonstrating appropriate play, and other beneficial interactions with animals. The involvement of animals in therapy can also assist students in learning how to discuss shame, blame, and/or guilt that may be associated with trauma or abuse from their past (Tedeschi et al., 2019).

The human-animal bond can also help to create a trusting relationship between the student and the animal-assisted school counselor (Tedeschi et al., 2019). Parish-Plass (2018) completed a study on a

Figure 4.7 Art therapist, Diana Gibson, and her canine partner, Sketch, facilitate art therapy with two teens.

group of maltreated children, aged 7 to 11 years old, in residential care. This population can be more likely to distrust adults due to traumatic experiences such as abuse and neglect by other adults in their lives. Parish-Plass found that the group who participated in AAC formed a stronger therapeutic alliance with their counselor after three sessions versus the non-AAC treatment group. After the completion of all eight sessions, there was no significant difference in the therapeutic alliance, but findings show that the incorporation of animals in play therapy, may have expedited the formation of the therapeutic alliance (Parish-Plass, 2018). Though AASC has been shown to be beneficial and is increasingly popular, practitioners should not be remiss of differing perceptions of animals related to culture, religion, and animal-related traumas. School counselors can increase their cultural awareness through cultural responsiveness, knowledge of diversity, and assessment of students.

Bringing It All Together

AASC practitioners are called to follow professional standards and competencies identified by the school counseling and AAC fields. This chapter offered a recommendation for AASC competencies that can be applied in school settings. AASC practitioners should be well trained in competencies for knowledge, skills, and attitudes to ensure the effectiveness of their AASC program and interactions with students and staff. Practitioners should also put the welfare of the animal and the student at the forefront of their work. Competent AASC practitioners and animal partners promote the integrity of the AASC field.

References

American Counseling Association. (2014). *ACA code of ethics.* https://www.counseling.org/resources/aca-code-of-ethics.pdf

American School Counselor Association (ASCA). (2019). *ASCA school counselor professional standards & competencies.* https://www.schoolcounselor.org/getmedia/a8d59c2c-51de-4ec3-a565-a3235f3b93c3/SC-Competencies.pdf

American School Counselor Association (ASCA). (2022). *ASCA ethical standards for school counselors.* https://www.schoolcounselor.org/getmedia/44f30280-ffe8-4b41-9ad8-f15909c3d164/EthicalStandards.pdf

Binfet, J. T., & Hartwig, E. K. (2020). *Canine-assisted interventions: A comprehensive guide to credentialing therapy dog teams.* Routledge. 10.4324/9780429436055

Center for Disease Control and Prevention. (2021). *This week is dog bite prevention week.* CDC. https://www.cdc.gov/healthypets/connect/newsletter/dog-bite-prevention-week.html

Fine, A. H., Tedeschi, P., Morris, K., & Elvove, E. (2019). Forward thinking: The evolving field of human-animal interactions. In A. H. Fine (Ed.), *Handbook on animal assisted therapy* (5th ed., pp. 23–41). Elsevier/Academic Press. 10.1016/B978-0-12-801292-5.00003-1

Hartwig, E. K. (2020). Advancing the practice of animal-assisted counseling through measurable standards. *Journal of Creativity in Mental Health, 16*(4), 482–498. 10.1080/15401383.2020.1792382

Jones, M. G., Rice, S. M., & Cotton, S. M. (2019). Incorporating animal-assisted therapy in mental health treatments for adolescents: A systematic review of canine assisted psychotherapy. *PLoS ONE, 14*(1), 1–28. 10.1371/journal.pone.0210761

Meints, K. & de Keuster, T. (2009). Brief report: Don't kiss a sleeping dog: The first assessment of "The Blue Dog" bite prevention program. *Journal of Pediatric Psychology, 34*(10), 1084–1090. 10.1093/jpepsy/jsp053

Parish-Plass, N. (2018). *The influence of animal-assisted psychotherapy on the establishment of the therapeutic alliance with maltreated children in residential care.* Master's thesis, University of Haifa. 10.13140/RG.2.2.36514.25280

Schuck, S. E. B., Fine, A. H., Abdullah, M. M., & Lakes, K. D. (2019). Animal assisted interventions for children with disorders of executive function: The influence of humane education and character development on the P.A.C.K. model. In A. H. Fine (Ed.) *Handbook on animal assisted therapy* (5th ed., pp. 299–311). Elsevier/Academic Press. 10.1016/B978-0-12-815395-6.00019-5

Stewart, L. A. (2014). *Competencies in animal assisted therapy in counseling: A qualitative investigation of the knowledge, skills and attitudes required of competent animal assisted therapy practitioners.* Doctoral dissertation, Georgia State University. 10.57709/5496621

Stewart, L. A., Chang, C. Y., Parker, L. K., & Grubbs, N. (2016). *Animal-assisted therapy in counseling competencies.* American Counseling Association, Animal-Assisted Therapy in Mental Health Interest Network. https://www.counseling.org/docs/default-source/competencies/animal-assisted-therapy-competencies-june-2016.pdf?sfvrsn=14.

Tahan, M., Saleem, T., Sadeghifar, A., & Ahangri, E. (2022). Assessing the effectiveness of animal-assisted therapy on alleviation of anxiety in pre-school children: A randomized controlled trial. *Contemporary Clinical Trials Communications, 28*, 1–6. 10.1016/j.conctc.2022.100947

Tedeschi, P., Jenkins, M. A., Pariah-Plass, N., Olmert, M. D., & Yount, R. A. (2019). Treating human trauma with the help of animals: Trauma-informed intervention for child maltreatment and adult posttraumatic stress. In A. H. Fine (Ed.), *Handbook on animal assisted therapy* (5th ed., pp. 363–380). Elsevier/Academic Press. 10.1016/B978-0-12-801292-5.00022-5

Trevathan-Minnis, M., Johnson, A., & Howie, A.R. (2021). Recommendations for transdisciplinary professional competencies and ethics for animal-assisted therapies and interventions. *Veterinary Sciences, 8*(12), 303. 10.3390/vetsci8120303

Chapter 5

Training in AASC

Kim Sullivan[1] and Amy Blasingame[2]
[1]*Heart and Soul Counseling;* [2]*Coppell Independent School District*

Box 5.1

Chapter 5 Scenario

Rosalie is excited about the possibility of bringing Hank to school as her school counseling partner. As a member of several therapy dog Facebook groups, Rosalie is aware that some school counselors have received minimal training for bringing their animals to school and others have received more intensive training. The ones who have received comprehensive AASC training provide information about competencies and training programs that are specifically designed for professional therapy animal teams. She recognizes that she has an ethical obligation to receive training and supervision to be competent in the services she provides to children in schools. However, she's not clear on what guidelines and requirements there are for AASC training. Furthermore, she's not sure what she and Hank should consider when choosing an AASC training program. She looks at Hank and says, "Are you ready to do what it takes so that we're both prepared to work together in schools?" Hank responds by running over to her, sitting in front of her, and looking expectantly for a pet or maybe even a treat. Rosalie is going to start today by looking for an AASC training program that can best prepare them to make an impact on children in schools.

As Rosalie is becoming aware of in the opening scenario, successfully and ethically integrating an animal partner with school counseling involves quality training in AASC. This chapter covers training needed for both the school counselor and the animal partner for them to work together as an AASC team. Both humans and animals require introductory and advanced training in AASC as both are being called to operate in new ways. The school counselor will be working with a partner of a different species, responsible for communicating and understanding their partner as well as acting as something of a translator for the students in the school. The animal partner, on the other hand, is being asked to work in a new and unfamiliar environment. They may be asked to join in with the counselor's work throughout the day, interacting with many types of students in a variety of situations. By participating in training, skills practice, and supervision, the AASC team will be better prepared to work together in supporting their student population.

Building on Chapter 4's presentation of AASC competencies, this chapter will begin by addressing the question of "why do we need training?" by acknowledging standards in the animal-assisted interventions field and exploring the ethical importance of AASC-specific training. Once the "why" has been established, this chapter will explore the "how." The many training, certification, and registration

DOI: 10.4324/9781003392415-5

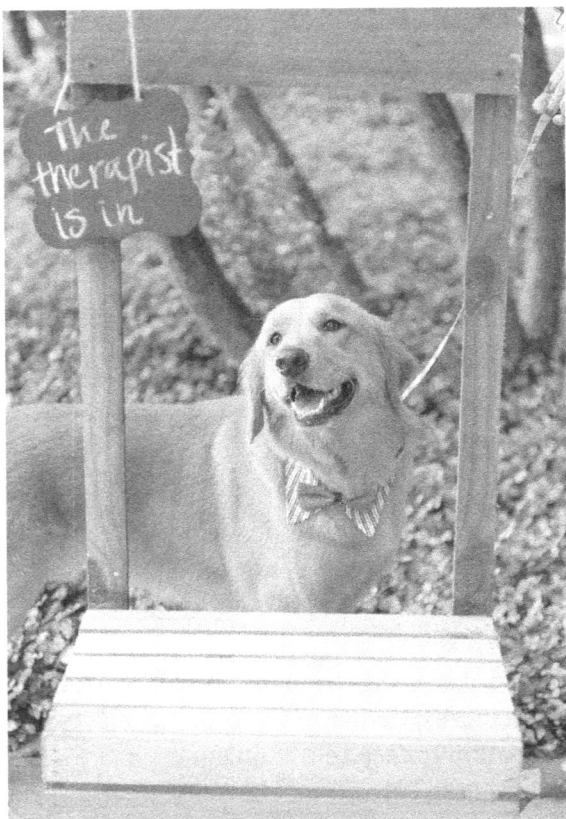

Figure 5.1 Crystal Perez's canine partner, Neo, is ready to do therapy!.

options available for human/animal teams coupled with the lack of specific guidelines within the mental health profession can leave an aspiring AASC practitioner feeling very confused. Although this chapter is not intended to replace actual AASC training, it will provide suggestions so that school counselors and their future animal partners can begin to prepare for training. Its goal is to clarify options by summarizing the training that is available for counselors and animal partners now, covering both volunteer and professional therapy animal training. Finally, drawing from research and experience in the field, this chapter will conclude by offering recommendations for choosing an AASC training program (Figure 5.1).

Literature Review

It's important to begin by recognizing standards in the animal-assisted intervention field. Chandler (2017) noted that the competent practice of animal-assisted counseling (AAC) requires compliance with (1) animal-assisted intervention and animal welfare organizations' standards of practice; (2) ethical codes of mental health organizations; (3) local, state, and federal guidelines related to animal welfare; and (4) standards that consider multicultural attitudes and beliefs about working with animals. Insufficient training could put the AASC practitioner, students, or the animal partner at risk. A therapy animal lacking essential skills might be unable to join with a student on a school counseling lesson, a therapy animal that has not passed a profession-based evaluation may snap at unexpected or rough petting, a school counselor may miss their animal's stress signals, or a student's unwillingness to participate with an animal might go unnoticed resulting in increased stress for the student or the animal. At its worst, an animal partner might end up injured or develop a fear of students, a child might experience an injury or a fear of that species of animal. These risks can be greatly reduced by school counselors and their animal partners participating in AASC training and supervision. Chandler asserted practitioners using AAC should have the following skills in order to reduce risk: complete training in AAC, facilitate a client screening prior to AAC services, review AAC-specific informed consent, recognize how to prevent animal-transmitted diseases, assess and respond to animal stress and welfare during sessions, develop clinical goals as part of an AAC treatment plan, and assess client progress.

Promoting Student and Animal Welfare

As much as the school counselor relies on their animal partner to provide comfort to students and staff, the animal also relies on the counselor to be their leader and protector. Ng (2019) found if a handler behaves in an irresponsible manner, it reduces the efficacy and well-being of interactions. School counselors need to adhere to appropriate training methods in order to facilitate positive experiences between animal partners and the students with whom they will be interacting within the school setting.

All services provided to students in a school counseling program should be offered with the goal of promoting student safety and welfare. Services that could inhibit student safety could impact the student academically, psychologically, and emotionally. Hartwig (2020) identified that practitioners who do not receive AAC training and supervision could cause harm in various ways. This list was adapted to apply to AASC as follows:

- an animal partner without sufficient training or temperament could injure a student
- a school counselor might fail to assess a student's interest or willingness to work with an animal partner
- a school counselor could ignore animal partner stress during a lesson or group, which could lead to student or animal injury and increased fear
- the likelihood of animal-transmitted diseases may increase by not requiring hand washing and assessment of both human and animal health
- the school counselor may not know how to effectively incorporate animals into the school counseling process through goal-setting, treatment planning, and AASC interventions.

These examples of potential harm can be avoided through sufficient training. Practitioners who are dedicated to AASC training will be prepared for assessing student interest in AASC, promoting positive student-animal interactions, decreasing the potential for human- and animal-transmitted diseases, and demonstrating clinical AASC skills and interventions.

Another topic that begs to be addressed is the welfare and safety of those animals that are providing the therapeutic benefits. As reported by Ng (2019), research supports that animals experience many of the same emotions that people do. It can be therefore considered that they are also vulnerable to the effects of experiencing the strong emotions that accompany trauma. In training and preparation for school counseling work, consideration must be given for the self-care of the animal to avoid over stimulation or burn-out, just as school counselors must also give mind to these aspects for themselves. In order to do this, a school counselor will need to have the ability to identify and interpret their animal partner's stress signals. They will also need to have a plan for providing breaks and flexibility for adapting their routine when the situation warrants. Additionally, they will need a strong relationship with their animal partner, providing connection to anchor their animal partner while navigating the stresses of the day. As noted by Mariti et al. (2018), dogs have the ability to form strong attachments with humans, feeling more stress when in the presence of a stranger and more relaxed in the presence of their attachment figure. Ng (2019) asserted that we have an ethical responsibility to our animals because we are asking so much of them – in the school setting, the counseling animal will be asked to interact with strangers in an environment full of unfamiliar sights, smells, and sounds. The animal may at times experience petting in ways they are not used to, be asked to perform tricks or follow cues, and be away from home for a prolonged amount of time. School counselors have much to learn about preventing harm and promoting positive human-animal interventions prior to bringing their animal partner to school.

Linkage to ASCA Standards

School counselors are called to follow ethical codes to uphold the integrity of the profession, promote the ethical practice of school counselors, and ensure the well-being of children in schools. The American School Counseling Association (ASCA) Ethical Standards (2022, p. 4) state that school counselors should "practice within their competence level and develop professional competence through training and supervision." Furthermore, these standards compel school counselors to "engage in routine, content-applicable professional development to stay up to date on trends and needs of students and other stakeholders, and regularly attend training on current legal and ethical responsibilities" (ASCA, 2022, p. 8). The ethical standards provide clear guidelines that school counselors are required to develop and maintain professional competence through training and supervision. These standards set a precedent for school counselors to seek out and participate in training and supervision in AASC that promotes the welfare of children.

The ASCA Professional Standards and Competencies provide further support for AASC training. Professional standard B-PF 3 h asserts that school counselors should "engage in continual professional development to inform and guide ethical and legal work" (ASCA, 2019, p. 3). Professional standard B-PF 4 states that school counselors should "stay current with school counseling research and best practices," "conduct and analyze self-appraisal and assessment related to school counseling professional standards and competencies," and "develop a yearly professional development plan to ensure engagement in professional growth opportunities related to relevant professional standards and competencies and personal limitations" (p. 3). These standards make it clear that school counselors are tasked with engaging in training and supervision in order to develop competencies in AASC (Figure 5.2).

Integrating AASC Competencies

Now that it has been established that the AASC professional has both professional and ethical obligations to seek specialized training, this section will define the recommended content for that training. The previous chapter identified research by Stewart et al. (2016) who conducted a qualitative study on AAC competencies with 20 practitioners who were considered experts in the AAC field. These competencies highlighted specific knowledge, skills, and attitudes that AAC practitioners should be able to demonstrate. Seeking to specify these requirements even more, Hartwig (2020) surveyed 38 AAC researchers, program directors, practitioners, and graduate students involved in the AAC field.

Figure 5.2 A therapy dog-in-training practices how to greet a friendly stranger.

The outcomes revealed four crucial knowledge content areas, all pertaining to a mental health professional's working relationship with their animal partner. Those four areas were (1) how animals are incorporated into counseling settings; (2) ethical implications of AAC; (3) how to work as a team with an animal partner; and (4) establishing and maintaining a working relationship with an animal partner. Quantitative outcomes from this study identified that practitioners interested in pursuing AAC as a specialization area should complete an average of 117 training hours, 22 live supervised experience hours, and 141 post-training supervised experience hours. These measurable standards provided specific guidance on the quantity of training, supervision, and experience for AAC training programs.

Chapter 4 recommended AASC competencies in the areas of Knowledge, Skills, and Attitudes. As a review, the first area of AASC Knowledge Competencies encompassed the field of AASC (e.g., its history, current literature, ethics, interventions, and risk management), the AASC animal partner (e.g., species-specific information, care, health needs, and positive training methods), and the AASC professional's school population (e.g., understanding of the effects of the human-animal bond and diversity considerations). This section included training as a way of gaining knowledge and supervision as a means of solidifying and extending AASC knowledge.

The second area of AASC Skills Competencies extends professional skills to include the counselor's own animal partner. Basic skills such as creating and maintaining a therapeutic relationship, communication, counseling skills, application of clinical theory, choice giving, and cultural responsiveness are also applied to the animal partner in AASC. Other skills are called for due to the inclusion of the AASC partner. Informed consent, continuing assessment of students and the animal partner, limit setting, facilitating interventions, advocating for an animal partner, and ending AASC services in a positive and healing manner are all necessary.

Finally, the area of AASC Attitudes Competencies seeks to outline ways that the AASC professional maintains the integrity of their profession and their animal partner's role through their professional identity, expressed values, advocacy, participation in research, and continuing professional development. All three of these competency categories promote the breadth and reach of knowledge, skills, and attitudes needed to be a successful AASC team.

Current Training in AASC

With a clearer understanding of the ethical guidelines and animal welfare considerations that oblige school counselors to get training and supervision in AASC and the professional competencies needed to be an AASC practitioner, this section will explore current training in AASC. In the school counseling field, there are two types of therapy animal teams: volunteer therapy animal teams and professional therapy animal teams. These types of teams differ in purpose, length, and intensity of training for school settings, as outlined in Table 5.1.

Table 5.1 Comparison of Volunteer and Professional Therapy Animal Teams in Schools

Information Category	Volunteer Therapy Animal Team	Professional Therapy Animal Team
Service Provider	School volunteers (e.g., reading program volunteers, career day speakers)	School professionals (e.g., school counselors, school social workers, school psychologists, Communities In Schools site coordinators)
Scope of Program	Team works with students who are identified for select services	Team is responsible for developing an AASC program that meets a variety of student and school needs
Educating Others	Team educates classes, groups, or individual students on appropriate ways to interact with animal partner	Team introduces and advocates for AASC program and animal partner at faculty meetings, school events, and potentially School Board meetings to educate those in the community about current research and the benefits of having animal partners in schools
Independence Within School Setting	Team must have another professional present (e.g., teacher, librarian, school counselor)	Team services provided by school professionals, so no other professionals required to be present
Location	Team typically visits classrooms or library	Team has office in school and can provide services throughout school
Treatment Plan	Team does not generally provide services as part of a student treatment plan	Services offered by teams are goal-directed and an intentional part of a student treatment plan

(Continued)

Table 5.1 (Continued)

Information Category	Volunteer Therapy Animal Team	Professional Therapy Animal Team
Services	Team is responsible for providing limited volunteer services for specific students or classrooms	Team delivers specialized, goal-focused interventions for a diverse group of students with a variety of learning needs and abilities; AASC services include schoolwide, classroom, group, and individual services
Length of Visits	Visits are short duration (two hours or less)	Team may be on campus for part or all of school day and on certain days of the week
Training	Training is typically a one-day or online training, animal health assessment, and a team evaluation	Training is typically more intensive with 100+ hours of training specific to AASC, animal health assessment, AASC team evaluation, AASC skills practice, and clinical supervision
Continuing Education	Continuing education training generally not required, but team may need to be reevaluated every two years and update animal health records	Specific requirements for continuing education in the field of AASC, update health records, and reassess animal behavior and engagement in continuing AASC services
District-required Professional Development	Team does not participate in district professional development	Team is asked to present information about AASC at district professional development to promote interest and growth in the program to other professionals

Volunteer work can provide a great introduction for the school counselor who is considering working with their pet in AASC. Trainings typically require a low time commitment yet provide introductory learning in essential skills that can be applied to AASC. Through the training, a school counselor can learn about facilitating brief interactions between their animal and strangers, interpreting their animal's body language, and setting healthy limits for their animal partner. The animal can also benefit by learning to meet a wider variety of people than it would typically meet, mastering basic commands, and learning to focus on cues from its human partner. As will be shown later in this chapter, all these skills translate easily to the school environment. An added benefit of volunteering is that the school counselor and their animal partner can sample working together, potentially before making a sizable time, financial, and emotional investment into the AASC training. Volunteer therapy animal programs do well in preparing a human/animal team for short volunteer visits such as a canine-assisted reading program. However, they are not designed for preparing a school counselor for working with their animal partner on mental health goals as part of a comprehensive AASC program, which involves specialized AASC knowledge, skills, and practice.

In addition to volunteer therapy animal programs, there are some online animal-assisted certification programs. Online training programs, though convenient and often less expensive than in-person training, provide a wealth of information about animal behavior and training, animal welfare, legal and ethical issues, working with special populations, and applications of animal-assisted interventions.

While these trainings can help develop knowledge competencies, they typically do not involve the opportunity to learn AASC-specific knowledge, practice AASC skills with their own animal partner, and provide counseling with their animal partner in the presence of a qualified supervisor that can provide feedback and evaluation.

An online search for "animal-assisted school counselor training" reveals the wide variety of training available. The professional is left with a dizzying selection of choices: volunteer or professional training, online or in-person, brief seminars to intensive programs, and those affiliated with colleges or universities versus those presented by individual training organizations. The next section will delve into recommendations for an AASC training protocol that offers guidance for school counselors considering becoming an AASC team.

Recommended AASC Training Protocol

Like Rosalie and Hank in this chapter's opening scenario, many school counselors and their potential animal partners find themselves asking the question of "Which program should I choose?" Having one's animal partner with them at school presents complexities that are outside the scope of volunteer training – as a school counselor will likely be designing animal-assisted interventions to support their students and meet school goals, adjusting their schedule to include their animal partner's needs, and including their animal in responding to students needing extra emotional support. Daily routines such as going to the rest room, meeting with caregivers, walking down hallways between classes, and getting lunch all now need the extra consideration of how to best meet the animal partner's needs. Unexpected situations also must be prepared for, such as fire and safety drills. What plan will be followed should the counselor need to focus all their attention on a student in the midst of a classroom animal-assisted lesson on social skills? What steps can a counselor take for training themselves and their animal partner to best ensure the physical and emotional safety of their students, themselves, and their animals? Even smaller critter therapy partners need special training as they will be asked to fill a larger, potentially more interactive role than that of a classroom pet. To help address these concerns, the authors have drawn from current research and their own experience to make recommendations on what to look for in an AASC training program.

Prerequisite Training – Introduction and Mastery of Basic Skills

Mastery of basic skills lays an important foundation for both school counselors and animal partners in AASC. Just as most certified school counselors were required to have prerequisite training as demonstrated by a graduate degree and classroom experience in education, a school counselor entering AASC training should have already learned and practiced the critical skills required of all school counselors. This will allow a training program to focus on learning and applying the many specialized skills needed in AASC without having to spend valuable time teaching basics that could be learned elsewhere. For the school-based practitioner, meeting their state's requirements for certification as a school counselor (or other type of school-based practitioner) is recommended.

Basic prerequisite skills are also needed for the animal half of the team. As recommended by Otto et al. (2021), training in basic obedience prepares an animal for a future work-specific evaluation. For a canine partner, using the American Kennel Club (AKC) Canine Good Citizen is recommended. This test is made up of ten steps considered to be "ten essential skills for every dog" (AKC, 2022): (1) accepting a friendly stranger, (2) sitting politely for petting, (3) appearance and grooming, (4) loose leash walking, (5) walking through a crowd, (6) sit, down, and stay on cue, (7) come when called, (8) behave politely around other calm dogs, (9) reaction to a loud noise, and (10) supervised separation. All of these skills will translate into AASC – for example, a therapy dog may need to walk beside their human partner through a crowded hall during a fire drill. Using a screening tool such as the CGC gives the practitioner the opportunity to see their animal through another's eyes, potentially avoiding the overlooking of behaviors or challenges that may impede an animal's ability to happily function as an AASC animal partner. Unlike volunteer therapy animal evaluations, the CGC is a generalized evaluation, offered by CGC evaluators across the United States, is readily available, and can be taken without becoming affiliated with a volunteer organization. Like volunteer evaluations, it also considers the handler's relationship with their canine.

What if a chosen animal partner is a guinea pig, rabbit, or miniature horse? Evaluations for non-canine animal partners are not as common, but still an important first step in training for AASC. Since there is not an equivalent screen to the CGC for non-canines, evaluations from volunteer organizations may be used as an alternative. Pet Partners, self-described as "the nation's most diverse and respected nonprofit registering handlers of multiple species" (Pet Partners, 2023), offers evaluations for cats, rats, birds, rabbits, guinea pigs, pigs, llamas, alpacas, horses, and donkeys in addition to dogs. Love on a Leash evaluates cats and rabbits, basing their evaluations on veterinary recommendations (Love on a Leash, 2023). The recently formed Miniature Equine Therapy Standards Association (METSA) offers evaluations for miniature horses, donkeys, and mules (METSA, 2020). All of these evaluations offer a method of objectively evaluating a future animal partner's appropriateness for AASC. However, it should be remembered that these evaluations are directed toward skills necessary for volunteering in a volunteer capacity and environment and may include behaviors that do not as readily translate to the school environment.

Preparation for the evaluation begins at home, regardless of the species involved, with the test items on the evaluation serving as a guide for training. Familiarity and ease around many different types of people in different environments is one of the most important skills a future animal partner can learn (Binfet & Hartwig 2020). An AASC animal partner will be interacting with a diverse assortment of students, teachers, and staff each day. Some interactions will be brief, such as greeting students as they move toward their morning classes. At other times the animal may take part in more complex AASC interventions, like working together with students to learn relaxation skills before testing. Chandler (2017) suggests experiences that help a dog see going out and greeting strangers as a happy experience. Introduce new people and situations gently and in small steps, then explore more complex environments as the animal partner grows in confidence (Figure 5.3).

Figure 5.3 Gordon shows that unique resources, such as rolling dice, may help integrate animal partners into the AASC process.

A school counselor's relationship with their AASC partner is a vital part of their work. Students will see and learn from their interactions, potentially learning as much or more about human relationships than from their classroom lessons. For this reason, it is important to start with a training program that values those qualities they wish to convey – those of respect, value, and teamwork. At some point in their training journey, an aspiring animal-assisted school counselor will undoubtedly join up with a professional trainer.

Researchers and professional organizations encourage people to use positive reinforcement techniques, such as rewarding positive behaviors with treats or verbal cues, rather than aversive training tools, such as shock collars or physical corrections (American Veterinary Society of Animal Behavior, 2021; Ziv, 2017). The Association of Professional Dog Trainers (APDT, 2023) takes this further by stating, "Trainers who use aversive tools such as choke collars, prong collars, shock collars (including 'stim-collars' and 'e-collars'), bonkers, shaker-cans, citronella spray, water spray, leash-pop/ leash-corrections (with any type of collar/harness), yelling, or any other technique designed to cause fear, pain, or startle in the dog are not practicing the least aversive, minimally aversive approach as described and used within APDT". By choosing a trainer that uses positive reinforcement training only, they will have a better chance of upholding these values. If possible, practitioners should watch the trainer in action with other clients and/or discuss preferred training methods with the trainer before working with them. Practitioners should ask themselves the question, "Will using this training method improve or damage my relationship with my pet?" And, if one finds oneself being instructed to act in ways that are contrary to one's values, do not hesitate to advocate for one's pet.

Finally, the future AASC team should seek consistency by continuing to practice skills even after the screening evaluation has been passed. At home, keeping all four feet on the floor to be petted, staying in a specific safe space to "settle" when visitors drop by, and sitting before their food is placed on the ground help a pet generalize skills and practice them in different situations. This can be especially difficult with multiple human members in a household, but so important to a pet's learning. When everyone in a family takes part, a pet will have the added benefit of learning to follow cues from multiple people – something they may be called on to do at school with students, too. Outside of the home, consider regular outings to pet-friendly restaurants and shopping locations, or perhaps accompanying their human to visit their office at school on a weekend when students are not likely to be encountered. Casual meetings such as these give the counselor the opportunity to observe interactions between their dog and the people they meet, taking notice of their pet's preferences (for example, how it likes to be touched and where, does it like for people to bend over or to squat down to pet). By taking these steps, the AASC practitioner will gain valuable learning that will help in the next stage of their journey.

AASC Knowledge – New Learning for Human and Animal Team Members

Once the future AASC team has already met their professional and basic animal training prerequisite skills, the school counselor will then be able to focus their training on learning the specialized knowledge needed for AASC. Much of the learning involves the human partner, so the authors recommend an initial learning portion that is human-only. The human partner has much to cover, considering that the school counselor will be working and translating for a different species. Otto et al. (2021) recommend training in zoonotic disease management and the interpretation of stress behaviors in their therapy animal. Likewise, Ng (2019) states, "being able to recognize the behavioral signs of stress is the first essential lesson for the handler; being proficient in responding to these signals is the second" (p. 63).

The AASC Knowledge Competencies set forth in Chapter 4 offer a comprehensive framework for AASC training as well as a guide in evaluating potential AASC training programs. Foundational knowledge should be adequately covered, including a review of the history of animals in school settings and current knowledge in the field as reflected by recent research and literature. Professional topics such as ethics, diversity, interventions, and risk management may already be familiar to the counselor but will need to be addressed from an AASC point of view, helping the counselor to adjust their understanding to include their future animal partner. Significant time should also be spent learning about the counselor's chosen species of animal partner, with the content covering animal care, communication, positive training, and health and wellness needs. Coverage of the human-animal bond, both as it relates to the school counselor's connection with their animal partner and as it relates to future connections with students and staff, is vital to training. Finally, the program should provide supervision throughout the training – providing feedback to the school counselor as they work to internalize this new knowledge so that they will be ready to apply it in practical situations.

AASC Skills – Transforming Knowledge into Skills

Just as school counselor education programs include experiential learning, the authors propose that a quality AASC training program should also offer the opportunity for practice with a school counselor's own future animal partner. In doing this, both the school counselor and animal partner will be able to develop their specialized skill set together. Practice provides a setting in which the school counseling team learns to apply knowledge gained during the previous section of training. Consequently, the AASC Skills Competencies involve practical application of AASC Knowledge Competencies. With these points in mind, the authors propose that trainers use the following strategies for AASC skills training:

- Role plays that allow AASC practitioners to practice the animal greeting, informed consent, responding to animal communication, animal choice, and AASC interventions
- Practicum sessions with volunteer clients that give AASC practitioners the opportunity to use basic counseling skills, apply their clinical theory, facilitate goal setting, use limit setting skills, demonstrate cultural responsiveness, and facilitate interventions and student-animal relationship
- Treatment and lesson plans to ensure AASC practitioners can link student goals to specific AASC interventions
- AASC Skills Checklist (Appendix A) completion so that AASC practitioners can reflect on their counselor-animal relationship, cultural responsiveness skills, assessment of students and animal partner, and confidence
- Recertification process to ensure that practitioners have a process for assessing animal partner well-being over time and when it's time to terminate AASC services for students and the animal partner
- Clinical supervision to assess practitioner skills during the training program and when AASC team is working in their school site.

Trainers can use all of these strategies to create more comprehensive AASC training for teams that allows for teams to scaffold skills by practicing some skills through role plays and later more advanced skills in practice sessions or with students in a school setting.

In this section, the authors will provide some additional information about each AASC skill related to what trainers can focus on or emphasize during an AASC training program.

1   Practitioner-Animal Relationship – Applying the knowledge of the human-animal bond to building a stronger connection with their own animal partner, school counselors and their animal partners work together throughout their AASC training. Counselors look out for their animal partner's needs, respond to an animal partner's need for a break, and maintain safe distances between their own animal partner and others in the training. The team relationship can also be demonstrated by emerging animal skills such as waiting quietly or settling during human-human interactions, and loose leash walking.

2   Animal Greeting – Trainers should provide opportunities for AASC practitioners to practice teaching others how to greet their animal partner. Trainers can demonstrate these skills and then have teams practice with peers, family members, and then eventually volunteer clients or students.

3   Animal Communication – Using knowledge about positive and stress signals in their animals, the counselor identifies their own animal partner's common (and sometimes subtle) communication. Practitioners should be fluent in animal communication and able to clearly recognize physical and verbal signals that their animal partner shows to indicate calm states and stress signals.

4   Cultural Responsiveness – Applying knowledge of diversity awareness, counselors examine their own beliefs about animals as well as those beliefs of their student population. Training programs should incorporate methods for broaching cultural conversations related to AASC and integrating cultural responsiveness based on student beliefs and experiences with animals.

5   Basic Counseling Skills – Building on mastery of prerequisite basic counseling skills and utilizing earlier training of those skills as applied to AASC, counselor training should involve practice through role playing and, later, through practice with volunteer clients. For example, counselors who are proficient in the skills of reflecting content, tracking, and reflecting feeling during a non-directive school counseling intervention might find it difficult to adjust to reflecting their animal partner's actions and feelings at the same time as their student's. Learning to reflect content, feelings, and behaviors of both students and the animal partner at the same time are important AASC basic skills.

6   Student-Animal Relationship – Practitioners should have opportunities to demonstrate how they facilitate the relationship between a student (or group of students) and the animal partner. This can involve comments about how the animal interacts with the child and how the child responds to the animal. The practitioner can learn ways to promote positive human-animal interactions through relationship-building activities, such as dog puzzles.

7   Animal and Student Choice – Training should involve the counselor practicing the process of allowing both the animal and student to choose if they want to be involved in various interactions and interventions. If an animal indicates they do not want to participate, they may be ready to take a break or may be experiencing stress or disinterest in the activity.

8   Limit Setting – Setting limits is a therapeutic response to potential actions that could cause physical harm or stress to the animal partner or student. The RUF protocol, adapted from Landreth (2023) and noted in Chapter 4, is recommended as it preserves the therapeutic alliance, addresses the student's motive, keeps the limit firm, and proposes an alternative. This method involves the following: Recognize what the person wants, Underscore the limit, and Focus on an alternative. As an example, Rosalie might respond to a student trying to give Hank a human hug by using the RUF method in this way: (1) Recognize what the person wants – "You really want to hug Hank," (2) Underscore the limit – "But Hank isn't for hugging that way." (3) Focus on an alternative – "You can scratch his chest or hug this stuffed toy instead."

9   Assessment of Students – As a part of risk management, counselors learn to identify potential strengths and difficulties in AASC, such as students who may not be appropriate due to allergy or

behavioral concerns. Practicing AASC with actual clients in training and post-training supervision gives practitioners an opportunity to navigate and consult on AASC challenges.

10 Assessment of Animal Partner – Combining risk management and animal welfare knowledge, the counselor applies their knowledge to their animal partner throughout the training to ensure that AASC is a good fit for them. It is possible for an animal partner to possess all prerequisite skills and still express discomfort with some or all aspects of AASC. Training activities such as role plays and practice interventions will help counselors make more detailed assessments of their animal partner's strengths and limitations.

11 Confidence – Trainers should assess for practitioner's ability to demonstrate confidence in AASC skills during the training program. If practitioners are not confident in their facilitation of skills during the program, they may need additional training or practice before bringing their animal partner to a school setting to work with children.

12 Informed Consent – AASC training programs may provide sample informed consent forms. The training program should offer opportunities to practice reviewing informed consent with students by describing topics such as school counselor/animal partnership, health protection, benefits and risks of AASC, and the animal's right to choose in AASC interactions.

13 Clinical Theory – Utilizing graduate training in clinical theories and post-graduate experience in using a theory, school counselors should be able to apply a primary counseling theory with the addition of their animal partner. Training should include opportunities to apply their theory in AASC practice sessions and in treatment and lesson plans.

14 Goal Setting – Considering basic training skills and knowledge of interventions, the counselor practices setting goals with AASC in mind. Training should involve actual practice in creating treatment and lesson plans for student services that include measurable goals for students.

15 Facilitating Interventions – With the knowledge of a variety of AASC interventions, training should offer the opportunity to practice facilitating those interventions through methods such as role play. While special trick training is not necessary, counselors may find it to their advantage to teach their animal partner new skills such as giving a "high five" or rolling foam dice, to be integrated into AASC interventions.

16 Termination – Taking into consideration knowledge gained in the areas of the human-animal bond, ethics, and animal well-being, counselors consider their student population's attachment bond with their animal partner and develop plans for a healthy, positive ending to the school year. Training should also cover identification and planning for unforeseen events, such as illness or death of the animal partner.

The above points are given in brief, not as an exhaustive list, but to provide examples and guidance in the recommended skills that will better prepare a team for meeting students in a school setting. One may notice a pattern where each of these items includes application of knowledge gained in the first portion. It is critical to the success of the team to demonstrate mastery of these applications together before encountering actual clients. More than just points for evaluation, each item also gives direction for practice.

AASC Attitudes – Discovering Your Professional Identity

Chapter 4 included a list of recommended AASC Attitudes Competencies. Although less tangible than skills, an AASC practitioner's attitude is no less important to their profession. Through the attitudes reflected by professional identity, values, advocacy, research, and professional development, an AASC counselor influences the attitudes of those around them. Videos and literature read during training expose counselors to new viewpoints, encouraging them to explore issues and ideas that they might not have considered before. Counselors might reconsider the importance of understanding animal stress signals or better understand training from a dog's point of view. Counselors also become aware of small words with large impact on attitudes – for example replacing the phrase "*using animals at school*" to "*partnering* with an animal at school" to convey the team approach more accurately to AASC.

AASC Supervision – Application in a Real World

Prerequisites lay a foundation, knowledge building sets up a framework, skills practice and attitudes fill in that framework with walls and a roof – now it is time for supervision to complete the structure and add uniqueness to the AASC's training. Just as each school counselor found areas of strengths and specialties – possibly focusing on at risk students, elementary, or secondary students – they will now have an opportunity to identify strengths and challenges as an AASC team.

Once an AASC team has passed their AASC evaluation, they are ready to further develop their skills by interacting with real students. Much as counselor education programs offer in-class practice first, then practicum experience with supervision, and then a supervised internship, the authors also recommend a similar process with an AASC practicum followed by a supervised internship. The in-person practicum allows for the application of knowledge and skills while learning specifics such as writing session notes and other documentation, learning and receiving feedback on recorded sessions, and evaluating the animal partner's acceptance of a variety of interventions (e.g., do they prefer nondirective or more directive interventions?).

How much time is recommended for supervision? Hartwig's (2020) study revealed an average of 22.24 practicum hours followed by 141 post-training hours of experience as recommended by those professionals surveyed. The authors suggest at least 20 hours for practicum, made up of direct and indirect experience, followed by at least 100 post-training hours. We (the authors) also propose a requirement of at least ten hours spent in either group or individual supervision so that the AASC team can continue to process challenges, gain feedback, and grow as a team. It should be noted that few training programs include a practicum section working with a counselor's own animal. There is also a gap in the number of programs that offer supervision as part of their certification process.

What happens during supervision? In a practicum setting, before training is complete, AASC teams work with volunteer child clients on basic goals, such as regulation strategies. Practicum sessions are typically individual sessions so that the AASC counselor can receive feedback and make adjustments with one client before attempting more complex work in school settings. Supervisors observe live sessions and record observations, noting strengths and areas of growth. These initial practicum sessions are critical for AASC practitioners to gain confidence and establish strong AASC skills before offering services to their school population. Post-training supervision is equally important, with AASC training graduates meeting together with a supervisor for case consultation, observation of recorded sessions, sharing AASC interventions, discussion of strengths, and increasing awareness of progress and areas of growth.

In order to support the development of AASC competencies, an AASC Skills Checklist was developed and is available in Appendix A. This checklist is based on the AASC Skills Competencies and describes what should be demonstrated for each competency. Supervisors can use this checklist by watching live or recorded lessons or sessions and then using the rating and comments on the form to provide feedback to AASC teams. Similarly, AASC practitioners can review recorded sessions (with caregiver permission) and complete the AASC Skills Checklist or complete the checklist after facilitating an AASC intervention with a student, group, or class. This checklist can be used in AASC program training to support AASC skills development and assessment.

Applying AASC Training to Primary-Level Schools

This section will explore how training will vary depending on the ages of the students one works with at a school. Another factor to consider is how training might need to be modified when working with students who have special needs. Regardless of the ages of students that an AASC practitioner is working with, it can be very helpful to make an introductory video to share with students, staff, and families before the first introduction of the animal partner to the campus to go over some of the basic concepts such as how to greet the animal, likes/dislikes of the animal, and any other safety protocols that need to be put in place.

When working with younger children, it is helpful to start from the very basic levels of knowledge. Jalongo et al. (2004) asserted procedures on allergies, safety, sanitation, cultural differences, and fear of animals should all be considered when bringing animals into the classroom. First and foremost, students need to know that before and after they interact with an animal in the classroom, they must wash their hands or use hand sanitizer. They are old enough to understand what germs are and how they make people and animals sick. This would be a great opportunity to partner with the school nurse to ensure all involved are using consistent vocabulary and protocol on this very simple, but important piece. Also, it is essential to know which students have reported pet allergies. The nurse will be able to share this information with the school counselor since many younger children are not aware of whether they have allergies or not.

Before every visit the school counselor makes to a classroom, teachers should review the established procedures for staying healthy and safe with the students (Baumgartner & Cho, 2014). Teachers are also one of the best resources for finding out if there are any cultural differences to consider or if any students have a fear of animals. The school counselor will need to be proactive and devise a plan on how to handle situations where a student is afraid, and consult with teachers and family so everyone is on the same page. Having contact information on any communication that is sent out via newsletter/ emails will help with staying informed of any concerns that families may have regarding the animal partner.

So what happens next? It is time to go into classrooms. Depending on what kind of animal the counselor has, it is helpful to have a visual aid to show what the animal might look like when they are happy, relaxed, and anxious/irritated. It is important to model for students how to greet the animal in various areas of the school, because younger students are more prone to crowd around the animal and want to touch it any time they see it. Students also need to know what to do if a fire drill or shelter-in-place ever occurs and the animal partner is with the counselor. If a counselor wants to work with students individually in a primary/elementary setting, the animal partner can be incorporated into play therapy interventions. A counselor might find that training in play therapy will be most beneficial in meeting the developmental needs of younger students. In one study about animal-assisted therapy, researchers found that children used their imagination to help "make unconscious connections" while listening to stories and as a result would choose to talk to a puppet or to the dog about their feelings, and often touch or hug the dog afterward which decreased their anxiety about sharing (Reichert, 1994). The majority of the AASC services with younger children in schools will address emotional regulation when they are feeling anxious, overwhelmed, or sad. More information about individual and small group interventions will be addressed later in this book (Figure 5.4).

Figure 5.4 Certified therapy dog, Stanley, shows a relationship-building activity that is used with students in school.

Applying AASC Training to Secondary-Level Schools

One might wonder how different it can be working with your animal partner in a middle or high school versus a primary or elementary school. The answer: it is on the opposite end of the spectrum. In secondary campuses, the environment is not as controlled as in elementary where teachers have students completing daily routines and walking in a more organized way in the hallways. Secondary campuses have crowded passing periods, the students are bigger in size, louder, and have less time to leave classrooms to visit with counselors. It is difficult for counselors to schedule visits to classrooms due to concerns teachers have with the lack of instructional time. Students are also trying to work through issues of depression and anxiety, gender identity and expression, suicidal ideation, self-harm, peer pressure, and college and career planning with increased pressure to exceed in all areas of life. By this age, many students have been exposed to pets or have pets of their own, so this is an advantage for secondary counselors and their animal partners. Overall, students are more developmentally mature and have basic knowledge about pets. A counselor must still address some of the same things that would be addressed with elementary students in the beginning. However, it should be a faster process to start implementing AASC with students.

Initially, before having students meet an animal partner, distribute an introductory video that addresses the basics of greeting the animal and its likes and dislikes to all students via weekly newsletters and possibly during an advisory period if they have one. Requesting that their teachers allow the students to watch the video during their class to help ensure more students will watch it. It is

Figure 5.5 Stanley and a student participate in a bonding activity in school.

never ideal to have the animal partner walking through crowds, so avoid it whenever possible to prevent incidents that might scare or hurt the animal. Students of this age may be familiar with their own allergies and able to verbally communicate this but consulting with the school nurse is highly recommended.

Many teens value the social aspects of their lives. When considering training and how best to deliver interventions to secondary students, training in animal-assisted small groups would be helpful because students get the social interaction time with peers and interact with the animal partner, making it possible to participate in therapeutic activities, as well as having processing time to talk about their feelings with the animal present. In one study, a high school counselor discussed how she considers her dog a "relaxing agent" and students often "indirectly communicate" with her as they are interacting with her dog, Roscoe (Anderson & Olson, 2010). In another animal-assisted model that was studied in a school, it was discovered that students and dogs have nonverbal interactions, and as a result, students learn how to decode nonverbal communication and apply this skill to their interactions with people (Anderson & Olson, 2010). This social skill is applicable to the general and special education students alike. In the same study, Anderson and Olson (2010) found that having a dog provided an outlet for middle school students to be friendlier with each other. Finally, another training option for secondary school counselors would be to learn more about activity therapy such as sand therapy and expressive art, that can be incorporated with AASC. These interventions could be used when meeting individually with students or in small groups. Expressive art and sand therapy provide opportunities for youth to express their ideas, feelings, and beliefs through what they create. AASC practitioners can use processing questions to incorporate the animal partner. The animal partner also provides a safe and nonjudgmental presence as youth are completing expressive interventions. AASC training should include curriculum in which practitioners learn AASC interventions for different age groups of students and opportunities to practice facilitating these interventions with their animal partners (Figure 5.5).

Applying AASC Training to Students with Special Needs

Lastly, when working with students with special needs, whether elementary or secondary, the school counselor should consult with the special education teacher about specific skills needing to be worked on and what the developmental levels of the students are. This data will be necessary for designing lessons for individuals, small groups, or classrooms. ASCA ethical standard A.10.i discusses that school counselors need to be aware of the strengths and weaknesses of learners with special needs while using best practices to support them academically and emotionally (ASCA, 2022). The counselor and animal partner will be able to work with the students and do lessons; however, one will need to adapt them and adjust the pace to meet each student's developmental needs. One option for introducing an animal partner to a class is to bring a stuffed animal that resembles the animal partner into the special education classroom. This allows time for the school counselor to model for the students how to properly interact with the animal and have them practice with the stuffed animal. If any students are fearful of meeting the animal partner, there can be a discussion that addresses how students have a choice, just like the animal does, in any interactions in AASC. School can be a safe place for students to work through their fears through several brief AASC visits (Baumgartner & Cho, 2014). Special education students and classrooms can benefit from individual and classroom AASC visits and services to help them work on specific goals to promote student success.

Trauma-Informed and Diversity Considerations

It is important for the AASC practitioner to remember that not all students and teachers will hold the same positive associations with animals that the practitioner does. As noted in the previous chapter, attitudes may be shaped by cultural, religious, or family values. Other students may wish to engage with the animal partner, but are held back by physical or emotional limitations. Interactions may be difficult because of the use of a device such as a wheelchair, or they may have reduced ability to control impulsive behaviors such as movements or vocalizations. Still other students may have high or low sensory thresholds, leading to either avoidance of the animal's smell or texture or to a sensory-seeking approach such as rough petting. They may even be aware of these differences and reluctant to engage out of fear of scaring the animal.

Perry (2014) defines trauma as "a psychologically distressing event that is outside the range of usual human experience, often involving a sense of intense fear, terror and helplessness" (p. 15). He goes on to report that it is estimated that about five million children experience some kind of trauma yearly. With these facts in mind, it is probable to assume that a number of the AASC team's student population will have experienced at least one trauma event. Animal-related trauma events are especially important to the AASC team as negative experiences with an animal in the past can affect a student's perception of the therapy partner in the present. For example, a child may generalize that a specific breed of dog is prone to bite and so avoid interacting with a canine partner that resembles that breed. Ludy-Dobson and Perry (2010) point out that trauma can affect children in multiple ways, all of which can bear importance on AASC. Early childhood trauma disrupts the healthy development of neural systems that are used in forming relationships and in regulating the stress response. In short, a student is unable to form a relationship with a school counselor and animal partner if their brain is focused on keeping them safe from perceived threats. This student is more likely to notice small movements of the therapy animal, interpreting them as threats. A "doggie smile" (sign of pleasure) may be misinterpreted as a snarl, for example. An added concern is that small actions by the animal, such as an inadvertent light scratch during an intervention, may be experienced as an attack on safety and result in increased fear.

All of these concerns can be addressed by a strong training program, beginning with the school counselor's training. Diversity, multicultural considerations, and trauma-informed care are all topics typically covered in school counseling programs. These topics should be readdressed in an AASC training program, with focus on specific applications to AASC. Development and practice of skills are also of great importance in these situations as it is the application of these skills that will enable the school counselor to create and maintain a safe environment, inviting all to participate on a level at which they feel comfortable. Some skills that the AASC team may find most useful in addressing diversity and trauma concerns are:

- Therapeutic limit setting that maintains safety without laying blame
- Knowledge of stress signals and signs of pleasure in your animal partner, coupled with the ability to monitor for these continuously and skills to intervene (or remove the animal) if needed.
- Skills in planning back-up interventions or adjusting existing interventions as unpredictability or lack of organization may decrease students' sense of safety
- Relationship-building skills such as making connecting statements (for example, "Hank noticed that you are sitting quietly. He is sitting quietly near you, too.") as Ludy-Dobson and Perry (2010) relate that healthy relationships are at the core of healing from trauma and loss.
- Choice-giving as presented by Landreth (2023), which gives students a sense of safety and control.

Canine partners, especially large ones, can be trained to remain sitting during initial greetings, or taught tricks that facilitate building a connection without direct contact.

Most importantly, the AASC counselor must know their own student population. Using and reviewing an AASC informed consent form with students can help identify potential considerations or challenges before any interactions take place. AASC counselors are encouraged to continue assessing student attitudes and needs both during and after interventions by asking questions such as, "What does this intervention mean to you?" or "How do you feel about this kind of animal?"

Before leaving the topic of trauma and diversity considerations in training, the animal partner's point of view must be considered as well as that of the students'. Like people, animals also have the ability to make associations, form connections, and experience trauma (Ng, 2019). A dog that has never met a man with a beard may react with fear, barking, or growling at their first encounter. Training in meeting a diverse group of people is crucial to helping a therapy dog generalize their concept of "friendly stranger." Screening tools, training, and evaluations are important in identifying the presence (if any) of triggers or areas of stress, particularly in animals that may have been acquired as rescues or later in their lives.

Finally, practice is the key to strengthening and generalizing skills for both school counselor and animal partner. Repetition with a variety of students in varied situations builds the team's ability to move through interventions confidently. It helps the animal partner learn what is expected of them and helps them to feel more at ease. All while building the ability to lead students in a consistent, predictable manner that emphasizes safety (Figure 5.6).

Bringing It All Together

School counselors wishing to find training in AASC often find themselves at a loss, faced with a variety of program formats: volunteer, professional, online, in-person, brief, and intensive, to name a few. Ethical principles, ASCA Professional Standards, and AAC/AASC competencies guide the school counselor on a quest to develop skills so they can support the students' social, intellectual, and emotional growth. Based on current research and our own experience in the field, we (the authors) recommend a robust program that includes training for both the school counselor and animal partner in AASC. Both will need to work together as they learn new knowledge, master skills, and practice in

Figure 5.6 Gordon high fives a child and shows that a quality training program benefits everyone.

controlled and school settings. We also set forth a framework of skills, guiding the AASC team as they learn as well as setting a standard for evaluation before moving into practice with students. A quality training program, such as the one outlined in this chapter, will help the AASC counselor to meet their goals for all of their student population.

References

American Kennel Club (AKC) (2022). *Canine Good Citizen (CGC)*. https://www.akc.org/products-services/training-programs/canine-good-citizen/

American School Counselor Association (ASCA). (2019). *ASCA school counselor professional standards & competencies*. https://www.schoolcounselor.org/getmedia/a8d59c2c-51de-4ec3-a565-a3235f3b93c3/SC-Competencies.pdf

American School Counselor Association (ASCA). (2022). *ASCA ethical standards for school counselors*. https://www.schoolcounselor.org/getmedia/44f30280-ffe8-4b41-9ad8-f15909c3d164/EthicalStandards.pdf

American Veterinary Society of Animal Behavior. (2021). *Position statement on humane dog training*. https://avsab.org/wp-content/uploads/2021/08/AVSAB-Humane-Dog-Training-Position-Statement-2021.pdf

Anderson, K. T., & Olson, M. R. (2010). "Dog"gone crazy schools: Models for incorporating dogs into the school setting. *Children, Youth and Environments, 20*(1), 318–328. https://www.jstor.org/stable/10.7721/chilyoutenvi.20.1.0318

Association of Professional Dog Trainers (APDT). (2023). *Official APDT position statements*. https://apdt.com/about/position-statements/

Baumgartner, E., & Cho, J. (2014). Animal-assisted activities for students with disabilities: Obtaining stakeholders' approval and planning strategies for teachers. *Childhood Education, 90*(4), 281–290. 10.1080/00094056.2014.936221

Binfet, J. T., & Hartwig, E. K. (2020). *Canine-assisted interventions: A comprehensive guide to credentialing therapy dog teams*. Routledge. 10.4324/9780429436055

Chandler, C. K. (2017). *Animal assisted therapy in counseling* (3rd ed.). Routledge. 10.4324/9781315673042

Hartwig, E. K. (2020). Advancing the practice of animal-assisted counseling through measurable standards. *Journal of Creativity in Mental Health, 16*(4), 482–498. 10.1080/15401383.2020.1792382

Jalongo, M. R., Astorino, T., & Bomboy, N. (2004). Canine visitors: The influence of therapy dogs on young children's learning and well-being in classrooms and hospitals. *Early Childhood Education Journal, 32*(1), 9–16. 10.1023/B:ECEJ.0000039638.60714.5f

Landreth, G. L. (2023). *Play therapy: The art of the relationship* (4th ed.). Routledge. 10.4324/9781003255796

Love on a Leash. (2023). *Become a member*. https://www.loveonaleash.org/become-a-member/

Ludy-Dobson, C. R., & Perry, B. D. (2010). The role of healthy relational interactions in buffering the impact of childhood trauma. In E. Gil (Ed.), *Working with children to heal interpersonal trauma: The power of play* (pp. 26–43). Guilford Press.

Mariti, C., Carlone, B., Sighieri, C., Campera, M., & Gazzano, A. (2018). Dog behavior in the Ainsworth Strange Situation Test during separation from the owner and from the cohabitant dog. *Dog Behavior*, *4*(1), 1–8. 10.4454/db.v4i1.76

Miniature Equine Therapy Standards Association (METSA). (2020). *Qualification evaluation*. https://www.miniatureequinetherapy.org/qualification

Ng, Z. (2019). Advocacy and rethinking our relationships with animals: Ethical responsibilities and competencies in animal-assisted interventions. In P. Tedeschi & M. Jenkins (Eds.), *Transforming trauma: Resilience and healing through our connections with animals*. Purdue University Press. https://www.jstor.org/stable/j.ctv2x00vgg.6.

Otto, C. M., Darling, T., Murphy, L., Ng, Z., Pierce, B., Singletary, M., & Zoran, D. (2021). 2021 AAHA working, assistance, and therapy dog guidelines. *Journal of the American Animal Hospital Association*, *57*(6), 253–277. 10.5326/JAAHA-MS-7250

Perry, B. D. (2014). *Helping traumatized children: A brief overview for caregivers*. Child Trauma Academy. https://www.childtrauma.org/trauma-ptsd

Pet Partners. (2023). *Careers at Pet Partners*. https://petpartners.org/about/careers/

Reichert, E. (1994). Play and animal-assisted therapy: A group treatment model for sexually abused girls ages 9–13. *Family Therapy*, *21*(1), 55–62.

Stewart, L. A., Chang, C. Y., Parker, L. K., & Grubbs, N. (2016). *Animal-assisted therapy in counseling competencies*. American Counseling Association, Animal-Assisted Therapy in Mental Health Interest Network. https://www.counseling.org/docs/default-source/competencies/animal-assisted-therapy-competencies-june-2016.pdf?sfvrsn=14.

Ziv, G. (2017). The effects of using aversive training methods in dogs—A review. *Journal of Veterinary Behavior: Clinical Applications and Research*, *19*, 50–60. 10.1016/j.jveb.2017.02.004

Preparing the School for an Animal Partner

Kristina Kern

Austin Independent School District

Box 6.1

Chapter 6 Scenario

Rosalie and Hank just completed an AASC training program together. After their hard work, they earned certification as an AASC team and are excited to begin the next chapter. It helps, too, that Rosalie advocated with her district to allow Hank to attend school with her. Of course, there are still many steps Rosalie should take before Hank is introduced to students and staff at her school. As a school counselor, Rosalie must ensure that all feel welcome. "All" includes the students who may be uncomfortable with or fearful of dogs. Rosalie will be creating plans and accommodations to ensure that the students and staff feel safe at school with Hank present. Rosalie will facilitate this by teaching her school community all about Hank – from his likes and dislikes to when it's okay to greet him. It's easy for Rosalie to educate others about Hank because she loves talking about him. Rosalie is excited to implement her canine partner into her individual, small group, and classroom counseling lessons, as she knows he will become an integral part of her school counseling program. By building her AASC program ahead of Hank's arrival, Rosalie is confident Hank's first steps on campus will be successful.

There are many factors to consider when a school counselor develops an AASC program at their school. By planning and preparing for multiple scenarios for the animal partner, the school counselor allows themself an optimal experience for all parties involved. Questions like "Where will the pet relief area be?," "How many hours a week will the animal come to school?," and "What items should I bring to my school to create a welcoming environment for my animal when working at school?" should be answered prior to the arrival of the animal partner. Clear communication with staff members, administration, students, and families is critical. In fact, the process of communicating to all stakeholders starts long before the animal arrives. Providing families with the AASC team's certification and credentials, the protocol for interacting with the animal partner, and opportunities to ask questions and share concerns helps ease the transition from a school *without* an animal partner to a school *with* an animal partner. Composing a welcome letter, developing a presentation about the animal partner to be shared with the community, and creating an informed consent are important components to complete before the arrival of an animal partner. This chapter provides the school counselor with ideas and tools on how to help introduce an animal partner to the school.

DOI: 10.4324/9781003392415-6

Literature Review

When considering the introduction of an animal partner to school, studies show that the "benefits definitely outweigh the disadvantages" (Anderson & Olson, 2010, p. 11). However, counselors may struggle with a starting point. Ensuring an animal has the right temperament and training is important. In fact, the American Counseling Association (ACA) Code of Ethics clearly states, "Counselors practice in specialty areas new to them only after appropriate education, training, and supervised experience (ACA, 2014, p. 8). While developing skills in new specialty areas, counselors take steps to ensure the competence of their work and to protect others from possible harm (Hartwig, 2020). Chapter 4 presented AASC competencies for the ethical practice of AASC. These competencies asserted that practitioners receive AASC training that includes AASC-specific knowledge, assessment of AASC skills, and supervision by an AASC supervisor. Therefore, school counselors should not bring an animal partner to their school until they've completed AASC-specific training, skills assessment, and supervision. In a study on measurable standards in AAC, Hartwig (2020) identified that practitioners should "complete an average of 117 training hours, 22 live supervised experience hours, and 141 post-training supervised experience hours" (Hartwig, 2020, p. 1). By developing a skillset and collecting valuable experience, a school counselor and their administration can feel assured that both the school counselor and the animal partner (i.e., the AASC team) have taken appropriate steps to help the school feel safe with an animal.

Once a school counselor and their animal partner have received the proper training, the school counselor can begin to consider how to introduce the animal to the school. Receiving buy-in from the school, district, and community are helpful steps in easing the transition. School counselors should also collaborate with their administration on ways to notify students' caregivers. Anderson and Olson (2010) recommended sending a letter home on the first day of school introducing the AASC team. Other school counselors may choose to inform their families in person at a "Meet the Teacher" night, by email, or even by a campus newsletter. The need to keep families informed and educated is an important step. In fact, obtaining support from caregivers is encouraged as they can be strong advocates for the animal partner and the school counseling program (Anderson & Olson, 2010). By working with families in tandem, the school counselor has the opportunity to proactively plan accommodations for students who may be allergic to the animal or not interested in interacting with the animal due to cultural reasons. This helps to prevent potentially harmful situations and emphasizes the expertise and competency of the school counselor (Figure 6.1).

School counselors should also recognize and communicate the role and purpose of the animal partner's presence on campus. This is important for those community members who are skeptical of an animal being available to students on campus. Most likely, the animal partner will serve to meet the social-emotional needs of students. Social-emotional needs can encompass a child's self-awareness, their self-management, their social awareness, their relationship skills, and their decision-making skills. Anderson and Olson note that students can feel empowered by teaching dogs skills. The time and discipline it can take for a child to commit to teaching an animal something is helping them with their own management of their body. This also helps students hone social skills and increase their self-esteem. When an animal follows a student's cue, the positive sense of self that develops can translate into other domains of the student's life. Overall, the introduction of an animal partner should be a carefully considered process involving all stakeholders to help ensure the safest and most positive experience for the animal partner and the community.

Figure 6.1 Hank's first day of school.

Linkage to ASCA Standards

ASCA Professional Standards and Competencies as well as ASCA Ethical Standards are helpful frameworks when building a school counseling program. When introducing an animal partner to a school counseling program, it is important to consider the role ASCA standards and competencies already play in the AASC program. For instance, school counselors are asked to "inform caregivers of the school counseling program's mission and standards in academic, career, and social-emotional domains that promote and enhance the learning process and outcomes for all students" (ASCA, 2022, p. 7). The school counselor can advocate for the importance of including an animal partner in a school counseling program by connecting the role of an animal partner to the mission of the school counseling program or district. Animal partners have the capability to develop students' social and emotional learning skills. Providing the connection gives the program added value.

In addition, ASCA Ethical Standards state that "all students have the right to a physically and emotionally safe, inclusive and healthy school environment, both in-person and through digital platforms, free from abuse, bullying, harassment, discrimination and any other forms of violence" (ASCA, 2022, p. 1). All students need to be considered when developing an AASC program. This includes students who are afraid of animals and may, perhaps, have had a traumatic experience involving an animal. How does the school counselor continue to provide a physically and emotionally safe school environment? The school counselor will need to put in safety measures for the animal and the students to provide a level of comfort. Normalizing for all members of the campus community that a student will never be obligated to interact with an animal partner is a way to provide relief to the students who don't want to interact with an animal.

School counselors can also create space for students to face their fears around an animal by offering them time with the animal. The school counselor is supervising the animal partner's mood and behavior at all times. When an animal partner is visiting a classroom in which the school counselor is aware of a child who may be frightened, the counselor can observe the animal partner's behavior and share observations with the student. Phrases like "I'm noticing his calm body, so if someone wanted to give him a pet right now, I think he may like that" or "Do you notice how his mouth is open and looks like a smile? That open mouth and relaxed body means he feels relaxed and interested in meeting you." In fact, ASCA Ethical Standards state that school counselors should "provide opportunities for all students to develop a positive attitude toward learning, effective learning strategies, self-management and social skills and an understanding that lifelong learning is part of long-term career success" (ASCA, 2022, p. 3). An opportunity to learn that an animal can be safe is such a powerful lesson for those who have previously had a negative experience with an animal.

ASCA Professional Standards state that "effective school counseling is a collaborative process involving school counselors, students, families, teachers, administrators, other school staff and education stakeholders" (ASCA, 2019, p. 2). Working alongside families, staff, and students when introducing the animal partner to the school eases the process for all involved. Finally, a school counselor should "demonstrate leadership through the development and implementation of a school counseling program" (ASCA, 2019, p. 2). Animal partners are not part of every school counseling program. Therefore, taking the necessary steps to develop an effective AASC program demonstrates a school counselor's leadership skills.

Steps to Preparing Schools for an Animal Partner on Campus

There are many steps to take before bringing an animal partner on campus. To begin, a school counselor will need to provide the appropriate documentation to the school and district leaders. As a school counselor, providing training certificates, up-to-date immunization records, and proper liability insurance for the animal alleviates stress for those uncertain of the AASC team's credentials. The school counselor will provide the paperwork to their principal or other district leader well in advance of the arrival of the animal partner on campus. As discussed earlier in the book, gaining district buy-in is a pivotal point for a school counselor taking the journey of incorporating an animal partner into a school counseling program. The initiative a school counselor takes to provide copies of credentials, medical records, and insurance assures the campus and district leaders of the school counselor's competency.

Once a school counselor collects this documentation, they will need to be ready to tap further into their creativity because there are several other types of documentation that allow them to produce new, exciting content for their community to use. Sure, immunization records aren't all glitz and glam, but other documents a school counselor creates to promote an animal partner can be fun and exciting.

AASC Family Survey

School counselors get the opportunity to envision how they'd like to create their AASC program. This author recommends that a school counselor create a survey to collect information from caregivers and families about their thoughts on having an animal partner join the school community. The AASC Family Survey can be found in Appendix A. This survey can be used or modified by AASC practitioners. Each school counselor must consider their school climate and culture to decide which questions work best for their campus.

Welcome Letter

A school counselor can put caregivers at ease by sending a welcome letter home with students. An AASC welcome letter is an official way to introduce an animal partner to the community. Below are ideas to consider including in a welcome letter:

- Animal partner's name, age, and/or breed
- Animal partner's certification and qualifications
- Anticipated schedule for the animal partner (e.g., "on campus Tuesdays and Thursdays from 9 am-12 pm")
- Benefits of having an animal partner on campus
- Acknowledgment that all needs will be considered including those with aversions to animals and allergies to animals
- How to contact the school counselor

The school counselor can also include pictures of their animal partner to create excitement around the animal's arrival. The school counselor should be ready to receive an influx of communication varying from additional questions to comments of enthusiasm. Figure 6.2 presents an example of a welcome letter that this author provided to all families before bringing her animal partner on campus.

Frequently Asked Questions Page

An AASC Frequently Asked Questions (FAQ) page on a school counselor webpage is an additional tool that not only gives families the opportunity to learn about an animal partner's credentials, but also, gives a school counselor the chance to proactively provide answers to the questions they think they will most likely receive such as, "How many hours of training did you and your animal receive?" or "What were some of the components of the test you and your animal partner had to pass in order to receive certification?" The school counselor should work with their administration to decide when and how the most appropriate way will be to distribute the information. The school counselor should also connect with the nurse during this process to document and ensure that all students who are allergic to the animal partner are known by the school counselor and the nurse. Perhaps animal allergy information has never been collected due to the fact that it was not relevant information for the school. However, if an animal will be providing frequent campus visits, knowing animal allergies is critical information. Communicating and partnering with families will ease this process of onboarding an animal's presence to the campus. Figure 6.3 is an example of an AASC FAQ page for an animal partner.

Signs

In addition to a Welcome Letter and an FAQ page, the school counselor can create signage to be posted in the school on how to appropriately greet an animal partner while in school. Before an animal partner arrives on campus, it is critical to teach others how to safely greet an animal. A phrase that can be used as a reminder to students and staff on how to greet an animal partner is to "be a tree" (Doggone Safe, 2018) (Figure 6.4).

Dear Families,

As one of the school counselors at Mills, Ms. Kern is excited to continue to build a positive climate and culture as our students continue growing both academically and socially/emotionally.

We're writing to inform you of the newest staff member at Mills. His name is George, and he is a certified therapy dog. George received his Canine Good Citizen certificate in September 2020 and is certified to work with children through the Animal Assisted Counseling Academy at Texas State. He meets Austin ISD's requirements for having a therapy dog at school. In order to obtain these certifications, George had to pass several evaluations as well as be approved by his veterinarian for his temperament.

At Mills, George will accompany Ms. Kern (at most) 2 days a week and will help build relationships with students. Research has shown that therapy dogs help with emotional regulation and tend to create a comfortable, warm setting. While it seems that many students are ecstatic about having a dog at school, it's likely that others will be more hesitant or even afraid. Please be aware that no student is obligated to interact with George. Students will be encouraged to wash their hands before and after petting George to avoid the spread of dander. Under rare circumstances, students with severe allergies may need different accommodations. If your child has allergies, or you do not wish to have your child to interact with George for any reason, please don't hesitate to contact Ms. Kern directly.

Thank you for all you do to support your child.

With kindness,

Kristina Kern and George

Figure 6.2 Welcome letter example.

FAQs about George!

Who is the dog at my child's school?

George is a French bulldog and is certified to work in an elementary school. He will most likely work at Mills at most two times a week. When he is not at school, he lives with our school counselor, Ms. Kern. He is 1 year old, and his birthday is on February 16th! George loves people, his family and treats!

What does George do at school?

George will have many different jobs at Mills. He is available for scheduled pets with students. He will also work with Ms. Kern as a therapy dog. He can help kids reach goals related to self-esteem, emotional regulation, friendship, or attention issues among many others. He is here to support.

I'm worried about allergies. Is that being considered?

Ms. Kern coordinates with our nurse so she is aware of students who have allergies (If you have not communicated this allergy with the nurse, please contact Ms. Kern). Before George comes into the school, he is cleaned to significantly reduce any dander (George likes baths!). One of Ms. Kern's protocols is that students wash their hands before and after working with George. Also, Ms. Kern's room is cleaned daily. Remember, no student is obligated to interact with George!

My child is afraid of dogs. What should I do?

Please let Ms. Kern know if your child has an aversion to dogs. There are several rules that Ms. Kern and George follow at school to ensure that all our students and staff feel safe. That is a primary focus of this program.

What is George's training?

George went to a 10-day board and train program to learn his basic manners in the summer of 2020. He also earned his American Kennel Club (AKC)'s Canine Good Citizen (CGC) certificate in September 2020. He and Ms. Kern, then, participated in Texas State's Animal Assisted Counseling Academy throughout the summer of 2021. The program was over 120 hours of training over the course of several weeks to prepare for his evaluation. He passed his certification test to be a therapy dog, and the certificate is in the counseling office. Ms. Kern and George are currently under supervision by Dr. Elizabeth Hartwig at Texas State University.

If you have any questions or concerns, please feel free to contact Ms. Kern!

Figure 6.3 FAQ page example.

The school counselor may have students on campus who want to run up to an animal partner and pet them right away. Teaching students the safe way to greet a dog, for example, is a lesson they can carry forward and teach others. In fact, animals may find it aggressive for a person to reach over them and pat them on top of the head. By grounding one's feet, dropping one's arms, and letting a dog engage first, it provides comfort to the animal. After a dog sniffs the person who wants to greet the dog, the person can slowly lower their body to be at the same level and then can begin gently petting the

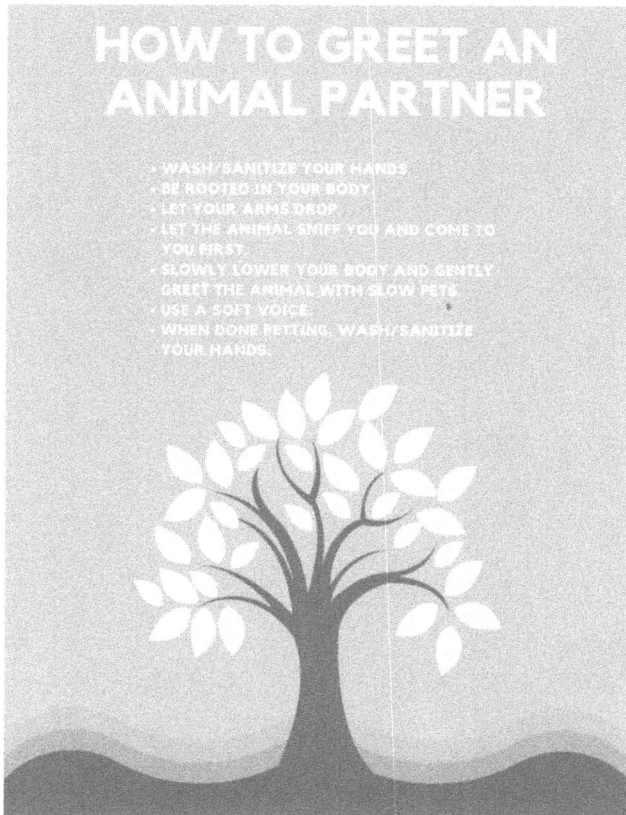

Figure 6.4 Visual aid poster on how to greet an animal partner.

animal. Posting signage, such as in Figure 6.5, promotes safety and welfare for students and animal partners. Also, as most educators know, a visual aid can be incredibly helpful for students.

Informed Consent

Informed consent and assent are integral parts of an ethical AASC program. It helps students and caregivers know about various aspects of the AASC program and working with an animal partner. The school counselor should use an informed consent form and process specifically for students working directly with the animal partner. This form should be covered and provided in the AASC training program. By having informed consent for students to work with an animal partner, it ensures full awareness of the benefits and risks involved in AASC. In addition, it deters the risks of liability occurring, and finally, it's a way to protect and advocate for the animal partner. Each animal is unique, and it will be important to consider if there are certain behaviors or noises that may concern a person. A comprehensive training program should provide a template of an informed consent as a foundation of items to include in an informed consent. While reading this book is an important step in gaining knowledge in this topic, it is critical to attend a training on this subject matter as well and practice facilitating informed consent in the training.

When you see an animal in the hall...
- **Stay with your teacher.**
- **Remain quiet.**
- **Wave to the animal with your finger.**
- **Give the school counselor and the animal room to pass.**

Figure 6.5 "When You See an Animal in the Hall" sign.

Space and Supplies for Animal Partner

Paperwork isn't the only thing a school counselor does to prepare for an AASC program. A school counselor will also need to consider the space their animal partner will be using. It's important to create a space that welcomes the animal partner. As part of the AASC team, a school counselor is always the animal partner's advocate and voice. School counseling offices vary in size and location, but there will certainly need to be a space somewhere on campus that meets the needs of the animal partner. An animal partner will need access to water, a place where they can rest, and a place to relieve themself. These are all areas to consider when creating a safe space for the animal partner. Animal partners have the choice to participate or not participate in a counseling session. Students also have a choice to have or not have an animal partner join a counseling visit. Therefore, when designing a space, there must be ways for a school counselor's animal partner and others to have separation. An animal partner must have a space they call their own in the school counselor's office. For example, having a large dog crate that includes the animal partner's bed, water bowl, and toys provides a space where the animal partner had a place to refuel and relax.

Acclimating the Animal Partner

To help an animal partner get adjusted to a school environment, it's a good idea for a school counselor to bring their animal partner to school before students have arrived. Perhaps, visiting the campus over the summer to better acclimate the animal partner to the environment is a safe, more convenient way to meet the animal partner's needs. Have them sniff around without other humans around and begin the rhythm and routine of arriving for their "new job" as this will also be part of the school counselor's new rhythm and routine. When brainstorming where a pet relief area may be, a school counselor can collaborate with their administration. School counselors can explore outside areas where their animal partner may feel comfortable. An example of this was when a colleague selected a grass area near the staff parking lot and off campus for their animal partner. This allowed her and her animal partner to have a space where the animal could have no interruption during pet relief. This also helped the animal partner understand where it was okay to have a potty break instead of, perhaps, on the school playground. The intentionality behind each detail of an animal partner's time on campus is critical. In addition, it helps build a sense of structure to the AASC program.

Apparel

As a school counselor continues to make decisions on how they will introduce their animal partner to the school, a school counselor must consider what will be both appropriate apparel for themselves and for their animal partner. This author recommends that school counselors wear close-toed and flat shoes, a small bag or fanny pack to hold treats and hand sanitizer, and business casual clothes that allow flexibility in movement when walking an animal partner. The animal partner should have an identifiable vest or bandana that indicates they are an animal partner, such as a vest that reads "Certified Therapy Dog" or an AASC-related bandana. Similar to humans, an animal partner having a "uniform" is a great way for the animal to know when they are working.

To Leash or Not to Leash

Although the topic of leashes may not pertain to all animals, it is important to consider the role of a leash in an AASC program. For critter animal partners, a specific habitat or space is created in a school counselor's office space to meet the needs of the critter, and therefore, a leash does not play a critical role. However, for an animal partner such as a dog, leashes play an important safety role for both the school community and the animal partner. Leashes provide safety for the animal partner and "felt safety" to students, staff, and families.

School counselors must consider when to leash and when not to leash. Setting these expectations at the start of the program is critical. At no point should a canine partner be unleashed outside of the school counselor's office in open spaces, such as the hallway, administration office, or gym. Students, staff, and families should be assured that the school counselor will be with the animal partner at all times and will also have the animal partner leashed when not facilitating sessions in a counseling space. By doing so, this brings assurance to students and staff who may have some discomfort or fear about the animal partner. With the set expectation that the animal partner is with the school counselor, it allows all members of the community to feel safe.

However, there are times where having an animal partner off leash can play a significant role. Once again, setting these expectations of when to leash and when not to leash early in the program helps bring a sense of calm and understanding for all those involved in the program. For counseling purposes, a canine partner may be taken off leash in the school counselor's office or a classroom where counseling groups are held. Before doing so, it's important to review expectations with the students and/or staff that are in the space. Ensure that the students and/or staff know the expectations such as to wash their hands before and after petting the animal partner, how to greet the animal partner, and reminders of stress signals of the animal partner. Students and staff should verbally agree to the animal partner being off leash before taking the animal partner off leash. Animal partners can have very impactful moments off leash in a small group or individual setting. Receiving permission and setting expectations with the group and/or individual before unleashing an animal partner sets a positive tone for the session. Finally, it's important to lock the counseling office door or ensure that the animal partner will not leave the counseling office space when off leash. As so often happens, school counselors may be interrupted by a knock at their door followed by someone opening their door. Therefore, building in safety protocols and procedures so that the only times in which the animal partner is unleashed is when they are in the counseling office. Having an animal partner off leash is an exciting opportunity for the animal partner and the students, but all parties involved need to feel safe and secure in order to have a productive and meaningful session.

Introducing the Animal Partner Presentation

Communication is critical throughout the process of introducing an animal partner to a school community. As discussed earlier in the chapter, receiving input from families, collaborating with campus and district leaders, and educating every stakeholder about how to work with an animal partner are critical pieces to ensure the success of this additional component to a school counseling program. Another consideration is how the school counselor will teach the school community about appropriate ways to interact with an animal partner. Options for introducing an AASC team to the school include a presentation in each classroom, a schoolwide presentation, and a recorded video with animal partner. These are all ideas to help a school counselor create a presentation that works for each AASC team and their school. It should be noted that regardless of when and how the introduction occurs, reminders will be given each time a school counselor and their animal partner visit a classroom. Students will need to be reminded that they are to wash their hands before and after petting an animal partner, when it is appropriate and not appropriate to approach the animal partner, how many people can be around the animal partner at a time, and an animal partner's stress signals. This is part of the world of education: providing reminders to students.

Regardless, choosing how to introduce an animal partner is a fun opportunity. The school counselor gets to teach their school how to make the experience a positive one for the students and for their animal partner. The school counselor gets to teach their community what an animal partner is and how, where, and when to interact with their animal partner. Ideas to make a presentation engaging include sharing an animal partner's likes and dislikes, sharing an animal partner's age, history, and breed, and providing glimpses into their personality – whether that is through photos or videos or stories about the animal partner. Additionally, helping students learn how to pet an animal partner and notice stress signals in an animal partner are great ways to educate the school. The following items should be considered when developing a presentation (Figure 6.6):

• What an animal partner is and their role at the school
• What an animal partner does at school
• History, age, and breed of the animal partner
• Health and safety procedures and protocols when interacting with the animal partner
• What to do if you are not interested in the animal partner
• How, when, and where to greet the animal partner
• How, when, and where *not* to greet the animal partner
• Signs the animal partner is happy

Figure 6.6 George, an animal partner in Austin, Texas; photo used for an introductory presentation.

- Signs the animal partner is stressed
- Likes and dislikes of the animal partner
- Pictures of the animal partner

Depending on the age level, school counselors should create a presentation that is short and educational for their school community. The method in which a school counselor intends to introduce their animal to their school will set the tone of how the school counselor wants their animal partner treated. The introduction *should* take time and careful consideration. Luckily for the reader of this book, if they implement the steps provided in this chapter, the school counselor is helping to ensure an animal partner is cared for in a safe and happy way.

So far, this chapter has reviewed the following considerations: necessary paperwork to demonstrate competency and qualifications to provide AASC services to the campus, preparations for a space to welcome an animal partner to a safe environment, surveys for stakeholders to complete before an animal partner arrives on campus, ways to communicate to students, staff, and families that an animal partner will be arriving on campus soon, and ideas on how to introduce an animal partner to campus. The final piece is just as important as these prior steps. It's now time to build a system and schedule that works best for an AASC team for the school days ahead.

Program Schedule

School counselors are flexible people who will pivot to meet the needs of their students, and in this case, to meet the needs of their animal partner, too. When deciding how often and how long an animal partner will be at school, it is key for the school counselor to start with a small plan and grow from there. This means to start with shorter visits one day a week and build towards longer hours and/or multiple workdays per week. The school counselor and animal partner should be creating realistic and achievable goals to build towards an ideal schedule that will work for the team. Depending on the comfort level of the animal partner and the school counselor, the amount of time spent at a school per week as an AASC team will vary. Regardless, an AASC team wants to continuously be experiencing little successes so that the team is building confidence in themselves and in their program.

A planned schedule wouldn't be what it is without the unpredictable and unplanned circumstances that occur sometimes. It is critical to let students and staff know that even with a schedule, an animal partner may not be able to meet all their scheduled visits. A school counselor may have to explain to their students that just like humans, animals can get sick, too. School counselors must continuously remind themselves that they are their animal's advocate. There may be certain days that an animal partner is scheduled to attend school but as the advocate, the school counselor notices their behavior (e.g., the animal is sick) and can tell they are not up to working with students that day. A school counselor may have six scheduled visits to classrooms in a day and notice that after classroom visit number four, the animal partner is exhausted. It is up to the school counselor – the advocate – to make the decision to speak up for the animal partner and promote animal welfare.

When building a schedule, school counselors will need to consider the services they'd like to offer to their campus and how people can access said services. Here are some questions to consider about the AASC program:

- Will the animal partner participate in classroom visits?
- Will the school counselor and the animal partner provide individual counseling services?
- Will the animal partner participate in small group counseling?
- How can people access the services offered by the AASC team?
- Will the school counselor have an online scheduler that teachers can access?
- Will people email the school counselor to request individual informed consent forms?
- Will the school counselor have an AASC services interest form that is accessible to all?

These are questions that only the school counselor can answer. When introducing an animal partner to the school, however, it is important to have thought through these scenarios so that the school counselor can provide clear answers to their community on how and when the AASC team is available.

For instance, the school counselor may decide that they will attend school with their animal partner for the first four hours of their Friday. The first hour and a half could be individual check in sessions with students. Following the individual sessions, the school counselor provides their animal partner with a scheduled break. Afterward, the school counselor accesses the online scheduler they've given to every teacher to see which teachers signed up for classroom visits that day in the two-hour window that has been set aside for classroom visits. As the advocate, the school counselor has strategically created the visit to be in 30-minute windows. However, the school counselor has planned for every visit to be 20 minutes maximum so as to provide the animal partner and the school counselor breaks in between each classroom. Finally, during the last half hour of the animal partner's time at school, the school counselor provides their animal partner with a potty break and returns to their office to catch up on emails and voicemails. Perhaps responsive services are in order and the AASC team is on the way to another classroom. If in the last half hour, the school counselor notices their animal partner is completely spent and has instead chosen to put on some quiet music, turn off the lights, and work quietly at their computer, allowing their animal partner to have their own quiet time to drink water and rest. Every school counselor and every animal partner have different styles, paces, and ways of serving their school. As the school counselor continues to build their relationship with their animal partner, the school counselor will continue to adjust and develop a schedule and system that works for themselves, for their animal partner, and for the students they serve (Figure 6.7).

In all these instances, it is incredibly important that the school counselor partner with their administration. Before the arrival of an animal partner on campus, school counselors should work with an administrator to see what a realistic and reasonable schedule looks like for the school counselor and for the animal partner. For example, it will be critical to receive permission from an administrator to leave campus during the school day to either pick up the animal partner, drop off

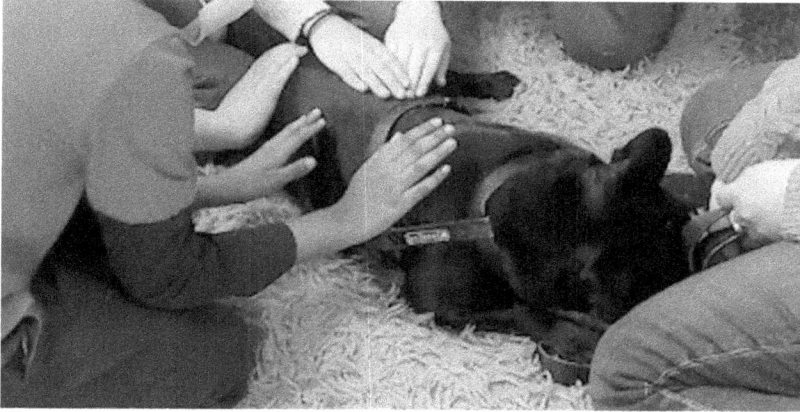

Figure 6.7 George visiting a classroom.

the animal partner, or both. School counselors might not be able to schedule a four-hour workday for an animal partner if a principal explicitly states to a school counselor that they will not be given travel time during the day to drop off an animal partner at home. During the first few weeks of implementation of the program, communicating with the campus leader should occur on a frequent basis. Process with them what is and isn't working regarding the AASC program. The relationship developed between a school counselor and a principal is one of the most important relationships on campus. With the support and trust from an administrator, a school counselor can effectively promote and deliver AASC program services.

Swag

As a bonus, when introducing an animal partner to a school, school counselors have yet another opportunity to be creative. Get others engaged and excited by promoting an animal partner program through stickers, magnets, or even baseball cards. These may be made available in the front office and the school counselor may carry them around to hand out to students or provide them to teachers to use in their classroom as they see fit (Figure 6.8).

Figure 6.8 Animal partner sticker examples.

Participation and engagement are ways to evaluate the overall feeling of the animal partner's presence. As one can see, the preparation for the arrival of an animal partner requires thoughtful action steps. By considering the documentation, the space, the communication, and the system and schedule, a school counselor is setting themselves up for a successful school counseling program involving an animal partner.

Trauma-Informed and Diversity Considerations

When starting an AASC program, it is expected that the students, staff, and families will have a wide range of thoughts, beliefs, and opinions about the animal partner. While many may have had positive experiences with animals in their past, there may be students, staff, and/or family members of students who have had a traumatic experience with an animal. As referenced earlier in this chapter, before introducing the animal to the campus, the school counselor has an opportunity to collect information from stakeholders and learn about the fears a student may have about the animal partner. An effective way to capture any and all concerns about an animal arriving on campus is to provide a survey to stakeholders. A school counselor can use all communication platforms available to them in order to reach all families. Whether that be an email by their homeroom teacher, or a newsletter sent by the principal, the school counselor can access all the available communication pathways to assess the climate around an animal. Receive input and feedback on how best to support each individual struggling with the fear they have about the animal's arrival. Brainstorm and co-create safety plans with individual students who may be scared or afraid of an animal partner's presence. Develop goals with individual students who are hoping to build a positive relationship with the animal partner. These are important considerations when introducing an animal partner to the campus.

In addition, depending on the cultures of a school community, there may be families in the school community who hold a belief that animals, particularly dogs, are unclean and impure. Therefore, once again, the school counselor has an opportunity to seek to understand their community before the animal arrives. The school counselor should be able to broach cultural conversations related to AASC with students and their families. Perhaps, the school counselor considers including this as a slide in the PowerPoint presentation that will be shared with every classroom before the arrival of the animal partner in which the school counselor teaches the role of the animal partner and explores cultural beliefs. There are certainly thoughtful ways to carefully prepare for a successful beginning of an animal partner on campus and proactively taking steps to address these considerations will ease the process of adding an animal partner to a school counseling program.

Bringing It All Together

The introduction of an AASC animal partner to a school campus is an exciting time. Throughout this chapter, the author introduced various resources for preparing the school for an AASC program and animal partner. Documentation such as AASC team credentials, proof of training and/or certification, current immunization records, proof of liability insurance, a welcome letter, an FAQ page, and informed consent provide school staff, students, and caregivers with information about a school counselor's expertise, training, and plans for the AASC program. Examples were provided of some documentation to assist and inspire school counselors. In addition, school counselors learned the importance of creating a safe space for the animal partner. Space includes not only a place where an animal can rest but also where an animal may go to relieve themselves. Also, throughout the chapter, communication was reiterated as a key component in introducing an animal partner to a school. From partnering with the nurse to help identify all students with an allergy to educating all students on what an animal partner is, school counselors learned how critical it is to be communicative throughout the process of introducing an animal partner to a campus. Finally, school counselors were provided ideas and examples on how to build a system and schedule for their animal partner. There are truly many components that must come together to ensure that the introduction of an animal partner is a positive experience for all. An AASC program has the potential to create systemic change in the lives of students. By following these action steps shared in this chapter, school counselors are preparing themselves to be a successful AASC team.

References

American Counseling Association. (2014). *Code of ethics.* https://www.counseling.org/resources/aca-code-of-ethics.pdf

American School Counselor Association. (2019). *ASCA school counselor professional standards & competencies.* https://www.schoolcounselor.org/getmedia/a8d59c2c-51de-4ec3-a565-a3235f3b93c3/SC-Competencies.pdf

American School Counselor Association. (2022). *ASCA ethical standards for school counselors.* https://www.schoolcounselor.org/getmedia/44f30280-ffe8-4b41-9ad8-f15909c3d164/EthicalStandards.pdf

Anderson, K. T., & Olson, M. R. (2010). *"Dog"gone crazy schools: Models for incorporating dogs into the school setting. Children, Youth and Environments*, 20(1), 318–328. https://www.jstor.org/stable/10.7721/chilyoutenvi.20.1.0318

Doggone Safe (2018). *Be a tree program.* https://doggonesafe.com/be-a-tree

Hartwig, E. K. (2020). Advancing the practice of animal-assisted counseling through measurable standards. *Journal of Creativity in Mental Health*, 16(4), 482–498. 10.1080/15401383.2020.1792382

Assessment in AASC

Krista K. Schultze
Marion Independent School District

Box 7.1

Chapter 7 Scenario

Rosalie and Hank have had such a positive impact in their school that counselors on other campuses are beginning to inquire about adopting a similar program at their school. The superintendent has unallocated funding that he could devote to training additional counselors in animal-assisted school counseling (AASC), but there are other programs more directly linked with learning and academics for that funding as well. He approaches Rosalie to request any data she has collected that shows the impact that Hank and her intervention services have had on student outcomes. Rosalie has collected a variety of outcome data related to interventions used in the areas of personal, social/emotional development, and college/career planning and how Hank was utilized in these domains to contribute to student learning and growth. The superintendent will use this data to assess the AASC program in his district, which will drive decisions about the future growth of the program.

Assessing learning environments, campuses, districts, teachers, personnel, curriculum, and students is a normal part of the educational system today. State standardized testing results guide teacher development needs, campus accountability, funding distribution, and student intervention courses (Every Student Succeeds Act, 2015). It is no longer good enough to assume that a new curriculum results in better student outcomes. Schools need proof. It is not good enough to suggest that all demographic groups are learning equitably. We need data to support this. The mentality of "if it ain't broke, don't fix it" no longer applies as maintenance is not desired, but rather constant growth of our students (Studer et al., 2006). Knowing where students are now, and where they end up after implementing a new curriculum, intervention, or program is a necessary and often required component of today's educational system.

Counseling programs are not immune to the need for assessment either. Assessment data can be used to plan, develop, and evaluate a comprehensive counseling program (American School Counselor Association (ASCA), 2019; Carey & Dimmitt, 2008; Even & Williams, 2018). They can be used to determine what interventions a student needs, as well as gauge the effectiveness of those utilized on academic, social/emotional, and career planning goals. Assessments can be used as a tool to advocate for counseling program needs as well. As a school support service, evaluating the effectiveness of a counseling program on student learning can further justify the role of counseling in the overall school system. At the end of the day, the primary mission of the educational system is to promote student achievement and

DOI: 10.4324/9781003392415-7

even support services needed to validate their contribution to this cause (U.S. Department of Education, 2011; Sink, 2009; Studer et al., 2006). AASC can be an effective component of counseling programs and contribute to student achievement. Planning and utilizing assessment data to support this claim will be vital to maintaining an effective data-driven AASC program.

Literature Review: AASC Assessment Cycle

The process of school counseling is fluid, dynamic, and usually cyclical in nature as shown in Figure 7.1. It begins by identifying a need or problem, formulating a strategy to address it, gathering data before, during, and after an intervention, reflecting on outcome data, and making adjustments or finding new problems to continue the cycle (ASCA, 2019, 2021). Assessment and evaluation are linked throughout many of the steps in this process. AASC does not change these steps; the same framework can be utilized in an AASC program. The same assessment strategies used in other types of school counseling can be applied to AASC. In this chapter, we will review the various types of assessment and examples used in school counseling. Note that assessment is linked to all three school counseling domains – academic, career planning, and social/emotional development – so the examples presented hereunto are not inclusive of all possible methodologies for all possible domains, mindsets, and behaviors. We present mere examples to model the various methodologies that can be used in AASC (ASCA, 2019).

In today's society, school counseling programs must be data-driven, and conducting a needs assessment is the first step in ensuring this occurs (see Figure 7.1; ASCA, 2019; Carey & Dimmitt, 2008). This step identifies what problems or gaps exist within the campus or an individual student that can be addressed by the counselor. Tables 7.1 and 7.2 identify some of the data that can be gathered in the needs assessment process. The amount of data available to counselors can be overwhelming, but not all data is gathered at all times. Some of these data sources are released at regular intervals (i.e., report

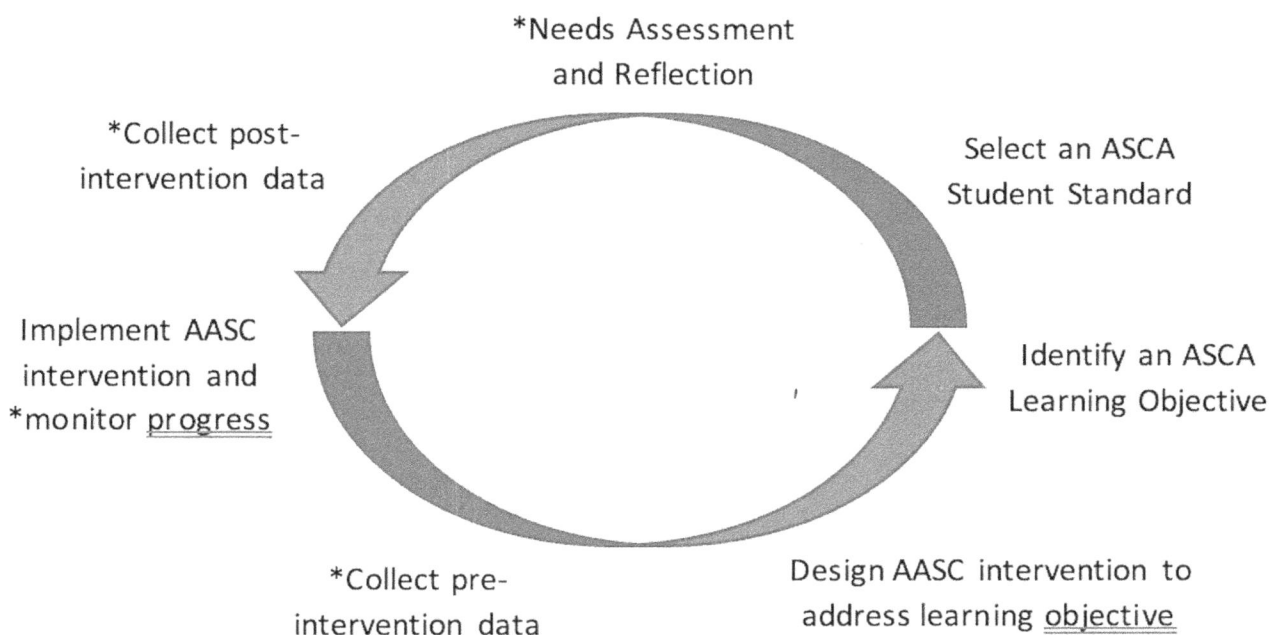

Figure 7.1 AASC data-driven counseling cycle.

Table 7.1 Campus-Wide Data Sources for Needs Assessment

Example	Purpose
Achievement Data	
School accountability report	Review trends by subject, grade, or subpopulation to identify gaps
National standardized test results (e.g., PSAT, SAT, ACT, AP, ASVAB)	Review overall participation and scores. Disaggregate the data by subpopulation to identify gaps
Course enrollment data	Review program enrollment data for equitable distribution of subpopulations across Advanced Placement, dual credit, dual enrollment, and technical education courses
Failure report	Review for trends in number of failures, subject-area failures, or subpopulation failures
College application reports	Analyze for equitable distribution and overall completion rate
Attendance Data	
Average daily attendance reports	Review absence and tardy reports to identify trends
School activity sign-in sheets	Review student and parent participation in various events
Behavior Data	
In-school suspension reports	Identify common themes for placement (e.g., insubordination, vaping, fighting), seasonality trends, as well as population distribution
Alternative education placement reports	Identify common themes for placement (e.g., drug possession, fighting, possession of weapons), seasonality trends, as well as population distribution
Referrals reports	Identify common themes for write-up (e.g., insubordination, disrespectful behavior), seasonality trends, as well as population distribution
National/State Reports	
SAMHSA National Survey on Drug Use and Health; National Substance Use and Mental Health Services Survey	Identify national and state trends relating to academics, career needs, and social/emotional issues
Perception Data	
Parent survey data	Use of qualitative and quantitative responses to identify needs from a parents' perspective regarding any of the three ASCA domains (e.g., academic, career development, social/emotional) Example: Parent knowledge of FAFSA and comfort level with completing the application independently

(Continued)

Table 7.1 (Continued)

Example	Purpose
Student survey data	Use of qualitative and quantitative responses to identify needs from a students' perspective regarding any of the three ASCA domains Examples: Students self-described level of stress, along with known coping strategies; Student survey on post-secondary interests could drive campus recruitment efforts
Teacher/staff survey data	Used to identify needs from a teachers' perspective regarding any of the three ASCA domains Example: Teachers rank a variety of counseling-related services that they believe are most needed
Universal Screeners	
BASC2-BESS, Perceived Stress Survey	Used to screen for various academic, behavioral, or emotional skills as compared to state and national standards. ASCA does not endorse using these for diagnostic assessment as that is outside the scope of a school counselor

Table 7.2 Individual Data Sources for Needs Assessment

Example	Purpose
Achievement Data	
Student transcript	Identify if the student is on track to graduate based on credits. Identify academic areas of strengths and weaknesses
Student report card or progress reports	Identify student progress towards credits. Identify academic areas of strengths/weaknesses
Student standardized test reports (e.g., state assessments, AP, SAT, PSAT, ACT, AP)	Identify if a student is on track for post-secondary steps
Attendance Data	
Student attendance record	Identify trends in time of day missed or seasonality of absences. Identify correlations between absences and grades
Behavior Data	
Student disciplinary record	Identify areas for personal growth
Diagnostic Reports	
Medical diagnosis	Identify if students need additional support services. Recognize interventions that may be more effective based on diagnosis

(Continued)

Table 7.2 (Continued)

Example	Purpose
Perception Data	
Student oral or written response during responsive service setting	Identify appropriate services to meet their needs
Student oral or written response during a classroom guidance, small group, or individual meeting	Identify appropriate services to meet their needs
Standardized Achievement Tests	
Iowa Assessments CogAt	To compare student achievement in various subjects to national standards. ASCA does not endorse using these for diagnostic purposes as it is outside the scope of the school counselor

Sources: (Dimmitt, 2009; Even & Williams, 2018; Simon et al., 2018).

cards), whereas others are released only once or twice a year (i.e., school accountability). Others are always available, so can be compiled as convenient or as needed (i.e., disciplinary reports; universal screeners). To prevent information overload, a data review calendar can help divide up data collection and analysis throughout the year into manageable pieces.

The needs assessment phase may identify several target areas that the school counseling program can address. For example, Donohue et al. (2018) used a universal screener (e.g., Behavioral Assessment System for Children-Behavioral and Emotional Screening System (BASC-BESS)) to identify students in emotional distress that could use social-emotional support like individual or small group counseling. Likewise, Smith et al. (2010) administered a counseling topic interest survey to high school students that led to the development of a new health and wellness curriculum delivered by the counseling department. When gathering data in this phase, counselors should ensure that needs identified are within the scope of the counseling department by identifying a corresponding match in ASCA's student mindsets and behaviors (ASCA, 2021). The next step in the data-driven counseling cycle is designing an intervention or strategy to target the learning objective. The counselor should decide at this step if an animal-assisted intervention would be in the student's best interest. Chapters 9 and 10 address how to develop and plan AASC interventions to meet student goals.

Creating Data-Driven AASC Lesson Plans

The AASC Lesson Plan provides a framework for designing appropriate interventions, but also for preemptively identifying the types of data needed to ensure adjustments to the intervention are needed, learning objectives met, and impact to the campus is assessed. Various forms of data – formative, outcome, and implementation – are included in this document. The Lesson Plan begins with a Lesson Plan Info section. In this section, basic data about the lesson is identified, such as the name of the AASC practitioner and animal partner, theory used, target audience, and lesson plan title. For types of lesson plan, practitioners can choose between schoolwide, classroom, small group, or individual counseling service types. In order to indicate the type of evidence base that supports this lesson, options include best practice, action research, evidence-based, and research-informed. Best practice denotes that others in the field use the intervention as an accepted and respected practice. Action research is an intervention that conducts some form of research in the process of the intervention. Evidence-based means that this intervention has been identified through multiple research studies with significant results as an evidence-based practice. Research-informed implies that research has supported this practice, but there is not enough research to identify it as an evidence-based practice. Figure 7.2 provides an example of this section of the lesson plan.

Lessons should target student standards and focus on one or more learning objectives. Figure 7.3 shows an example of this section of the AASC Lesson Plan. Notice that a specific ASCA Mindset and Behavior (ASCA, 2021) is listed as well as a measurable learning objective.

Practitioners should identify and prepare any materials needed for each lesson. For some activities, there may be a lot of materials or preparation and for others there are limited supplies needed. In this example (Figure 7.4), there is only a survey needed for the activity. The strategies the students will learn do not involve any supplies.

The next section describes how the AASC practitioner will facilitate the lesson. Writing this out in a lesson plan ensures that the practitioner has a plan for teaching the content, involving the animal partner, and assessing for animal welfare. The topics in this section include: introduce lesson topic/focus, communicate the lesson objective, teach content, practice content, involve animal partner, assess for animal welfare, and summarize/close. Figure 7.5 provides an example of this section.

Lesson Plan Info	
AASC Practitioner	Krista Schultze
AASC Animal Partner	Snickers, guinea pig
Counseling Theory Used	Solution-focused therapy
Lesson Plan Title	Managing My Stress
Type of Lesson	☐ Schoolwide ☐ Classroom ☒ Small-Group ☐ Individual Counseling
Target Audience	6th Graders
Evidence Base	☒ Best Practice ☐ Action Research ☐ Evidence-Based ☐ Research-Informed

Figure 7.2 AASC lesson plan info section.

ASCA Student Standards Targeted		Student Learning Objectives
Identify 1–2 student standards relevant for this targeted group and goal		For each of the selected student standards, write 1–2 learning objectives
M&B#	Mindsets & Behaviors Statement	Student Learning Objectives
B-SMS 7	Effective coping skills	Students will learn and practice four regulation strategies to regulate their body during times of academic and personal stress.

Figure 7.3 AASC lesson plan student standards and objectives section.

Materials:	
For Activity: Perceived Stress Survey	For Animal Partner: N/A

Figure 7.4 AASC lesson plan materials section.

Describe how you will:	
Introduce Lesson Topic/Focus:	Students identify factors that may stress Snickers. They identify how they may know if Snickers is stressed and what Mrs. Schultze could do to help him when he gets stressed.
Communicate the Lesson Objective:	Students are given the schedule for the next six weeks which includes learning four new regulation strategies.
Teach Content:	Students will learn a new regulation strategy each week. Students share if they utilized the previous week's strategy and if it's a strategy that they found effective. The four regulation strategies include: 1. deep breathing 2. stretching 3. reading 4. collaborative discussions
Practice Content:	Students will first observe if Snickers is demonstrating positive signals (e.g., coming close to students, making happy sounds) or stress signals (e.g., hiding, running away quickly). Students will make guesses about what might be causing Snickers stress, if anything, and what they can do to decrease his stress (e.g., talking softly, giving him space). Mrs. Schultze will share what helps Snickers feel safe. As students learn each regulation strategy, they will practice in class. Mrs. Schultze will notice strengths in the students as they develop and utilize regulation skills. After learning the regulation skill, they will check back with Snickers. They will see if Snickers is interested in playing or showing stress signals.
Involve Animal Partner:	See "Introduce Lesson Topic/Focus" and "Practice Content"
Assess for Animal Welfare:	Students are encouraged to help observe Snickers and to let Mrs. Schultze know if he appears stressed. If he does exhibit signs, the counselor moves him to a dark location so he can feel safer. They then discuss the importance of engaging regulation strategies early.
Summarize/Close:	The sixth week is designed as a wrap-up session. Students rank the four strategies they have learned in order to most effective to least effective for them.

Figure 7.5 AASC lesson plan description section.

Formative assessment involves the collection of practitioner and participant feedback data throughout the intervention allowing for alterations to intervention methodology (Simon et al., 2018). In the AASC Lesson Plan, this type of data can be found in the Data Collection Plan. The section on Formative data is especially effective with long-term interventions like small group sessions that last several weeks. For example, a counselor is teaching a small group of elementary boys about deep breathing exercises. The first session is held immediately after physical education class. The boys are energetic and struggle to settle down and learn breathing techniques. A formative assessment shows that only one of the five boys actually performs a breathing cycle correctly. Rather than move forward to the next lesson in the subsequent week, the counselor schedules a time other than after physical education class or after recess, to conduct the lesson again. This gives the students an opportunity to perfect the breathing technique when they are calm and can focus on the technique without distraction. The formative assessment process allows modifications throughout an intervention process making it more effective at meeting the learning objective (Dimmitt, 2009; Simon et al., 2018).

The first part of this section is the Participant Data Plan. This includes the number of students, number of sessions, length of sessions, and other process-related data (Dimmitt, 2009). We are at a period in time where counselors have to provide evidence of program reach and direct student service support. Implementation data is the evidence needed to advocate for our profession (Studer et al., 2006). It can include counseling center sign-in sheets, small group counseling attendance logs, caregiver evening turn-out numbers, FAFSA completion rates, and college/technical school/military recruitment event counts.

Data used to assess the effectiveness of interventions in meeting learning objectives is termed "outcome data" and is listed as such in the AASC Lesson Plan (Dimmitt, 2009; Simon et al., 2018). Outcome data is generated by comparing pre-intervention and post-intervention measures. For example, Garcia et al. (2021) administered a survey to ninth-grade students regarding their vocational confidence before and after use of a Career Information System for objectives related to career planning. Compared to the control group, students using the Career Information System had significantly lower career decision-making difficulties. Data can be collected to address academic interventions as well. Luck and Webb (2009) collected reading and math achievement scores using the Florida Comprehensive Assessment Test before and after implementation of the Student Success Skills Program at an elementary campus. Results indicated that the students in the program had significantly greater mean improvement scores in reading and math resulting in continued use of the program for the next several years (Luck & Webb, 2009). Figure 7.6 provides an example of the Data Collection Plan and Follow-Up Plans section.

Outcome data can also be collected when working with small groups or individuals as well (Sowell et al., 2020). For example, research has shown that the goal attainment scale (-2, -1, 0, 1, 2) used on a recurring basis throughout counseling services can be used to assess changes to various academic or behavioral objectives. It was proven to be an effective tool in working with adolescents struggling with homework completion rates (Brady et al., 2014).

Linkage to ASCA Standards

ASCA recognizes the importance of assessment to comprehensive school counseling programs, and this also applies in AASC. Various standards and competencies specifically reference the use of assessment and evaluation. AASC practitioners should be aware of these standards and competencies and how their practices align with them. Table 7.3 lists the ASCA Professional Standards and Competencies for Counselors that address assessment practices (ASCA, 2019). Those standards specifically related to

Data Collection Plan	
Participant Data Plan:	
Anticipated number of students:	15 students
Planned length of lesson(s):	6 weeks, 30-minute session/week
ASCA Student Standards Data Plan:	
Pre/Post Assessment Items: 1. Perceived Stress Survey 2. Average academic test scores	
Outcome Data Plan:	
☒ Academic Achievement: Average test scores before/after ☐ Attendance: ☒ Behavior: Average number of days students feel stress, Average number of coping skills students know	
Follow-Up Plans	
Plans for students who missed lesson: Plan for students who didn't demonstrate mastery or missed lesson: Since this is a six-week program, the counselor can assess for mastery at each step and modify subsequent lessons for students who need additional support. Some students may need more guidance than others. Individual sessions between weekly meetings may be necessary for some students.	

Figure 7.6 AASC lesson plan data collection and follow-up section.

Table 7.3 Assessment-Related ASCA Standards and Competencies for Counselors

Standard	Description
B-PA 2	Identify gaps in achievement, attendance, discipline, opportunity, and resources
B-PA 3	Develop annual student outcome goals based on student data
B-PA 4	Develop and implement action plans aligned with annual student outcome goals and student data
B-PA 5	Assess and report program results to the school community

Sources: (ASCA, 2019).

interventions and strategies for student learning objectives can be met through implementation of AASC. For example, the action plan listed in standard B-PA 4 could include various animal-assisted interventions designed to meet the outcome goals created from a needs assessment. In these cases, outcome data related to AASC should be collected and shared to support the intervention's use in meeting student needs. The importance of this is highlighted in standard B-PA 5 where AASC data would be shared with community stakeholders.

Sharing outcome data is not limited to ASCA's Professional Standards, it is also referenced in ASCA's Ethical Standards. When collecting and sharing student assessment data though, a variety of ethical considerations should be taken into account. Table 7.4 lists the ASCA (2022) Ethical

Table 7.4 ASCA Ethical Standards Related to Assessment

Standard	Description
A.3.c	Use data-collection tools adhering to standards of confidentiality as expressed in A.2.
A.3.d	Review and use school and student data to assess and address needs, including but not limited to data on strengths and disparities that may exist related to gender, race, ethnicity, socioeconomic status, disability, and/or other relevant classifications.
A.3.e	Deliver research-based interventions to help close achievement, attainment, information, attendance, discipline, resource, and opportunity gaps.
A.3.f	Collect and analyze participation, ASCA Mindsets & Behaviors, and outcome data to determine the progress and effectiveness of the school counseling program.
A.3.g	Share data outcomes with stakeholders.
A.4.c	Identify and examine gaps in college and career access and address both intentional and unintentional biases in post-secondary and career counseling.
A.7.c	Assess student needs to determine if participating in the group is appropriate for the student.
A.7.f	Use data to inform group topics, establish well-defined expectations, and measure the outcomes of group participation.
A.7.g	Reflect on group outcomes and determine adjustments that may improve future group interventions.
A.14.a.	Use only valid and reliable research-based tests and assessments that are culturally sensitive, in the student's preferred language, and free of bias.
A.14.b	Adhere to all professional standards and regulations when selecting, administering, and interpreting standardized assessment tools, and only use assessment instruments that are within the scope of practice for school counselors and for which they are licensed, certified, competent, and trained to use.
A.14.c	Follow confidentiality guidelines when using paper or electronic assessment instruments and programs.
A.14.d	Consider the student's developmental age, language skills, home language, and competence level when determining an assessment's appropriateness.
A.14.e	Use multiple data points, both quantitative and qualitative whenever possible, to provide students and families with complete and accurate information to promote students' well-being.
A.14.f	Provide interpretation, in the student's preferred language, of the nature, purpose, results and potential impact of assessment/evaluation measures in terms students and parents/ guardians can understand.
A.14.g	Monitor the use of assessment results and interpretation and take reasonable steps to prevent others from misusing the information.
A.14.h	Use caution when selecting or using assessment techniques, making evaluations, and interpreting the performance of populations not represented in the norm group on which an instrument is standardized.
A.14.i	Conduct and disseminate the results of school counseling program assessments to determine the effectiveness of activities supporting students' academic, college/career, and social/ emotional development through accountability measure.
B.1.e	Adhere to the Protection of Pupil Rights Amendment when using universal screeners, surveys, or needs assessments by informing parents/guardians prior to their use in accordance with school district policies and local, state, and federal law.

Standards related to assessment and data collection. Not all of these are related to AASC directly, but counselors that involve an animal partner should be keenly aware of those that are. For example, Standards A.3.f, A.3.g, A.14.h, and A.14.i reference the collection and dissemination of participation and outcome data. As schools consider expanding (or not expanding) AASC programs to other campuses, this implementation and outcome data would be a key source of information in justifying that decision. Counselors should keep an accurate record of this data to share with stakeholders. Data from the first year of implementation may not show significant results; however, in order to remain ethical, data has to be presented accurately. Less than stellar results in the first year or two of the program could be attributed to the newness of the techniques and need for additional practice. This also goes back to the need for formative assessment throughout interventions so modifications can continually be made toward meeting learning objectives. Another theme that resonates throughout these assessment-related standards is the adherence to confidentiality of private information obtained through assessment. One of the benefits of having an animal partner is that it does not pose additional threats to privacy. Practices that are generally used to maintain confidentiality should continue to be enforced in the animal-assisted settings. School counselors using AASC should review these standards and the possible implications to their practices.

Assessment in Primary-Level Schools

The examples that follow provide insight into the assessment process of AASC at the primary level. Using the counseling process from Figure 7.1 as a guide, forms of assessment (e.g., need, formative, outcome, and implementation) are identified in various scenarios.

Individual Session Assessment

A first-grade student, Hector, is having a hard morning so his homeroom teacher sends him to see Ms. Lopez, the school counselor. He enters the room crying and is visibly upset. This is Hector's first time in the counseling office, but Ms. Lopez has been told that he has struggled since August with his emotions. The counselor introduces herself, along with her animal partner, a canine named Buster. She asks how Hector is feeling and he confirms that he is sad. The counselor then asks the student "how big is your sadness on a scale of one to five" using the scale in Figure 7.7.

Hector states that he is at level five. When asked why he is feeling this way, Hector tells the counselor that he lost his lunch box this morning. Ms. Lopez recognizes that Hector needs help with ASCA Behavior Standard, B-SMS 7, Effective coping skills (ASCA, 2021). Ms. Lopez progresses through a lesson that covers size of emotions versus size of your problems. Using Buster as a reference, the counselor and Hector come up with possible problems that Buster may have on each level of the scale and what his energy and response may look like with each type of problem. They then relate this to the size of Hector's lunch box problem and what an equal-sized reaction would

Figure 7.7 Emoji sadness scale.

look like. At the end of the session, Ms. Lopez asks Hector to rate the size of his sadness, which he identifies as a level two. The counselor follows up with the teacher afterward to see how Hector's day has progressed. The teacher states that Hector had a successful day and may benefit from additional meetings with the counselor as his emotions tend to impact his academic success. AASC Lesson Plan 7.1, which can be found in Appendix B, presents an example of an AASC Lesson Plan for this individual counseling session.

The various forms of data collected with Hector are identified in Lesson Plan 7.1. Note that the AASC Lesson Plan does not include "needs assessment" data as the lesson plan is utilized after a need has already been addressed. In this example though, the informal data from Hector and the teacher is enough information to warrant an initial session. Remember that counseling is cyclical in nature, so this is not likely the last time Ms. Lopez will meet with Hector. It sounds like he may need additional support in regulating his emotions with the end goal of work completion and test performance enhancement. The type of data gathered will continue to change as she learns more about Hector and his needs.

Classroom Guidance Intervention

College and career planning is one of the three ASCA domains that counselors address (ASCA, 2019). This is expected to be addressed at all grade levels moving from career awareness to career exploration. Mr. Wang is a counselor at Goodchild Elementary School where he serves grades three through five. He decides to use a research-proven ten-week program on career exploration with the fifth graders at his school which concludes with a career fair where students will create and display a trifold display board about a job they have researched (Edwin & Prescod, 2018). Mr. Wang decides to involve his animal partner, a lionhead rabbit named Loyal, to deliver the lesson material. For example, lesson two looks at the multiple intelligences theory, so he has students rationalize which intelligence is Loyal's strength based on what they know about him. They then discuss in small groups what their own strengths may be. Students are led through various activities each week that culminate in a small research project about a career they may be interested in exploring more. As students explore their own career, they brainstorm a job for Loyal as well. The counselor develops a trifold display board for Loyal that may be a social worker, counselor, lettuce farmer, or hairdresser as examples. Each week, the counselor conducts a formative assessment using either verbal call-outs or written responses. Edwin and Prescod (2018) suggest the use of a worksheet where students match various jobs to the appropriate career clusters to assess the effectiveness of lesson seven in comparing the various career clusters. AASC Lesson Plan 7.2 in Appendix B demonstrates how this lesson was planned and facilitated.

At the career fair, Loyal's board draws just as much attention as the students' own since they played a part in developing his future as a food sensory technician, otherwise known as a lettuce taster. To further engage students and provide cross-disciplinary lessons, the counselor could even ask students how they could determine which types of lettuce Loyal enjoys most. If time permits or maybe at a different time, this could be implemented as part of a future lesson with students on nutrition and healthy choices. Figure 7.8 shows Loyal enjoying his lettuce.

Assessment in Secondary-Level Schools

This section will explore the assessment process of AASC interventions at the secondary level. The domains of academic, career planning, and social-emotional learning are addressed at these levels as well, but the approaches to implementation usually differ (ASCA, 2019). Assessment practices for each example are included.

Figure 7.8 Therapy rabbit, Loyal, eating lettuce.

Classroom Guidance Intervention

The school principal meets with Mr. Flores, the school counselor, about the increasing number of students receiving disciplinary action on their campus related to vaping. On average, one student per week is receiving a consequence for this action. This is in line with recent data from the U.S. Department of Health and Human Services which expressed that 28% of students have reported using an e-cigarette in the last 30 days (Cullen et al., 2019). This is an alarming number for two reasons. First, the various chemicals inhaled into the lungs damage these organs, yet students believe they are safe since they are advertised as water vapor. Second, students who are caught with e-cigarettes at school are missing instruction due to disciplinary action they receive. It is a growing concern that the principal feels the school should address with the student body. They agree on a learning objective: Students will learn how vaping relates to their overall physical health in order to make more informed decisions. AASC Lesson Plan 7.3 in Appendix B shows this planned lesson.

Mr. Flores decides to collaborate with the nurse to provide classroom guidance on the dangers of vaping (Cullen et al., 2019). In order to engage students more in the discussion, he brings his bulldog partner, Scoot, with him to the lesson. Using AASC techniques, the counselor guides students through conversations related to animal ethics. Students are given an index card. On one side, students list things that Scoot needs to be adequately cared for. On the back, they list all the things that could be dangerous for Scoot that they should protect him from. They discuss what good animal husbandry looks and does not look like from these responses. Included in that discussion are topics like providing adequate nutrition and access to a veterinarian. They also discuss making sure Scoot does not have access to things that may hurt him. This leads into the conversation on vaping and taking care of one's own body as well. In all, the lesson lasts 45 minutes.

After the counselor has addressed the entire campus through this guidance lesson, he pulls disciplinary data for the months prior to the lesson including the number of students assigned in-school suspension (ISS) or alternative education program (AEP) for vaping. Mr. Flores collects outcome data in the months following the lesson as well. Although not drastic, post-intervention data suggests the program did positively impact the number of students having disciplinary consequences for vaping. The counselor reflects on his practices and asks the principal if he can go into classrooms at the beginning of the year next year to deliver the vaping curriculum, as well as collaborate with counselors on other campuses to do the same. In this way, the measure will be more preventative and reach students before any receive disciplinary consequences for this behavior.

Small Group Intervention

A group of sixth-grade teachers approach the counselor regarding their students' ability to manage stress this year. Although some students are managing the transition to middle school well, several others have intense periods of stress that impact their academic ability. Since it is not a grade-level inclusive issue, the counselor believes this could best be handled through small group sessions, but she needs to identify which students to include in the group. The counselor decides to use a research-proven universal screener, the Perceived Stress Scale (PSS), to rank which students would be good candidates for the small group sessions (Cohen et al., 1983). The PSS is a brief, fourteen-question survey that the counselor uses with the sixth-grade social studies classrooms with consent from the students' caregivers. In all, she identifies 15 students with elevated perceived stress scores who may benefit from small group instruction on stress management. After obtaining caregiver consent to attend the group and participate in AASC services, the counselor begins the first session. As a warm-up activity, students complete a questionnaire about their knowledge of stress, coping mechanisms, management techniques, and current stress level. AASC Lesson Plan 7.4 in Appendix B describes this lesson.

While they complete the survey, Mrs. Schultze looks up their current academic test scores and computes an overall test average for each student. Since teachers are worried about the impact that stress is having on students' academics, this information will be used as baseline data. This becomes the first session in a six-week AASC program focused on recognizing stress and practicing various coping techniques. They begin by learning to identify when Mrs. Schultze's animal partner, a guinea pig named Snickers, starts to get stressed, and how they can help regulate his stress levels. Each week, students learn a new stress management strategy including deep breathing, meditation, grounding exercises, and time management skills. As a warm-up each week, students share how they used one of the previous week's strategies when they started to feel overwhelmed. Figure 7.9 shows how Snickers helps a child practice regulation skills.

In the last week of the program, the students take the same questionnaire again and pre-intervention and post-intervention results are compared. Although most of the students in the group knew what stress was before the group started, they had little knowledge of how to manage it. Following the intervention, students were able to identify coping mechanisms and formative assessment results indicated regular use of these strategies. An added benefit was the increase in test scores, which Mrs. Schultze can report to stakeholders to justify how AASC impacts student academics. The counselor could follow up with students again in a month or two to determine if they have retained their knowledge of stress coping mechanisms as long-term outcome data.

Trauma-Informed and Diversity Considerations

The first part of this chapter identified campus-wide data that could be collected for conduction of a needs assessment. It is important to disaggregate different sources of data to analyze results for various subpopulations. For example, disaggregating data for participation in Advanced Placement course testing. This may include analyzing participation rates by gender, race, ethnicity, socioeconomic status, ability/disability, etc. to determine gaps in participation rates. As school counselors collect and analyze data, looking at the big picture provides useful insights, but looking at subpopulation data can bring to light inequities that a school counseling program can address (ASCA, 2022).

Figure 7.9 AASC deep breathing technique.

Special consideration should be given to using AASC with students with learning and behavioral difficulties. Research regarding the incorporation of animals in the classroom highlighted the positive influence of various animals on cognitive skill, motivation, social functioning, and motor skill development for all ages of students, but especially those with autism spectrum disorder, emotional disturbances, and sensory processing disorders (Brelsford et al., 2017; Knowles et al., 2021; Juríčková et al., 2020). Similar experiences may be achieved with the integration of animals in a school counseling environment as well.

Regardless of who is being assessed, school counselors should consider the diversity of participants in their program and ensure the assessment tool is appropriate for each specific client (Sink, 2009). First, the human-animal bond is different between cultural groups, so interventions that take into consideration the relationship between a client and the animal partner or interventions that bring the animal's perspective into consideration may produce unexpected results (Adekson, 2019; Studer et al., 2006). These results may be due to cultural differences in the way animals are viewed, rather than individual perspectives on the larger circumstance or experience being investigated. The same would be true of individuals who have experienced trauma, especially when animals were present or involved. Counselors should assess clients without predispositions based on their own experiences, as other's experiences can influence their response to interventions in unexpected ways. Understanding the student's views and perspectives can produce more accurate assessment results (Adekson, 2019; Studer et al., 2006).

Bringing It All Together

Assessment is a necessary component of today's comprehensive counseling programs that assists with program planning, meeting student needs, and advocating for the profession. Although the assessment process itself does not change based on the use of AASC, the data gathered can justify the value of an AASC program. There are various forms of assessment used in counseling programs including needs assessment, outcome evaluation, formative assessment, and implementation data. Needs assessment includes gathering academic, attendance, disciplinary records, universal screening data, or perception data to determine what learning objectives the counselor needs to prioritize for classroom guidance, small group lessons, or individual counseling sessions. Once interventions are initiated, outcome, formative, and implementation data are used to justify their effectiveness. Outcome data measures if an intervention met the learning objective it was intended to accomplish. Formative data is collected throughout the duration of the intervention to allow for modification based on how students are responding. Finally, implementation data includes the number of students participating, the intervention time, caregiver meeting logs, and participation rates in community events. Counselors identify when their animal partner is involved in these implementation records to advocate for continued use of this resource. AASC is a valuable tool to address the academic, career planning, and social/emotional development domains at all grade levels; however, assessment data must be collected to prove the effectiveness to all stakeholders. AASC practitioners should remain cognizant of this need and rely on constant reflection through the assessment process to modify their program and more effectively serve the students at their school.

References

Adekson, M. O. (2019). Multicultural awareness, knowledge, and skills. In M. O. Adekson (Ed.), *Handbook of counseling and counselor education*. Routledge. 10.4324/9781351164207

American School Counselor Association (ASCA). (2019). *ASCA school counselor professional standards & competencies*. Author. https://www.schoolcounselor.org/getmedia/a8d59c2c-51de-4ec3-a565-a3235f3b93c3/SC-Competencies.pdf

American School Counselor Association (ASCA). (2021). *ASCA student standards: Mindsets & behaviors for student success*. https://www.schoolcounselor.org/getmedia/7428a787-a452-4abb-afec-d78ec77870cd/Mindsets-Behaviors.pdf

American School Counselor Association. (2022). *ASCA ethical standards for school counselors*. Author. https://www.schoolcounselor.org/getmedia/44f30280-ffe8-4b41-9ad8-f15909c3d164/EthicalStandards.pdf

Brady, J., Busse, R. T., & Lopez, C. J. (2014). Monitoring school consultation intervention outcomes for data-based decision making: An application of the goal attainment scaling method. *Counseling Outcome Research and Evaluation*, 5(1), 64–70. 10.1177/2150137814527605

Brelsford, V. L., Meints, K., Gee, N. R., & Pfeffer, K. (2017). Animal-assisted interventions in the classroom - A systematic review. *International Journal of Environmental Research and Public Health*, 14(7), 669. 10.3390/ijerph14070669

Carey, J., & Dimmitt, C. (2008). A model for evidence-based elementary school counseling: Using school data, research, and evaluation to enhance practice. *The Elementary School Journal*, 108(5), 422–430. 10.1086/589471

Cohen, S., Kamarck, T., & Mermelstein, R. (1983). A global measure of perceived stress. *Journal of Health and Social Behavior*, 24(4), 385–396. 10.2307/2136404

Cullen, K. A., Gentzke, A. S., Sawdey, M. D., Chang, J. T., Anic, G. M., Wang, T. W., Creamer, M. R., Jamal, A., Ambrose, B. K., & King, B. A. (2019). E-cigarette use among youth in the United States, *JAMA*, 322(21), 2095–2103. 10.1001/jama.2019.18387

Dimmitt, C. (2009). Why evaluation matters: Determining effective school counseling practices. *Professional School Counseling*, 12(6), 395–399. 10.1177/2156759X0901200605

Donohue, P., Goodman-Scott, E., & Betters-Bubon, J. (2018). Using universal screening for early identification of students at risk: A case example from the field. *Professional School Counseling*, *19*(1), 133–143. 10.5330/1096-2409-19.1.133

Edwin, M., & Prescod, D. (2018). Fostering elementary career exploration with an interactive, technology-based career development unit. *Journal of School Counseling*, *16*(13). http://www.jsc.montana.edu/articles/v16n13.pdf

Even, T. A., & Williams, M. A. (2018). Assessment in K-12 school counseling. In B. McHenry, K. C. MacCluskie, & J. McHenry (Eds.), *Tests and assessments in counseling* (pp. 172–190). Routledge. 10.4324/9781315279534-12

Every Student Succeeds Act, 20 U.S.C. § 6301. (2015). https://www.congress.gov/bill/114th-congress/senate-bill/1177

Garcia, E. A., McWhirter, E. H., & Cendejas, C. (2021). Outcomes of career information system utilization among first-year high school students. *Journal of Career Development*, *48*(5), 767–780. 10.1177/0894845319890930

Juríčková, V., Bozděchová, A., Machová, K., & Vadroňová, M. (2020). Effect of animal assisted education with a dog within children with ADHD in the classroom: A case study. *Child and Adolescent Social Work Journal*, *40*(3), 433. https://doi-org.libproxy.txstate.edu/10.1007/s10560-020-00737-6

Knowles, C., Shannon, E. N., & Lind, J. R. (2021). Animal-assisted activities in the classroom for students with emotional and behavioral disorders. *Children and Youth Services Review*, *131*. 10.1016/j.childyouth.2021.106290

Luck, L., & Webb, L. (2009). School counselor action research: A case example. *Professional School Counseling*, *12*(6), 408–412. 10.1177/2156759X0901200609

Simon, T., McLain, J., Powell, L., & Cox, E. (2018). Data and assessment in school counseling. In L. A. Wines & J. A. Nelson (Eds.), *School counselors as practitioners* (pp. 294–322). Routledge. 10.4324/9781315175645-11

Sink, C. A. (2009). School counselors as accountability leaders: Another call for action. *Professional School Counseling*, *13*(2), 68–74. 10.1177/2156759X0901300202

Smith, L., Davis, K., & Bhowmik, M. (2010). Youth participatory action research groups as school counseling interventions. *Professional School Counseling*, *14*(2), 174–182. 10.1177/2156759X231153347

Sowell, S. M., Hunter, Q., Richey, K. G., & Baxter, C. (2020). Demonstrating school counselor efficacy in individual interventions using single-case research design: A guided process. *Professional School Counseling*, *23*(1_part_3), 1–9. 10.1177/2156759X20904491

Studer, J. R., Oberman, A. H., & Womack, R. H. (2006). Producing evidence to show counseling effectiveness in the schools. *Professional School Counseling*, *9*(5), 385–391. 10.1177/2156759X0500900405

U.S. Department of Education. (2011, October 20). *Mission*. https://www2.ed.gov/about/overview/mission/mission.html

Chapter 8

Theoretical Applications of AASC

Heidi Schilling[1] and Joy Cannon[2]

[1]Alpenglow Counseling, LLC; [2]Inkling Therapy PLLC

Box 8.1

Chapter 8 Scenario

Rosalie and Hank are excited to begin working with a student, Grace, who is a new student on the caseload. Grace is an intelligent, enthusiastic 12-year-old, who loves interacting with Hank. Grace was referred to Rosalie because she exhibits anxiety that manifests in perfectionism, such as redoing school assignments several times, turning in assignments late because she is revising them, not turning in work because it is not "good enough," wanting to please others, and becoming upset when she makes even a minor mistake on a test. As a result of these tendencies, Grace is also what one may consider a "dream" client, as she engages well in school counseling sessions, is compliant, and enjoyable to be around. Because Grace is so cheerful and easygoing, Rosalie wants to be mindful that AASC interventions are intentional, aim to reduce the presenting problem (i.e., anxiety), and do not become another place where Grace feels she has to please.

To address these factors, it is important that Rosalie has a primary theoretical orientation. Using a theory will help Rosalie to conceptualize Grace's presenting issues, have a pathway for supporting Grace in working toward her treatment goal, choose specific animal-assisted school counseling (AASC) interventions to meet Grace's goal, and use theoretical skills and techniques that support AASC and Grace. Rosalie needs to utilize a counseling theory in her work with Grace that integrates her AASC work with Hank. The following chapter will help you to better understand some of Rosalie's theoretical options and identify which theoretical approach may be best for Rosalie and Hank.

Counseling theories are models or principles used to explain human behavior and the process of change in counseling. Counseling theories guide evidence-based practices, lead to positive outcomes, and advance the counseling profession. Therefore, theory is an important part of school counseling. This chapter will review three counseling theories often used in school counseling settings. First, the authors will give a brief history of cognitive-behavioral therapy, solution-focused therapy, and person-centered therapy with descriptions of key concepts and play therapy applications in each approach. The authors will highlight connections between professional ethical standards and elements of these theoretical approaches. A discussion of the application of these theories with children and adolescents based on development stages follows, as well as how to utilize theories with AASC in primary and secondary levels. This chapter will end by exploring the fitness of these theories in working with trauma and diverse populations.

DOI: 10.4324/9781003392415-8

Literature Review

Professional associations direct counselors to utilize clinical theory as a foundation. The American Counseling Association (ACA) code of ethics section related to professional responsibility states, "When providing services, counselors use techniques/procedures/modalities that are grounded in theory and/or have an empirical or scientific foundation" (ACA, 2014, p. 10). ACA (2014, Section A.2.b.) also directs counselors to share purposes, procedures, risks, and benefits which may differ based on the counselor's theory as part of informed consent.

Theories assist counselors in conceptualizing individual needs, defining roles, treatment planning, group screening, program creation, intervention selection, informing decisions, assessing progress, and protecting clients from therapist bias or power differentials, especially in the complex environments of schools (Lemberger-Truelove et al., 2020). Counselors often set goals with students to work on from the first interaction to the last lesson, group, session, or conversation. The goal helps guide the entire process. Without a theory, a counselor will have difficulty identifying and working on clinical goals with students. Lemberger-Truelove et al. propose that school-based practitioners must "adopt theory that includes each of the following constituents necessary to suggest an evidence-based outcome: 1) qualities of students and school environments, 2) empirical and professional endorsements, 3) school counseling customs, and 4) methodological relevance" (2020, p. 4). Although broad, nondirective play therapy's objectives (such as positive self-regard) contribute to students' freedom from internal distractions as well as links to better learning potential. Landreth (2023) emphasized grounding concepts of personality theory so that counselors provide consistent safety and sensitivity to the individual. One sensitivity of stakeholders may be related to misunderstanding regarding the use of toys and/or the involvement of animals. Ray (2011) acknowledged and provided guiding examples on communicating about therapeutic play in school counseling. Later in the chapter, the authors will connect the principles of all three theories of focus to specific behavior competencies outlined by ASCA as well as the evidence basis for use of these theories in AASC.

Animal-assisted counseling (AAC) is not to be used as a stand-alone intervention (Endenburg & Van Lith, 2010). Stewart et al. (2016) developed AAC competencies, now endorsed by ACA, for integrating AAC into the practitioner's current counseling model or theory by using AAC "to enhance the therapeutic process rather than as a stand-alone intervention" (p. 5). Practitioners of AASC should therefore be able to describe links between animal interactions and concepts of their theory (Figure 8.1).

Cognitive-Behavioral Therapy

Cognitive-behavioral therapy (CBT) is an evidence-based practice that many practitioners utilize (Schott, 2021) with the overall intent to provide psychoeducation, help one develop effective coping skills, restructure thoughts, change behavior, and manage feelings in a healthy manner. CBT is a collaborative therapy, is often short-term, directive, and is goal-focused with actionable steps for change (Schott, 2021; Chandler, 2017). This theory has many uses including reducing depression and anxiety, improving communication, overcoming fears, developing mindfulness skills, increasing self-esteem, enhancing confidence in oneself, and challenging unhelpful and maladaptive thought patterns (Schott, 2021). Clients examine their thoughts, feelings, and behaviors through CBT. A core concept of this approach is that thoughts, feelings, and behaviors are all connected and influence each other. CBT focuses on both behavioral and cognitive changes. See key concepts of CBT in Figure 8.2.

Schott (2021) noted that CBT has been studied more than any other intervention. Ongoing research continues to demonstrate the effectiveness of CBT in treating a wide range of mental health difficulties.

Figure 8.1 Denali, a therapy dog, happy at work.

Research has also shown that CBT is empirically sound when used with children and adolescents, as well as with adults (Shelby & Berk, 2009). However, there are some drawbacks to using CBT with children. Since CBT relies on cooperation between the child and counselor this can be difficult when children are not self-referred nor have the insight into why they are in therapy in the first place (Knell, 1995). Further, the cognitive component of CBT often depends on sophisticated mental abilities for the child to be able to learn the skills utilized, ones that children have yet to develop (Knell, 1995; Shelby & Berk, 2009). Children and some adolescents may struggle with other components of CBT as well. These components may include finding talk therapy boring, difficulty with tracking thoughts, feelings, behaviors, or following through with "homework" assignments outside the therapy room (Shelby & Berk, 2009). These possible limitations have led clinicians to wonder if CBT can be as effective with children as it is with adults (Knell, 1995).

To bridge this gap in treatment, cognitive-behavioral play therapy (CBPT) was developed in the 1990s, by blending behavioral and cognitive interventions with the play therapy model (Knell & Dasari, 2009). Play therapy is described by Knell (1995, p. 8) as being "an attempt by the child to explore, gain mastery, and develop understanding." She goes on to note that since children are often not able to adequately express themselves verbally due to their developmental stage, they instead, express themselves through play. In CBPT, a child communicates their thoughts, feelings, perceptions, and conflicts through play (Knell, 1995). Play can be a means of communication and a way that behavior strategies are practiced, learned, or applied (Knell, 1995). Schaefer and Drewes (2009) assert that play is important to utilize in the treatment of young children because it is "a universal expression of children"

Key Concepts of CBT

Thoughts, feelings, behaviors, and physiological responses are all connected.

Thoughts and actions impact feelings.

Automatic thoughts and core beliefs impact one's worldview.

Develop skills for more adaptive thoughts/behaviors to replace maladaptive ones

Collaboratve, structured, directive, and goal-oriented

Emphasizes empirical interventions and empirical examination of treatment goals

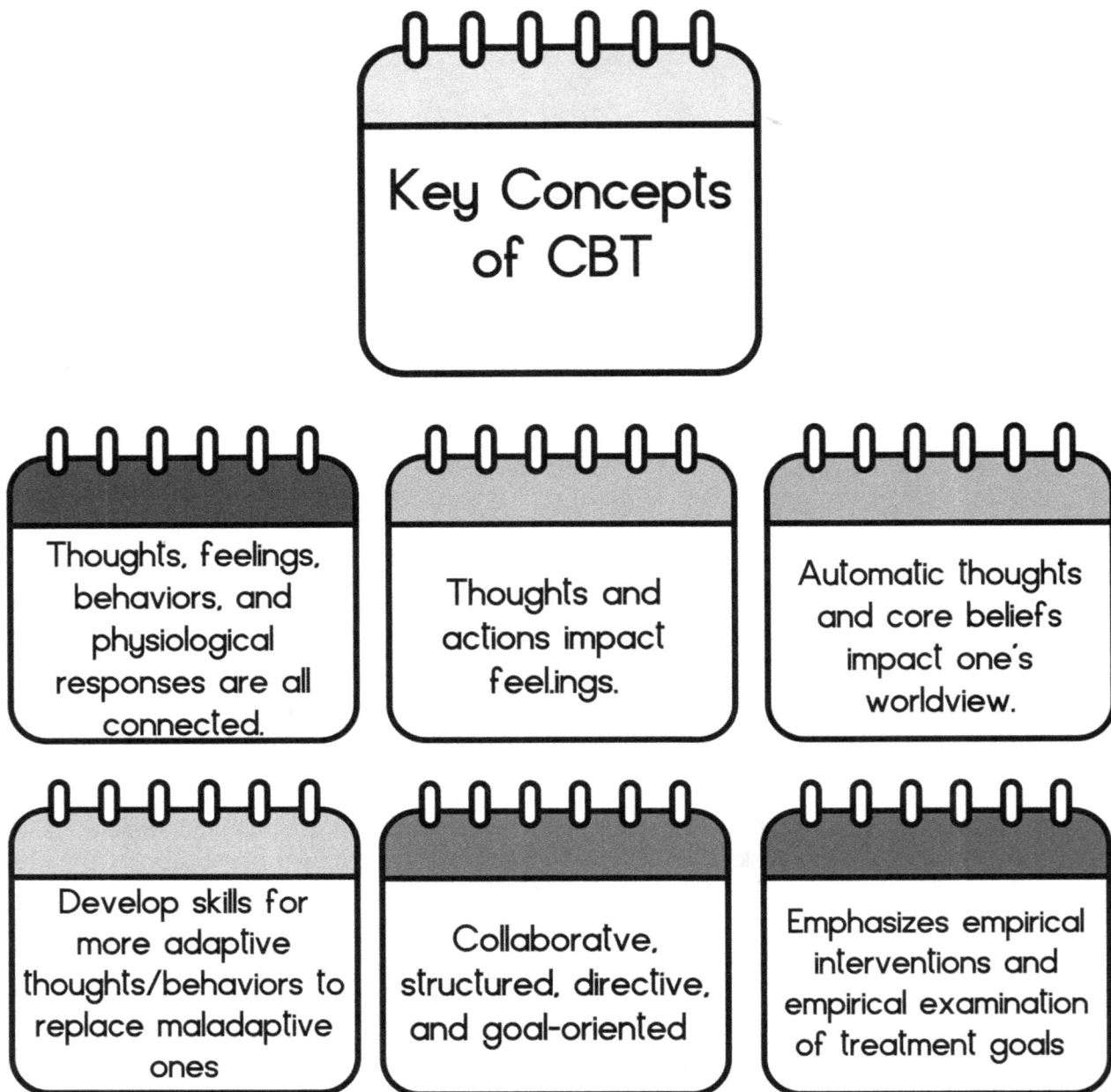

Figure 8.2 Key concepts of cognitive-behavioral therapy.

(p. 3) and is critical to a child's development. Play therapy helps create a therapeutic relationship with children, signals that a child can be a child, and the presence of toys suggests a safe place for the child (Schaefer & Drewes, 2009). Prior to the introduction of CBPT, play therapy was often nondirective and only guided by the child (Knell & Dasari, 2009). Further, the child being an active participant in change had not been sufficiently acknowledged in previous interventions, even behavioral interventions (Knell & Dasari, 2009).

CBT interventions were integrated into the play therapy model as they allow for the child's involvement in therapeutic change in a way that other child interventions do not (Knell, 1995). A child becomes more of an active participant in change when cognitive interventions are included, and this can result in increased understanding and insight (Knell, 1995). CBT by nature is more collaborative, and CBPT tends to be more structured and goal-directed (Knell & Dasari, 2009) than using nondirective play therapy. Lastly, utilizing the play therapy paradigm with CBT components integrated allows for CBT interventions to be employed in a way that takes into consideration a child's developmental level (Shelby & Berk, 2009), thus making it more appropriate for them.

While CBPT is often utilized with children, there are benefits to using it with adolescents as well. Frey (2009) outlines several reasons. First, adolescents can have a different emotional level than their cognitive level, which would make play effective for them to address this difference in development. Adolescents can be resistant to talk therapy, and therefore play-based activities, instead of just verbal-based therapy, can be beneficial. CBPT can also help when a youth is experiencing denial or lack of awareness of their symptoms or problems and work towards them gaining greater insight. Lastly, if an adolescent has delayed development or cognitive abilities, CBPT may be more appropriate than traditional talk therapy (Frey, 2009). Both CBT and CBPT are appropriate for school settings due to being short-term, research based, and goal oriented, as well as because they consider the developmental needs of children. Further, CBT and CBPT can also be utilized easily with an animal partner, thus making this theory suitable for AASC.

Applying CBT to AASC

There are many animal-assisted interventions that are applicable to CBT theory (Chandler, 2017). Chandler notes that the therapeutic relationship between the student and the animal can be utilized to help the student express feelings or identify beliefs. There are many skills a student can practice with the animal partner in a variety of ways. By involving the animal partner, the school counselor can model appropriate social behaviors for the student and then have the student practice with the animal themselves. Structured activities can also involve the animal to help the student practice and master skills. When the student engages with the animal to perform tricks or commands, this is an opportunity for the student to rehearse new and functional behaviors. The school counselor can provide feedback to students about their interactions with the animal partner, leading to the student identifying adaptive behaviors in place of maladaptive ones, as well as reinforce the learning of prosocial behaviors. It should be noted that practicing behaviors with an animal is likely to be more fun and less threatening than trying new behaviors with a person, especially for children and adolescents (Chandler, 2017).

Additionally, CBT-based goals in schools are consistent with the goals of AASC. These parallel goals include: helping build rapport between the student and the school counselor, increasing trust within relationships to adults such as teachers and staff, processing and sharing of feelings, working to have the student gain insight into the connection between their thoughts, feelings, and behaviors, helping the student understand how these three elements impact their school success, enhancing prosocial classmate interactions, and creating successful outcomes to increase a student's self-worth and confidence to learn.

By integrating CBPT and AASC together, these two approaches offer a playful approach to helping students change their thoughts and behaviors to achieve social-emotional goals in school. The relationship with the animal partner facilitates more ways to play. It also provides another tool in the student's immediate experience to which the school counselor can respond. An important aspect of CBT is humor, which can be utilized through the aid of playing with the animal (Chandler, 2017). Animal-assisted interventions have many benefits, which are similar to the benefits of play therapy. These include developing empathy, increasing motivation for attendance, creating a safe and comforting place, aiding in therapeutic rapport, offering unconditional acceptance, allowing a child to be a child, and improving mood (Endenburg & Van Lith, 2010; Lange et al., 2007; Weston, 2010).

Solution-Focused Therapy

Solution-focused therapy (SFT) is one of the most prominent theoretical approaches used with children and adolescents in schools (Carlson, 2016; Kim et al., 2017; Paolini, 2016). SFT is a strengths-based approach that helps people work toward goals by focusing on their capabilities and resources. This theoretical approach originated in the 1970s by founders, Berg and de Shazer, and associates at the Brief Family Therapy Center in Milwaukee, Wisconsin (De Jong & Berg, 2013). This future-focused approach is rooted in postmodernism and social constructivism (Hartwig, 2021). Rather than focus on problems or dysfunction, SFT directs counselors to see students as experts in solving their own problems. This approach emphasizes student abilities while using the client's language to identify existing strengths. SFT highlights what is possible, exceptions to the problem, and past solutions. SFT therapists view the child as capable and competent. Through SFT, the client self-evaluates and sets goals for their desired future (Bavelas et al., 2013).

SFT has been recognized as an evidence-based practice and beneficial approach in addressing academic concerns (Kim et al., 2019; Kim & Franklin, 2009). As a culturally affirming approach, SFT practitioners honor the culture of their clients and allow their clients to identify goals and solutions that fit their beliefs and values (Kim et al., 2015; Meyer & Cottone, 2013; Suitt et al., 2016). In schools, SFT can help students address challenges, while increasing self-efficacy and a sense of control (Kvarme et al., 2010). SFT has been applied in schools with individuals, groups, classrooms, and through a whole-school approach (Berg & Shilts, 2005). Numerous outcome studies of SFT in schools have been conducted (Hartwig & Taylor, 2022). A meta-analysis by Hsu et al. (2021) identified that SFT is effective in addressing behavioral problems in children and adolescents. With ample evidence of the effectiveness of SFT in schools, this approach can be a great fit for school counselors who connect with the key concepts and strengths-based qualities of SFT.

Figure 8.3 identifies the eight key concepts of SFT (De Jong & Berg, 2013). These key concepts highlight important elements of this strengths-based approach and can be applied well to school settings. For example, the concept "small steps can lead to big changes" can help children set and achieve smaller goals rather than trying to tackle large goals that may seem unachievable. The concept of "if it's not working, do something different" can help a student learn to try something new if how they're trying to address a problem isn't working. The SFT concept of "the future is both created and negotiable" means that a child's past doesn't dictate their future. They can work toward a preferred future by focusing on what they want in their life, rather than on past challenges.

SFT has also been applied to play therapy with children. Solution-focused play therapy (SFPT) emerged as a play-based approach that integrates the key concepts, skills, and techniques of SFT (Hartwig, 2021; Leggett, 2017; Nims, 2007; Taylor, 2019). SFPT is based on the core belief that children are competent and have the abilities they need to solve the presenting problem (Hartwig & Taylor, 2022). SFPT is grounded in neurobiological and developmental concepts that integrate both nondirective and directive skills (Hartwig, 2021). SFPT employs play therapy toys, materials, resources, and activities to help children work toward goals (Taylor, 2019). Hartwig (2021) identified and described 12 basic skills used in SFPT that were based on De Jong and Berg's (2013) 20 Skills for Not Knowing. As both a nondirective and directive approach, SFPT provides a space for school-based practitioners to use nondirective skills, such as reflection of behavior and feeling, for young children who do not need to respond verbally in play therapy, and more directive skills, such as open-ended

Key Concepts
of SFPT

If it isn't broken,
don't fix it.

If it works,
do more of it.

If it's not working,
do something
different.

Small steps can lead
to big changes.

The solution isn't
necessarily related
to the problem.

Solution-building
language is different
from problem talk.

No problems
happen all the time.

The future is both
created and
negotiable.

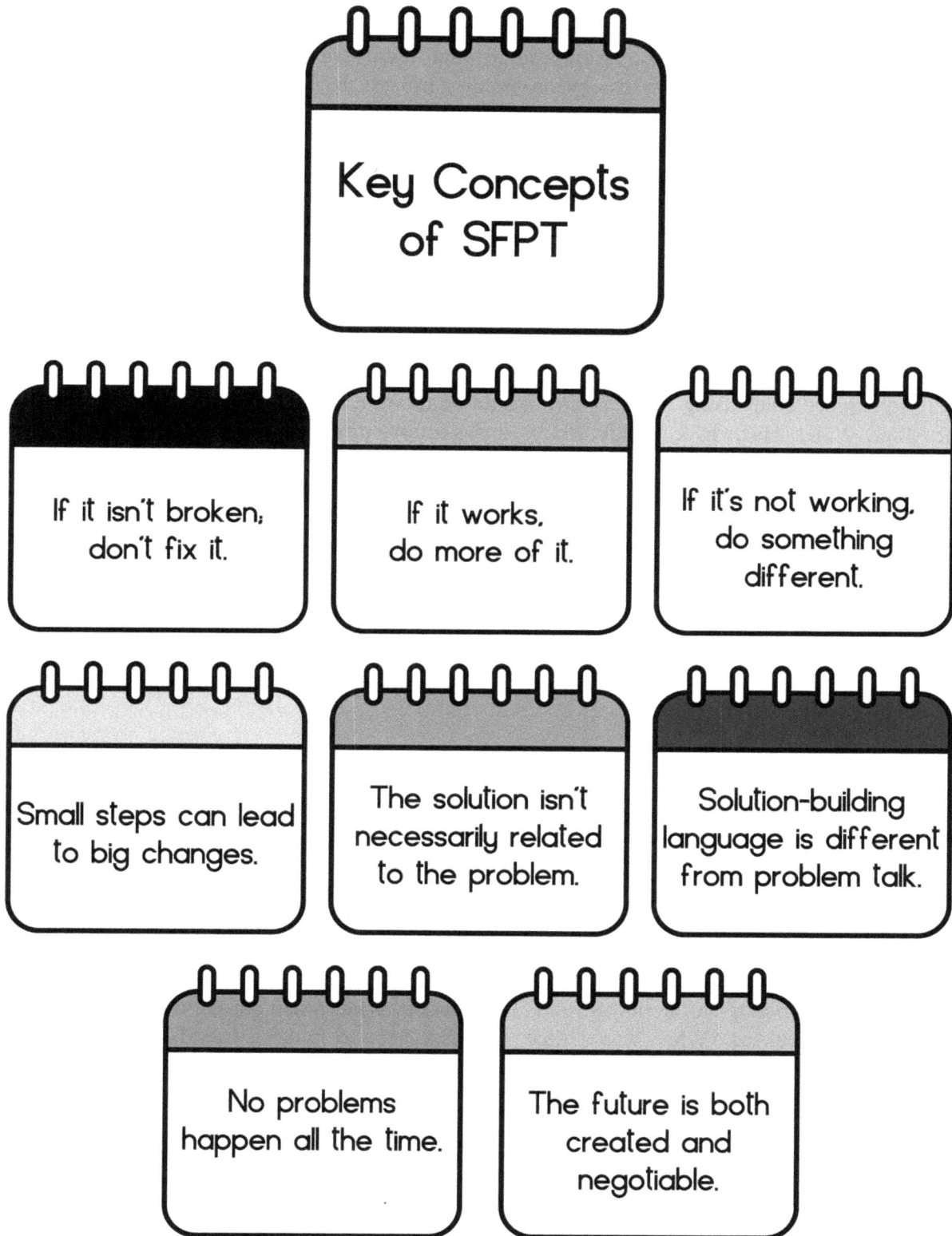

Figure 8.3 Key concepts of solution-focused play therapy.

questions and exploring client meaning, for children who can and choose to respond verbally. SFPT honors the developmental need for play expression in place of verbal responses with young children and adapts to become more interactive and conversational when used with older children and teens.

Goal setting is an important part of the solution-building process. By helping students focus on what they want in the future using SFPT, they may be more motivated to make the small changes that lead to significant growth. Hartwig and Taylor (2022) identified how to use goal setting in schools with SFPT. They described the five stages of solution building: (1) Describing the problem and best hopes, (2) developing well-formed goals, (3) searching for solutions, (4) end-of-session feedback, and (5) evaluating client progress (p. 135). They elaborated on ways to set goals with children in schools using sandtray and puppets as play-based interventions. Kim et al. (2017) highlighted the specific advantages of using SFT in school settings. They noted that this approach is especially portable to nonclinical settings at school, such as playground conflicts or staff/caregiver consultations. SFT can also be adapted to Independent Education Program goals by using discrete goals and the scaling technique (Kim et al., 2017).

One way to explore goals using SFPT is through an adaptation of the miracle question technique called the Magic Wand (Hartwig & Taylor, 2022). In this intervention, the school counselor and child create a wand using expressive art materials, such as star cut-outs, sequins, pipe cleaners, and ribbons. After they have created their wands, the counselor asks the child, "Imagine that this is a magic wand, and by waving your wand, you could make the problems or challenges in your life disappear. What will be different in your world?" (p. 136). This expressive intervention offers a play-based way for children to discuss how they would like their life to be different and potentially better. The school counselor and child can then explore what small steps the child could take to work toward this better world. The systemic nature of SFPT includes involvement with and external resources from caregivers, teachers, school counselors, and others, making it very useful in school counseling programs (Hartwig, 2021; Hartwig & Taylor, 2022).

Applying SFT to AASC

Bringing SFT and AASC together provides many opportunities for a student to experience success. Interactions with an animal partner can create moments for the child to practice new skills (Chandler, 2017). For example, a student struggling with giving a presentation in class due to anxiety can practice in front of the animal partner without judgment, leading the student to feel more confident. The counselor can ask the student to identify what made them successful in that moment and then help the student generalize it to the classroom setting. Another SFT example is having the student create a puppet show with the animal partner (Hartwig, 2021). The student can use puppets to teach the animal partner ways to make friends on the playground. The animal partner, through the counselor, can ask exception questions, such as "When was a time you were able to make a friend?" or the miracle question, such as "If [that puppet] were really good at making friends, what would they say or do to make a new friend?" Ultimately, focusing on the abilities of the student and the animal will help children find solutions in school.

One study sought to explore the effectiveness of SFT and AAC in youth ages 10 to 18. Hartwig (2017) examined the effectiveness of the Human-Animal Resilience Therapy (HART) intervention, which was a 10-session curriculum that incorporated play-based activities, such as sandtray and expressive art. Using a randomized comparison trial, the study evaluated the HART intervention. Outcomes indicated that children made significant improvements in anxiety, depression, and disruptive behavior in only ten weeks with this strengths-based intervention.

Integrating SFT and AASC in school settings can be a great way to help children identify their strengths and capabilities and achieve goals with the support of an animal partner. Pichot (2012) asserted that both SFT and animal-assisted work maintain six common values: (1) Respect for life and change, (2) Respect for culture and everyone's unique way of viewing the world, (3) Belief in hearing and respecting the wisdom of those with whom we are working, (4) Belief that the interaction should always be purposeful and with the end result in mind, (5) Belief that partnership is the most effective strategy, and (6) Belief that small steps can make a big difference. Though students may have lost hope, SFT practitioners believe in future possibilities with similar openness to life as the AASC practitioner watches for animal partners to initiate change in others' demeanor. Careful listening and intentional conversations help SFT practitioners understand others' uniqueness and in the same way, AASC practitioners observe each individual animal's communication for the sake of safety and respect.

Pichot (2012) frequently observed animals behaving unexpectedly to communicate needs that were unnoticed by humans. Respect for the student as the expert in their own life resembles respect for a dog's warning signals when children repeatedly step on the dog's tail. "Unless we really understand and respect the animal's unique way of interacting and communicating, we may miss early warning signals of discomfort in a situation" (Pichot, 2012, p. 16). Protocols for human-animal interactions, much like well-worded questions in SFT, ensure that both AASC and SFT techniques intentionally harmonize with desired outcomes. And whether the relationship is between human and animal or school counselor and student, SFT and AASC emphasize the importance of relating as partners who enhance the others' experience. The enriching experiences of combining solution-focused and animal-assisted work are built on gentle nuzzles, light pats, head nods, shifts in perspective, and single steps forward (Pichot, 2012).

Person-Centered Therapy

Another theory that can be applied to AASC is person-centered therapy (PCT). PCT was originally developed by Rogers (1942). Rogers identified 19 propositions of person-centered theory, asserting that each person is an organized whole whose behavior aligns toward a goal of self-actualization within a phenomenal field that is their reality. Individuals form their idea of self as they experience their perceptual field and differentiate. Congruence of experiences and self-concept leads to freedom and adjustment while incongruence is experienced as tension, maladjustment, or defending against a perceived threat. In the absence of threat, people can integrate, gain understanding, grow, and change (Rogers, 1965). This nondirective approach to counseling has the foundational belief that people do not need directive activities or questions to work toward healing, but rather the core conditions of empathy, congruence, and unconditional positive regard to access their own potential.

Axline, a student and colleague of Carl Rogers, applied person-centered theory to her work with children (Landreth, 2023). Axline (1947, 1964) wrote about the core concepts of nondirective play therapy and its eight basic principles. See Figure 8.4.

Landreth (2023) brought together the key concepts of PCT, Axline's basic principles, and the modality of play therapy to establish and operationalize child-centered play therapy (CCPT). In CCPT, the genuine, warm, and accepting relationship is the change agent, and play functions as the language of the child (Ray, 2011). By adopting certain beliefs about children consistent with PCT, following in play as an active participant when invited, providing toys as creative materials for self-expression, and setting limits only when needed, CCPT therapists help children process their experiences and heal by their innate potential (Landreth, 2023; Ray, 2011). Using intentionally selected play materials and symbolic play makes the child's challenging experiences manageable and safe to express through the

Basic Principles of Nondirective Play Therapy

Must develop a warm, friendly relationship with the child

Accepts the child unconditionally, without wishing the child were different in some way

Establishes a feeling of permissiveness in the relationship so that the child feels free to express self

Recognizes and reflects the feelings of the child to create understanding for the child

Respects the child's innate ability to solve his or her own problems and offers the opportunity to return responsibility to the child

Does not attempt to direct the child's actions or conversation, but allows the child to lead the way

Recognizes the gradual nature of the child's process and does not try to rush counseling

Establishes only those limitations that are necessary to anchor the child's counseling to the world of reality

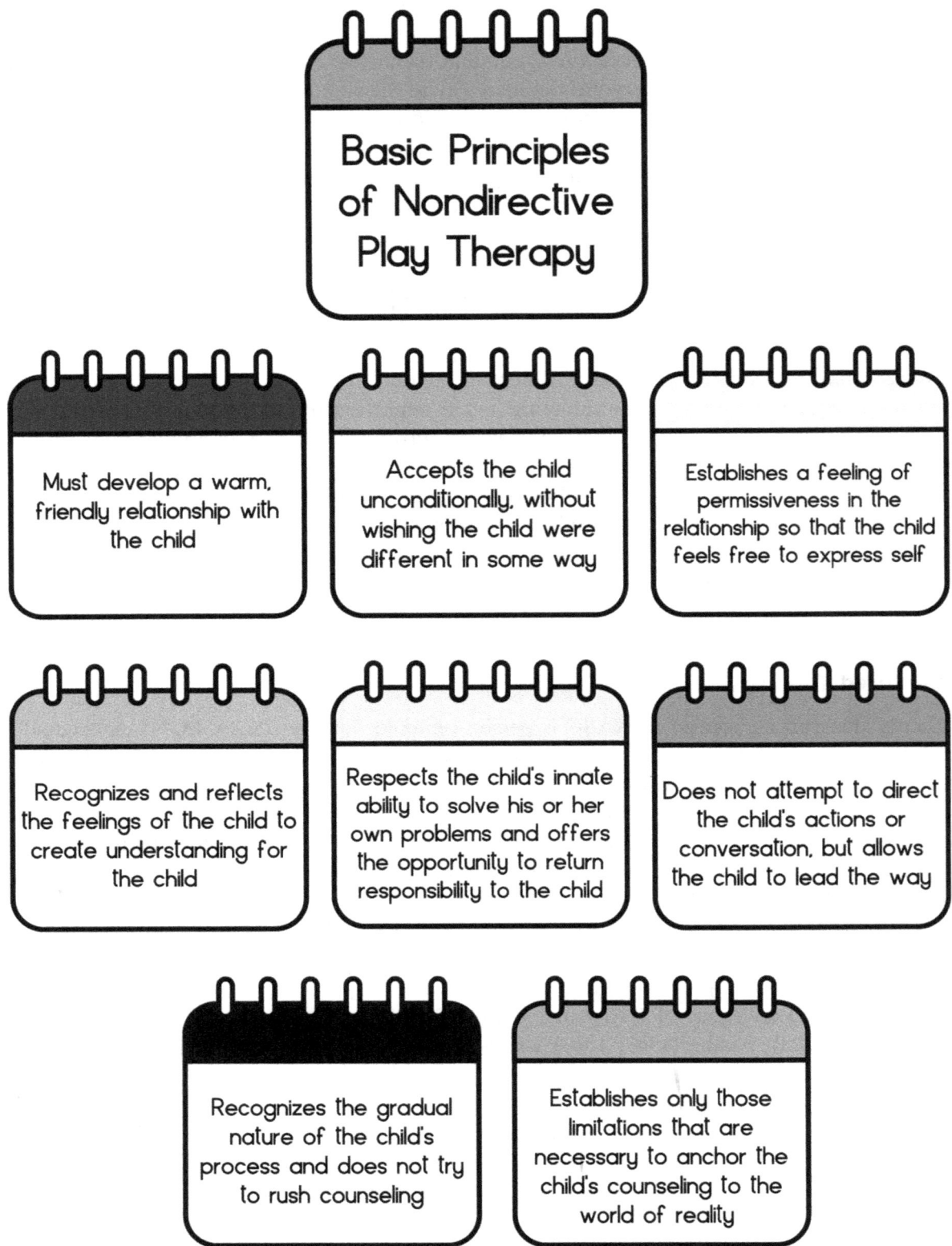

Figure 8.4 Basic principles of nondirective play therapy.

language of play. Ray (2011) identifies basic CCPT skills as open posture, tone of voice, tracking behavior, reflecting content, reflecting feeling, facilitating decision making, returning responsibility, facilitating creativity, esteem-building, responses about the relationship, reflecting larger meaning, and therapeutic limit setting. In order to avoid restricting the child's self-direction to the counselor's direction, the objectives of CCPT are broad: positive self-concept, self-responsibility, self-acceptance, self-reliance, decision making, feeling of control, sensitivity to the coping process, internal ability to evaluate, and trust in self (Landreth, 2023).

A host of studies have been conducted on the use of CCPT in school settings. For decades, researchers have found outcomes of academic improvement, decreased disruptive and externalizing behaviors, and improved teacher/student relationships as well as better communication and emotional expression (Ray, 2011). This demonstrates that even while CCPT uses a nondirective approach, it can be an effective modality to help children in schools.

Applying PCT to AASC

PCT or CCPT can be incorporated with AASC wherein students experience Rogers' core conditions of empathy, congruence, and unconditional positive regard through the animal partner and school counselor. Relating to the animal partner facilitates more ways to express beliefs about self and others. As the presence of another child in group play therapy demonstrates safety to a reluctant participant (Landreth, 2023), so, too, can the school counselor's care for and acceptance of an animal partner demonstrate safety to a reluctant student in AASC.

Two doctoral dissertations have explored the bringing together of CCPT and AAC. Austin-Main (2018) explored registered play therapists' experiences using "child-centered canine-assisted play therapy" (CC-CAPT) with children under 12 years old to support the previously anecdotal knowledge base for CC-CAPT. Broad themes emerged about preparation and the relationships with multiple sub-themes in each area. One major finding was how "the child and the dog can interact in ways that the therapist and child may not" (p. iii). The therapeutic relationship shifted from a practitioner-child dyad to a triad with child as director, therapy dog as connector, and counselor as facilitator. Austin-Main's inductive analysis study illuminates what CC-CAPT-trained counselors do to remain true to the tenets of CCPT and use the same facilitative skills. Practitioners described using clinical judgment to balance their attention and continue providing a truly healing, expressive space. Austin-Main asserted that play therapists need competence in professional counseling skills and play therapy skills before incorporating CC-CAPT into their practice.

Talley (2021) explored the integration of CCPT and AAPT, called "child-centered canine-assisted play therapy" (C3APT), using a constructivist grounded theory approach. This study explored this approach with four children who received C3APT services. From this study, the author identified three major themes: 1) Principles of C3APT, 2) procedures of C3APT, and 3) relational dynamics. Both dissertations notably advocated for safety of all, exploring ways to mitigate risk, supplemental materials such as a den or safe retreat for the animal, the triadic nature of relationships, roles for dogs in pretend play, and ways to introduce the animal without directing play (Austin-Main, 2018; Talley, 2021).

Linkage to ASCA Standards

The American School Counselors Association (ASCA) professional standards and competencies exist to aid school counselors in self-assessment and formulating their professional development plan. These standards outline the importance of counselors using clinical theory to help guide goals and treatment.

The ASCA (2022) ethical standards also direct the use of clinical theories to prevent harm and provide informed consent. Additionally, in these standards, cognitive-behavioral therapy, solution-focused therapy, and person-centered therapy are each recognized explicitly as effective and evidence-based professional foundations which contribute to social and emotional development of students (ASCA, 2019). Below is a review of the various professional standards and competencies and how they apply to clinical theories.

ASCA Professional Standards and Competencies

ASCA Professional Standard B-PF 1 has two parts to it that identify the importance of clinical theory for school counselors. First, B-PF 1c clearly states that school counselors need to utilize a theory and then goes on to list various theories that are successful, including the three theories being discussed in this chapter. The standard states that counselors "use established and emerging evidence-based counseling theories and techniques that are effective in a school setting to promote academic, career and social/emotional development, including but not limited to rational emotive behavior therapy, reality therapy, cognitive-behavioral therapy, Adlerian, solution-focused brief counseling, person-centered counseling and family systems" (ASCA, 2019, p. 3). Standard B-PF 1d identifies the importance of using theories in all therapeutic settings. It states, "use counseling theories and techniques in individual, small-group, classroom, and large-group settings to promote academic, career, and social/emotional development" (ASCA, 2019, p. 3), indicating that no matter where a counselor works within a school, it is important they utilize a theory.

ASCA Professional Standard B-SS 3 identifies the need for counselors to provide counseling short-term both individually and in a small-group settings. Under B-SS 3a, it further directs school counselors to identify students in need and provide short-term individual and small-group counseling (ASCA, 2019). This is relevant to theory as some theories, such as SFT, are brief approaches, meaning that counselors work with children on smaller goals (e.g., learning two regulation skills) in a short-term timeframe rather than on a large goal (e.g., decreasing multiple symptoms of anxiety) over a long-term timeframe. Without a theoretical approach, a school counselor may also struggle to identify what the student's needs are or how to help them work toward a goal without having a clinical theory to guide them. Together, the identified ASCA standards provide the basis for theoretically informed AASC. Further, all three theories discussed in this chapter are based on research, recognized explicitly by ASCA in B-PF 1c, and related to social/emotional development by encouraging the potential in students.

ASCA Ethical Standards

The ASCA Ethical Standards (2022) were created to identify ethical behavior for school counselors to adhere to, to assure the highest level of integrity and professionalism are preserved. The ethical standards serve as a guide for school counselors to promote ethical behavior and to maintain high standards of professionalism and integrity in the school counseling field. Ethical Standard B.3.b asks school counselors to "maintain professional competence in current school counseling issues and topics" and standard B.3.e. compels counselors to "engage in routine, content-applicable professional development to stay up to date on trends and needs of students and other stakeholders, and regularly attend training on current legal and ethical responsibilities" (ASCA, 2022, p. 8). These two ethical standards indicate the need for school counselors to stay informed of school counseling issues and how to address and support the needs of the students. The professional standards indicate that theories need to be evidence-based, while the ethical standards describe the importance of counselors being knowledgeable about current trends. Additionally, clinical theory is one aspect of a school counselor's competency set that needs to be maintained. School counselors being up to date on their clinical theory will help them to best meet the needs of their students. Without a full understanding of one's theory, a school counselor will struggle to support their students and will have difficulty identifying effective and appropriate interventions.

Applying Theories in Primary-Level Schools

In this section, we'll explore how to apply CBT, SFT, and PCT to AASC in primary-level schools. When choosing a theory, it's important that school counselors identify a theory that fits with their personal beliefs and values about how clients change. For example, if a practitioner sees changes in thoughts, feelings, and behaviors as a way that clients change, then CBT would be a good fit. If a practitioner believes that clients have internal strengths and external resources that can help them take small steps toward change, then SFT would be an ideal choice. Lastly, if a practitioner believes that clients change best within a self-directed environment in which directive activities and questions are not needed, then PCT would be a great option.

The school counselor's theoretical orientation should not change based on the client's age or presenting problem. Rather, the school counselor should take into consideration the age, developmental level, and goals of the child and then adapt the approach accordingly. All three theoretical approaches can be beneficial in primary schools due to the developmental level of children and utilization of play within the theories, which has been noted as an important part of treatment of children (Schaefer & Drewes, 2009).

When choosing an intervention, it is important that the school counselor chooses one that focuses on the student's specific goals. For example, if the child needs to work on identifying and expressing emotions, the counselor would use an intervention that focuses on that goal (e.g., Emotion Balls). It is key that school counselors know how to plan interventions to meet the specific individual, group, and classroom goals for children in schools.

Appendix B includes lesson plans for AASC interventions that apply CBPT and CCPT with children at the primary level. The first intervention, Lesson Plan 8.1 (Appendix B), is called Emotion Balls, and is described using CBPT. This activity helps children learn to identify emotions, which is important for emotion regulation. The goal of this activity is for the animal partner to find each emotion ball so that the animal can help the child talk about emotions. The student hides the emotion balls and each time the animal finds an emotion ball, the counselor asks the student to talk about a time when they felt that way. Through processing the activity, the child can also work to build skills to effectively manage various emotions. This intervention fits CBPT theory due to the direct nature of the activity and the student being involved in their treatment through play. It also focuses on the student's thoughts, feelings, behaviors and how these are all connected, as well as teaches the student skills. Figure 8.5 shows an example of a school counselor facilitating the Emotion Balls intervention.

The second intervention, Lesson Plan 8.2 (in Appendix B) called Nondirective Play Therapy is an example of using CCPT and AASC together. This activity allows a student to guide the play with an animal partner present. The counselor does not provide expectations or directives about the play. The school counselor uses the CCPT basic skills identified by Ray (2011) to acknowledge the child's play and interactions with the animal. This intervention is an example of CCPT due to the play being the function of communication for the student, acceptance and unconditional positive regard provided

Figure 8.5 A school counselor facilitates the Emotion Balls intervention.

by the counselor, and the nondirective nature of the therapy. Figure 8.6 shows a practitioner and child in a CCPT session.

Applying Theories in Secondary-Level Schools

In general, youth at the secondary-level schools, such as middle and high schools, often have more advanced cognitive skills than younger children. AASC interventions with older children and adolescents can involve more directive activities and questions but should also be balanced with solid basic skills. Below are examples of AASC interventions using CBT and SFT that could be facilitated with secondary-level students.

The CBT intervention, Animal Obstacle Course Challenge, is presented in Lesson Plan 8.3 (Appendix B). This intervention involves an obstacle course where the student leads the animal through a course they have created for the animal. By creating the course and leading the animal through it, it provides an opportunity for the adolescent to practice various skills, such as problem solving or frustration tolerance. The student can also explore how to overcome life obstacles by learning how to navigate the course. This intervention can also change a student's emotional state. If the student is in a hypoarousal state ("shut down"), then creating the obstacle course will get them moving, likely resulting in the student becoming more regulated. Figure 8.7 shows a child and animal partner engaging in this intervention.

Figure 8.6 Teri Mills-Manuel works with a child in a CCPT session.

This intervention fits into CBT theory for several reasons. It focuses on skill building and learning effective coping strategies to learn how to manage challenges. Through the use of processing questions, the student can identify maladaptive thoughts and behaviors, how they impact their emotional/physiological state, and work to identify more adaptive thoughts and behaviors. The student can practice these more adaptive thoughts/behaviors through the obstacle course. Lastly, this activity provides an opportunity for the student to experience a change in an emotional state in the moment.

The SFT intervention, The Floor is Lava, is described in Lesson Plan 8.4 (Appendix B). This AASC intervention focuses on helping youth identify strengths and what is improving for them week to week. The student has to get from one end of the room to the other by jumping through different colored hula hoops, choosing their own path to the other side. Each hula hoop color represents a different prompt or question. All prompts/questions are based on SFT beliefs that children have strengths, resiliency, and have the resources to achieve their own goals (Hartwig, 2021). Examples of the prompts/questions are "Name a strength," "What has been better for you this week compared to last?," "What is a coping skill you have been using that is working well?," and "What is something you can do differently this week that may be helpful?" (Figure 8.8).

This intervention further fits into SFT theory due to its focus on solutions rather than the problems and its attention on what is changeable. The intervention is also grounded in the present and future rather than emphasizing the past.

Figure 8.7 A student encourages Hank through an obstacle course.

Trauma-Informed and Diversity Considerations

In terms of diversity considerations, all three theoretical approaches discussed in this chapter have addressed the importance of diversity in literature. Hays (2019) explores ways in which CBT can be made more culturally responsive. One method Hays recommends is using the ADDRESSING model to recognize nine cultural influences and related groups: Age and generational influences, Developmental or other Disability, Religion and spiritual orientation, Ethnic and racial identity, Socioeconomic status, Sexual orientation, Indigenous heritage, National origin, and Gender (pp. 12–13). AASC practitioners can begin with a self-assessment of themselves. They also can consider similar aspects of the ADDRESSING model regarding their animal partner, such as breed, age in animal years, health issues, adoption type, previous history with trauma, and/or training methods. After a self-assessment, AASC practitioners can seek to learn more about these cultural factors from students.

SFT has embraced concepts of neurobiology as this theory has developed into a more trauma-informed approach. Concepts such as understanding regulation and dysregulation (Siegel & Payne Bryson, 2011), bottom-up processing, and the six Rs of healing trauma (ChildTrauma Academy, 2017) are important components to integrate into SFT work with children in schools. Hartwig (2021) describes how a child petting a dog supports the six Rs of healing trauma and demonstrates child-animal co-regulation. Furthermore, a wealth of research on SFT in schools demonstrates efficacy with diverse populations including: LatinX, African American, North American, European, Chinese,

Figure 8.8 A student high-fives Denali.

and Korean communities (Kim et al., 2017). SFT is a culturally responsive approach since the SFT practitioners believe in the concept of the client as expert in their lives and the therapist leading from one step behind, meaning the therapist guides the session but allows the client to make their own choices and create their own solutions. SFT has also been established as an affirming approach for the LGBTQIA+ community. Ouer (2016) described how to support queer clients in reaching their clinical goals by emphasizing the hope, resilience, and resources already present within this population.

CCPT values the child leading in their play and thus is seen as a client-centered and culturally affirming approach. CCPT counselors release the child's inner-directional and self-healing power (Landreth, 2023). This focus on following the child's lead honors the intersections of diversity and trauma that any individual may experience. CCPT reflections aid students in learning to respect themselves, accept their feelings, and eventually to accept themselves.

Bringing It All Together

Theoretical frameworks such as CBT, SFT, and PCT provide key concepts, techniques, and skills that guide AASC practitioners in helping students succeed in school. In this chapter three theoretical orientations were presented and applied to AASC. Throughout this chapter, the reader was introduced to theoretical applications that can help children set and achieve goals in school, as well as AASC interventions that apply those theories to work toward specific goals. AASC practitioners should be guided by a theoretical approach that aligns with their values about how children change and can be facilitated with an animal partner in a school setting. With this knowledge, one likely also has a better understanding of which theory they would utilize, thus being able to identify skills, techniques, and interventions best suited for Rosalie when providing school counseling with Hank, leading to a successful reduction in Grace's symptoms. Choosing and applying a theoretical approach to AASC helps school counselors have a guiding map of how to help children succeed in school with the support of a present and nonjudgmental animal partner.

References

American Counseling Association. (2014). *ACA code of ethics.* Author. https://www.counseling.org/resources/aca-code-of-ethics.pdf

American School Counselor Association. (2019). *ASCA school counselor professional standards & competencies.* Author. https://www.schoolcounselor.org/getmedia/a8d59c2c-51de-4ec3-a565-a3235f3b93c3/SC-Competencies.pdf

American School Counselor Association. (2022). *ASCA ethical standards for school counselors.* Author. https://www.schoolcounselor.org/getmedia/44f30280-ffe8-4b41-9ad8-f15909c3d164/EthicalStandards.pdf

Austin-Main, J. (2018). Understanding child-centered canine assisted play therapy: A qualitative collective case study [ProQuest Information & Learning]. In Dissertation Abstracts International Section A: *Humanities and Social Sciences* (Vol. 79, Issue 3–A(E)).

Axline, V. M. (1947). *Play therapy: The inner dynamics of childhood.* Houghton Mifflin Co.

Axline, V. (1964). *Dibs: In search of self.* Ballentine Books.

Bavelas, J., De Jong, P., Franklin, C., Froerer, A., Gingerich, W., Kim, J., Korman, H., Langer, S., Lee, M. Y., McCollum, E. E., Jordan, S. S., & Trepper, T. S. (2013). *Solution focused therapy treatment manual for working with individuals: 2nd version.* Solution Focused Brief Therapy Association. https://www.sfbta.org/resources/Documents/SFBT_Revised_Treatment_Manual_2013.pdf

Berg, I. K., & Shilts, L. (2005). *Classroom solutions: WOWW approach.* Brief Family Therapy Center.

Carlson, M. A. (2016). Using solution-focused brief therapy in schools. *Communique, 46*(2), 26–28.

Chandler, C. K. (2017). *Animal assisted therapy in counseling* (3rd ed.). Routledge. 10.4324/9781315673042

ChildTrauma Academy. (2017). *Neurosequential Model of Therapeutics© core slides.* https://childtrauma.org/wp-content/uploads/2018/01/CTA_NMT_Core-Slides_2018r.pdf.

De Jong, P., & Berg, I. K. (2013). *Interviewing for solutions* (4th ed.). Brooks/Cole.

Endenburg, N., & van Lith, H. A. (2011). The influence of animals on the development of children. *The Veterinary Journal, 190*(2), 208–214. https://doi-org.libproxy.txstate.edu/10.1016/j.tvjl.2010.11.020

Frey, D. (2009). Building self-esteem, coping skills, and changing cognitive distortions. In A. A. Drewes (Ed.), *Blending play therapy with cognitive behavioral therapy: Evidence-based and other effective treatments and techniques* (pp. 373–399). John Wiley & Sons, Inc.

Hartwig, E. K. (2017). Building solutions in youth: Evaluation of the Human-Animal Resilience Therapy intervention. *Journal of Creativity in Mental Health, 12*(4), 468–481. 10.1080/15401383.2017.1283281

Hartwig, E. K. (2021). *Solution-focused play therapy: A strengths-based clinical approach to play therapy.* Routledge. 10.4324/9780429354984

Hartwig, E. K., & Taylor, E. R. (2022). Small steps can lead to big changes: Goal setting in schools using solution-focused play therapy. *International Journal of Play Therapy, 31*(3), 131–142. 10.1037/pla0000179

Hays, P. A. (2019). Introduction. In G. Y. Iwamasa & P. A. Hays (Eds.), *Culturally responsive cognitive behavior therapy: Practice and supervision* (pp. 3–24). American Psychological Association. 10.1037/0000119-001

Hsu, K.-S., Eads, R., Lee, M. Y., & Wen, Z. (2021). Solution-focused brief therapy for behavior problems in children and adolescents: A meta-analysis of treatment effectiveness and family involvement. *Children and Youth Services Review, 120.* 10.1016/j.childyouth.2020.105620

Kim, J. S., & Franklin, C. (2009). Solution-focused brief therapy in schools: A review of the outcome literature. *Children and Youth Services Review, 31*(4), 464–470. 10.1016/j.childyouth.2008.10.002

Kim, J. S., Franklin, C., Zhang, Y., Liu, X., Yuanzhou, Q., & Chen, H. (2015). Solution-focused brief therapy in China: A meta-analysis. *Journal of Ethnic & Cultural Diversity in Social Work, 24*(3), 187–201. 10.1080/15313204.2014.991983

Kim, J. S., Jordan, S. S, Franklin, C., & Froerer, A. (2019). Is solution-focused brief therapy evidence-based? An update 10 years later. *Families in Society: The Journal of Contemporary Social Services*, *100*(2), 127–138. 10.1177/1044389419841688

Kim, J. S., Kelly, M., & Franklin, C. (2017). *Solution-focused brief therapy in schools: A 360-degree view of the research and practice principles* (2nd ed.). Oxford University Press.

Knell, S. M. (1995). *Cognitive-behavioral play therapy*. Jason Aronson, Inc.

Knell, S. M., & Dasari, M. (2009). CBPT: Implementing and integrating CBPT into clinical practice. In A. A. Drewes (Ed.), *Blending play therapy with cognitive behavioral therapy: Evidence-based and other effective treatments and techniques* (pp. 321–352). John Wiley & Sons, Inc.

Kvarme, L. G., Helseth, S., Sorum, R., Luth-Hansen, V., Haugland, S., & Natvig, G. K. (2010). The effect of a solution-focused approach to improve self-efficacy in socially withdrawn school children: A non-randomized controlled trial. *International Journal of Nursing Studies*, *47*(11), 1389–1396. 10.1016/j.ijnurstu.2010.05.001

Landreth, G. L. (2023). *Play therapy: The art of the relationship* (4th ed.). Routledge. 10.4324/9781003255796

Lange, A., Cox, J., Bemert, D., & Jenkins, C. (2007). Is counseling going to the dogs? An exploratory study related to the inclusion of an animal in group counseling with adolescents. *Journal of Creativity in Mental Health*, *2*(2), 17–31. 10.1300/J456v02n02_03

Leggett, E. S. (2017). Solution-focused play therapy. In E. S. Leggett, & J. N. Boswell (Eds.), *Directive play therapy: Theories and techniques* (pp. 59–79). Springer Publishing Co.

Lemberger-Truelove, M. E., Ceballos, P. L., Molina, C. E., & Dehner, J. M. (2020). Inclusion of theory for evidence-based school counseling practice and scholarship. *Professional School Counseling*, *23*(1_part_3), 6–13. 10.1177/2156759×20903576.

Meyer, D. D., & Cottone, R. R. (2013). Solution-focused therapy as a culturally acknowledging approach with American Indians. *Journal of Multicultural Counseling & Development*, *41*(1), 47–55. 10.1002/j.2161-1912.2013.00026.x

Nims, D. R. (2007). Integrating play therapy techniques into solution-focused brief therapy. *International Journal of Play Therapy*, *16*, 54–68. 10.1037/1555-6824.16.1.54

Ouer, R. (2016). *Solution-focused brief therapy with the LGBT community: Creating futures through hope and resilience*. Routledge. 10.4324/9781315744360

Paolini, A. C. (2016). Utilizing solution focused brief counseling with primary and middle school grades: Helping the perpetrator and the victim mitigate effects of bullying. *International Review of Social Sciences and Humanities*, *10*(2), 50–60.

Pichot, T. (2012). *Animal-assisted brief therapy: A solution-focused approach*. Routledge. 10.4324/9780203830826

Ray, D. C. (2011). *Advanced play therapy: Essential conditions, knowledge, and skills for child practice*. Routledge. 10.4324/9780203837269

Rogers, C. R. (1942). *Counseling and psychotherapy: Newer concepts in practice*. Houghton Mifflin.

Rogers, C. R. (1965). *Client-centered therapy: Its current practice, implications, and theory*. Houghton Mifflin.

Schaefer, C. E., & Drewes, A. A. (2009). The therapeutic powers of play and play therapy. In A. A. Drewes (Ed.), *Blending play therapy with cognitive behavioral therapy: Evidence-based and other effective treatments and techniques* (pp. 3–15). John Wiley & Sons, Inc.

Schott, E. (2021). *LGBTQI Workbook for CBT*. Routledge. 10.4324/9781003089285

Shelby, J. S., & Berk, M. S. (2009). Play therapy, pedagogy, and CBT: An argument for interdisciplinary synthesis. In A. A. Drewes (Ed.), *Blending play therapy with cognitive behavioral therapy: Evidence-based and other effective treatments and techniques* (pp. 17–40). John Wiley & Sons, Inc.

Siegel, D. J., & Payne Bryson, T. (2011). *The whole-brain child: 12 revolutionary strategies to nurture your child's developing mind*. Bantam Books.

Stewart, L. A., Chang, C. Y., Parker, L. K., & Grubbs, N. (2016). *Animal-assisted therapy in counseling competencies*. American Counseling Association, Animal-Assisted Therapy in Mental Health Interest Network. https://www.counseling.org/docs/default-source/competencies/animal-assisted-therapy-competencies-june-2016.pdf?sfvrsn=14

Suitt, K. G., Franklin, C., & Kim, J. S. (2016). Solution-focused brief therapy with Latinos: A systematic review. *Journal of Ethnic & Cultural Diversity in Social Work*, *25*(1), 50–67. 10.1080/15313204.2015.1131651

Talley, L. P. (2021). Child-centered canine-assisted play therapy: An investigative look at integrating therapy dogs into child-centered play therapy [ProQuest Information & Learning]. In Dissertation Abstracts International: *Section B: The Sciences and Engineering* (Vol. 82, Issue 8–B).

Taylor, E. R. (2019). *Solution-focused therapy with children and adolescents: Creative and play-based approaches.* Routledge. 10.4324/9781315166674

Weston, F. (2010). Using animal assisted therapy with children. *British Journal of School Nursing, 5*(7), 344–347. 10.12968/bjsn.2010.5.7.78286

Chapter 9

AASC Classroom and Schoolwide Interventions

Melissa Whitsett[1] and Heather C. Trupia[2]
[1]*Liberty Hill Independent School District;* [2]*Hays Consolidated Independent School District*

Box 9.1

Chapter 9 Scenario

Hank stands at his post, tail wagging, just down the hall from the cafeteria each morning as children approach and ask to pet him. Rosalie smiles and reminds the crowd of giggling children to form a line and that no more than two at a time may be petting him. They wait eagerly for Hank to give them a sniff, then come down to his level to pet him under the chin, around his ears, and on his back. Rosalie is glad that she took the time to use what she learned in her animal-assisted school counseling (AASC) training to teach the children how to interact with Hank, therefore making his mental and physical welfare a priority. After their interaction with Hank, students continue on to breakfast. Breakfast numbers have increased at this Title I school, where all children receive free breakfast, since Rosalie and Hank took over this post. Students have made a connection, "If I get breakfast each morning, I can pet Hank most days". When the line of students is not long, students may opt for a second pet on their way out of the cafeteria as well. Morning interactions with Hank have made a big impact on the start of the day for many students. There are fewer instances of hungry children waiting to eat until lunch, and there are many more smiling students walking down the hallway to class.

   From their morning duty vantage point, Rosalie and Hank can also be waved down for some assistance when a student is struggling to come to school that day. Several times a week, you will find a student with drying tears, being brave and finding comfort as they walk with Rosalie and Hank to their classroom. From there, Hank visits with classes and students in an effort to increase attendance numbers and remind them of the schoolwide attendance incentive, "Popcorn and Paws". Rosalie is grateful for the training she has had in ensuring Hank's ethical and safe involvement in schoolwide and classroom activities. His presence has supported her Tier 1 efforts in addressing the social-emotional, and behavioral needs of all students, and fostered a greater positive impact on the school environment than she could have imagined.

School counselors are charged with a variety of duties during the school day. One of the most critical responsibilities is to connect and build rapport with students in order to be successful in supporting social-emotional well-being, behavior improvement, empathy development, enhancing coping skills, and building a growth mindset. Success in these areas will likely lead to improved attendance, confidence, and enhanced academic and problem-solving skills. Bringing in an animal partner can be a special addition to a Comprehensive School Counseling program that helps to support all these skills and more (Figure 9.1).

DOI: 10.4324/9781003392415-9

Figure 9.1 Walking Ahsoka with a double-handled leash.

Through the ages, many expressions for a dog's love, loyalty, and friendship have been shared. As they show a willingness to accept humans as they are with tail wags, kisses, and snuggles, one can see why it is widely accepted that dogs are our best friends. Dogs demonstrate a relational nature when they interact with children through play and support the child's ability to perceive congruence and unconditional positive regard from the dog (Talley, 2021). This may be why it seems so easy for children to feel instantly safe and at ease with a family pet or a canine counseling partner. Students who may not have healthy, secure attachments at home may find joy, connection, and comfort with an AASC animal partner at school, which can lead to a rewarding relationship with both the counselor and the dog.

Classroom lessons and schoolwide initiatives are a vital part of a school counseling comprehensive program that seeks to serve students through a multi-tiered system of supports (MTSS). The MTSS system is an evidence-based framework that uses student data to provide tiered interventions to support academic growth, career development, and social-emotional learning (Sink, 2016). Goodman-Scott et al. (2020) identified the tiered services as:

- Tier 1 – classroom instruction and schoolwide initiatives.
- Tier 2 – individual and group counseling, collaboration with school personnel, families, and community stakeholders.
- Tier 3 – indirect services for students, such as referrals to outside resources and consultation.

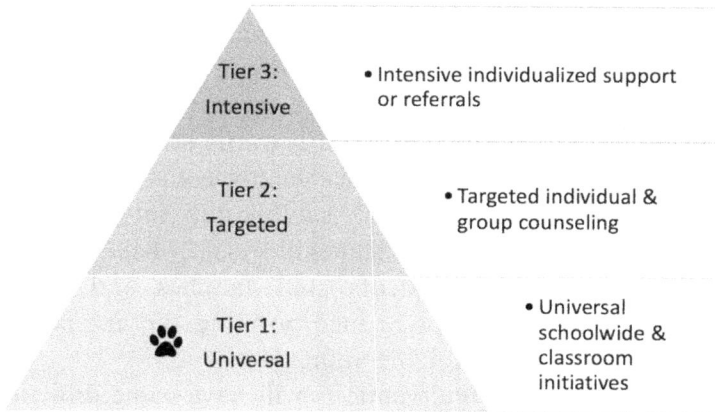

Figure 9.2 MTSS model.

This chapter focuses on Tier 1 interventions, which offer broad services through classroom instruction and schoolwide programming (Figure 9.2).

By providing Tier 1 interventions, AASC teams are able to influence every child in the school. This chapter offers examples of schoolwide and classroom AASC interventions school counselors can utilize and build upon. While the main focus is centered around working with a canine partner, the activities and interventions can be modified for other animal partners.

Literature Review

The Center on Positive Behavioral Interventions and Supports (2023) defines Tier 1 systems as regular, proactive, and preventative. The American School Counseling Association (ASCA, 2021) notes that through direct and indirect student services, school counselors provide Tier 1 support through classroom instruction, schoolwide initiatives and activities, collaboration, and data-driven, evidence-based prevention. This makes school counselors part of the educational process that affects academic outcomes (Webb et al., 2005). The interventions that school counselors provide to improve the social and emotional well-being of students are linked to academic success and behavior development. Student well-being and receptiveness to learning are connected (Henderson et al., 2020). Students with higher levels of social-emotional well-being master academic concepts more effectively, have increased academic engagement, and have fewer absences from school. Along with the growing evidence that supports AASC animal partners having a positive effect on students' well-being in school, animals in schools can promote a positive attitude toward learning, inspire more participation in learning activities, and reduce negative behaviors such as aggression and work avoidance (Grové et al., 2021). Animals in the classroom can encourage relationship building, trust, and nurturing skills and enhance students' ability to focus as they seek interactions and connection with the non-judgmental animal partner (Chandler, 2017). In fact, the growing body of research suggests that canine partners, in particular, support children physiologically, emotionally, socially, and physically. Children appear to perceive these trained animal partners as non-judgmental, without the expectations and complications that human relationships have, thus being valuable sources of social support (Friesen, 2010).

Collaboration with staff, families, and students, and integration of Tier 1 AASC interventions into the school culture will facilitate a sense of connection and trust between the AASC team (i.e., the school counselor and animal partner) and everyone involved in the school community. Trust and connection are the building blocks that can lead to a stronger sense of belonging, well-being, and overall positive outcomes (Grové et al., 2021) for students and for the AASC program. With expanding research shedding a positive light on the presence of animals within the educational setting, such as improved attentiveness and responsiveness, improved focus, and positive attitude towards school (Gee et al., 2017), AASC interventions can be an integral part of a comprehensive school counseling program. Grové et al. (2021) recommended several key considerations to successfully integrate AASC interventions into Tier 1 Services: (1) gaining the support of the stakeholders, (2) flexibility of the diverse needs of the school and students (3) training of the students, staff, families, and any other stakeholders, (4) training for the animal and for the counselor in incorporating the animal into a comprehensive school counseling program, and (5) planning for the animal's welfare.

School counselors looking to learn about Tier I AASC interventions will have some difficulty in finding relevant research on AASC Tier 1 interventions. While there are some qualitative articles, personal anecdotes, and school-related news stories about the positive impact an animal partner can have on students and staff in a school, much research is still needed in this area to support a data-driven program. Further research and more rigorous data on AASC Tier 1 interventions can explore the beneficial effects an animal partner can have on the school environment, students, staff, and AASC programs.

Linkage to ASCA Standards

ASCA outlines the professional standards and competencies (ASCA, 2019) and ethical standards (ASCA, 2022) for school counselors through specific mindsets and behaviors that school counselors need to meet the support Pre-K through 12 students. There are four specific standards that are integral to the development and implementation of Tier 1 services for an AASC program.

ASCA Professional Standards and Competencies

ASCA Professional Standard B-SS 1 states that school counselors "design and implement instruction aligned to ASCA Student Standards: Mindsets & Behaviors for Student Success in large-group, classroom, small-group and individual settings" (ASCA, 2019, p. 2). Animal partners are able to support student mindsets and behaviors in large-group and classroom settings. Tier 1 supports build a strong foundation to an AASC program because they expand services to a larger group and focus on preventative services. Having an animal partner interacting alongside the school counselor with students in larger settings can increase positive attitudes about school and create a sense of belonging. Animal partners being present during transition times, classroom lessons, and lunch time are a few of the ways to do this. An animal partner can also enhance classroom lessons on social-emotional topics such as empathy, responsibility, and identity development. Time spent with them can aid in school engagement and reduce anxiety for challenging work and reduce anxiety for challenging work.

ASCA Professional Standard B-SS 2 states that school counselors "provide appraisal and advisement in large-group, classroom, small-group and individual settings" (ASCA, 2019, p. 2). The foundation of effective Tier 1 services is using data to inform services that are most needed. By utilizing the AASC Lesson Plan, as discussed in Chapter 7, practitioners can design lessons that include how they will gather formative data to assess student needs in order to adapt and build supplementary interventions around skill deficits, struggles, and needs.

ASCA Ethical Standards

In terms of ASCA ethical standards related to schoolwide programs, school counselors are called in standard A.5 to "act to eliminate and/or reduce the potential for harm to students and stakeholders in any relationships or interactions by using safeguards, such as informed consent, consultation, supervision and documentation" (ASCA, 2022, p. 3). This goal of preventing harm is important for students and animal partners, alike. School counselors who have an animal partner must ensure that students, staff, and animals involved in large-group services are participating in ways that promote positive human-animal interactions and prevent harm. Some ways to do this are teaching and practicing proper greeting of the animal partner, limiting the number of students petting the animal at the same time, giving reminders or cues for students to follow petting and behavior expectations when interacting with or around the animal partner, and routine hand washing. AASC practitioners can also promote animal welfare by watching for signs of stress, limiting the animal partner's time at school, having a safe place for them to rest, and allowing the animal partner to choose if they want to participate or not in an activity.

Another ethical standard identified by ASCA is focused on acknowledging that bullying, discrimination, hate incidents, harassment, and bias are violations of federal law. Standard A.11 compels school counselors to "facilitate and monitor schoolwide prevention of bullying, harassment, discrimination, hate and bias through active practices that support a positive school climate, culture and belonging" (ASCA, 2022, p. 5). Tier 1 AASC interventions support this by strengthening students' social-emotional learning and can improve children's engagement in learning (Harris & Binfet, 2022). AASC practitioners can also plan more targeted bullying prevention activities, such as Lesson Plan 9.4 in Appendix B: PAWs Down Against Bullying. A school counselor has many responsibilities to students under the ASCA ethical standards (2022). AASC interventions can support a school counselor's work in fostering psychosocial development and being responsive to student mental health needs.

AASC Schoolwide and Classroom Lessons for Primary Schools

Schoolwide lessons should begin before your animal partner comes to campus. Building a positive atmosphere and rapport is just the beginning of having an animal partner in school for AASC lessons and interventions. Chapter 6 provides guidance on introducing your animal partner, teaching expectations for greeting and petting, and facilitating informed consent. Setting standards for interactions with your animal partner doesn't stop at first-time introductions. They must be reinforced daily and retaught as necessary throughout the school year. These steps should be addressed prior to more intentional Tier 1 AASC services being provided to students. This section presents guidance on facilitating Tier 1 interventions and describes several AASC lesson plans for schoolwide and classroom instruction and support.

While some school counselors travel to classrooms to do lessons, others have classrooms of their own to do the lessons. Having a dedicated classroom for counseling lessons has several benefits when it comes to having an animal partner. It can become a home away from home for the animal partner. The standard of atmosphere and behavior can more easily be set for their well-being, and the animal partner may be more comfortable opting out of participating when needed if they have their own safe space (e.g., a comfy bed) to go to. In the following example, Rosalie and Hank demonstrate a class coming to the AASC team classroom.

Rosalie stands at the door to greet the second-grade class coming to her room. As students arrive, they are eager to not only greet her, but Hank as well. She gains their attention to give them a reminder to greet him properly, just as they have practiced before so that Hank is comfortable with so many children approaching him. They step forward to let Hank have a sniff if he chooses and give him a soft pet on his chest or back, which are his favorite places to be petted. They've practiced this before and know that they have a whole class to get inside the room. Rosalie also gets greetings that vary from salutes, waves, heart-hand signals, or a quick hug. Students can look at the sign hung outside the classroom for greeting ideas. Students walk in calmly and sit on the carpet in a circle. They know Hank will more than likely want to walk around the circle for another greeting if they are calm. As predicted, Rosalie and Hank, with his tail wagging, walk around the circle so that students can give him a little longer of a pet. Hank often senses who needs a little more time and lingers in front of those students a little longer before making sure to say hello to each and every student in the circle. This is the way each class begins, unless Hank gets tired. Rosalie always allows him to decide to curl up on his comfy bed. If students don't get to greet him at the beginning of class, they know they'll likely get a goodbye at the end of class if he hasn't gotten up or joined in the lesson before that. Rosalie has had many conversations with students about this and they have learned empathy for the busy days that Hank has and are okay with letting him sleep. They, too, look out for Hank's well-being.

In the circle, at the beginning of guidance lessons, Rosalie uses a mood check-in process. Some days they take turns around the circle, and other times they raise their fingers up to give a number to go along with a picture of how they are feeling (see Figure 9.3). They decide which mood they feel according to the various pictures of Hank. Of course, Rosalie helps Hank share how he's feeling that day too!

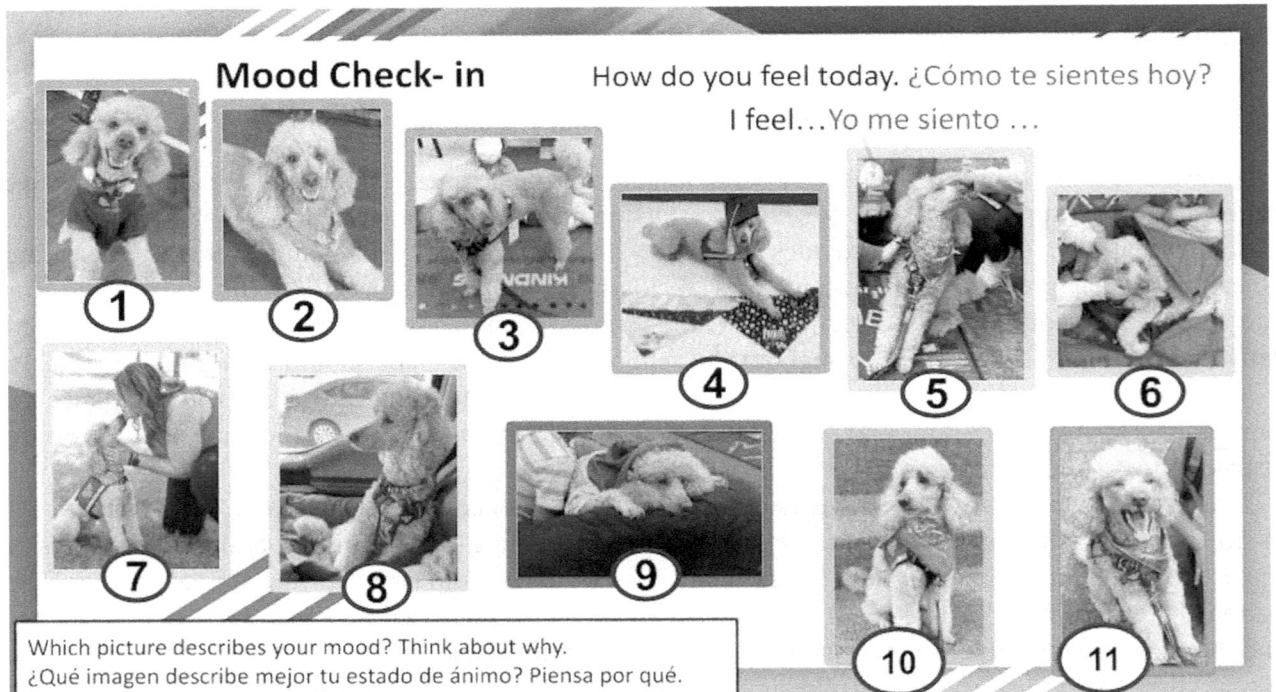

Figure 9.3 Mood check in.

Schoolwide Lessons

One schoolwide intervention that does not require a lot of planning or supplies is called Weekly Student Greeting presented in AASC Lesson Plan 9.1, which can be found in Appendix B. For this intervention, the AASC team chooses a centralized place where the team can greet students coming to or leaving school. This intervention allows the greatest number of students to see and greet the AASC team. This intervention can be planned for a certain day of the week (e.g., every Friday) or on the days when the animal partner is on the school campus. This intervention has the potential to increase mood, relationship-building skills, and comfort with students and staff.

Using the example of Rosalie and Hank, students in that school may be eager to see Hank and his wagging tail every Friday. Hank may sense when a student needs a little more attention from him. He builds morale and reinforces school as a welcoming and safe place to be. In this way, If and when a crisis should occur, students will already be familiar with, and likely even have a strong bond with, the animal partner. This weekly post also gives the counselor a chance to have mini check-ins with students in need of connection and encouragement to be in school. For students who feel anxious to be in school or are in need of frequent reminders of social-emotional learning strategies they may be working on, this intervention gives students a positive and consistent beginning to the day. An animal partner's presence and influence can be felt, even on days when they are not there. Having an animal partner can positively accelerate students' relationship with the counselor. Their connection to the counselor can increase exponentially through their relationship with the animal partner. There will likely be many questions and comments such as: "Where is Hank today?", "Is today Hank's rest day?", "Will Hank be here tomorrow?", and "I bet Hank was tired today and needed a rest". Having a mini stuffed animal in the likeness of the animal partner available for use when they are not there can be helpful for comfort or conversation at times (Figure 9.4).

Another schoolwide intervention is called Get Caught Being Pawsitive. This initiative is described in AASC Lesson Plan 9.2 (Appendix B). For this intervention, the school counselor can use the morning announcements to share about the concept of kindness or read a brief book about kindness. Teachers or the AASC team can then facilitate classroom discussions about kindness through the lens of the animal partner, which can be referred to as being "pawsitive". The next step in this intervention is to have students and staff notice people being pawsitive. School counselors can provide forms for students and staff to submit names and examples of people being pawsitive. Having a "Pawsitive Wall of Fame" can also be a way to show all the students and staff who were caught being kind to others (Figure 9.5).

Figure 9.4 Ahsoka with Ahsokita.

Figure 9.5 Let's Celebrate Paws-itivity activity.

This strengths-based intervention helps children focus on demonstrating kind behavior to peers and provides incentives for doing so.

Classroom Lessons

Developing and exploring self-concept and identity is an important journey for children in school. AASC Lesson Plan 9.3 (Appendix B) presents a classroom lesson on exploring identity. This lesson includes a discussion of what identity means and what we notice and don't notice about the animal partner. Students make an outline of the animal partner or their own pet to explore what qualities they have on the inside and what qualities they show us on the outside Then students discuss their own personal qualities that they show and perhaps some they don't show to others. AASC practitioners can use the discussion questions to process the intervention with the class. This lesson plan serves as a large group intervention to support student self-concept and identity development. Figure 9.6 shows an example of school counseling partner, Stella, who showed children her many kind and caring qualities.

During some lessons, animal partners will play an active role, while in others a more passive role. In the active role, animals are participating in the activity. This may include the animal demonstrating skills, walking through an obstacle course, or finding emotion balls around the room. In the passive role, the animal partner may be in the room, but not actively engaged in the activity. Just the presence of an animal can make a difference. Even if the animal is not there that day, AASC practitioners can use processing questions, such as "What would Hank do?" or "How would Hank feel if …?" to explore

Figure 9.6 AASC canine partner, Stella.

student beliefs and promote critical thinking. The animal partner engaging in both active and passive roles in AASC interventions can be beneficial for students.

AASC Schoolwide and Classroom Lessons for Secondary Schools

Middle and high schools are busy buildings. Kids aren't walking in straight, orderly lines anymore. There are loud bells throughout the day. Counselors likely have a smaller office with a whole lot of traffic going past the door. There's an energy about the building and lots of movement and noise. This is also a tumultuous time in the lives of students. They are learning how to become more independent. Their hormones are all over the place, and they are expected to keep track of multiple classes with various assignments and responsibilities. They are also navigating social pressures. This is such an important time for School Counselors to be a part of their journey. Making time to share Tier 1 AASC interventions with classrooms and the student body can help to reduce the number of walk-ins and crisis situations. The more time secondary school counselors can spend in classrooms and with the whole student body, the more it can help to foster a closer relationship between counselor and student.

Considering all the moving parts of a secondary school, special awareness is vital when planning an animal partner's schedule and how to best create a connection between the animal and the school. Secondary counselors may not be able to go to classrooms as often as elementary counselors. Animal partners may only be at school on certain days and during certain times in this busy environment. Even with these possible limitations, there are ways to reach a majority of the students on campus. This section offers some ideas for Tier 1 AASC interventions on secondary campuses.

There are several ways that AASC teams can work with the administration and the district office to create a strong, interactive presence on campus and throughout the district. Here are some recommendations:

• Get a staff badge that can hang on the animal partner's collar. For example, everyone loves Gus's badge (see Figure 9.7). It is commented on and giggled about daily. It sparks conversation between the counselor and students, staff, and families.
• Make sure the animal partner is added to staff birthday lists.
• Celebrate their birthday with a fun treat, take pictures or a video and send to staff to share with their classes and during video announcements if the school has those.

Figure 9.7 Gus with his employee badge.

- Celebrate National Therapy Animal Day in April in a similar way.
- Create a business card or trading cards with their picture and some fun facts that can be passed out to students.
- Create stickers or other items with their pictures that can be handed out to everyone, or given out as rewards.
- Get their yearbook picture taken.
- Create social media profiles (with district approval) that can be followed by students. This can be a great place to share counselor news and tips.
- Create short videos that teachers can share about social-emotional learning.
- Apps that can show your animal partner talking can be a fun way to send videos to individual students or classrooms.
- Connect with sports teams, fine arts groups, or other clubs to see if they can make a bandana, bowtie, or some other small trinket your animal partner can wear to support events on campus.

Building the animal's presence on campus and across the district allows students to feel a connection with them even if they haven't met or interacted yet. By making the animal a visible and active part of the school community, students can feel a sense of connection and belongingness.

Schoolwide Lessons

Including an animal partner in schoolwide initiatives can be a great way to inspire participation and connection among all students. Many students may not ever work with an animal partner individually or in a small group setting. Creating schoolwide lessons allows the animal to be seen and interactive even if it's digitally. The AASC Lesson Plan 9.4 (Appendix B), called PAWs Down Against Bullying, is a schoolwide intervention involving a canine partner. It could be adapted to another kind of animal partner. The lesson includes daily announcements and activities to engage the whole campus. In this lesson, the AASC practitioner uses a talking animal application, such as My Talking Pet (Sharemob Ltd., 2018). Throughout the week, students will take part in short lessons and interactive activities that seek to expand their knowledge about bullying and ask them to think critically and thoughtfully about themselves and others. This intervention is a fun way to involve the animal partner in promoting bullying awareness and prevention (Figure 9.8).

Figure 9.8 Canine partner, Holly, demonstrates the My Talking Pet app.

Classroom Lessons

For older children and teens, it's important for them to know what helps them feel safe and secure. These skills can help children in the future to set appropriate boundaries, participate in healthy relationships, and promote self-care. The classroom lesson, Personal Space and Needs, AASC Lesson Plan 9.5 in Appendix B, addresses the topics of personal safety, security, and boundaries. The lesson begins by asking the animal to sit inside a hula hoop (Figure 9.9).

The practitioner will ask the students to brainstorm what things belong in their personal space (e.g., water, treats, toys, belly rubs) and things that don't belong in their personal space (e.g., mean people, aggressive animals, harmful food). They will then write these down on bone-shaped paper (or just small pieces of paper). The students will place the small bones inside the hula hoop or outside the hula hoop according to where they belong. Students will then discuss as a group what belongs and doesn't belong in their own personal space. This lesson encourages students to consider self-awareness, confidence, personal safety, and self-advocacy. Having an animal partner serve as an example for this lesson can provide students with a sense of safety and help the students relate their ideas and experience with the animal.

Figure 9.9 Zoe demonstrating the Personal Space and Needs lesson.

By providing classroom instruction and whole school activities, the school counselor uses the MTSS model to offer services to the broader school community. Tier 1 counseling services allow AASC teams to deliver engaging and preventative content that reaches across classrooms. Including an animal partner in Tier 1 interventions can be a helpful tool that encourages student engagement, connection, and belongingness.

Trauma-Informed and Diversity Considerations

One of the magical things about working with animals is their ability for unconditional positive regard. They don't care how a student has struggled in school, how a student looks, or what kind of trauma a student has experienced. They simply want positive interaction. This makes them a valuable addition to an AASC program that seeks to support all students. An AASC team has a greater chance of establishing a positive rapport with a student because of the power of human-animal interaction (Binfet & Hartwig, 2020). This rapport-building experience is grounding and adds a feeling of safety as the students observe the animal's ability to trust the counselor, giving them permission to trust. The attention in the room can also be directed towards the animal, helping the students to feel less observed, scrutinized, or judged. The counselor might talk directly to the animal instead of the students. For example, the counselor may notice that the animal partner is showing stress after hearing several beeps over the loudspeaker. The counselor can acknowledge and respond to the animal's stress signals by using a calm tone of voice, being curious about the sounds, and petting the animal softly. The counselor can then ask the students how they respond when they feel scared or anxious. As students connect the animal partner's response to their own responses, they can recognize similarities and discover new ways of coping. Utilizing touch, narration, indirect questions, and other AASC interventions helps the counselor to do trauma-informed work with students. Animals can help decrease student resistance and create a more open and emotionally safe space for students (Lange et al., 2007).

Connecting AASC interventions with school initiatives that support trauma history, diversity, and disabilities can support a school's goal of reaching and advocating for all students. Students can build self-esteem by learning how to teach the animal new cues or skills and demonstrating their success to teachers, staff, or families. Training an animal can also encourage patience as the student must allow the animal to process information and learn the new skill in their own time. Training work creates the opportunity for increasing self-confidence, pride in one's work, empathy for another living being, assertiveness, and other social, emotional, and behavioral goals (VonLintel & Bruneau, 2021). Some students may benefit from learning more about animal behavior and training at school as they take that information home to work with their own animals and families. Becoming an "expert" can help to build compassion, concentration, and empathy as well as leadership skills as they become the teacher. A student's desire to work with the animal can further motivate them to want to come to school and work (Chandler, 2017). See children in Figure 9.10 drawing pictures of canine partner, Ahsoka, who is very loved by the children in her school.

Facilitating a classroom lesson that focuses on learning how to interact with an animal can help students become advocates for positive human-animal interactions. AASC Lesson Plan 9.6 (Appendix B), Become a Dog Advocate, is a multi-session lesson that helps students who may have a history of animal-related trauma or fears to learn how to advocate for safety between animals and humans. The lesson teaches students about animal body language and how to properly greet and interact with animals. Throughout the lesson, students will learn how to teach others how to advocate for dogs, thus building leadership skills and interpersonal relations.

Figure 9.10 Children drawing pictures of Ahsoka.

Bringing It All Together

Whether it's connecting with students individually in the school environment, in classrooms, or with the whole student body, working with an animal partner can be a beneficial and rewarding partnership. From Pre-K through senior year, an animal partner can assist in better connecting a school counselor with their students, staff, families, and communities. By integrating the animal partner into the school culture, supporting school initiatives, and interacting in specific interventions, animals can help reduce stress, increase empathy and feelings of safety in school, and encourage students to participate in school (Lange et al., 2007). All of the beneficial effects of an AASC team can impact the student's academic journey. Counselors can work with their campus and district to create an AASC program that supports a feeling of connection for students and families. Counselors can develop and deliver classroom interventions and schoolwide initiatives that support academic, social, emotional, and behavioral goals. In these ways, animal partners will support comprehensive school counseling programs and be the catalyst to help students thrive.

References

American School Counselor Association. (2019). *ASCA school counselor professional standards & competencies.* Author. https://www.schoolcounselor.org/getmedia/a8d59c2c-51de-4ec3-a565-a3235f3b93c3/SC-Competencies.pdf

American School Counselor Association. (2021). *The school counselor and multitiered system of supports.* Author. https://www.schoolcounselor.org/Standards-Positions/Position-Statements/ASCA-Position-Statements/The-School-Counselor-and-Multitiered-System-of-Sup

American School Counselor Association. (2022). *ASCA ethical standards for school counselors.* Author. https://www.schoolcounselor.org/getmedia/44f30280-ffe8-4b41-9ad8-f15909c3d164/EthicalStandards.pdf

Binfet, J. T., & Hartwig, E. K. (2020). *Canine-assisted interventions: A comprehensive guide to credentialing therapy dog teams.* Routledge. 10.4324/9780429436055

Center on Positive Behavioral Interventions and Supports. (2023). *Tier 1.* https://www.pbis.org/pbis/tier-1

Chandler, C. K. (2017). *Animal assisted therapy in counseling* (3rd ed.). Routledge.

Friesen, L. (2010). Exploring animal-assisted programs with children in school and therapeutic contexts. *Early Childhood Education Journal, 37*(4), 261–267. 10.1007/s10643-009-0349-5

Gee, N. R., Fine, A. H., & McCardle, P. D. (Eds.) (2017). *How animals help students learn: research and practice for educators and mental-health professionals.* Routledge.

Goodman-Scott, E., Betters-Bubon, J., Donohue, P., & Olsen, J. (2020). *Making MTSS work.* American School Counselor Association. https://admin.schoolcounselor.org/getmedia/cdb8dc40-b550-4b50-8918-8fbec4c9969e/WEB072220_Handout.pdf

Grové, C., Henderson, L., Lee, F., & Wardlaw, P. (2021). Therapy dogs in educational settings: guidelines and recommendations for implementation. *Frontiers in Veterinary Science, 8.* https://www.frontiersin.org/articles/10.3389/fvets.2021.655104/full

Harris, N. M., & Binfet, J.-T. (2022). Exploring children's perceptions of an after-school canine-assisted social and emotional learning program: A case study. *Journal of Research in Childhood Education, 36*(1), 78–95. 10.1080/02568543.2020.1846643

Henderson, L., Grové, C., Lee, F., Trainer, L., Schena, H., & Prentice, M. (2020). An evaluation of a dog-assisted reading program to support student wellbeing in primary school. *Children and Youth Services Review, 118.* 10.1016/j.childyouth.2020.105449

Lange, A., Cox, J., Bemert, D., & Jenkins, C. (2007). Is counseling going to the dogs? An exploratory study related to the inclusion of an animal in group counseling with adolescents. *Journal of Creativity in Mental Health, 2*(2), 17–31. 10.1300/J456v02n02_03

Sharemob Limited. (2018). *My talking pet.* https://apps.apple.com/us/app/my-talking-pet/id1427290424

Sink, C. A. (2016). Incorporating a multi-tiered system of supports into school counselor preparation. *The Professional School Counselor, 6*(3), 203–219. http://tpcjournal.nbcc.org/wp-content/uploads/2016/09/Pages203-219-Sink.pdf

Talley, L. P. (2021). Child-centered canine-assisted play therapy: An investigative look at integrating therapy dogs into child-centered play therapy [ProQuest Information & Learning]. In *Dissertation Abstracts International: Section B: The Sciences and Engineering* (Vol. 82, Issue 8–B).

VonLintel, J., & Bruneau, L. (2021). Pathways for implementing a school therapy dog program: Steps for success and best practice considerations. *Journal of School Counseling, 19*(14). http://www.jsc.montana.edu/articles/v19n14.pdf

Webb, L. D., Brigman, G. A., & Campbell, C. (2005). Linking school counselors and student success: A replication of the student success skills approach targeting the academic and social competence of students. *Professional School Counseling, 8*(5), 407–413.

AASC Individual and Small-Group Interventions

Amanda Arriola[1], *Kristen Turpin*[2], *and Crystal Reese*[2]
[1]*New Braunfels Independent School District;* [2]*Manor Independent School District*

Box 10.1

Chapter 10 Scenario

Rosalie and Hank have worked hard to create an animal-assisted school counseling (AASC) program at their school that is positive, impactful, welcoming, and safe for students, staff, and families. The students have received Hank's presence at school positively, and he has been invited to student presentations, classroom parties, and sporting events. Hank is also recognized by caregivers and stakeholders in the community. Hank has been included in school performances and has been an active member of many restorative circles with students experiencing conflict with one another. Rosalie and Hank greet students upon their arrival to school and wish students a great day at dismissal, with Hank giving tail wags to students leaving and trying to get any last belly rubs for the day. Hank has also been included in classroom incentives. Classrooms can earn a "Hank Visit" which may include recess, special prizes "from Hank," or lunch time with Hank. Hank has hosted schoolwide reading events. Students who have displayed kindness and support to one another can earn a "Hank's Hero" award, which is highly coveted by students. Hank hosts "Pen Paws," a program that allows students to write to Hank about their feelings, thoughts, or any questions they have. Hank responds to every letter with a "paw-written" note. This is a very popular intervention, and students eagerly await a response. In fact, this program has become so popular that students have written multiple times. Hank's presence and love for all have helped to build a supportive campus community.

Another major component of Rosalie and Hank's work is the AASC interventions facilitated at the individual and group levels. While Rosalie and Hank have been able to impact the entire school community through schoolwide services, many individual and group interventions have been established to support students based on teacher, staff, and caregiver referrals. These interventions have been a wonderful addition to the services that are offered to students and have helped students work through their social and emotional challenges. Rosalie and Hank have received a multitude of requests to support students of various ages, cultures, and situations. The vast array of student needs has prompted the development of a variety of AASC interventions that fit different situations to provide the most impactful support to students.

To have a robust AASC program, working with individuals and groups is essential. This chapter discusses the impact of AASC on individuals and groups in a school setting and how the ability to create and implement AASC interventions enhances individual and group work. According to the American School Counselor Association (ASCA, 2012) National Model, school counselors develop

DOI: 10.4324/9781003392415-10

Figure 10.1 Connections with Hank include students writing to him as a "Pen Paw" and Hank writing back to them.

their program through four components: define, manage, assess, and deliver. For AASC teams this involves defining professional and student standards, managing program planning and focus, assessing the program, and delivering direct and indirect student services. AASC interventions, which are a part of the delivery component, are a large part of how counselors engage with students to increase positive behaviors and decrease negative behaviors. In the school setting, school counselors strive for students to increase success in school and, depending on the nature of the presenting problem, improve positive peer relationships, coping skills, and/or situations outside of the classroom or at home (Figure 10.1).

Through the delivery component of the ASCA model, AASC teams can provide interventions to any student whose immediate personal concerns or problems put the student's continued educational, career, personal, or social development at risk. This can include preventive, remedial, or crisis situations. Responsive services are implemented through individual or small-group counseling, as well as through crisis response. This aligns perfectly with the support an AASC program can provide. Individual and group counseling interventions that involve an animal partner allow for creativity, new experiences, and unbiased support from the animal. Confiding in pets to "discuss" difficult life situations can greatly relieve stress (Walsh, 2009). The animal offers nurturance through a presentation of unconditional acceptance and interaction (Chandler, 2017). AASC interventions provide support for students in ways school counselors cannot always reach through traditional counseling methods.

Literature Review

Interventions for both individuals and small groups are an imperative and critical part of the school counselor role. The American School Counselor Association (ASCA) has guidelines for all counselors to follow to ensure all students receive what they need to be successful not only academically, but personally and socially. ASCA (2021) promotes a three-tier model called the Multi-Tiered System of Supports (MTSS). Figure 10.2 displays the MTSS framework with a focus on the interventions covered in this chapter.

Tier 1 interventions on the MTSS model focus on classroom-based lessons and programs in which the entire school body is involved. An example of an AASC Tier 1 intervention is the "Hank's Hero" award that Rosalie created in the initial scenario. This is a schoolwide recognition program that is something each student works to obtain. Tier 2 interventions target students with more specific needs. These services are delivered to children through small groups and individual counseling. Tier 2

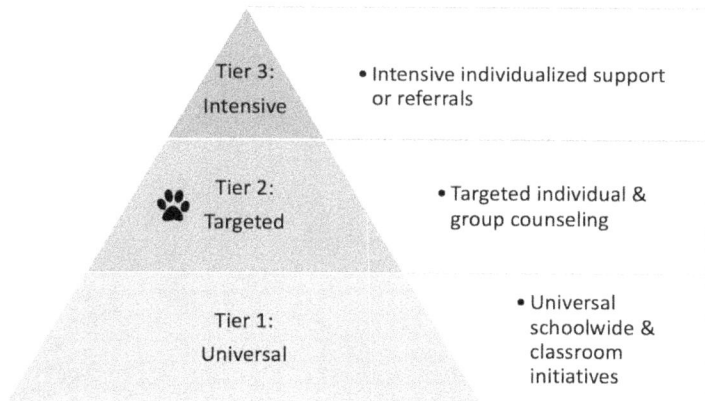

Figure 10.2 MTSS framework.

interventions are focused on students who need more support than Tier 1 alone. Small group and individual work done in Tier 2 has shown a success rate of 67% positive impact on students (Crone et al., 2010). Involving an animal partner in a Tier 2 intervention could be done in multiple ways, such as having the animal participate in lunch bunch groups, check in and check out meetings with students (Maynard et al., 2014), or small groups focusing on a variety of topics such as grief, anxiety, friendship skills, and bully prevention. In this chapter, school counselors will learn different ways to implement and execute Tier 2 interventions. Tier 3 interventions involve indirect student support, such as consultation, collaboration with other professionals, and referrals to outside agencies. According to Putz (2014), involving an animal partner has been shown to have numerous benefits including "facilitating trust, connection, communication, and relieve anxiety" (p. 9). The presence of the animal can facilitate a trust-based relationship between the client and counselor while also creating a fun and playful atmosphere (Chandler, 2017). Because of this, it is understandable that a common benefit of using AASC interventions in schools is that animals create an environment where children feel safe and accepted and goals can be reached.

Over the past several decades animal partners in schools have grown in popularity. The benefits are numerous, and counselors are seeing positive results through their work. An animal partner has a unique way of creating belonging for students, staff, and the school community. In an AASC program, the animal partner is accessible to all students and brings a sense of connection and unity to the school community. Research over the past 30 years indicates that canine partners offer physiological, emotional, social, and physical support for children (Friesen, 2010). In addition, dogs provide a nonjudgmental presence and level of comfort that humans cannot. Students may believe that if the dog trusts the counselor, then the students can trust them, too (Reichert, 1998). Researchers have found that in schools, canine partners lead to less negative comments between students, increased use of praise, decreased distractibility, improved relationships, increased eye contact, more appropriate voice tone with others, decreased tantrums, and decreased learned helplessness (Martin & Farnum, 2002).

Multiple studies show the benefits of AASC, particularly in the school setting. Granger et al. (1998) found that in schools AASC has led to less negative comments between students, decreased distractibility, and improved relationships. Hergovich et al. (2002) identified that AASC increased autonomy in problem solving and empathy. Many people associate AASC with reading programs. Although very beneficial, animal partners can provide a multitude of interventions that are focused on social-emotional goals. According to Bueche (2003, p. 46), "the results are quite extraordinary, the

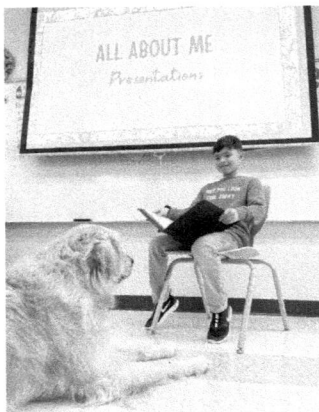

Figure 10.3 Hank provides support to student during oral presentation.

student who has social fears and is terrified to read out loud forgets about what they can't do. Dogs are magical catalysts" (Figure 10.3).

In addition to individual interventions, the AASC team can be effective in group settings. An integral part of the school counselor's role is to provide groups for students that target specific needs. Zents et al. (2017) found that canine partners have the capacity to reach all individuals regardless of their functioning level, which makes them especially appealing for working in schools. This same concept can be applied to group work. Despite what each group member brings to the group, all can benefit from the AASC interventions used in the group format. For example, Schuck et al. (2015) revealed that children diagnosed with attention deficit hyperactivity disorder (ADHD) who were involved in a cognitive-behavior therapy group with a canine partner demonstrated lower severity of ADHD symptoms than children in the group without a dog. Similar to the individual interventions mentioned above, a school counselor can apply AASC techniques in group settings, such as asking the group members what they think the animal partner is thinking or feeling, taking time to connect with the animal partner at the beginning and end of group, and noticing significant human-animal moments or responses during group.

While the benefits are many, attention must be paid to ensuring a safe environment for the counselor, animal partner, students, and staff. Proper education for students on how to greet the animal partner and how to touch the animal is imperative. School counselors also commit to grooming their animals, ensuring all vaccinations are current, and receiving consent from caregivers before facilitating Tier 2 interventions. At the beginning of each school year, a school counselor within an AASC program is diligent in ensuring the school nurse has notified them of any allergies, has sent correspondence home to all caregivers to notify them of the AASC program, and has provided all health records to the school administration team. The school counselor informs staff weekly as to when the animal will be at school for that week and has created a request form for classrooms to request visits. The animal partner is always under the supervision of the school counselor and is always on a leash (for canine partners) when at school in open areas, such as classrooms or hallways.

This section explored various studies focused on Tier 2 AASC services. Overall benefits of individual and group services in an AASC program include the many ways to partner with the animal to meet the vast array of needs that students bring. The natural way in which students can bond and connect with animal partners enhances this work making it impactful and meaningful. The rapport built between the client and the animal may increase client motivation to attend therapy and allow clients to experience genuine acceptance by a living being (Chandler, 2017). Chandler (2017) suggests, "children seem to perceive therapy dogs as a neutral or nonjudgmental participant in the therapeutic or classroom environment, and thus the therapy dogs serve in a supporting role for social, emotional, and academic achievements by the children" (p. 336). The impact of AASC and the variety of ways in which an animal can serve are numerous, as are the opportunities to be creative in partnering with your animal. It is important to remember that school counselors are "partnering" with their animals and that in all interventions they are mindful of their animal's needs as much as the students. There is such an opportunity for growth and reaching students in a different way that makes this work extremely fulfilling and joyful.

Linkage to ASCA Standards

ASCA (2019) supports school counselors' efforts to help students focus on academic, career, and social/ emotional development so they can achieve success in school and are prepared to lead fulfilling lives as responsible members of society. The school counselor's role is to enhance students' social and emotional development along with their academic success. ASCA has compiled professional standards and competencies which outline the mindset and behaviors school counselors need to meet the rigorous demands of the school counseling profession and the needs of Pre-K through 12 students (ASCA, 2019). These standards and competencies are outlined to be a tool for school counselors, school administrators, and school counselor education programs. They can be used to self-assess, align with professional development goals, set professional appraisals, and guide services for ensuring that students graduate with the appropriate skills and knowledge. There are several specific standards described in this section that are integral to the development and implementation of Tier 2 services for an AASC program.

ASCA Professional Standards and Competencies

ASCA Professional Standard B-SS 1 states that school counselors "design and implement instruction aligned to ASCA Student Standards: Mindsets & Behaviors for Student Success in large-group, classroom, small-group and individual settings" and standard B-SS 2 asserts that school counselors "provide appraisal and advisement in large-group, classroom, small-group and individual settings" (ASCA, 2019, p. 2). These standards are aligned directly to the implementation of Tier 2 services. School counselors can use the AASC Lesson Plan to create and implement lessons that promote student success, appraisal, and advisement with the support of an animal partner.

ASCA Professional Standard B-SS 3 compels school counselors to "provide short-term counseling in small-group and individual settings" (ASCA, 2019, p. 2). This standard encourages school counselors to offer targeted individual counseling and small-group services to support student needs. AASC interventions with individual students should involve the animal in working toward specific treatment goals for the student. Counselors facilitating AASC small groups should have lessons that clearly state procedures and desired outcomes. These small groups target goals that all group members share, such as increasing social skills or gaining coping strategies to manage anger. Counselors can also pre-assess students who will be participating in the groups and conduct a post-assessment at the end of the group to evaluate the impact of the group. Conducting pre- and post-assessments is best practice, and evaluates the effectiveness of the AASC groups in schools.

ASCA Professional Standard B-PF 1d encourages counselors to "use counseling theories and techniques in individual, small-group, classroom and large-group settings to promote academic, career, and social/emotional development" (ASCA, 2019, p. 2). Chapter 8 explores how to apply counseling theories in AASC. Theories can be applied in both individual and small-group services. AASC practitioners can work with their animals and students in a variety of school settings to help students work toward specific goals.

Another standard that aligns with AASC is ASCA Professional Standard B-PA 3b. This standard asks school counselors to "write goals in a measurable format such as the SMART goal format and include baseline and target data within the goal statement" (ASCA, 2019, p. 6). AASC practitioners should develop specific goals for individual and group services. For example, if Rosalie and Hank are working with a Pre-K student on social and emotional growth, a goal might be to increase the student's ability to recognize, identify, and work through his emotions. Ideally, the AASC team will use interventions that specifically target those skills for the student and will provide him with skills that will allow him to be successful in and out of the classroom.

ASCA Ethical Standards

In terms of ethical guidelines related to individual and small-group services, school counselors are bound in Ethical Standard A.1 to "provide culturally responsive counseling to students in a brief context and support students and families/guardians in obtaining outside services if students need long-term clinical/mental health counseling" (ASCA, 2022, p. 1). School counselors can utilize goal-focused interventions to offer brief, targeted individual and group services. Since school counselors do not provide long-term counseling to students, they work closely with families to make appropriate referrals as needed. In Ethical Standard A.7, school counselors are called to "offer culturally sustaining small-group counseling services based on individual student, school and community needs; student data; a referral process; and/or other relevant data" (ASCA, 2022, p. 4). AASC practitioners should be aware of cultural beliefs about animals and use culturally responsive practices to ensure students feel safe and have a choice in participating in AASC services. Chapter 11 provides more guidance on cultural considerations in AASC.

AASC Individual and Group Interventions in Primary-Level Schools

Students in primary schools are starting their educational journey. They are beginning to learn how to be learners and listeners, how to express emotions, and how to be social with other people outside of their household. These children are adjusting to school for the first time. Many students struggle with the structure, particularly with following rules and procedures. In AASC, the school counselor and animal can teach and work on these primary skills. Animal partners support this work by expressing behaviors that show enjoyment and tolerance. Animal partners also have the opportunity to choose how they want to participate in activities. These interactions with children can teach positive social skills for children, such as how to express their feelings and how to make choices and set limits. It is important to note that using AASC in schools offers amazing support to the school and students but should not necessarily be the first form of support for students. Other interventions that can be considered for students include individual behavior charts, preferential seating, reminders to stay on task, and/or providing visual schedules. Involving an animal partner is a complimentary and supportive form of intervention provided by trained AASC professionals (Figure 10.4).

When planning individual counseling with a student, AASC practitioners should develop specific mental health goals with which the animal can be involved in supporting. Let's consider the example of Lily, a Pre-K student at Rosalie and Hank's school. Lily struggles with being able to identify and work

Figure 10.4 Hank and student participate in a painting activity.

through her emotions. There are many times when the school counselor must intervene in the classroom because Lily has an outburst and is unable to say what she is feeling and why she is frustrated or angry. The goal that Lily will be working on is to identify two coping skills for managing her anger in class. As a beginning step towards that goal, she has been working with the AASC team on identifying her emotions and how to work through them. The counselor has provided individual AASC services to Lily so that they can work together to target those skills. One example of an AASC individual intervention that they might use is called Emotions Hide and Seek, which is AASC Lesson Plan 10.1 available in Appendix B. Emotions Hide and Seek is an intervention for primary students who struggle with being able to identify their emotions. This intervention helps students identify different physiological changes that happen when they are experiencing different emotions. They can also discuss positive and negative behaviors that are associated with various emotions, such as smiling when happy or shaking when scared. One coping skill they can learn in this intervention is to use relaxed breathing with Hank. They can learn how to breathe calmly and slowly, like Hank does when he is relaxed, when they begin to get angry and feel signs in their body that they are becoming dysregulated. The goal is for Lily to learn that emotions are okay and that she can use the tools she's learned in counseling, such as relaxed breathing, when she feels angry to express that emotion in a safe way (Figure 10.5).

Another common goal in counseling for primary-level students is identifying feelings. Children experience a lot of different feelings at school, such as sadness for being away from caregivers, anger at another student for taking something from them, or happiness for getting a good grade on an assignment. Young children are learning how to identify and express their feelings in the school setting. Let's explore another illustrative example with Amaya, who is a kindergarten student at Rosalie and Hank's school. This is Amaya's first time in school and the first time being away from home. According to Amaya's teacher, she spends most of her day sad or crying; in the cafeteria or any place where her teacher is not with her, she has an even harder time. Amaya's teacher worries that her being so sad is also causing her to have accidents and she is unable and unwilling to participate in the academic activities that are being presented to her in class. Rosalie, Hank, and Amaya have been working together to come up with different strategies to help Amaya work through her emotions and have social and academic success. One of the interventions that Rosalie and Hank worked on with Amaya is *"Hank's Feelings Chart,"* which Rosalie created. Multiple pictures of Hank with different facial expressions and in a variety of environments on a large poster board, allow students to connect with Hank and realize that all people have feelings. The feelings are not labeled, allowing students to use

Figure 10.5 A student partners with Hank to self-regulate.

Figure 10.6 A student is able to identify feelings with Hank using "Hank's Feelings Chart".

their own experiences and interpretations and to select what feelings they are having that match Hank's feelings. Having feelings similar to Hank's provides safety and validation. This intervention can be found in Appendix B as AASC Lesson Plan 10.2 – The Many Feelings of Hank (Figure 10.6).

AASC provides school counselors with the tools to incorporate small-group interventions. AASC practitioners incorporate group curricula based on the needs of the school. AASC Lesson Plan 10.3

available in Appendix B presents an example of a small-group curriculum for primary students called Paws and Pals. This group teaches positive social skills to children with the help of the animal partner.

AASC Individual and Group Interventions in Secondary-Level Schools

Today's adolescents and teens face a variety of challenges in school including academic and social pressures. Prolonged exposure to stress can have adverse effects on a child's behavior, ability to learn, and overall health that can span the course of their life (Meints et al., 2022). As a rising number of young people report symptoms of stress, anxiety, and depression, the need for effective interventions in school settings continues to increase. This can be tricky because many adolescents and teens may find it awkward to discuss their feelings or share personal experiences with a counselor. In their article, Zents et al. (2017) shared a scenario where a student was initially reluctant to speak to their school psychologist but was provided an opportunity to care for the psychologist's canine partner each day. As his relationship with the dog developed, he became more comfortable with the school psychologist and gradually began to open up. Animals offer an unbiased and affirming perspective that can be important to many secondary students.

Various studies have shown the positive impact on students from having an animal present at school. In their article on the effect of animal partners on children with severe emotional disorders, Anderson and Olson (2006) found that having an animal present in the classroom contributed to a decrease in episodes of emotional crisis, improved attitudes towards school, and student capacity to learn lessons related to responsibility, respect, and empathy. AASC has also been shown to be effective in decreasing the symptoms of stress and anxiety in students in the school setting. Meints et al. (2022) found that dog-assisted interventions significantly reduced stress in students with and without special education needs. These studies support AASC as a beneficial approach in schools.

Individual counseling in schools offers the maximum amount of confidentiality and allows the counselor and animal partner to provide one-on-one attention to a student who may be struggling. Students in individual counseling may benefit from interventions that are tailored specifically to their needs. An animal partner can enhance the therapeutic environment, bring a relaxing presence to sessions, and add some fun and variety to therapeutic interventions. AASC Lesson Plan 10.4 in Appendix B provides a fun and engaging individual counseling activity that focuses on student strengths. In this activity, the student identifies challenges that the animal partner may experience and challenges they experience. Then the student uses problem-solving skills to help the animal go through a hula hoop of challenges. The student processes with the counselor what strengths and skills they use to cope with challenges and how they helped the animal partner go through the hoop. This intervention can be used with students working on self-esteem, self-concept, and problem-solving goals (Figure 10.7).

Small-group counseling is time effective because a school counselor can connect with multiple students during a session versus just one. It also provides a space for students to connect with peers who may be facing similar circumstances to themselves. Small groups also alleviate some of the intimidation and awkwardness that a student may initially feel when working one-on-one with a counselor. There are many ways that an AASC team may work with groups. This can be explored through another illustrative example:

At the beginning of the semester, Rosalie sent out a needs assessment to students in grades 9 through 12 to get an idea of which topics might be most beneficial for counseling small groups. Amira, Michelle, and Khloe, all high school sophomores, indicated that they would benefit from support with test anxiety. After meeting with each girl individually to determine their interest and discuss the format of

Figure 10.7 A student works with Cleo to complete the hula challenge.

Figure 10.8 Gracie, the therapy rabbit, helps a student regulate through touch.

the group, Rosalie obtains caregiver consent for participation and begins meeting with her "Girl Power" small group once a week for eight weeks with a targeted goal of decreasing feelings of anxiety in the classroom setting. Lesson Plan 10.5 (Appendix B) presents the Mindful Moment intervention that Rosalie and Hank use with their students in a small-group setting to reduce feelings of stress and anxiety and teach effective coping strategies to use when testing. The following activity has been formatted for use with a rabbit but could be adapted to use with a variety of animal partners (Figure 10.8).

This section provided examples of Tier 2 services that can be implemented with an animal partner. AASC interventions involve the animal in helping children work toward specific goals at both primary and secondary school levels. These services should be part of a comprehensive school counseling program that is designed to meet the needs of students in your school.

Trauma-Informed and Diversity Considerations

As animal enthusiasts, eager school counselors may assume that all members of their school community are just as willing and ready as themselves to welcome an animal partner into the school community.

However, when considering how to incorporate AASC into work with individuals and small groups, it is important to consider the needs of the school population with whom the AASC team will be working. The school counselor should consider things such as cultural sensitivities, beliefs and values about different animal partners, and possible health concerns, such as allergies. Grové et al. (2021) recommended that counselors observe student's body language when the animal is present or send out a survey to staff members asking for feedback about having an animal partner on campus.

Prior to beginning small group or individual counseling with an animal partner, the school counselor should talk with each student about their prior knowledge of and experience with animals. Some children may have had a negative experience with animals, such as being bitten or snapped at by a dog or having a pet guinea pig die unexpectedly. Providing AASC services without prior knowledge of students' experiences could have adverse effects. In their study, Zents et al. (2017) point out the importance of taking faculty perceptions about animals on campus into account. Participants in their study reported that some staff members were afraid of dogs while others enjoyed seeing the dog on campus and saw the dog as very effective in helping students. AASC teams may opt to introduce their animal partner and address any questions during a faculty meeting prior to the start of the school year. Additionally, caregivers may have concerns regarding allergies or cleanliness in regard to having an animal on campus. Psychoeducation and an opportunity for stakeholders to ask questions and voice concerns are key when implementing AASC on campus. Figure 10.9 is an example of a letter that can be sent out to all caregivers at the beginning of the school year and included in registration packets for any students who transfer in mid-year. This letter demonstrates how to introduce an animal partner, shares information about the AASC team's training, and describes the procedures and safeguards that have been put in place for the AASC team.

In addition to providing information to the families of each student, an AASC practitioner should ensure that every caregiver is given the opportunity to opt out of their child participating in activities

---

Campus Therapy Dog Information

Dear Parents and Guardians:

Our school is very excited to welcome Hank, our campus therapy dog. Miss Rosalie, School Counselor, and her canine partner, Hank, have completed 120 hours of training through the Texas State University Animal Assisted Counseling Academy. As a prerequisite to the training, Hank received his Canine Good Citizen Certificate through the American Kennel Club, which is combined with his certification from the AACA. Miss Rosalie and Hank's combined training included a rigorous evaluation as well as completion of supervised clinical practicum with clients aged 4-13.

Safety is our number one priority and numerous safeguards have been put in place prior to students meeting Hank. Before Hank visits classrooms, all students and staff will go through a pre-teach lesson with Miss Rosalie where they will learn about canine body language, and how to appropriately greet and interact with Hank. While on campus, Hank will always be in the presence of Miss Rosalie and canine interaction skills will continue to be taught and reinforced throughout the year.

Please note that parents and guardians do have the option to submit an opt-out form which would allow your child the option of engaging in an alternate activity (e.g., reading in a neighboring classroom or the library) during Hank's visit to their classroom.

If you have any questions or concerns, please feel free to contact Miss Rosalie via email or phone M-F during school hours.

Figure 10.9 Sample letter to parents and caregivers to introduce animal partner.

with the animal partner. The school counselor can work closely with the campus administration to create a plan for any students who choose to opt out of engaging with the animal partner. If a caregiver signs the opt-out form, their child will not receive targeted services with the animal partner and will be given the option to work in a neighboring classroom or visit the school library during any animal partner classroom visits. It's important to note that the animal partner may be present in the hallway or during schoolwide events (Figure 10.10).

When working with students of diverse abilities, taking the animal's temperament, energy level, and size into consideration to find the right fit is important. The school counselor should consult with the child and other stakeholders in the student's life, such as teachers and caregivers, to ensure that the animal partner and student are set up for success. Sandt (2019) gives the example of a canine partner working with medically fragile students. In this scenario, it is suggested that the counselor meet with the student's teacher first to assess the location for potential visits, discuss logistics, such as mobility of students, and identify medically fragile equipment, such as catheters or feeding tubes. They can also determine outcome goals and how the animal partner can support student goals with each student. AASC animal partners should be exposed to and assessed around assistive equipment, such as wheelchairs and head supports, prior to working with children who use these supportive resources.

When working with students of any ability, it is crucial to review human-animal interaction etiquette and teach about the "language" that the animal uses to communicate (Sandt, 2019). This teaches students how to appropriately interact with the animal and helps them avoid behaviors such as sticking fingers in the animal's mouth, pulling tails or fur, and attempting to lie on or ride on the animal. In a

---

Therapy Dog Opt Out Form

All students will have the opportunity to interact with the campus therapy dog, Hank. However, if you choose to have your child not interact with the dog, you may opt out by signing this form and returning it to the office. If your child is visiting the counselor's office on a day when Hank is present, we will make sure that Hank is not in the office while your child speaks with Miss Rosalie. In addition, if the therapy dog is requested to visit your child's classroom, your child will be given the option to read in a neighboring classroom or the library during Hank's visit. Hank may be on the front porch for morning arrival on the days that he is here, and we will do our best to make sure that the dog is not near your student in these settings.

If you do not send this form back with your signature, then it is our understanding that you are giving permission for your child to interact with the therapy dog. If you do choose to turn this form in, please return it to the front office within 2 school days.

Therapy Dog Opt Out

By signing this form, I am stating that I do NOT give my consent for my child to interact with the therapy dog and that it is my wish that my child be given the opportunity to engage in an alternate activity during the therapy dog's visit to my child's classroom.

_____   _____
Child's Name   Child's Home Room Teacher

_____   _____
Parent/Guardian Signature   Date

Figure 10.10 Therapy dog opt-out form.

setting where students may be differently abled, collaborating with the teacher or caregiver to deliver this information is ideal. The counselor can share their knowledge of the animal partner and their needs while the teacher will know how to best deliver the information to students.

Bringing It All Together

AASC teams can support their school communities in a wide variety of ways including responsive services provided through individual and small-group counseling sessions. One-on-one sessions with an AASC team could work well for students who would benefit from individual attention, do not feel comfortable disclosing information in front of peers, or have very specific needs. In these instances, an animal partner could alleviate any initial awkwardness and add a fun element to therapeutic interventions when working toward the students' goals. AASC in a small-group setting might work best for students who are working towards a common goal. Bringing an animal partner into a group setting helps students make connections to the animal and to each other and can also make group activities more engaging.

When working with individuals or groups in schools, it is important to advocate for the needs of the animal partner and to educate students, staff, and campus stakeholders on animal communication and welfare. Additionally, counselors should take into consideration any cultural sensitivities, differing perceptions of dogs, or possible health concerns such as allergies that students, staff members, or caregivers may have. Psychoeducation and an opportunity for members of the school community to learn about the animal, ask questions, and voice any concerns can help ensure that everyone feels safe and that the AASC team is set up for success.

The presence of animal partners in schools has been proven to have a myriad of positive effects on students' social and emotional wellness as well as their academic success (Putz, 2014). AAIs in schools have also been linked to improvements in behavior, attention, mood, and cognitive development in school settings (Brelsford et al., 2017). With thorough preparation, clear communication, and a passion for what they do, AASC teams have the potential to positively impact their school communities through individual and small-group AASC interventions.

References

American School Counselor Association. (2012). *ASCA national model: A framework for school counseling programs*. Author. https://www.schoolcounselor.org/About-School-Counseling/ASCA-National-Model-for-School-Counseling-Programs#:~:text=%E2%80%9CThe%20ASCA%20National%20Model%3A%20A,student%20achievement%2C%20attendance%20and%20discipline

American School Counselor Association. (2019). *ASCA school counselor professional standards & competencies*. Author. https://www.schoolcounselor.org/getmedia/a8d59c2c-51de-4ec3-a565-a3235f3b93c3/SC-Competencies.pdf

American School Counselor Association. (2021). *The school counselor and multitiered system of supports*. Author. https://www.schoolcounselor.org/Standards-Positions/Position-Statements/ASCA-Position-Statements/The-School-Counselor-and-Multitiered-System-of-Sup

American School Counselor Association. (2022). *ASCA ethical standards for school counselors*. Author. https://www.schoolcounselor.org/getmedia/44f30280-ffe8-4b41-9ad8-f15909c3d164/EthicalStandards.pdf

Anderson, K. L., & Olson, M. R. (2006). The value of a dog in a classroom of children with severe emotional disorders. *Anthrozoös, 19*(1), 35–49. 10.2752/089279306785593919

Brelsford, V. L., Meints, K., Gee, N. R., & Pfeffer, K. (2017). Animal-assisted interventions in the classroom—A systematic review. *International Journal of Environmental Research and Public Health, 14*(7), 669. 10.3390/ijerph14070669

Bueche, S. (2003, February 1). Going to the dogs: Therapy dogs promote reading. *Reading Today, 20*(4), 46.

Chandler, C. K. (2017). *Animal assisted therapy in counseling* (3rd ed.). Routledge. 10.4324/9781315673042

Crone, D. A., Hawken, L. S., & Horner, R. H. (2010). *Responding to problem behavior in schools: The Behavior Education Program* (2nd ed.). Guilford Press.

Friesen, L. (2010). Exploring animal-assisted programs with children in school and therapeutic contexts. *Early Childhood Education Journal, 37*(4), 261–267. 10.1007/s10643-009-0349-5

Granger, B. P., Kogan, L., Fitchett, J., & Helmer, K. (1998). A human-animal intervention team approach to animal-assisted therapy. *Anthrozoös, 11*(3), 172–176. 10.2752/089279398787000689

Grové, C., Henderson, L., Lee, F., & Wardlaw, P. (2021). Therapy dogs in educational settings: Guidelines and recommendations for implementation. *Frontiers in Veterinary Science, 8.* https://www.frontiersin.org/articles/10.3389/fvets.2021.655104/full

Hergovich, A., Monshi, B., Semmler, G., & Zieglmayer, V. (2002). The effects of the presence of a dog in the classroom. *Anthrozoös, 15*(1), 37–50. 10.2752/089279302786992775

Martin, F., & Farnum, J. (2002). Animal-assisted therapy for children with pervasive developmental disorders. *Western Journal of Nursing Research, 24*(6), 657–670. 10.1177/019394502320555403

Maynard, B. R., Kjellstrand, E. K., & Thompson, A. (2014). Effects of check and connect on attendance, behavior, and academics: A randomized effectiveness trial. *Research on Social Work Practice, 24*(3), 296–309. 10.1177/1049731513497804

Meints, K., Brelsford, V. L., Dimolareva, M., Maréchal, L., Pennington, K., Rowan, E., & Gee, N. R. (2022). Can dogs reduce stress levels in school children? Effects of dog-assisted interventions on salivary cortisol in children with and without special educational needs using randomized controlled trials. *PLoS ONE, 17*(6), 1–26. 10.1371/journal.pone.0269333

Putz, J. N. (2014). *Animal-assisted therapy and its effects on children in schools.* St. Catherine University repository website. https://ir.stthomas.edu/ssw_mstrp/376/

Reichert, E. (1998). Individual counseling for sexually abused children: A role for animals and storytelling. *Child and Adolescent Social Work Journal, 15*(3), 177–185.

Sandt, D. D. (2019). Effective implementation of animal assisted education interventions in the inclusive early childhood education classroom. *Early Childhood Education Journal, 48*(1), 103–115. 10.1007/s10643-019-01000-z

Schuck, S. E. B., Emmerson, N. A., Fine, A. H., & Lakes, K. D. (2015). Canine-assisted therapy for children with ADHD: Preliminary findings from the Positive Assertive Cooperative Kids study. *Journal of Attention Disorders, 19*(2), 125–137. 10.1177/1087054713502080

Walsh, F. (2009). Human-animal bonds II: The role of pets in family systems and family therapy. *Family Process, 48*(4), 481–499.

Zents, C. E., Fisk, A. K., & Lauback, C. W. (2017). Paws for intervention: Perceptions about the use of dogs in schools. *Journal of Creativity in Mental Health, 12*(1), 82–98. 10.1080/15401383.2016.1189371

Chapter 11

Student-Affirming AASC

Jennifer H. Greene-Rooks[1] and Wanda Montemayor[2]
[1]*Texas State University;* [2]*Community Arts LLC*

Box 11.1

Chapter 11 Scenario

Rosalie partners with Hank to support all students by using gender-affirming AASC interventions. Saige, a student at Rosalie's school, identifies as nonbinary and uses they/them pronouns. Saige is an intelligent, creative, and high-achieving student who has struggled with how to advocate for themself with peers and adults who misgender them by referring to them as "she" or "her." With permission from Saige's parents, Rosalie and Hank facilitate the Gender Unicorn activity (Trans Student Educational Resources, 2015). Rosalie shares how sometimes Hank expresses that he is stressed, and other children don't understand what he is communicating. She describes how she advocates for Hank by removing him from stressful interactions and taking him to her office where he can take a break. With the Gender Unicorn activity, Saige explores their gender identity and expression. They share how sometimes they feel misunderstood like Hank and need a break from stressful encounters with peers. Rosalie and Saige discuss how Saige can advocate for themself in times of stress by talking with a caring teacher or taking a break to the counseling office. Through this AASC intervention, Rosalie and Hank provide a safe environment in which Saige can take steps to manage stress and promote positive mental health.

Understanding and incorporating gender-affirming competencies on campus are important because marginalized groups, such as the LGBTQIA+ community, experience a much higher rate of violence and have greater mental health needs (Kosciw et al., 2022). The term LGBTQIA+ refers to Lesbian, Gay, Bisexual, Transgender, Queer/Questioning, Intersex, Asexual, and all sexual and gender minority people. Another term used as an umbrella term is the queer community. By integrating a trained animal partner into a school setting, school counselors can create a more affirming environment for all students including students in the queer community. LGBTQIA+ students who attend schools with more LGBTQIA+ resources and support feel safer, have higher attendance, and higher GPAs (Kosciw et al., 2022). Utilizing AASC focused on safety and belonging for LGBTQIA+ students can be part of making schools safer for these students. Some of the goals of using AASC with queer youth are to create a safe space that affirms all identities, promote the use of pronouns, create and respect boundaries including healthy consent, help youth feel more grounded, reduce anxiety, and reduce dysphoria.

It is critically important to design interventions that promote acceptance and celebration of sexual and gender diversity and support young adult development from an affirming lens. Counselors and

DOI: 10.4324/9781003392415-11

mental health professionals should come prepared with specific knowledge of the psychological needs of the LGBTQIA+ community. This chapter delves into literature on the queer community, school counseling standards, creating a safe and equitable environment at primary and secondary schools, and AASC interventions that are gender-affirming for students and staff. By creating more counseling services that are gender-affirming, the well-being of the students is improved because gender expression becomes more normalized.

Literature Review

LGBTQIA+ students continue to face hostile school climates in the areas of school safety, anti-LGBTQIA+ harassment, assault, and discriminatory policies (Kosciw et al., 2022). Almost 82% of LGBTQIA+ students reported feeling unsafe at school due to personal characteristics, with 68% of these students feeling unsafe specifically due to sexual orientation, gender expression, or gender identity. Queer students also experienced verbal and physical harassment, as well as physical and sexual assault at school. It is not surprising that as incidents of victimization increased, feelings of school belonging for LGBTQIA+ students decreased. A hostile school environment adversely impacts students' academic achievement and mental health (Kosciw et al., 2022).

Some of the policies and practices that help LGBTQIA+ students feel safer and more connected at school are not universally available at schools (Kosciw et al., 2022). These affirming policies and practices include having Gay Straight Alliances/Gender and Sexuality Alliances (GSAs), access to inclusive curricular resources, the presence of supportive educators, and LGBTQIA+ inclusive and supportive school policies. Even having safe space designators, such as posters or stickers, increased the likelihood that faculty and staff would intervene on behalf of LGBTQIA+ students.

For transgender and gender non-conforming (TGNC) students specifically, hostile school climates have denied acknowledgment or use of their pronouns, not utilized their preferred name, denied appropriate restroom and locker room facilities, and prevented participation in sports that align with their gender. Sports participation for LGBTQIA+ students increases school belonging and mental health, yet many aren't able to or don't feel safe participating (Clark & Kosciw, 2022). AASC allows school counselors to create safe spaces for students to be accepted by a caring and unbiased animal partner (Figure 11.1).

Linkage to ASCA Standards

The American School Counseling Association (ASCA, 2022c) identifies in their position statement that school counselors are compelled to "safeguard the well-being of transgender and nonbinary youth" and "recognize all students have the right to be treated equally and fairly, with dignity and respect as unique individuals, free from discrimination, harassment and bullying based on their gender identity and gender expression" (para. 1). ASCA provides specific guidance for school counselors to respect and use chosen names as well as pronouns that align with students' gender identity, use chosen names on student records as appropriate (i.e., caregivers are aware of the name change) even without a legal name change, ensure access to gender-appropriate bathrooms and locker rooms, and ensure access to sports and other extracurricular activities, among other things (ASCA, 2022c). Another ASCA position statement (2022b) asserts that school counselors should "promote equal opportunity and respect for students regardless of sexual orientation, gender identity or gender expression" and "recognize the school experience can be significantly more difficult for students with marginalized identities. School counselors work to eliminate barriers impeding LGBTQIA+ student development and achievement" (para. 1). This includes providing nonjudgmental and accepting

Figure 11.1 Canine partner, Luna, helps students reach counseling goals one belly rub at a time.

counseling services, advocating for them as needed, understanding intersecting identities, practicing cultural competence, providing safe spaces, advocating for inclusive curriculums and school policies, addressing absenteeism, identifying resources, and providing training, among other things (ASCA, 2022b). AASC teams can promote equal opportunity and respect for all students by creating an affirming counseling office, following ASCA guidance, and advocating for marginalized students through inclusive AASC services.

The ASCA Professional Standards and Competencies and Ethical Standards outline mindsets and behaviors that school counselors need to uphold the demands of the school counseling profession for Pre-K through 12 students. Professional Standard B-PF 6 encourages school counselors to "demonstrate understanding of the impact of cultural, social and environmental influences on student success and opportunities" (ASCA, 2019, p. 2). ASCA's Ethical Standards (2022a) do not specifically use the terms LGBTQIA+ or TGNC but there is specific mention of school counselors' responsibilities to marginalized populations including advocacy for access and inclusion for all students regardless of "gender identity, gender expression, [or] sexual orientation" (p. 5). Throughout ASCA's Ethical Standards, school counselors are compelled to ensure equitable access for students, which includes LGBTQIA+ students. Furthermore, ASCA includes sexual orientation and gender identity in the areas of diversity that school counselors need to understand and affirm. The promotion of using AASC with LGBTQIA+ youth to address and mitigate negative influences on this population is a relevant way to address these standards and competencies.

Using AASC to Support LGBTQIA+ Students in Schools

School counselors can utilize AASC to support LGBTQIA+ students in primary and secondary schools by thoughtfully including AASC as a part of their comprehensive school counseling program. AASC can be implemented at each level of intervention (i.e., Tier 1, 2, or 3 services). One way to utilize AASC to support queer students is by identifying their and their animal partner's pronouns when leading individual, group, or classroom lessons to create a safe space where having self-identified pronouns is part of the climate. Including pronouns as an integrated part of groups and other interactions lets students know that it's safe to share their pronouns, which creates dialog and inclusiveness in the classroom (Figure 11.2).

In a qualitative study on the protective role of animals for transgender youth, Wenocur et al. (2022) identified two primary themes. The first theme emphasized the importance of animal partners in providing emotional and social support to youth. Four subthemes emerged that highlight how animals facilitate support: being a calming presence, offering safe physical touch, promoting healthy behaviors, and providing affirmation. Students may feel more able to cry and express themselves when an animal partner is present in counseling (Wenocur et al., 2022). LGBTQIA+ youth may be able to have more open and difficult conversations in the presence of a therapy animal than they would otherwise engage in. Safe physical touch, especially petting or cuddling with a canine partner or critter counselor, is reported to reduce anxiety and provide positive mental health implications for clients. For LGBTQIA+ youth with dysphoria regarding their gender or other aspects of identity, "having that unconditional dog or cat sitting there is kind of soothing," which may mitigate those dysphoric feelings (Wenocur et al., 2022, p. 20).

Another theme that emerged from Wenocur and colleagues' (2022) study was desired social support. The subthemes that emerged within this theme included the importance of peer acceptance and support, the need for such supports to be trans-competent, and the value of supports that enhance self-advocacy skills. Participants reflected that, as youth, they would have appreciated the support of other TGNC youth that was not readily available in their communities or online. Clinician participants also spoke to the importance of TGNC youth having peer support that can be found through group counseling in a way that individual counseling does not provide. Additionally, clinicians shared the acceptance that animal-assisted counseling can provide for TGNC youth. When providing support for TGNC youth, it is important that the support be trans-competent, meaning that facilitators are knowledgeable about transgender issues and advocate for TGNC youth. School counselors need to ensure that they

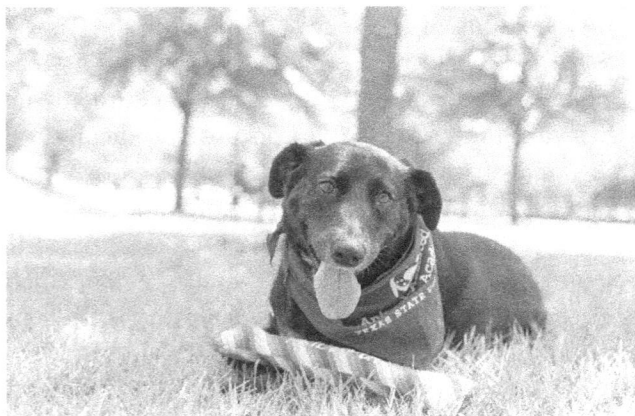

Figure 11.2 Sadie plays with her "Pride Pup" toy.

themselves, teachers, and fellow students are able to provide trans-affirming support. AASC can be utilized to support that learning. In addition, AASC can help TGNC students learn self-advocacy, such as in the example with Saige and as suggested by Wenocur and colleagues (2022) research.

Student-Affirming AASC in Primary-Level Schools

Students in primary-level or elementary schools are going through huge developmental changes physically, mentally, socially, and emotionally (Lally & Valentine-French, 2019). According to Erikson, they are addressing the task of industry versus inferiority by developing self-efficacy. School counselors can support LGBTQIA+ students by helping them to feel safe and find ways they feel capable to develop healthy self-efficacy. During late elementary school, many students are approaching or entering puberty and experiencing the hormonal and developmental shifts that entails. Elementary school is a time when students are developing their self-concept as learners and people and develop skills such as decision-making, problem solving, communication, and other life skills (ASCA, 2019). School counselors in elementary schools are tasked with meeting the academic, social, and emotional needs of children in middle to late childhood.

School counselors are a critical part of primary schools and their work can be supported and broadened by the inclusion of AASC. Schools, as a microcosm of society, are diverse learning environments. Elementary school counselors meet the diverse needs of all students through creating and implementing a comprehensive school counseling program that is geared toward diverse students. Including a trained animal partner may help with meeting the needs of all diverse students. School counselors can use AASC with their trained animal partners in whole school initiatives, classroom lessons, small groups, as well as individual work. There are two lesson plans provided to support queer students in primary-level schools. Lesson Plan 11.1 in Appendix B presents the "Our Families" intervention. In this activity, the school counselor and students read a book about families and discuss what makes family members different and special, including pets. Students then draw a picture or create a collage of their family and share about their family with the group. The AASC practitioner shares about the animal partner's family. In Lesson Plan 11.2 (Appendix B), "Affirming Each Other," the practitioner uses different books to show how children express themselves in different ways, such as the clothes they choose to wear. The school counselor can bring different bandanas or capes for the animal partner to try on and discuss with the group (Figure 11.3).

Figure 11.3 Sullivan shows off her star cape.

LGBTQIA+ students and families are an integral part of elementary school communities so it is critical that school counselors implement AASC in a way that supports them. Affirming LGBTQIA+ students and families includes: inclusive language in materials, inclusive curricular resources such as queer characters and families in lessons and books, small groups modeling affirming practices, individual counseling focused on the needs of queer students, and responsive crisis intervention. Including an animal partner through AASC allows for many opportunities to encourage all students. Some considerations in using AASC in elementary schools with the queer community include the following:

1   Know state and local laws that may support or deny support for LGBTQIA+ youth since these are changing rapidly. This can also be an area of advocacy for school counselors.
2   Know professional guidance for working with queer students, such as the ASCA Ethical Standards and Position Statements. When this conflicts with local and state laws, consultation or legal support may be necessary.
3   Learn school district policies on providing support services for the queer students. When districts do not have supportive policies or the policies are harmful, this is another way school counselors can get involved in advocacy.
4   Ensure that you have caregiver permission to meet with students in small groups or individually on an ongoing basis.

School counselors may be limited in the scope of services they can provide for queer youth in a school setting. AASC practitioners can offer youth and their caregivers referrals and resources to local agencies, therapists, books, and websites that may offer more targeted LGBTQIA+ support outside of school.

Student-Affirming AASC in Secondary-Level Schools

Students in middle and high school are in early to late adolescence and are experiencing many changes in their bodies, social circles, and emotions that characterize the transition between childhood and adulthood. Hormonal changes are significant and the associated developmental stages can be quite challenging for students. School counselors are trained to work with students going through these developmental changes and to develop comprehensive school counseling programs to address their needs (ASCA, 2022b; ASCA, 2022c). AASC can and should be integrated into secondary school counselors' work as a part of a comprehensive program to meet the needs of students as each level of the pyramid of intervention (i.e., whole school, classroom, small group, and individual intervention).

Considerations for Using Student-Affirming AASC in Individual Counseling

When working one-on-one with an LGBTQIA+ student, the school counselor can include their animal partner in ways that communicate congruence, empathy, and unconditional positive regard. For example, when using expressive arts techniques, the school counselor can have their animal partner use basic skills, such as reflection of content and open-ended questions, to track the student's artwork or feelings. The school counselor could use phrases such as "Hank, do you see Saige coloring that picture? What feelings do you think are in their artwork? Do you think that they are ready to talk about their feelings?" or "Hank noticed that you colored all of that black. What would you like to share with him about that?" The student can choose whether or not to share more about their art or what they're experiencing emotionally (Figure 11.4).

Figure 11.4 Chango loves to support middle school students through expressive art activities.

For queer students who are struggling with attendance, possibly due to not feeling safe at school, the school counselor's animal partner can be a part of helping students to feel safe. One way to do this is to offer a daily attendance check-in with the animal partner. The student can have a set time before school to come to the AASC office and give the animal partner some pets and treats. The animal partner can be a motivator to attend and participate in school and counseling activities (Lange et al., 2007).

AASC can be used to help students who are dysregulated. Body movement and connecting to the animal companion can soothe distress. It can be helpful for students to notice and talk about how dysregulation impacts the animal partner. Additionally, other grounding techniques such as mindfulness and journaling can be utilized while in the calming presence of the AASC animal partner.

Considerations for Using Student-Affirming AASC in Small Groups

All school counseling groups should be affirming groups, even those that have a focus other than diversity and acceptance such as: loss and grief groups, anger control groups, new student groups, friendship groups, groups for students experiencing family transitions such as divorce, groups for students with an incarcerated or deported parent, groups to support students at risk, and groups that support LGBTQIA+ students or TGNC students. In the experiences of one school counselor, their AASC animal partner was particularly helpful for a TGNC student who was experiencing homelessness. Their favorite part of the week was group therapy that included the school counselor's animal partner. With the animal partner, the TGNC student was able to experience unconditional acceptance. The school counselor and their animal partner were able to model consent for physical touch regarding the animal partner sitting on the student's lap. The student reported that having the animal partner nearby made them feel at home, a monumental grounding for a homeless individual.

It can be helpful to institute a Bill of Rights for the animal partner, and a Bill of Rights for group members. Lesson Plan 11.3 (Appendix B) presents guidelines for this activity. The Bill of Rights explores the importance of students developing a sense of self, defining ways to feel safe, and creating boundaries for themselves. This can also lead to a discussion about how to respect others' boundaries and the availability to advocate for their needs and limits. The school counselor can also use the Bill of Rights to promote the use of appropriate pronouns for group members. Group members can practice using different pronouns with the animal partner. While animal partners may respond positively to different pronouns, this may not be true for TGNC students. It's important to maintain that there is a

Figure 11.5 Marisa and her canine partner, Nimah, show their pride flag in their team photo.

distinction between animal partners and the experience of students. Animal partners would respond differently if a person treated them unkindly, such as yelling at them. Being treated with kindness and respect can look different for different species and different individuals. It's important to treat others as they want to be treated, and AASC can support the exploration of these social interactions.

Groups can be an ideal way to incorporate AASC into student-affirming services. Lesson Plan 11.4 in Appendix B provides a five-week group curriculum called True Colors. In this group, members will cover topics, such as learning how to be an ally and create awareness about bullying. This group provides activities that integrate the animal partner into each session. These sessions can be modified according to the needs of students in a particular group (Figure 11.5).

Trauma-Informed and Diversity Considerations

ASCA recognizes that school counselors must address the needs of students who have experienced trauma (ASCA, 2022d), including their LGBTQIA+ students. A trauma-informed school is a place where all students are safe, affirmed, and welcomed (ASCA, 2022d). School counselors must work as a team with other school personnel to implement trauma-informed practices at their schools. School counselors should keep in mind the following considerations when integrating an animal into a school environment.

In a study on integrating AAI with Trauma-Focused Cognitive Behavioral Therapy, researchers found that AAIs did not improve trauma symptom severity and that some participants even declined to participate (Allen et al., 2022). While limitations in that study existed, it's notable that using an exposure-based therapy with AAI may not be the best fit for school-based groups designed to reduce trauma. Another consideration is to assess if students have previously had negative animal interactions or trauma related to an animal (e.g., a dog bite, and attack by a loose dog in the neighborhood). Ascertaining if students have had a traumatic experience with an animal could inform whether and how to involve the AASC animal partner with a particular student or students. AASC informed consent procedures provide a process for assessing if students have had negative experiences with animals and if they are interested in AASC services.

Additionally, school counselors who are considering the implementation of AASC at their schools will need to take into account any cultural beliefs and practices regarding particular animals. Cultural beliefs about a particular animal could affect how students react to and accept the school counselor's animal partner. Despite these considerations, there are many benefits to utilizing AASC in schools, particularly to support LBGTQIA+ students.

Bringing It All Together

It is important that school counselors are inclusive and practice cultural humility as a critical part of their work with students. Additionally, ASCA has offered guidance on how to do that in their ethical standards (2022a) and position statements on the topics (2022b, 2022c). Identifying at-risk students in school is critical to ensuring that efforts are made to make sure all students feel safe and able to be successful in school. LGBTQIA+ students have faced hostile school environments that adversely affect their sense of safety and belonging as well as academic achievement (Kosciw et al., 2022). Integrating AASC into schools' comprehensive school counseling programs is one way to help queer students feel safe and connected by creating a welcoming and affirming school environment. AASC is a unique, progressive approach to counseling that allows students to experience the nonjudgmental presence of an animal partner through targeted AASC interventions and services that promote acceptance and equality for all students.

References

Allen, B., Shenk, C. E., Dreschel, N. E., Wang, M., Bucher, A. M., Desir, M. P., Chen, M. J., & Grabowski, S. R. (2022). Integrating animal-assisted therapy into TF-CBT for abused youth with PTSD: A randomized controlled feasibility trial. *Child Maltreatment*, *27*(3), 466–477. 10.1177/1077559520988790

American School Counselor Association. (2019). *ASCA school counselor professional standards & competencies*. Author. https://www.schoolcounselor.org/getmedia/a8d59c2c-51de-4ec3-a565-a3235f3b93c3/SC-Competencies.pdf

American School Counselor Association. (2022a). *ASCA ethical standards for school counselors*. Author. https://www.schoolcounselor.org/getmedia/44f30280-ffe8-4b41-9ad8-f15909c3d164/EthicalStandards.pdf

American School Counselor Association. (2022b). *The school counselor and LGBTQ+ youth*. Author. https://www.schoolcounselor.org/Standards-Positions/Position-Statements/ASCA-Position-Statements/The-School-Counselor-and-LGBTQ-Youth

American School Counselor Association. (2022c). *The school counselor and transgender and nonbinary youth*. Author. https://www.schoolcounselor.org/Standards-Positions/Position-Statements/ASCA-Position-Statements/The-School-Counselor-and-Transgender-Gender-noncon

American School Counselor Association. (2022d). *The school counselor and trauma-informed practice*. Author. https://www.schoolcounselor.org/Standards-Positions/Position-Statements/ASCA-Position-Statements/The-School-Counselor-and-Trauma-Informed-Practice

Clark, C. M., & Kosciw, J. G. (2022). Engaged or excluded: LGBTQ youth's participation in school sports and their relationship to psychological well-being. *Psychology in the Schools*, *59*(1), 95–114. 10.1002/pits.22500

Kosciw, J. G., Clark, C. M., & Menard, L. (2022). *The 2021 National School Climate Survey: The experiences of LGBTQ+ youth in our nation's schools*. GLSEN.

Lally, M., & Valentine-French, S. (2019). *Lifespan development: A psychological perspective* (2nd ed.). Open Education Resource. http://dept.clcillinois.edu/psy/LifespanDevelopment.pdf

Lange, A., Cox, J., Bemert, D., & Jenkins, C. (2007). Is counseling going to the dogs? An exploratory study related to the inclusion of an animal in group counseling with adolescents. *Journal of Creativity in Mental Health*, *2*(2), 17–31. 10.1300/J456v02n02_03

Trans Student Educational Resources. (2015). *The gender unicorn*. http://www.transstudent.org/gender

Wenocur, K., Matthews, M., & Kotak, N. (2022). Personal and professional perspectives on the protective role of animals for transgender youth: A qualitative analysis. *Human Animal Interaction Bulletin*, *13*(1), 14–29. 10.1079/hai.2022.0008

Chapter 12

Future Directions in AASC

Elizabeth Kjellstrand Hartwig
Texas State University

As this book comes to a close, it's important to explore takeaways from the book and consider where the AASC field goes from here. The aim of this chapter is to review highlights from the book, look at future directions in training, research, and practice, and share stories from the field. This chapter will be useful to practitioners who want to be a part of moving the field forward. It is hoped that the information presented in this chapter inspires stakeholders in the AASC field to contribute to the development of AASC.

AASC Overview

AASC is an exciting and dynamic practice in schools. This book began with an introduction to the field of AASC. Chapter 1 presented a rationale for the book and defined and noted examples of AASC terminology. An overview of each chapter and chapter sections was provided. The chapter concluded by offering guidance on how the book may best be used.

Getting approval for an AASC program is an important step in the development of a successful program. Chapter 2 provided guidance on questions to consider and address before seeking program approval. This chapter offered recommendations for addressing common questions related to training, liability, costs, and student and animal welfare. Included in Appendix A are forms that can be used to secure approval for an AASC program.

Dogs aren't the only animal partners working in school settings. Chapter 3 explored several common species that work in schools in addition to dogs, such as rabbits, guinea pigs, and cats. For each type of animal partner, an introduction to the species, beneficial qualities of that species, and welfare considerations for AASC were presented. The authors provided a description of service delivery with different species at the primary and secondary school levels. This chapter was enhanced with four lesson plans that can be found in Appendix B for working with different species in schools.

School counselors are charged with practicing within the boundaries of their professional competence. This means that practitioners need to seek out AASC training and supervision that aligns with competencies in this profession. Chapter 4 presented a description of AASC knowledge, skills, and attitudes competencies to support AASC teams in being sufficiently trained to provide services to children in schools. A list of these competencies can be found in Appendix A.

An effective AASC practitioner must possess the requisite knowledge, skills, and attitudes for working with an animal partner in schools. Chapter 5 explored the training involved in preparing AASC teams. This chapter explored the differences between volunteer and professional therapy animal training and presented steps to training including prerequisite training, AASC knowledge and skills training, skills practice in a practicum setting, and post-training supervision. Appendix A includes an

DOI: 10.4324/9781003392415-12

AASC Skills Checklist that can be used by practitioners and supervisors to assess and hone essential AASC skills.

There is a lot that goes into preparing the school for an animal partner. Chapter 6 delved into considerations for what practitioners will need to address when preparing their school to implement an AASC program. This chapter offered a wealth of resources and recommendations for communicating with students, caregivers, and staff about the AASC program, gathering necessary supplies, and ensuring animal welfare throughout this process. Practitioners will find an AASC Survey for Families to address questions about the program in Appendix A.

Data collection and assessment can be used as a tool for planning, evaluating, and advocating for the school counseling profession. Chapter 7 explored assessment practices in AASC. The author provided tools and methods for data collection that can be used for planning, evaluating, and advocating for the AASC program. This chapter identified how to create data-driven lesson plans. Appendix B includes four lesson plans from this chapter that offer examples of various assessment tools that can be used with AASC interventions.

School counselors should be proficient in applying a primary counseling theory to AASC. Chapter 8 described three theories frequently used in school settings that have a strong evidence base and are grounded in play therapy skills: cognitive-behavioral therapy, solution-focused therapy, and person-centered therapy. This chapter demonstrated the application of these theories through AASC interventions at primary and secondary schools. Appendix B includes four lesson plans that apply these different theories to play-based and expressive AASC interventions.

There is a range of services that can meet the social and emotional needs of children in schools. Chapter 9 described schoolwide and classroom-based AASC interventions. Considerations for working with animals in large groups and how to modify services to support animal welfare were shared. The authors included six lesson plans in Appendix B that describe AASC interventions for schoolwide and classroom services.

School counselors also provide more targeted services to students. Chapter 10 presented information about how to develop AASC interventions for individual and small-group services. The authors described individual lessons and group curricula that integrate an animal partner. In Appendix B, five AASC lesson plans are provided to employ interventions for small group and individual counseling services.

School counselors promote respect for all students and eliminate barriers impeding students from achieving in school. Chapter 11 described how AASC teams can support student-affirming services by emphasizing student competence and embracing diversity, equity, and inclusion. The authors presented AASC practices that celebrate culture, gender identity, sexual orientation, and disabilities. Appendix B includes four student-affirming AASC lesson plans.

This chapter focuses on identifying future directions in the field of AASC. The next sections explore future directions in training, research, and practice. This chapter will also share stories from the field from school therapy animal teams. As a wrap-up, this chapter identifies next steps for new AASC teams (Figure 12.1).

Future Directions in Training

Quality training is one of the most important elements in preparing AASC teams to be successful in schools. Chapter 5 described the differences in volunteer and professional therapy animal training and emphasized the importance of training that meets current standards, prevents liability, and promotes positive human-animal interactions. That chapter also offered a framework for training that aligns with the AASC competencies.

Figure 12.1 A child gets support from Ahsoka.

One of the biggest recommendations for future directions in training is the development of more AASC training programs. Few programs in the U.S. offer training specifically for school-based practitioners. AASC training should address topics discussed in this book and follow a similar protocol of prerequisite training, AASC knowledge and skills training, an AASC practicum for hands-on practice with their animal partner, and post-training supervision and consultation. The AASC Skills Checklist (Appendix A) can be used as a guide to develop and assess practitioner and animal partner skills. Practitioners interested in developing AASC training programs should have received extensive training and credentialing from a recognized AAI program. There should also be ample classroom and training spaces to ensure AASC teams-in-training have the room they need to practice and demonstrate skills. AASC trainers can enlist the assistance of other trainers, researchers, and supervisors in the field for consultation on training program development and implementation.

Future Directions in Research

Recent research and developments in the animal-assisted intervention (AAI) field have improved practitioners' understanding of the role of animal partners in helping children in schools reduce stress, improve academics, and increase social and emotional skills (Brelsford et al., 2017; Meints et al., 2022). This evidence base underscores the work that AASC programs do and demonstrates tangible benefits for animals in schools. As the practice of AASC continues to develop, there is a need to increase research in this field and the methodological rigor of the research conducted. McCune et al. (2014) recommended the utilization of control groups, sufficient sample sizes, consistent measures, and appropriate statistical methods to enhance the rigor of future studies. Studies using randomized controlled trials can support future meta analyses that examine how and to what extent AASC interventions can benefit students in schools. Research on how AASC influences specific treatment issues that school counselors address, such as anxiety, depression, social skills, aggression, and substance abuse, can be explored in future studies. Studies that seek to understand the perspectives and influence of AASC on diverse students, such as students of color and students in the queer community, can provide new insights into effective AASC practices. Studies on AASC interventions with varied species would inform the field of potential benefits or challenges with these animals in schools. There is a world of opportunity for research in the AASC field.

Future Directions in Practice

One aim of this text was to describe and simplify the process for developing an AASC program. As new fields of AAIs emerge, the public can sometimes be slow to fully accept an AAI practice without widespread integration of this practice, sufficient training opportunities, and a considerable evidence base. For years practitioners have partnered with animals in schools, but the practice of AASC is still developing. One way to enhance the practice of AASC is the creation of a professional association for AASC. This association could be housed within a larger organization, such as the American School Counseling Association, or be a standalone organization. This professional association can be comprised of dedicated professionals who are willing to put the time and energy into establishing a mission, board of directors, bylaws, and other resources that can further support the development of AASC programs. While this idea may seem like a big undertaking, many organizations have started with a small group of committed professionals who had similar goals and values and grew from that small group. The AASC field would be strengthened by more acceptance of this practice and a professional association.

Stories from the Field

In this section, school-based practitioners will share their own personal stories from the field of AASC. These practitioners work with their animal partners in schools across the United States with the goal of promoting social and emotional skills in children. Some of these practitioners share narratives of their AASC experiences in schools while others share recommendations for new AASC teams. Readers can find helpful takeaways and engaging moments of change from the stories of Summer and Croix, Lisa and Thor, Breanne and Mickey, Cortnie and Irie Grace, and Laura and Winnie.

Sommer Bowers Hynes and Croix

School District: River Falls School District, River Falls, Wisconsin
Years in the AASC Field: Three years (Figure 12.2).

Sommer Bowers Hynes shared the following about starting an AASC program:

> I would advise to advocate to your district to encourage your school to allow a therapy dog program! It has been such a rewarding experience and we feel like it has been a preventative approach, too, when it comes to supporting mental health needs in our building. We are seeing students that may not have traditionally come into the school counseling office. However, now they want to come see Croix or they have scheduled their own visit to meet with him. It allows us to connect with students and strengthen those relationships! Students and parents also love following him on Instagram so be sure to set up an account for your therapy animal! One more thing is to get a stamp made of your therapy animal's paw print because it comes in handy to sign yearbooks and thank you cards.

Sommer provides some helpful suggestions about starting an AASC program.

Lisa Klink and Thor

School District: Wayne Public School District, Wayne, New Jersey
Years in the AASC Field: Five years (Figure 12.3).

Figure 12.2 Sommer and Croix dress up as Hedwig and Harry Potter for homecoming week.

Lisa shared her story:

My name is Lisa Klink and my therapy dog is a five-year-old German Shepherd named Thor. He is certified with Bright & Beautiful Therapy Dogs. I am a special education teacher of 13 years at Schuyler-Colfax Middle School in Wayne, New Jersey with the Wayne Public School District. Thor and I have worked together as a team for five years. Thor was given to me to raise in a guide dog puppy raising program in 2018 when he was just seven weeks old. His main purpose was to be raised as a future guide dog. I raised Thor for a year and took him to work with me at the middle school during this time. The staff and students were incredibly receptive to Thor. They truly appreciated his mission in becoming a guide dog as well as the ability to personally de-stress with some pet therapy. During this time, I was also enrolled as a graduate student at Rowan University, and I wrote a thesis on the topic of animal-assisted therapy and its benefits in the classroom (Klink, 2019). Thor returned to the guide dog program at about a year and a half old, but unfortunately, he was not chosen to proceed in the guide dog program. However, the guide dog program allows puppy raisers a chance to adopt their dog back if they do not qualify for the program. I happily accepted Thor home when I was given this chance!

Due to his extensive socialization and guide dog training, I immediately took Thor to be tested with Bright & Beautiful Therapy Dogs at the beginning of 2020. When he passed the certification test, my middle school was grateful to have the opportunity to accept Thor back into the building as a therapy dog. Although schools closed to in-person instruction rather quickly for COVID protocols,

Figure 12.3 Lisa poses with Thor on her graduation day.

Thor spent his time home doing many virtual visits with the students. I wrote an article about this time that was published by the New Jersey Education Association (Klink, 2020).

Recently this year, Thor unfortunately suffered a serious medical setback when he was diagnosed with Intervertebral Disc Disease. Without any warning, he slowly started showing signs of paralysis in his back legs from what we would later find was a ruptured disc. Thor had to stop therapy visits at school and undergo major emergency back surgery that was incredibly expensive, to say the least. In this deeply tragic time, my middle school graciously organized a GoFundMe campaign to raise money to help Thor get back on his feet (literally!). Our campaign reached PIX 11 News. We were able to secure all the funds that Thor needed for surgery, hospitalization, and physical therapy rehabilitation. To say I am overwhelmed by the kindness, generosity, and love is clearly an understatement. I will never forget the true miracle of the community coming together to save my dog. It was so absolutely beautiful to watch staff, students, and their family and friends demonstrate support for Thor's mission to bring comfort to others. I am happy to report that he is doing well and continues his weekly school visits! An article and video about this event was featured on PIX 11 News (Vasil, 2023).

Thor usually attends school with me on Fridays, but he is welcome to come on any day I would like to bring him. Thor follows me to all of my classes, as my schedule requires me to move to different classrooms much like the students do. Once in the classroom, Thor has a blanket and soft collapsible crate set up that he can relax in. He loves being pet, brushed, and fed treats and ice cubes. By far, his favorite activity of the day is playing tennis ball with the students and staff in the gym.

He is a silly, vocal, and loving shepherd! I very frequently dress him up in funny headbands, bandanas, and outfits that coordinate to the various holidays throughout the year. The students and staff always find it amusing when he does this!

Lisa's story demonstrates the impact that animal partners can have on a school community and the love that a school community can have for a therapy dog.

Breanne Long and Mickey

School District: Lakeside Union School District, Lakeside California
Years in the AASC Field: Three years (Figure 12.4).

Breanne shared the following:

At the time that Mickey and I became a certified therapy dog team, I was going on my eigth year as a School Psychologist in the Lakeside Union School District. School was slowly starting back up in person after the spring and summer that COVID had hit. I had always hoped that one day I could bring therapy dog teams into our schools as I have loved and owned dogs my whole life and am such a strong believer in the sense of calm and comfort that dogs can give us. After adopting Mickey, it was obvious how people-driven he was and how amazing he was with my kids from the first day we

Figure 12.4 Breanne and Mickey Long.

brought him home. This intrigued me to start working with a trainer to see if we could work towards him passing the Alliance of Therapy Dogs exam.

During this process, I spoke with my principal and Special Education Director about the training Mickey and I were going through, all the items on the tests we would have to pass, the insurance we would carry, and the ways I would have him support students at our school. After they got the go-ahead from our Superintendent, Mickey and I passed our Alliance of Therapy Dog and Canine Good Citizen exams and we began the process of starting him at my school! (I am the first employee in my School District to implement dog therapy as a program, so this was very exciting for us!) I began this process by first bringing Mickey in to meet the teachers during an after-school meeting and allowing them to ask any questions they had. Next, I made "opt-out" forms to go home to the students' parents to give them information about the program we would be doing with Mickey and give them a form to opt-out of the "Mickey visits" if their child was allergic, had a dog phobia, etc. After waiting a couple of weeks for parents to ask questions and return these forms if needed, we then began our curriculum.

I made weekly visits into the classrooms with Mickey and came up with lessons where the students could read to Mickey in small groups, use their creativity to draw pictures and write stories about him, lead science experiments centered around him, and more. We've had so many special moments with so many different kinds of circumstances. For instance; Children overcoming their dog phobias and cuddling with him on the rug after a handful of visits, children who are shy or depressed, but suddenly they are lighting up and laughing with peers while petting Mickey in a group, children who do not speak due to a disability, but then began using words to say "bye" to Mickey, or ask for "dog." I could truly go on and on about all the special moments that have come from bringing Mickey into classrooms. It's something I wish every classroom at every school could experience!

Breanne described several ways in which Mickey has made a difference at her school.

Cortnie Wise and Irie Grace

School District: New Summit Charter Academy, Colorado Springs, Colorado
Years in the AASC Field: Two years (Figure 12.5).

Cortnie shares the following recommendations:

Watching kids make progress from the therapeutic benefits of canine interaction, on both good and bad days, warms my heart. I am truly grateful for working at a school and under an administration that knows and honors the incredible benefit of having animals at school. Since being on this journey, I have been blessed immensely by watching the unspoken interactions of unconditional love that are displayed between Irie and the students she serves. My greatest advice is to know your dog and to honor their limits. Watch them for communication and understand that they have needs too. Irie is very good at communicating with me when she is happy and feeling social versus when she is tired or bored and more of an introvert. It is my job as part of the therapy dog team to discern her needs and meet them for her. She remains a priority even while I am working. It is so important, too, to let them be a dog. She needs time to run, play, sleep where she wants, and interact with her brother (also an Australian Shepherd). When her work vest comes off then she knows that she can be at ease. That time is just as important for her well-being as any time that she is at work. Finally, I would just say that it is important that your school community is fully invested in animal-assisted interactions as

Figure 12.5 Irie Grace is ready to get some work done at her school.

well. It starts with administration and as with anything else, their belief in and support of an initiative is important. Irie is referred to as "fur-staff" at school and she is just as much a part of the community as anyone else. The animal being welcomed is crucial to your success as a team!

Cortnie provided some helpful guidance on supporting an animal partner both at school and home.

Laura Wheeler and Winnie

School District: Nottingham School District, Nottingham, New Hampshire
Years in the AASC Field: Two years (Figure 12.6).

Laura shares her story:

My family adopted Winnie in April 2021 when he was five years old. From the moment that we met him, we knew he was a special dog with empathetic super powers. After becoming a certified therapy team, Winnie began coming to school with me and quickly became the favorite staff member. Our school has never had a therapy dog before Winnie, so we were learning together how we could best impact our school community.

Perhaps one of Winnie's most impactful ways that he makes a difference is that he is the ultimate "social equalizer". He brings students together naturally and fosters a culture of inclusivity just by

Figure 12.6 Laura and Winnie Wheeler.

being a presence. Whether it is a group of students gathering to pet him in the hallway, a classroom setting where he is drawing a small group of students together, or recess where playing ball with Winnie provides an opportunity for being included in a game, Winnie brings students together. It is something so simple, yet so important. Students put aside their differences, have an opportunity to connect and talk with new peers, and feel a sense of belonging whenever Winnie is present. Soon after Winnie began coming to school, a student commented to me, "Winnie has helped me to make friends".

As a therapy team, Winnie and I are always learning new ways to make an impact, and I can truly say that he teaches me new things every day! We have so much to learn from animals, and integrating them into our school has changed our culture and climate in positive ways. Winnie and I look forward to continuing our work together!

Laura and Winnie demonstrate how an AASC team can bring children together.

What's Next for Future AASC Teams

What future stories could potentially be shared about AASC teams in schools? As this book comes to a close, this section will offer recommendations for what's next for future AASC teams. The first step is for practitioners to begin the process of seeking approval for an AASC program. Next, practitioners can make sure they have chosen an animal partner that is the best fit for AASC work. Animals should have the right temperament and enjoy being around a lot of strangers for this type of work. AASC teams are called to develop specific competencies in knowledge, skills, and attitudes. Practitioners should search for AASC training programs that can help them develop those competencies. Finding an AASC supervisor or consultation group can help practitioners develop strengths and work through challenges at their school site. After practitioners receive training and supervision, they can begin to prepare their school for having an animal partner on campus. As practitioners create their AASC program, they can consider how they will design schoolwide, classroom, small group, and individual lessons that apply their clinical theory and include ways to assess these interventions. Programs are designed to include AASC practices that celebrate students' diversity, culture, and abilities. As practitioners navigate the process of developing an AASC program, they should always advocate for their animal partner's well-being.

The goal of this book was to provide a framework for designing and implementing effective AASC programs in schools. This text sought to reduce variability in the AASC field by presenting a clear structure of competencies, training recommendations, assessment practices, theoretical approaches, and tiered interventions that best meet the social and emotional needs of students and uphold the welfare of animals. This book took readers on a journey from the foundations of AASC to future directions in AASC. Throughout the book, AASC forms were provided to guide practitioners as they traverse the program approval and implementation process. Readers were also presented with a myriad of AASC lesson plans that offer creative and educational lessons to employ with an animal partner. Practitioners have been equipped with a wealth of information about this field and guidance on how to develop the skills and competencies needed to be a successful AASC team. The future of the AASC field is calling for new AASC practitioners, researchers, trainers, and stakeholders to use the power of human-animal interaction to make a difference in children's lives.

References

Brelsford, V. L., Meints, K., Gee, N. R., & Pfeffer, K. (2017). Animal-assisted interventions in the classroom - A systematic review. *International Journal of Environmental Research and Public Health, 14*(7), 669. 10.3390/ijerph14070669

Klink, L. M. (2019). The effectiveness of animal-assisted therapy on the anxiety and school attendance of students with disabilities. [Master's thesis, Rowan University]. *Theses and Dissertations*, 2669. https://rdw.rowan.edu/etd/2669

Klink, L. M. (2020). *Thor the therapy dog delights, reassures Wayne students*. New Jersey Education Association. https://njeatogether.njea.org/thor-the-therapy-dog-delights-reassures-wayne-students/

McCune, S., Kruger, K. A., Griffin, J. A., Esposito, L., Freund, L. S., Hurley, K. J., & Bures, R. (2014). Evolution of research into the mutual benefits of human-animal interaction. *Animal Frontiers, 4*(3), 49–58. 10.2527/af.2014-0022

Meints, K., Brelsford, V. L., Dimolareva, M., Maréchal, L., Pennington, K., Rowan, E., & Gee, N. R. (2022). Can dogs reduce stress levels in school children? Effects of dog-assisted interventions on salivary cortisol in children with and without special educational needs using randomized controlled trials. *PLoS ONE, 17*(6), 1–26. 10.1371/journal.pone.0269333

Vasil, J. (2023). *Therapy dog Thor helped this NJ school community. Now they're helping him. PIX 11*. https://pix11.com/news/local-news/new-jersey/therapy-dog-thor-helped-this-nj-school-community-now-theyre-helping-him/

Appendix A

AASC Program Request Form

Date: _____

Practitioner Name: _____

School: _____

Please answer the following questions in the spaces provided regarding developing an animal-assisted school counseling (AASC) program at your school.

1   Describe your animal partner. Please include name, age, species, and information about their temperament.

2   Why do you think your animal partner would be a good fit for AASC work on a school campus?

3   What AASC training program are you planning to attend? *Please note that volunteer therapy animal training programs do not meet competencies for AASC.*

4   How many hours of AASC knowledge training, clinical experience, and supervision are provided by this training program?

   Knowledge hours: _____
   Clinical experience hours: _____
   Supervision hours: _____

5   What evaluations will you and your animal partner complete as part of the training program?

6   When will you and your animal partner need to be recredentialed or re-evaluated by the program through which you are being credentialed?

7   How do you plan to pay for the AASC training program? What financial support, if any, are you requesting from the district?

8   Animals must be cleared by a veterinarian to do AASC. Describe your animal's health and any potential health issues.

9   What are your goals for having an AASC program on campus?

10 How will your AASC program benefit the school's goals and mission?

11 How will your AASC program benefit student's social and emotional goals?

12 What feedback have you received from the students, school staff, and the community about an AASC program?

13 In what ways do you think AASC interventions could impact students in your school?

14 What questions do you have about implementing an AASC program?

Practitioner Signature _____ Date _____

I have read and give approval for the practitioner to pursue AASC training.

Principal Signature _____ Date _____

AASC Training Verification Form

Date: _____

Practitioner Name: _____

School: _____

Prior to implementing an animal-assisted school counseling (AASC) program, practitioners must have previously completed the AASC Program Request Form and received training in AASC. This form requests confirmation that practitioners have the necessary training and documentation in place prior to the implementation of an AASC Program. Attach the required documentation requested to this document.

1 What AASC training program did you attend? *Please note that volunteer therapy animal training programs do not meet competencies for AASC.* *Attach a copy of your AASC Certification or training certificates

2 How many hours of AASC training, clinical experience, and supervision were provided by this training program?
   Knowledge hours: _____
   Clinical experience hours: _____
   Supervision hours: _____

3 What evaluations did you and your animal partner complete as part of the training program?

4 When will you and your animal partner need to be recredentialed or re-evaluated by the program through which you are credentialed?

5 Animals must be cleared by a veterinarian to do AASC work. *Attach the Animal Health Screening Form.

6 Practitioners must have professional liability insurance. Do you have professional liability insurance that specifically covers animal-assisted services? *Attach the Professional Liability Insurance Form.

7 Students working directly with the animal partner will need to have a signed informed consent that covers AASC-specific topics. *Attach the AASC Informed Consent Form.

Animal Welfare Information

When will your animal partner be present at the school? Please include designated days and hours.

Where will the animal partner rest and take breaks when they are at school?

Where will your animal partner take restroom breaks and what are your plans for keeping that area clean?

What will you do with your animal partner if you need to attend to a crisis situation?

How will you promote positive human-animal interactions with your animal partner?

Please attach a copy of the following documents to this application before submitting:

- AASC Certification or training certificates
- Animal Health Screening Form
- Professional Liability Insurance
- AASC Informed Consent

Practitioner Signature _____ Date _____

I have read and give approval for the implementation of an AASC program on campus.

Principal Signature _____ Date _____

AASC Animal Health Screening Form

This form should be completed by the animal's veterinarian based on an exam that has been completed within the past year. This form requests information about the animal's temperament, vaccinations, and overall health. This form provides support for the animal to provide animal-assisted school counseling (AASC) services in a school. If you have any concerns about the animal, please discuss these with the caregiver prior to completing the form.

Animal Caregiver/Practitioner's Name: _____

Animal Profile

Animal Name: _____

Date of Birth: _____   Age: _____

Species: _____   Breed: _____

Describe animal's temperament: _____
_____

Describe any issues with temperament, anxiety, or aggression: _____
_____
_____

Animal Health

Last complete exam date: _____   Rabies vaccination date: _____

Annual fecal exam result: _____   Heartworm exam result: _____

Current medications: _____

Describe any conditions or disabilities the animal has and how this may impact therapy work:_____
_____
_____

Attestations

• This animal is current on all vaccinations.
• This animal does not display any signs of infectious or zoonotic diseases.
• This animal is free from internal and external parasites.
• I confirm that this animal is in good health as of the date of the last complete exam.
• I do not have reservations at this time about this animal providing AASC services.

Veterinarian Name (Print): _____

Signature: _____   Date: _____

AASC Presentation Slides

These sample AASC presentation slides provide guidance on topics to cover that are most relevant to seeking district support for an AASC program.

Meet Me and My Animal Partner

Why I'm Passionate About Having an AASC Program

What is AASC?

Animal-assisted school counseling (AASC) is a goal-directed process in which a trained school-based practitioner and their animal partner work together as a team in schools to promote social and emotional wellness in students using the power of human-animal interactions.

Benefits of AASC in Schools

- Promotes a positive attitude toward learning, inspire more participation in learning activities, and reduce negative behaviors such as aggression and work avoidance (Grové et al., 2021)
- Decreases symptoms of depression and anxiety in youth (Hartwig, 2017)
- Improves attentiveness, responsiveness, focus, and positive attitude towards school (Gee et al., 2017)
- Increases student perception of animals as non-judgmental and unconditionally accepting (Friesen, 2010)
- Promotes mindsets and behaviors for student success (Hartwig, 2024)

AASC & Multi-Tiered System of Supports

- Tier 1 – schoolwide services (e.g., anti-bullying, humane education, morning check ins)
- Tier 2 – targeted individual and small group counseling with animal partner
- Tier 3 – intensive individualized support and referrals (e.g., crisis support)

AASC Crisis Teams

- Practitioners trained in AASC can impact a wider population in the district by serving as an AASC crisis team when issues come up at various schools
- Crises on school campuses can range from individual student concerns, such as suicidal ideations or abuse, to schoolwide issues, such as natural disasters, neighborhood violence, or the death of a student or teacher
- AASC crisis teams can provide services to students who have been affected by crises
- AASC can help safely break through the barriers of isolation caused by crisis, allowing individuals to re-connect to their families, friends, peers, and other social supports.
- Animal partners can help those experiencing crisis feel safe, connected, and more able to share their thoughts and feelings

Common Concerns

- AASC training and supervision
- Student and staff education
- Risks and liability
- Established procedures

AASC Training & Certification

* Planned AASC training program:
* Dates:
* Hours/CEs of AASC training
  * Knowledge and skills: _____
  * Clinical Hours: _____
  * Supervision Hours: _____

AASC Program Fees

* Cost of program
* District support for AASC training
* AASC Program Request Form

Plans to Address Liability

- AASC training – preventing liability, learning processes for teaching others how to greet and interact with animal partner, recognizing and responding immediately to animal stress signals
- Informed Consent
- Professional Liability Insurance
- Promoting animal welfare – breaks, removing animal when stressed, assessing energy and engagement
- Animal Health Screening Form

Next Steps

- AASC Program Request Form
- AASC Training & Supervision
- AASC Training Verification Form
- School/District Approval
- Prepare school for animal partner
- Implement AASC program!

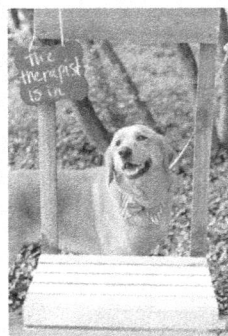

Questions?

References

* Friesen, L. (2010). Exploring animal-assisted programs with children in school and therapeutic contexts. *Early Childhood Education Journal, 37*(4), 261–267. https://doi.org/10.1007/s10643-009-0349-5

* Gee, N. R., Fine, A. H., & McCardle, P. D. (Eds.). (2017). *How animals help students learn: research and practice for educators and mental-health professionals.* Routledge.

* Grové, C., Henderson, L., Lee, F., & Wardlaw, P. (2021). Therapy dogs in educational settings: guidelines and recommendations for implementation. *Frontiers in Veterinary Science, 8.* https://www.frontiersin.org/articles/10.3389/fvets.2021.655104/full

* Hartwig, E. K. (2017). Building solutions in youth: Evaluation of the Human-Animal Resilience Therapy intervention. *Journal of Creativity in Mental Health, 12*(4), 468-481. https://doi.org/10.1080/15401383.2017.1283281

* Hartwig, E. K. (Ed.). (2024). *Animal-assisted school counseling.* Routledge.

AASC Competencies

AASC Knowledge Competencies		
Code	Competency	Description
K1	Training	School-based practitioners complete comprehensive training in AASC that includes AASC-specific knowledge, skills practice, attitudes, and clinical experience.
K2	Supervision	School-based practitioners participate in clinical supervision or consultation provided by an AASC supervisor to promote professional growth and learning. Practitioners understand how to self-assess AASC skills and integrate an assessment of skills provided by an AASC supervisor.
K3	History	School-based practitioners possess knowledge of the history of AAC, AASC, and teams working with children in schools.
K4	Literature	School-based practitioners read foundational and emerging literature and research related to AAC, AASC, and animals in school settings and are knowledgeable of current AASC language and terminology.
K5	Human-Animal Bond	School-based practitioners understand what the human-animal bond (HAB) is and the impact of HAB on children, family members, educators, administration, and school staff and on the AASC process.
K6	Animal Knowledge and Care	School-based practitioners understand species-specific information about their AASC animal partner including communication signals, physiology, behavior, and care. Practitioners are knowledgeable of their animal partner's strengths and limitations within AASC work.
K7	Animal Health and Wellness	School-based practitioners understand their animal partner's needs and provide access to water, rest time, and bathroom breaks. Practitioners attend to the wellness of the animal through regular veterinary care, vaccinations, nutrition, grooming, and exercise. Practitioners understand health implications of AASC and minimize the risks of animal- or human-transmitted diseases through handwashing and sanitation procedures.
K8	Positive, Non-Aversive Training	School-based practitioners possess knowledge of and use positive and non-aversive training techniques for animal partners working in school settings.
K9	Ethics	School-based practitioners understand ethical and legal implications of AASC. Practitioners seek consultation from AASC supervisors and peers to guide ethical decision making.
K10	Risk Management	School-based practitioners understand potential liability involved in practicing AASC and possess knowledge of risk-management strategies including limit setting, informed consent, and insurance coverage.

(Continued)

AASC Knowledge Competencies		
Code	Competency	Description
K11	Diversity Awareness	School-based practitioners understand the implications of the use of AASC with students with respect to race, ethnicity, age, sex, religion, sexual orientation, gender identity, gender expression, disability, economic status, and other diverse backgrounds.
K12	Interventions	School-based practitioners have knowledge of AASC interventions and how they can be applied to specific clinical goals for students in the school setting.

AASC Skills Competencies		
Code	Competency	Description
S1	Practitioner-Animal Relationship	School-based practitioners establish and maintain a strong working relationship with their animal partner. Practitioners advocate for the welfare of their animal partner in all AASC interactions. Practitioners demonstrate that they are not "using" an animal, but rather "partnering" with an animal.
S2	Animal Greeting	School-based practitioners show students, teachers, and staff how to greet animal prior to the person interacting with the animal partner. Practitioners guide the greeting interaction between the person and animal.
S3	Animal Communication	School-based practitioners recognize animal partner's communication signals, including positive and stress signals. School-based practitioners respond immediately to animal stress signals and implement strategies to ensure safety of the animal partner and students.
S4	Cultural Responsiveness	School-based practitioners evaluate and address their personal cultural influences, beliefs, values, and biases and avoid imposing these onto students. Practitioners broach cultural conversations related to AASC and make modifications to AASC interventions based on the needs, culture, values, and beliefs about animals that students, families, and staff may hold.
S5	Basic Counseling Skills	School-based practitioners exhibit proficiency in basic counseling skills within a school setting prior to the integration of AASC including showing empathy, respect, and unconditional positive regard toward the animal partner and students. Basic counseling skills include reflecting content and feeling, summarizing, and using open-ended questions.
S6	Student-Animal Relationship	School-based practitioners demonstrate facilitation of student-animal relationship so that a working alliance is developed.

(Continued)

AASC Skills Competencies		
Code	Competency	Description
S7	Animal and Student Choice	School-based practitioners recognize and assess the animal partner's and student's willingness, safety, and comfortability while participating in AASC interactions. Practitioners assert that both the animal partner and student have a choice in participating in interactions and interventions without judgment or consequences.
S8	Limit Setting	School-based practitioners demonstrate the ability to set limits when needed by using the RUF protocol: Recognize what the person wants, Underscore the limit, and Focus on an alternative. An example would be, "Jordan, I see you want to hug Hank, but he's not for hugging that way. You can pet him on the chest instead."
S9	Assessment of Students	School-based practitioners assess children's suitability to participate in AASC based on informed consent information, student behavior, and student interest.
S10	Assessment of Animal Partner	School-based practitioners continuously assess the animal partner's strengths, limitations, and appropriateness for AASC, regardless of the bond between the animal partner and practitioner. The practitioner can identify when it is appropriate to remove the animal partner from a particular session or retire them from the AASC program.
S11	Confidence	School-based practitioners demonstrate appropriate levels of self-assurance and trust in own ability and animal partner's ability to facilitate AASC interactions and interventions.
S12	Informed Consent	School-based practitioners facilitate and obtain AASC-specific informed consent.
S13	Clinical Theory	School-based practitioners apply a primary clinical theory in their AASC program (e.g., solution-focused, cognitive-behavioral, Adlerian). Through this theory, they use key concepts, therapist role, and techniques to provide AASC services and assess progress. School-based practitioners have knowledge of the difference between indirect and direct modalities and benefits and limitations of each in the school setting.
S14	Goal Setting	School-based practitioners establish appropriate goals with students and connect AASC interventions to students' goals.
S15	Facilitating Interventions	School-based practitioners select and facilitate appropriate AASC interventions for each student based on student goals and provide a rationale for activities and strategies utilized.
S16	Termination	School-based practitioners demonstrate the ability to end AASC services well through positive counseling termination strategies. Practitioners seek out consultation from AASC professionals and stakeholders if an adverse event and/or animal partner sudden death or illness is the cause of termination.

AASC Attitudes Competencies		
Code	Competency	Description
A1	Professional Identity	School-based practitioners demonstrate AASC professional identity in their work in schools and in professional settings. This includes knowledge of their role as both a practitioner and advocate for their animal partner and developing, maintaining, and continuously improving AASC knowledge, skills, and attitudes.
A2	Values	School-based practitioners support, advocate for, and endorse AASC professional values and respect animal autonomy and welfare. Practitioners demonstrate enthusiasm related to their work with students and animal partners.
A3	Advocacy	School-based practitioners advocate for their animal partner's welfare and wellness. Practitioners understand the potential for animal exploitation in a school setting and realize their responsibility to the animal partner.
A4	Research	School-based practitioners support and contribute to literature and research in AASC through participation in research, writing, and presenting in local, regional, national, and international trainings or conferences.
A5	Professional Development	School-based practitioners participate in opportunities to enhance and hone their AASC skills through continuing education, consultation, and professional development activities.

AASC Skills Checklist

Date: _____ AASC Team: _____
Lesson: _____ Student/Group: _____

This form is used to assess a school-based practitioner's animal-assisted school counseling (AASC) skills during a single lesson or session.

Ratings: N – Not applicable/No opportunity to observe; O – Does not demonstrate this skill; 1 – Demonstrates this skill minimally; 2 – Demonstrates this skill variably; 3 – Demonstrates this skill consistently.

Code	Competency	Description	Rating	Comments
Preliminary Skills				
S1	Practitioner-Animal Relationship	Establishes and maintains a strong working relationship with their animal partner. Advocates for the welfare of their animal partner in all AASC interactions.		
S2	Animal Greeting	Shows students, teachers, and staff how to greet animal prior to the person interacting with the animal partner. Guides the greeting interaction between the person and animal.		
S3	Animal Communication	Recognizes animal partner's communication signals, including positive and stress signals. Responds immediately to animal stress signals and implements strategies to ensure safety of the animal partner and students.		
S4	Cultural Responsiveness	Evaluates their personal cultural influences, beliefs, values, and biases and avoids imposing these onto students. Broaches cultural conversations related to AASC. Makes modifications to AASC interventions based on the needs, culture, values, and beliefs about animals that people may hold.		
Facilitative Skills				
S5	Reflection of Behavior	Demonstrates reflection of non-verbal behavior in relation to AASC interactions.		

(Continued)

Code	Competency	Description	Rating	Comments
S5	Reflection of Content	Demonstrates reflection of verbal content in relation to AASC interactions.		
S5	Reflection of Feeling	Demonstrates reflection of feeling in relation to AASC interactions.		
S5	Non-Verbal Skills	Demonstrates effective use of posture, eye contact, gestures, and proximity during AASC interactions.		
S5	Empathy	Communicates empathy, respect, and unconditional positive regard to student and animal.		
S5	Questions	Demonstrates appropriate use of open-ended and close-ended questions, with an emphasis on open-ended questions.		
S6	Student-Animal Relationship	Demonstrates facilitation of student-animal relationship so that a working alliance is developed.		
S7	Animal and Student Choice	Recognizes and assesses the animal partner and student's willingness, safety, and comfortability while participating in AASC interactions. Asserts that both the animal partner and student have a choice in participating in interactions and interventions without judgment or consequences.		
S8	Limit Setting	Demonstrates ability to set limits when needed by using the RUF protocol: Recognize what the person wants, Underscore the limit, and Focus on an alternative.		
S9	Assessment of Students	Assesses children's suitability to participate in AASC based on informed consent information, student behavior, and student interest.		
S10	Assessment of Animal Partner	Assesses the animal partner's strengths, limitations, and appropriateness for AASC, regardless of the bond between the animal partner and practitioner.		

(Continued)

Code	Competency	Description	Rating	Comments
S11	Confidence	Demonstrates appropriate levels of self-assurance and trust in own ability and animal partner's ability to facilitate AASC interactions.		
Therapeutic Intentionality Skills				
S12	Informed Consent	Facilitates and obtains informed consent for AASC services.		
S13	Clinical Theory	Applies a primary clinical theory in their AASC lessons and services.		
S14	Goal Setting	Establishes appropriate goals with students and connects AASC interventions to students' goals.		
S15	Facilitating Interventions	Selects and facilitates appropriate AASC interventions for each student based on student goals and provides a rationale for activities and strategies utilized.		
S16	Termination	Demonstrates the ability to end AASC services well through positive counseling termination strategies.		

Strengths:

Areas of growth:

AASC Family Survey

The purpose of this survey is to provide the school-based practitioner with information related to an AASC program on campus. As a reminder, the practitioner and the animal partner have completed many hours of training and supervision in order to bring this program to the school.

Student Name: _____

Student Grade Level: _____   Teacher: _____

1 What do you think might be benefits of having an animal partner on the school campus?

2 What current or former pets has your child had?

3 What animal or food allergies does your child have?

4 What positive experiences has your child had with animals?

5 What negative experiences, if any, has your child had with animals?

6 Is your child interested in AASC services and working with an animal partner, if that is an option?

7 What information might be helpful for the school counselor to know before your child interacts with the animal partner?

8 Are there any other questions or concerns you have about the AASC program?

Caregiver Name: _____

Phone #: _____   Email: _____

AASC Lesson Plan 3.1

Lesson Plan Info		
AASC Practitioner	Kimberly Scott	
AASC Animal Partner	Nibbles (Rabbit)	
Counseling Theory	Solution-Focused Therapy	
Lesson Plan Title	**Meet the AASC Team**	
Type of Lesson	☐ Schoolwide ☒ Classroom	☐ Small-Group ☐ Individual Counseling
Target Audience	Elementary or Secondary Students	
Evidence Base	☒ Best Practice ☐ Action Research	☐ Evidence-Based ☐ Research-Informed

ASCA Student Standards Targeted		Student Learning Objectives
Identify 1–2 student standards relevant for this targeted group and goal		For each of the selected student standards, write 1–2 learning objectives
M&B#	Mindsets & Behaviors Statement	Student Learning Objectives
M2	Sense of acceptance, respect, support, and inclusion for self and others in the school environment	Be able to identify positive qualities within themselves as well as be able to find common positive qualities with other students
B-SS 2	Positive, respectful, and supportive relationships with students who are similar and different from them	Learn about the similarities and differences between self and others in class
B-SS 3	Positive relationships with adults to support success	Be able to identify the school counselor as a helper in the school that supports students
		Learn about the extra support that the counselor has through psychoeducation regarding the animal partner

Materials:	
For Activity: Phone/tablet template of a blank screen Pencils Colored pencils, crayons, or markers Enlarged view of the template, either projected on the board or on a large paper that is visible to students	For Animal Partner: N/A

Describe how you will:	
Introduce Lesson Topic/Focus:	Introducing the role of the counselor, the counseling partner, and how to identify positive qualities
Communicate the Lesson Objective:	We will be learning about each other today and you will be meeting my counseling partner.
Teach Content:	The counselor will introduce themself and begin by writing keywords about their role on the template on the board (either poster sized or projected on board). • Encourager: help students through problems, but also celebrate accomplishments • Advocate: help students get what they need to be successful • Supportive: here to listen when you need extra help and to help find more support at school/community • Trustworthy: introduce the concept of confidentiality, will follow-through with what I say • Helper – love helping people and wants people to know that they can come to them on good days and on days when things are tough - can also introduce the self-referral system at this time to make an appointment. Introduce the counseling partner through a lesson about the animal. Have students help come up with what the animal's qualities might be. These should be reframed to positive qualities. For example, in the case of the rabbit that might appear to be "timid"/"shy," this can be reframed to "cautious" or "likes to be safe."
Practice Content:	Students will write their positive qualities and share them with others at their table groups or with the class depending on participation and time. Some students might need help reframing some of their traits.
Involve Animal Partner:	Animal partner will be present to introduce to students but will not be directly interacting with students at this time. The animal will be involved through educating students about rabbits and writing about the qualities/characteristics of the rabbit on one of the templates as a group.
Assess for Animal Welfare:	Animal partner will not be directly interacting with students due to the large classroom setting to ensure safety. If rabbit seems distressed, they will be put in quieter area that is more hidden from students.
Summarize/Close:	We were able to learn about each other's similarities and differences and you also learned about my role at the school as well as my counseling partner Nibbles. We are looking forward to working with you this school year and to continuing to get to know each of you.

Data Collection Plan	
Participant Data Plan:	
Anticipated number of students:	22–28
Planned length of lesson(s):	30–45 minutes

ASCA Student Standards Data Plan:

Pre/Post Assessment Items:
1. I can identify positive qualities about myself
2. I know who I can go to at school if I need support
3. I feel as though I am respected in my classroom.
4. I know that name of my counselor and the counseling partner

Outcome Data Plan:

☐ Academic Achievement:
☐ Attendance:
☒ Behavior: By allowing students to share positive similarities and differences in a controlled and respectful environment, students will view each other in a more empathic way. Students will also know who to ask for support in school, which will lower the reported behavior concerns in classrooms and encourage students to seek help when there is an issue.

Follow-Up Plans

Plans for students who missed lesson: Students will be able to attend a "make-up" lesson with other students during their intervention time.
Plan for students who didn't demonstrate mastery: Students who are not able to demonstrate mastery will be assessed for group counseling to determine if there is an additional need that can be met. Students that are not a good fit for group counseling will be considered for individual counseling.

AASC Lesson Plan 3.2

Lesson Plan Info

AASC Practitioner	Kimberly Scott
AASC Animal Partner	Mr. Pricklepants (hedgehog)
Counseling Theory	Solution-Focused Therapy
Lesson Plan Title	**Prickly Coping Strategies**
Type of Lesson	☐ Schoolwide ☐ Classroom	☒ Small-Group ☐ Individual Counseling
Target Audience	Elementary or Secondary Students	
Evidence Base	☒ Best Practice ☐ Action Research	☐ Evidence-Based ☐ Research-Informed

ASCA Student Standards Targeted / Student Learning Objectives

ASCA Student Standards Targeted		Student Learning Objectives
Identify 1–2 student standards relevant for this targeted group and goal		For each of the selected student standards, write 1–2 learning objectives
M&B#	Mindsets & Behaviors Statement	Student Learning Objectives
M2	Sense of acceptance, respect, support, and inclusion for self and others in the school environment	Be able to identify what makes them feel "unsure," unsafe, or anxious
B-SS 8	Advocacy skills for self and others and ability to assert self when necessary	Learn coping strategies to help with managing the feelings
B-SMS 7	Effective coping skills	

Materials:

For Activity: Clothespins	For Animal Partner: play pen

Describe how you will:	
Introduce Lesson Topic/Focus:	Coping strategies for when we feel unsure
Communicate the Lesson Objective:	We will be learning about our counseling partner, Mr. Pricklepants (the hedgehog), and what he does when he's unsure in a situation and learn what we do when we're unsure.
Teach Content:	The counselor will introduce bring out their counseling partner, Mr. Pricklepants, and will discuss what he does when he feels unsure about a situation. When he is not sure if he's safe, he will curl into a ball, hide his head, and his quills will stick straight up. What do you do when you're feeling unsure? Give students a chance to discuss what they do when they are feeling unsure or unsafe in a situation. Examples: pull their hood up, try to escape Discuss with students what situations make them feel that way. For each situation, students get their own "quills" by putting a clothespin on their shirt (if appropriate). In past sessions, coping strategies were discussed. Which coping strategies would help? Students remove "quills" when discussing appropriate coping strategies. Who would you go to for help?
Practice Content:	Students will identify triggers and coping strategies. They will also be able to observe Mr. Pricklepants when he is "unsure" and how he slowly is able to feel safe and comfortable in the situation.
Involve Animal Partner:	Mr. Pricklepants will be moving around his safe area/play area so that students are allowed to observe him.
Assess for Animal Welfare:	While it is common for him to curl into a ball at times, if he curls into a ball and appears distressed (e.g., quills out, not moving, head tucked) for an extended period, he will be moved back into his habitat away from students.
Summarize/Close:	You were all very brave in discussing what made you feel unsafe, or your triggers, and what can help you feel comfortable. Just like Mr. Pricklepants, sometimes we react a certain way to make sure that we're safe. In his case, he was safe, but he used his coping strategies of being still and listening to his body, to feel more comfortable. I would like you to keep track of when you feel unsure this week and use those coping strategies to get your quills to go back down.

Data Collection Plan	
Participant Data Plan:	
Anticipated number of students:	3–6
Planned length of lesson(s):	30 minutes
ASCA Student Standards Data Plan:	

Pre/Post Assessment Items:
1. I know what makes me feel unsafe
2. I can identify my triggers
3. I know how to calm my body when I don't feel sure about a situation
4. I know how to get help when I don't feel safe

Outcome Data Plan:

☐ Academic Achievement:
☐ Attendance:
☒ Behavior: Students are able to successfully identify triggers and appropriately use coping strategies. This is evidenced by data taken from the first session compared to the current session.

Follow-Up Plans

Plans for students who missed lesson: Students will be able to attend a "make-up" lesson during their intervention time.
Plan for students who didn't demonstrate mastery: Students that are struggling in the group setting might need to be assessed for their "fit" into the group. The student might need individual counseling or a referral to a community-based counselor (based on the need).

AASC Lesson Plan 3.3

Lesson Plan Info

AASC Practitioner	Kimberly Scott
AASC Animal Partner	Birdie (dog)
Counseling Theory	Solution-Focused Therapy
Lesson Plan Title	**Respect Agreement**
Type of Lesson	☐ Schoolwide ☒ Classroom / ☐ Small-Group ☐ Individual Counseling
Target Audience	Any level, from Pre-K through 12th Grades, including Special Education
Evidence Base	☒ Best Practice ☐ Action Research / ☐ Evidence-Based ☐ Research-Informed

ASCA Student Standards Targeted / Student Learning Objectives

Identify 1–2 student standards relevant for this targeted group and goal

For each of the selected student standards, write 1–2 learning objectives

M&B#	Mindsets & Behaviors Statement	Student Learning Objectives
M2	Sense of acceptance, respect, support, and inclusion for self and others in the school environment	Student(s) will: Discuss the ways that we will show respect for each other and our community through making a Respect Agreement
B-SS 2	Positive, respectful, and supportive relationships with students who are similar and different from them	Make expectations based on the Respect Agreement
B-SS 3	Positive relationships with adults to support success	

Materials:

For Activity: 5 large sheets of paper marker	For Animal Partner: n/a

Describe how you will:	
Introduce Lesson Topic/ Focus:	Students will determine the expectations and the consequences for when these expectations are not being followed.
Communicate the Lesson Objective:	We will be making a Respect Agreement, which will help us with how we would like to have respect shown to us, how we show respect to the counselor, how the counselor would like to have respect shown by students, and how we will show respect to our community (classroom).
Teach Content:	The counselor will have five large pieces of paper or can write on the board the headings: • Student-to-Student • Counselor-to-Student • Student-to-Counselor • All-to-Community • Students-to-Animal Partner The counselor will start with "Student-to-Student" and ask students how they would like to be treated by other students. Examples can include using kind words, sitting next to someone when they are alone. Counselor-to-student is how students want to have the counselor show them respect. Students might need to be reminded that they must be realistic and something the counselor is able to do. Student-to-Counselor is how the counselor would like to be shown respect. This is the counselor's time to discuss how she would like to be treated by the students. This can include following the voice level in the classroom, sitting in the seat the correct way with their feet on the floor. All-to-Community is how students will show respect to the classroom. This can include recycling materials in the classroom, picking up any trash, not writing on the tables. Student-to-Animal Partner is how the animal would like to be shown respect. This is animal dependent but for dogs, it could be related more to not poking the dog, pulling the dog's fur or tail. From the Respect Agreements, the students sign that they will show respect. Consequences can be discussed by students as well. If a student is shouting, the students might suggest that they are given a signal that they were too noisy. If a student is being rough with the animal, they might need to take a break and have the animal removed. From the Respect Agreement, common themes can be found, and overall expectations can be made, such as kind words to others, appropriate voice levels, walking when moving around the room, hands to self, pet the dog gently on his chest. All expectations should be worded as what a student should do and not the behavior that is undesired. Depending on the age level, the expectations could look different. It could be that students show respect by not having ear pods in or no electronic devices out during class. The expectations should be posted in the classroom all year. For younger students or students that are unable to read, visuals would be needed.
Practice Content:	Students will work together to come up with the Respect Agreement. They can discuss at table groups before discussing it with the group. The counselor should ask the students to

(Continued)

Describe how you will:	
	demonstrate each item to see if there is agreement between students and to make sure there are not any misunderstandings with that is being agreed upon. For example, "We're going to be using the appropriate voice level in this room. Can you let me hear what a voice level 0 (no voice) sounds like? What about a voice level 1 (whisper talk)? Remember that only the person right next to you should be able to hear you. Can you use a voice level 1 to say hello?"
Involve Animal Partner:	Animal partner will be present to demonstrate how the animal partner wants to be treated (pet on the chest, hand flat to give treats). Counselor will provide demonstration.
Assess for Animal Welfare:	Counselor will assess for animal partner's welfare by checking for signs of distress and if animal is fatigued. The quiet area for the dog (her crate) will be available to the dog when she needs a break.
Summarize/ Close:	We were able to work together to make a Respect Agreement and come up with our Expectations for the classroom and for when our animal friend, Birdie, visits. We also came up with consequences for when we are not following those expectations. I know that we are going to be working so hard together to follow our expectations and to make sure that we all feel supportive and welcome in here. When we do that, we're able to spend more time with our friend, Birdie, and to make sure that everyone stays safe.

Data Collection Plan	
Participant Data Plan:	
Anticipated number of students:	22–28
Planned length of lesson(s):	30–45 minutes
ASCA Student Standards Data Plan:	
Pre/Post Assessment Items: 1. I know how to show respect to others 2. I know how my counselor wants to be treated in her classroom. 3. I feel as though I have a voice in how I want to be treated at school. 4. I know what the expectations are when (animal name) is working with us.	
Outcome Data Plan:	
☐ Academic Achievement: ☐ Attendance: ☒ Behavior: By allowing students to come up with a Respect Agreement that they have helped make, the discipline referrals in the class will decrease. The pre-determined consequences will also help to deter maladaptive behavior.	
Follow-Up Plans	
Plans for students who missed lesson: Students will be able to attend a "make-up" lesson with other students during their intervention time. Expectations will also be reviewed before every classroom lesson. Plan for students who didn't demonstrate mastery: Students that are not able to demonstrate mastery will be assessed for group counseling to determine if there is an additional need that can be met. Students that are not a good fit for group counseling will be considered for individual counseling.	

AASC Lesson Plan 3.4

Lesson Plan Info			
AASC Practitioner	Kimberly Scott		
AASC Animal Partner	Squeakers (Guinea Pig)		
Counseling Theory	Solution-Focused Therapy		
Lesson Plan Title	**Overcoming Obstacles**		
Type of Lesson	☐ Schoolwide ☐ Classroom		☒ Small-Group ☒ Individual Counseling
Target Audience	Elementary or Secondary Students		
Evidence Base	☒ Best Practice ☐ Action Research		☐ Evidence-Based ☐ Research-Informed

ASCA Student Standards Targeted		Student Learning Objectives
Identify 1–2 student standards relevant for this targeted group and goal		For each of the selected student standards, write 1–2 learning objectives
M&B#	Mindsets & Behaviors Statement	Student Learning Objectives
M4	Self-confidence in ability to succeed	Be able to identify barriers that they experience
B-SMS 6	Ability to identify and overcome barriers	Identify ways/resources to help overcome barriers

Materials:	
For Activity: Large foam blocks or other safe material to build a maze for the animal partner	For Animal Partner: Ball for the animal partner to run in (optional)

Describe how you will:	
Introduce Lesson Topic/Focus:	Overcoming obstacles
Communicate the Lesson Objective:	We will be building a maze for our animal partner, Squeakers, to run through. We will be working together to make obstacles for him to see how he approaches them.
Teach Content:	Depending on the behavior of the animal partner, he might feel more comfortable in the maze with the ball rather than running on his own. This could be another discussion point for the students about how we feel more protected in certain situations if we have extra support. The student(s) will work together to build a maze and to make (safe) obstacles for him on the floor. While they are building the obstacles, students will be encouraged to share what obstacles they are dealing with in life. For younger students, this could be family issues or peer issues while older students might have similar issues or the issues could be related to post-secondary plans or academic issues. Once the maze is built, the students will observe Squeakers as he goes through the maze. Depending on the unpredictable nature of some animals, he will either refuse to go, find alternate ways, attempt to plow through the blocks, or give up.
Practice Content:	Students will discuss what would happen if they had the same behavior as the guinea pig to the obstacle. Here are processing questions: • "What would happen if you gave up on your college application? What options do you have? What would you be willing to try?" • "What do you normally do when faced with a challenge?" • "If you were able to find an alternate path to go around this obstacle, what would it be/what would it look like?" • "Who could support you or help you? What resources do you have available to you?"
Involve Animal Partner:	Squeakers, the animal partner, will be running through the maze after the maze is built by the students.
Assess for Animal Welfare:	If Squeakers is unable or unwilling to participate, he will be returned to his habitat, which could be a discussion point for students about giving up. If he is not in the ball, he will be assessed to make sure that he is comfortable, not in distress, and not fatigued.
Summarize/Close:	We were able to accomplish a few things today, work as a team, identify what our obstacles are, and discuss ways to overcome the obstacles. When faced with obstacles, just like our animal friend, you were able to identify what you could do, whether it was try to finish, find an alternative idea, or find someone or a resource to help you.

Data Collection Plan	
Participant Data Plan:	
Anticipated number of students:	1–6
Planned length of lesson(s):	30 minutes
ASCA Student Standards Data Plan:	

Pre/Post Assessment Items:
1. I can work together with others in the group (if group) or I can work through my challenges
2. I know what obstacles I am experiencing
3. I know who I can go to or what I can do to help when it's needed
4. I know my choices when experiencing an obstacle

Outcome Data Plan:

☒ Academic Achievement: Students are able to successfully work together as a group, identify their obstacles, and resources to help. This is evidenced by data taken from the first session compared to the current session.
☐ Attendance:
☐ Behavior:

Follow-Up Plans

Plans for students who missed lesson: Students will be able to attend a "make-up" lesson during their intervention/free period time.
Plan for students who didn't demonstrate mastery: Students that are struggling in the group setting might need to be assessed for their "fit" into the group. The student might need individual counseling or a referral to a community-based counseling clinic (based on the need).

AASC Lesson Plan 4.1

Lesson Plan Info		
AASC Practitioner	Jalen Evans	
AASC Animal Partner	Hank	
Counseling Theory	Dialectical Behavior Therapy	
Lesson Plan Title	**Waiting with Hank**	
Type of Lesson	☐ Schoolwide ☐ Classroom	☒ Small-Group ☐ Individual Counseling
Target Audience	Ages 5–8	
Evidence Base	☐ Best Practice ☐ Action Research	☒ Evidence-Based ☐ Research-Informed

ASCA Student Standards Targeted		Student Learning Objectives
Identify 1–2 student standards relevant for this targeted group and goal		For each of the selected student standards, write 1–2 learning objectives
M&B#	Mindsets & Behaviors Statement	Student Learning Objectives
B-SMS 2	Self-discipline and self-control	Students will learn and practice patience and self-control, while also learning to recognize and describe their thoughts and emotions related to waiting.

Materials:	
For Activity: Treats, Phone or Radio (For bell noise)	For Animal Partner: Kennel, water, treats, bed, leash

Describe how you will:	
Introduce Lesson Topic/Focus:	School counselor will introduce the topic of patience through questions about waiting for things. Counselor will ask questions such as: "Are there any time in your life when you have to wait for things?" "What happens when you have to wait for things?" Students will have to raise their hands to answer each question (practicing patience/delayed gratification).
Communicate the Lesson Objective:	Counselor will utilize developmentally appropriate language to describe the objectives for the lesson. An example of this may be: "Today we are going to practice waiting and Hank is going to help us."
Teach Content:	• School counselor will utilize developmentally appropriate language to teach the topic of patience and delayed gratification. An example of this may be: "Sometimes when Hank really wants a snack, it's so hard for him to wait. He starts to run all over the place and gets so excited. So, before he gets a treat, I have him do exercise and play with his toys so that he can practice waiting. This is called acting opposite so instead of Hank running around, we did play time and then he got rewarded. Waiting for things can be hard but if we practice, it can get a little easier. Patience with Hank is super important also so if we want to work with Hank, we must work on being patient and make sure not to scare him." • Check in with students to ensure that they are comprehending the topic and have the space to ask questions or relate to the topics and then continue to describe what we will do. "So. what we are going to do today is first practice waiting without Hank. I have a bell that we are going to listen for. Any time we hear the bell ring, we are going to raise our hand. Sometimes it will be slow and sometimes it will be fast, but we can't raise our hand before the bell rings. No matter how much we want to raise our hand beforehand, we're going to try and do the opposite, take a deep breath, and wait for the bell."
Practice Content:	School counselor will: • Play the bell noise • Have the students raise their hand every time the bell rings (the bell noise utilized in this activity shifted between a medium pace and then a slower one, forcing the students to focus and be patient) • After a few repetitions, process this activity. Praise the students for being patient. "Wow you were so patient." "How was that for you?"
Involve Animal Partner:	• The animal is the reward for the delayed gratification. The students get to engage with Hank when utilizing patience. • Discuss how they can use the patience or "waiting" skills they just learned when Hank joins the group and come up with a list of things that they can do to wait for him to approach them, this helps to avoid overwhelming him with pets all at once. • Allow therapy animal into session. Students will wait for Hank to approach and school counselor will remind them of the skills they came up with

(Continued)

Describe how you will:	
	• Each student will have the opportunity to engage with Hank • Process skills utilized in the engagement with Hank • "What was it like waiting for Hank?" • "What do you think Hank was thinking while we were waiting for him to come join us?" • "What do you think he was feeling?" • "What were you thinking? Feeling?" • "Was it difficult to wait for him?"
Assess for Animal Welfare:	Check Hank's body language to identify any stress signals. Remove Hank if students are not following rules for patient petting or respecting Hank's boundaries. Allow for Hank to enter his kennel if he does not want to participate.
Summarize/Close:	School counselor will close session by reviewing the activity and utilizing an exit ticket: "What are some times that you think you can practice waiting?"

Data Collection Plan

Participant Data Plan:

Anticipated number of students:	4
Planned length of lesson(s):	30 minutes

ASCA Student Standards Data Plan:

Pre/Post Assessment Items:
1. Observation of impulse control behaviors

Outcome Data Plan:

☐ Academic Achievement:
☐ Attendance:
☒ Behavior: Identify whether students are learning material to control impulses and gain self-control of behaviors and emotions

Follow-Up Plans

Plans for students who missed lesson: Provide brief review of this lesson in the next group.
Plan for students who didn't demonstrate mastery: Meet with student individually to assess additional needs.

AASC Lesson Plan 4.2

Lesson Plan Info

AASC Practitioner	Jalen Evans
AASC Animal Partner	Loyal
Counseling Theory	Cognitive Behavioral Therapy
Lesson Plan Title	**Compassionate Thinking**
Type of Lesson	☐ Schoolwide ☐ Classroom ☐ Small-Group ☒ Individual Counseling
Target Audience	Age 10+
Evidence Base	☐ Best Practice ☐ Action Research ☒ Evidence-Based ☐ Research-Informed

ASCA Student Standards Targeted		Student Learning Objectives
Identify 1–2 student standards relevant for this targeted group and goal		For each of the selected student standards, write 1–2 learning objectives
M&B#	**Mindsets & Behaviors Statement**	**Student Learning Objectives**
M 2	Sense of acceptance, respect, support, and inclusion for self and others in the school environment	Increase self-compassion of self through acts of self-compassion for the therapy animal, reducing negative self-talk and self-defeating thought patterns.
B-SMS 6	Ability to identify and overcome barriers	Explore student's negative or self-defeating thoughts and feelings of self and related behaviors. Identify alternate self-compassionate thoughts.

Materials:

For Activity: List of compassionate thinking phrases, paper, pen	For Animal Partner: Hay, water, tunnel, pellets, litterbox, x-pen

Describe how you will:	
Introduce Lesson Topic/Focus:	School counselor will introduce this topic as a way to help improve our thoughts, emotions, and behaviors and help us to utilize more compassion for ourselves.
Communicate the Lesson Objective:	School counselor will explain the objective differently based on the age group and developmental stage of the client. Overall, the objective of this lesson will be to explore the client's thoughts and feelings of self and client's behaviors in relation to thoughts of self; increase self-compassion and reduce negative self-talk.
Teach Content:	• School counselor will explain self-compassion. School counselor will explain that self-compassion includes being understanding of yourself when you fail, suffer, feel inadequate, aren't doing what you think you "should" be doing or what others think you "should" be doing, etc. • School counselor will explain that negative thinking patterns can lead to us feeling certain emotions that may contribute to us behaving in ways that are unhelpful • School counselor will explain that if we work on changing some of those negative thoughts and begin to practice self-compassion, we may begin to feel better about the situation or feel less intense emotions and think more clearly to make more helpful choices in behavior.

Practice Content:	• School counselor will explore client's most common negative thoughts and assesses unrealistic expectations of self (This could be related to academics, sports, debate, family roles, gender identity, etc.)
	• School counselor will provide student with an example of Loyal. Counselor explains that Loyal can decide whether he wants to participate in session.
	• School counselor will then ask questions about this example.
	  • Would we judge Loyal if he decided not to participate?
	  • Would we use should statements because we think Loyal "should" be behaving a certain way? (Such as, "He should be over here" "He shouldn't be hiding" "He should be wanting to cuddle")
	• School counselor will encourage the student to utilize compassion and think about why the animal might not want to participate.
	  • Student can provide examples: "He doesn't know me" "He could be tired" "He is just relaxing; nothing is wrong with that."
	• School counselor will highlight what the animal has accomplished "He is doing the best that he can" "Him being here today says something about who he is"
	• School counselor will cultivate positive alternate responses "I can tell he feels safe and that's good. Next time, maybe he'll come closer."
	• School counselor will assist the student in exploring their own situation and what they can tell themselves when they may not be meeting their own expectations or others'.

Involve Animal Partner:	See above for animal participation. Follow up and process questions are as follows: • What are some ways that Loyal can still be involved even if he does not want to physically participate?

(Continued)

Describe how you will:	
	• What are some ways that Loyal can still be involved even if he does not want to physically participate? • Sounds like you are understanding and supportive of [animal's name] during this time. • How can you use compassionate thinking in your own life? • What are some examples of things that you could tell yourself? Develop a list with the client. Bring a list of compassionate thinking phrases to help spark the discussion.
Assess for Animal Welfare:	Though Loyal would be present and involved in the session, his physical involvement would be limited. Since this session focuses on releasing expectations and "shoulds," there are no requirements of Loyal in this session. School counselor will verbally include Loyal into treatment and Loyal can choose to physically engage with the client at any time.
Summarize/Close:	End the session with a summarization of the topic above and review of the list that the client created. An exit ticket question could be: "What is one phrase on this list that you think you can utilize this week?"

Data Collection Plan	
Participant Data Plan:	
Anticipated number of students:	6
Planned length of lesson(s):	60 minutes
ASCA Student Standards Data Plan:	
Pre/Post Assessment Items: 1. The Self-Compassion Scale Youth Version (10-14; Neff et al., 2021)	
Outcome Data Plan:	
☐ Academic Achievement: ☐ Attendance: ☒ Behavior: Identify need for self-compassion skills to increase confidence in managing emotional and academic success.	
Follow-Up Plans	
Plans for students who missed lesson: Provide worksheet with examples utilized within the group. Plan for students who didn't demonstrate mastery: Provide individual session to gain feedback and re-assess student's needs.	

AASC Lesson Plan 7.1

Lesson Plan Info

AASC Practitioner	Ms. Lopez
AASC Animal Partner	Buster, canine
Counseling Theory	Cognitive Behavioral Therapy
Lesson Plan Title	**Size of Your Problem**
Type of Lesson	☐ Schoolwide ☐ Classroom	☐ Small-Group ☒ Individual Counseling
Target Audience	Hector	
Evidence Base	☐ Best Practice ☒ Action Research	☐ Evidence-Based ☐ Research-Informed

ASCA Student Standards Targeted		Student Learning Objectives
Identify 1–2 student standards relevant for this targeted group and goal		For each of the selected student standards, write 1–2 learning objectives
M&B#	Mindsets & Behaviors Statement	Student Learning Objectives
B-SMS 7	Effective coping skills	Students will categorize possible responses for challenging situations.

Materials:

For Activity: Emoji Sadness Scale	For Animal Partner: None

Describe how you will:	
Introduce Lesson Topic/ Focus:	Identify Hector's issue. Preliminary rating on emoji scale for baseline data
Communicate the Lesson Objective:	Discuss various reactions to challenging situations
Teach Content:	Introduce Buster, including Buster's role in the session. Using Buster as an example, student will identify various problems that Buster could encounter and will categorize them into various sizes of problems.
Practice Content:	Have Hector rate the size of the problem that brought him into the office.
Involve Animal Partner:	See "Teach Content"
Assess for Animal Welfare:	Student will help identify if Buster seems to be having any problems currently and how Buster may communicate that problem.
Summarize/Close:	Have Hector identify his sadness on the emoji scale again.

Data Collection Plan

Participant Data Plan:

Anticipated number of students:	1
Planned length of lesson(s):	30 minutes

ASCA Student Standards Data Plan:

Pre/Post Assessment Items:
1. Size of emotion on Sadness Emoji Scale
   a. Pre-assessment: 5/5
   b. Post-assessment: 2/5
2. Ability to recognize various sizes of problems

Outcome Data Plan:

☒ Academic Achievement: Improved test performance; Improved work completion rates
☐ Attendance:
☒ Behavior: Increased time-on-task through emotional regulation employment

Follow-Up Plans

Plans for students who missed lesson: N/A
Plan for students who didn't demonstrate mastery: Collect follow-up data from the teacher to identify if Hector needs additional lessons related to coping skills. She mentioned that his inability to regulate his emotions impact his test performance and work completion. Additional sessions would be necessary to impact this outcome data further.

AASC Lesson Plan 7.2

Lesson Plan Info

AASC Practitioner	Mr. Wang
AASC Animal Partner	Loyal, Dutch rabbit
Counseling Theory	Cognitive Behavioral Therapy
Lesson Plan Title	**Exploring Careers for My Future**
Type of Lesson	☐ Schoolwide ☒ Classroom	☐ Small-Group ☐ Individual Counseling
Target Audience	5th Graders	
Evidence Base	☐ Best Practice ☐ Action Research	☐ Evidence-Based ☒ Research-Informed

ASCA Student Standards Targeted / Student Learning Objectives

ASCA Student Standards Targeted		Student Learning Objectives
Identify 1–2 student standards relevant for this targeted group and goal		For each of the selected student standards, write 1–2 learning objectives
M&B#	Mindsets & Behaviors Statement	Student Learning Objectives
B-LS 7	Long- and short-term academic, career, and social/emotional goals	Students will analyze information from a variety of sources
		Students will create visual representations to clarify ideas, thoughts, and feelings

Materials:

For Activity:	For Animal Partner:
Copy of lesson plans from Edwin & Prescod (2018). Technology access so students can access information.	Playpen so Loyal can be visible in class yet contained. Food since lessons are 30 minutes long. Toys to keep him entertained and prevent boredom. Hand sanitizer for students.

Describe how you will:	
Introduce Lesson Topic/Focus:	Watch a brief video clip of *Zootopia* and discuss some of jobs that the animals have in the movie.
Communicate the Lesson Objective:	Each week has a different learning objective in this 10-week program. The teacher will introduce the lesson each week, as well as identify what step in the program the students are at each week so they can also develop time awareness.
Teach Content:	Teachers will follow the procedures as developed by Edwin & Prescod (2018).
Practice Content:	After the initial week's lesson, Loyal will be introduced to the classes. From the second week forward, Loyal will be used to practice each lesson before students apply the week's lesson to themselves. For example, students will create possible jobs that Loyal may be interested in. As students research information to include in their tri-fold displays, the counselor will develop a trifold for Loyal as well to use as an example.
Involve Animal Partner:	Loyal will be introduced to the program in week two during the Multiple Intelligences lesson. See "Practice Content"
Assess for Animal Welfare:	Notice signs of stress by Loyal's vocal or physical signs. The noise level in the class may be a source of stress, so it will be important to monitor him for stress and to communicate his needs to students as well. If Loyal needs a break, he does not have to be physically present each week. The classes can reference him without his presence if needed.
Summarize/ Close:	Career fair where students display their tri-fold display on a career of their interest.

Data Collection Plan	
Participant Data Plan:	
Anticipated number of students:	130
Planned length of lesson(s):	4 months; 10 lessons, 30 minutes
ASCA Student Standards Data Plan:	

Pre/Post Assessment Items:
1. Students will have a different topic related to career exploration each week.
   a. Counselor will use call-outs or written exit cards for formative assessment for the week
2. Development of a tri-fold display for a career of interest.
   a. Counselor can assess progress each week on this project

Outcome Data Plan:

☒ Academic Achievement:
   a. Number of students who complete a display board.
   b. Number of students who attend the career fair.
☐ Attendance:
☐ Behavior:

Follow-Up Plans

Plan for students who missed lesson or didn't demonstrate mastery: Since this is a 10-week program, the counselor can assess for mastery at each step and modify subsequent lessons for students who need additional support. Some students may need more guidance than others. Individual sessions between weekly meetings may be necessary for some students.

AASC Lesson Plan 7.3

Lesson Plan Info

AASC Practitioner	Mr. Flores
AASC Animal Partner	Scoot, canine partner
Counseling Theory	Cognitive Behavioral Therapy
Lesson Plan Title	**Caring for Animals and Our Bodies**
Type of Lesson	☒ Schoolwide ☒ Classroom · ☐ Small-Group ☐ Individual Counseling
Target Audience	9th–12th grade
Evidence Base	☒ Best Practice ☐ Action Research · ☐ Evidence-Based ☐ Research-Informed

ASCA Student Standards Targeted		Student Learning Objectives
Identify 1–2 student standards relevant for this targeted group and goal		For each of the selected student standards, write 1–2 learning objectives
M&B#	Mindsets & Behaviors Statement	Student Learning Objectives
M 1	Belief in development of whole self, including a healthy balance of mental, social/emotional, and physical well-being	Students will learn how vaping relates to their overall physical health in order to make more informed decisions.

Materials:

For Activity:	For Animal Partner:
Index card for each student	Water bowl, food bowl, toys

Describe how you will:	
Introduce Lesson Topic/Focus:	Introduce Scoot. Have students write on one side of the card all the things that Scoot needs so he can be taken care of. On the other side, write anything dangerous that he needs to be protected from.
Communicate the Lesson Objective:	Discuss the idea of animal husbandry and how this relates to humans taking care of themselves and others.
Teach Content:	The counselor and nurse present information on vaping and the dangers it presents to the human body using research-informed data.
Practice Content:	Using the index card from earlier, students identify any 'dangers' to Scoot that would be synonymous with vaping in humans. For example, if students wrote that they need to protect Scoot from chemicals, they would highlight or circle this line on their card.
Involve Animal Partner:	See "Introduce Lesson Topic/Focus"
Assess for Animal Welfare:	Animal ethics are a part of this lesson, so the counselor can interweave this idea throughout the lesson. When students discuss what Scoot needs to be taken care of, the counselor can identify the items she brought with her to corroborate their ideas. If he gets stressed, the counselor will care for him by removing him from the environment so he can rest and destress. Students could identify stress in this example as a danger to Scoot.
Summarize/Close:	See "Practice Content"

Data Collection Plan	
Participant Data Plan:	
Anticipated number of students:	500 students, 9th–12th grade
Planned length of lesson(s):	45-minute session. Sessions will be delivered in classrooms over the course of the month.
ASCA Student Standards Data Plan:	

Pre/Post Assessment Items:
1. Ability to identity needs for Scoot
2. Ability to identify things that may harm Scoot
3. Exit index card identifying which dangers to Scoot's are synonymous with vaping in humans.

Outcome Data Plan:

☐ Academic Achievement:
☐ Attendance:
☒ Behavior:
    a. Change in number of placements in In-School-Suspension (ISS) related to vaping
    b. Change in number of Alternative Education Placements (AEP) related to vaping

Follow-Up Plans

Plans for students who missed lesson: The counselor will call in students for small group lessons to cover the topic.
Plan for students who didn't demonstrate mastery: When students are placed in ISS or AEP, the counselor will meet with students individually for more intensive lessons, and possible referrals to local drug addiction programs.

AASC Lesson Plan 7.4

Lesson Plan Info

AASC Practitioner	Krista Schultze
AASC Animal Partner	Snickers, guinea pig
Counseling Theory	Solution-Focused Therapy
Lesson Plan Title	**Managing My Stress**
Type of Lesson	☐ Schoolwide ☐ Classroom ☒ Small-Group ☐ Individual Counseling
Target Audience	6th Graders
Evidence Base	☒ Best Practice ☐ Action Research ☐ Evidence-Based ☐ Research-Informed

ASCA Student Standards Targeted		Student Learning Objectives
Identify 1–2 student standards relevant for this targeted group and goal		For each of the selected student standards, write 1–2 learning objectives
M&B#	Mindsets & Behaviors Statement	Student Learning Objectives
B-SMS 7	Effective coping skills	Students will learn and practice four regulation strategies to regulate their body during times of academic and personal stress.

Materials:

For Activity: Perceived Stress Survey	For Animal Partner: N/A

Describe how you will:	
Introduce Lesson Topic/Focus:	Students identify factors that may stress Snickers. They identify how they may know if Snickers is stressed and what Mrs. Schultze could do to help him when he gets stressed.
Communicate the Lesson Objective:	Students are given the schedule for the next six weeks which includes learning four new regulation strategies.
Teach Content:	Students will learn a new regulation strategy each week. Students share if they utilized the previous week's strategy and if it's a strategy that they found effective. The four regulation strategies include: 1. deep breathing 2. stretching 3. reading 4. collaborative discussions
Practice Content:	Students will first observe if Snickers is demonstrating positive signals (e.g., coming close to students, making happy sounds) or stress signals (e.g., hiding, running away quickly). Students will make guesses about what might be causing Snickers stress, if anything, and what they can do to decrease his stress (e.g., talking softly, giving him space). Mrs. Schultze will share what helps Snickers feel safe. As students learn each regulation strategy, they will practice in class. Mrs. Schultze will notice strengths in the students as they develop and utilize regulation skills. After learning the regulation skill, they will check back with Snickers. They will see if Snickers is interested in playing or showing stress signals.
Involve Animal Partner:	See "Introduce Lesson Topic/Focus" and "Practice Content"
Assess for Animal Welfare:	Students are encouraged to help observe Snickers and to let Mrs. Schultze know if he appears stressed. If he does exhibit signs, the counselor moves him to a dark location so he can feel safer. They then discuss the importance of engaging regulation strategies early.
Summarize/Close:	The sixth week is designed as a wrap-up session. Students rank the four strategies they have learned in order to most effective to least effective for them.

Data Collection Plan	
Participant Data Plan:	
Anticipated number of students:	15 students
Planned length of lesson(s):	6 weeks, 30-minute session/week
ASCA Student Standards Data Plan:	
Pre/Post Assessment Items: 1. Perceived Stress Survey 2. Average academic test scores	
Outcome Data Plan:	
☒ Academic Achievement: Average test scores before/after ☐ Attendance: ☒ Behavior: Average number of days students feel stress, Average number of coping skills students know	
Follow-Up Plans	
Plan for students who missed lesson or didn't demonstrate mastery: Since this is a six-week program, the counselor can assess for mastery at each step and modify subsequent lessons for students who need additional support. Some students may need more guidance than others. Individual sessions between weekly meetings may be necessary for some students.	

AASC Lesson Plan 8.1

Lesson Plan Info		
AASC Practitioner	Elizabeth Hartwig	
AASC Animal Partner	Holly	
Counseling Theory	Solution-Focused Therapy	
Lesson Plan Title	**Emotion Balls**	
Type of Lesson	☐ Schoolwide ☐ Classroom	☐ Small-Group ☒ Individual Counseling
Target Audience	Primary School Level	
Evidence Base	☒ Best Practice ☐ Action Research	☐ Evidence-Based ☐ Research-Informed

ASCA Student Standards Targeted		Student Learning Objectives
Identify 1–2 student standards relevant for this targeted group and goal		For each of the selected student standards, write 1–2 learning objectives
M&B#	**Mindsets & Behaviors Statement**	Student Learning Objectives
M1	Belief in development of whole self, including a healthy balance of mental, social/emotional, and physical well-being	Identify and discuss feelings and emotions
B-SMS 1	Responsibility to self and actions	Gain insight into when one feels various emotions
B-SMS 7	Effective coping skills	Gain tools to manage feelings effectively

Materials:	
For Activity: Emotion Balls (balls with emotion faces on them)	For Animal Partner: Treats hidden with the emotion balls to help animal partner find them

Describe how you will:	
Introduce Lesson Topic/Focus:	The animal partner will find emotion balls to help the student talk about emotions and how to manage them effectively.
Communicate the Lesson Objective:	This activity helps a student learn emotion identification, which is important for emotional regulation. Through processing the activity, the student can also work to build skills to effectively manage various emotions.
Teach Content:	The student will hide the emotion balls around the room and the animal partner works to find the balls. Each time the animal finds an emotion ball, the counselor asks the child to talk about a time they felt that way. Throughout this activity, the counselor with identify strengths in the child.
Practice Content:	School counselor will use processing questions: • Talk about a time when you felt [this emotion]. • What led you to feel that way? • Who supported you when you felt that way? • What are some things you can do in the future to help cope with this feeling effectively? • What did you learn about your feelings from this activity?
Involve Animal Partner:	The animal partner finds the emotion balls.
Assess for Animal Welfare:	The animal should have access to water and a place to "stay." The counselor will assess the animal throughout activity to ascertain that the animal is engaged and stress-free. Breaks will be provided for the animal as needed. The animal has a choice to participate or not.
Summarize/Close:	The student will review what was learned and will practice identifying emotions throughout rest of the week.

Data Collection Plan	
Participant Data Plan:	
Anticipated number of students:	1
Planned length of lesson(s):	30–45 minutes
ASCA Student Standards Data Plan:	

Pre/Post Assessment Items:
1. Student's ability to identify different feelings
2. Student's ability to identify and practice various effective coping strategies

Outcome Data Plan:

☐ Academic Achievement:
☐ Attendance:
☒ Behavior: Child will be able to demonstrate one way of coping with a difficult emotion.

Follow-Up Plans

Plans for students who missed lesson: Counselor will plan for the student to make up the lesson when the student is present.
Plan for students who didn't demonstrate mastery: Counselor will revisit the lesson and may provide additional examples as needed. Counselor may provide an example related to the animal partner (i.e., "Holly feels frustrated when she has to stop playing ball").

AASC Lesson Plan 8.2

Lesson Plan Info

AASC Practitioner	Joy Cannon
AASC Animal Partner	Rufus
Counseling Theory	Child-Centered Play Therapy
Lesson Plan Title	**Nondirective Play Session**
Type of Lesson	☐ Schoolwide ☐ Classroom ☐ Small-Group ☒ Individual Counseling
Target Audience	Primary School Level
Evidence Base	☒ Best Practice ☐ Action Research ☐ Evidence-Based ☐ Research-Informed

ASCA Student Standards Targeted / Student Learning Objectives

Identify 1–2 student standards relevant for this targeted group and goal

For each of the selected student standards, write 1–2 learning objectives

M&B#	Mindsets & Behaviors Statement	Student Learning Objectives
M2	Sense of acceptance, respect, support, and inclusion for self and others in the school environment	Express thoughts and feelings through play
M4	Self-confidence in ability to succeed	Increase confidence by making choices through play
B-SS 3	Positive relationships with adults to support success	Develop relationship with counselor through play
B-SS 4	Empathy	Demonstrate empathy

Materials:

For Activity: Playroom with expressive toys in various play therapy categories	For Animal Partner: Treats as needed

Describe how you will:	
Introduce Lesson Topic/Focus:	The student will direct play with the animal partner present.
Communicate the Lesson Objective:	This activity allows the student to direct play without expectations for how to play. The student chooses what toys they will play with and how they will play with them.
Teach Content:	The school counselor introduces the play space and reminds the student how to keep self and animal safe: "This is the playroom and there are lots of toys as well as Rufus in here! We want to make sure that Rufus can play safely and happily. Let's check with Rufus during our playtime to make sure he is feeling safe and happy. Rufus can choose to play or not to play. You can play with the toys in a lot of ways you would like and with Rufus in the way he likes."
Practice Content:	The child plays in the play space. The counselor uses CCPT facilitative skills both from both their perspective and the dog's perspective. The counselor follows the child's play actively to communicate: I'm here; I hear you; I understand; I care.
Involve Animal Partner:	The animal partner is the counselor's partner in all play activities. The animal partner will be involved in activities that they choose/like. Counselor will reflect animal's behavior throughout play.
Assess for Animal Welfare:	The animal partner should be with the school counselor at all times and only be involved in activities that they like. For example, if the dog does not like to dress up, the school counselor could have different bandanas to use instead of costumes, or let the student know the dog does not like dressing up. The animal should have access to water and a place to be away from the play, if needed. The counselor will assess the animal throughout the activity to ascertain that the animal is engaged and stress-free. Breaks will be provided for the animal as needed.
Summarize/Close:	Notice and track the child's play and interactions with the animal partner. Enlarge meaning of play themes expressed by child across multiple sessions.

Data Collection Plan	
Participant Data Plan:	
Anticipated number of students:	1
Planned length of lesson(s):	30–45 minutes

ASCA Student Standards Data Plan:

Pre/Post Assessment Items:
1. Student's ability to express and process thoughts/feelings through play
2. Student's ability to demonstrate empathy through play
3. Student's ability to demonstrate confidence and self-discovery through play

Outcome Data Plan:

☐ Academic Achievement:
☐ Attendance:
☒ Behavior: Child will express 1-2 feelings during play.

Follow-Up Plans

Plans for students who missed lesson: The counselor will make a plan for the student to make up the lesson when the student is present.
Plan for students who didn't demonstrate mastery: Counselor will revisit the lesson until mastery is obtained.

AASC Lesson Plan 8.3

AASC Practitioner	Heidi Schilling
AASC Animal Partner	Denali
Counseling Theory	Cognitive Behavioral Therapy
Lesson Plan Title	**Animal Obstacle Course Challenge**
Type of Lesson	☐ Schoolwide ☐ Classroom ☐ Small-Group ☒ Individual Counseling
Target Audience	Primary School Level
Evidence Base	☒ Best Practice ☐ Action Research ☐ Evidence-Based ☐ Research-Informed

ASCA Student Standards Targeted		Student Learning Objectives
Identify 1–2 student standards relevant for this targeted group and goal		For each of the selected student standards, write 1–2 learning objectives
M&B#	Mindsets & Behaviors Statement	Student Learning Objectives
M1	Belief in development of whole self, including a healthy balance of mental, social/emotional, and physical wellbeing	Student will identify two feelings during play
M4	Self-confidence in the ability to succeed	Student will increase confidence by expressing thoughts
B-SMS 1	Responsibility to self and actions	Student will make choices during play
B-SMS 2	Self-discipline and self-control	Student will follow limits that are set
B-SMS 6	Ability to identify and overcome barriers	Student will demonstrate frustration tolerance

Materials:

For Activity: Various items to create an obstacle course: May include, but are not limited to hula hoop, tunnel, cones, jump hurdles, boxes, things to climb on or go under, puzzles, snuffle mat-anything in the environment that can create a safe obstacle	For Animal Partner: Treats as needed. Note: Dog agility equipment can be utilized but is not needed. Something to consider is that using items in the space allows for more creativity and participation by the student. However, dog agility equipment could be utilized in the beginning with a student who feels anxious by picking items. As the student gains more confidence, they could move to choosing their own items.

Describe how you will:	
Introduce Lesson Topic/Focus:	The student will lead the animal through an obstacle course that they have created for the animal.
Communicate the Lesson Objective:	By creating an obstacle course and leading an animal through it, this provides an opportunity for an adolescent to practice various skills (problem solving, frustration tolerance, etc.), while also beginning to explore how to overcome obstacles and/or what it can feel like to overcome obstacles. If a student is in a hypo-aroused state ("shut down"), this is also a good activity to get the adolescent moving, which may help change their emotional state.
Teach Content:	Discuss challenges in the animal's life and then discuss challenges in the student's life. The school counselor will use processing questions at the end (can choose a few relevant ones): • What was it like to do that activity? • What helped the animal succeed? What did you do to help the animal? • When did the animal face a challenge during this activity and what was leading to the challenge? • How did you know the animal was facing a challenge? • What helped the animal resolve the challenge It was facing? • Refer back to the challenges the adolescent mentioned in the beginning of the session … what can you do in your life to work through challenges? • Who can help you with challenges you face? How can they help you? • What unhelpful thoughts do you have about your challenges and how can you reframe them to more helpful ones (If youth is having a hard time doing this, student can identify thoughts they had about the animal's struggles and then practice generalizing to own situation). If the animal chooses his/her own path on the obstacle course and/or does not follow the student, this can be processed as well: • How did this feel? • What leads someone to not follow someone else? • How do you relate to this? If the purpose of the activity is to get the student moving, above process questions may be skipped. Focus on how they felt before the obstacle course, how they felt after, and what created the difference.
Practice Content:	The student will create the obstacle course using various items in the space. They will then identify challenges the animal may face during the course and/or can identify various parts of the course to represent challenges in their own life. The student will problem solve how to help the animal complete the obstacle course. If the animal does not complete any or all of the course, this can be processed.
Involve Animal Partner:	The student will lead the animal through the course.

(Continued)

Describe how you will:	
Assess for Animal Welfare:	The animal should have access to water and a place to "stay." The counselor will assess the animal throughout the activity to ascertain that the animal is engaged and stress-free. Breaks will be provided for the animal as needed. The animal has the choice not to participate. The student can choose which direction they would like the animal to go through the course, however, it is important to remind the student that the animal has a choice.
Summarize/ Close:	The student will review what was learned and will practice skills throughout the week.

Data Collection Plan	
Participant Data Plan:	
Anticipated number of students:	1
Planned length of lesson(s):	30–45 minutes
ASCA Student Standards Data Plan:	

Pre/Post Assessment Items:
1. Student's demonstration of acceptance of challenges
2. Student's ability to problem solve and identify ways to overcome challenges
3. Student's ability to effectively reframe unhelpful thoughts
4. Student's ability to tolerate and manage feelings effectively
5. Student's identification of benefit of being able to make own choices

Outcome Data Plan:

☐ Academic Achievement:
☐ Attendance:
☒ Behavior: Student will demonstrate ability to make choices in their play.

Follow-Up Plans

Plans for students who missed lesson: The counselor will make a plan for the student to make up the lesson when the student is present.
Plan for students who didn't demonstrate mastery: The student can continue to create an obstacle course for the animal partner in future lessons and continue to reflect on process questions.

AASC Lesson Plan 8.4

Lesson Plan Info

AASC Practitioner	Heidi Schilling
AASC Animal Partner	Denali
Counseling Theory	Solution-Focused Therapy
Lesson Plan Title	**The Floor is Lava**
Type of Lesson	☐ Schoolwide ☐ Classroom / ☐ Small-Group ☒ Individual Counseling
Target Audience	Secondary Level
Evidence Base	☒ Best Practice ☐ Action Research / ☐ Evidence-Based ☐ Research-Informed

ASCA Student Standards Targeted		Student Learning Objectives
Identify 1–2 student standards relevant for this targeted group and goal		For each of the selected student standards, write 1–2 learning objectives
M&B#	Mindsets & Behaviors Statement	Student Learning Objectives
M4	Self-confidence in the ability to succeed	Identify two personal strengths
B-SMS 6	Ability to identify and overcome barriers	Identify one thing that they could do differently
B-SMS 10	Ability to manage transitions and adapt to change	Identify two coping skills they are already using

Materials:

For Activity: Multiple hula hoops of different colors	For Animal Partner: Treats for animal as needed

Describe how you will:	
Introduce Lesson Topic/Focus:	The student will identify strengths and what is improving for them week to week through the use of a game and the animal partner.
Communicate the Lesson Objective:	The student will gain feelings of competency, come up with solutions, and try them out in the moment. The counselor lets the student know that the floor is "lava" and they cannot walk on it. The counselor identifies that the goal is for the student to get from one end of the room to the other, by jumping from hula hoop to hula hoop.
Teach Content:	Different colored hula hoops will represent a different prompt/question the student will have to answer. For example: • Red = Name a strength (or positive attribute). • Blue = What has been better for you this week compared to last? • Yellow = What is a coping skill you have been using that is working well? • Green = What is something you can do differently this week that may be helpful?
Practice Content:	The student can choose whichever pathway they want and will encourage the dog to follow their path. The student choosing their own pathway facilitates competence in self. Allowing the student to choose to change pathways if they are not feeling successful with the first path also helps to achieve feelings of competence. The student will answer the prompts. If the student or animal goes into the lava, the student will identify what they could do differently or how they can help the animal be successful (i.e., make changes/accommodations for the animal as needed).
Involve Animal Partner:	The animal partner will follow along and the student is encouraged to help the animal follow his/her path. The student and/or the counselor will answer prompts for the animal. The student will help identify what will help the animal be successful. If the adolescent is having a hard time naming their own strengths, they can start with the animal partner's strengths and then see if they can expand from the animal to themselves.
Assess for Animal Welfare:	The animal should have access to water and a place to "stay." The counselor will assess the animal throughout the activity to ascertain that the animal is engaged and stress-free. Breaks will be provided for the animal as needed. The animal has choice not to participate.
Summarize/Close:	The counselor can review the activity with student through the use of discussion/processing questions: • What helped you to be successful during the game? • What helped your animal partner be successful during the game? • How can you take what helped you and/or the animal partner be successful and generalize it to everyday life? If the student chose a different pathway than their initial choice: • What helped you to be more successful with a different path? • What might it look like to change a path (or part of a path) in real life?

Data Collection Plan	
Participant Data Plan:	
Anticipated number of students:	1
Planned length of lesson(s):	30–45 minutes

ASCA Student Standards Data Plan:

Pre/Post Assessment Items:
1. Student's ability to identify strengths
2. Student's ability to identify improvements from week to week
3. Student's ability to identify effective coping strategies they utilize
4. Student's ability to identify what they can do differently related to current challenges
5. Student's ability to focus on and identify solutions

Outcome Data Plan:

☐ Academic Achievement:
☐ Attendance:
☒ Behavior: Student is able to identify 1–2 personal strengths.

Follow-Up Plans

Plans for students who missed lesson: The counselor will plan for the student to make up the lesson when the student is present.
Plan for students who didn't demonstrate mastery: Counselor will revisit the lesson until mastery is obtained.

AASC Lesson Plan 9.1

Lesson Plan Info

AASC Practitioner	Heather Trupia
AASC Animal Partner	Ahsoka
Counseling Theory	Adlerian Therapy
Lesson Plan Title	**Weekly Student Greeting**
Type of Lesson	☒ Schoolwide ☐ Classroom ☐ Small-Group ☐ Individual Counseling
Target Audience	Grades Pre- K - 5
Evidence Base	☒ Best Practice ☐ Action Research ☐ Evidence-Based ☒ Research-Informed

ASCA Student Standards Targeted / Student Learning Objectives

ASCA Student Standards Targeted		Student Learning Objectives
Identify 1–2 student standards relevant for this targeted group and goal		For each of the selected student standards, write 1–2 learning objectives
M&B#	Mindsets & Behaviors Statement	Student Learning Objectives
B-SS-3	Positive relationships with adults to support success	Students will make connections and build a positive relationship with the counselor and the animal partner.

Materials:

For Activity: Animal Partner	For Animal Partner: Leash

Describe how you will:	
Introduce Lesson Topic/Focus:	The goal of this activity is to foster a positive school environment where students feel safe, and a sense of belonging and connection.
Communicate the Lesson Objective:	Students will engage with the counselor and animal partner to build connections and a positive relationship. This activity demonstrates Adlerian therapy's first phase of building a therapeutic relationship.
Teach Content:	Greetings and Discussions • Teach students how to approach the animal partner and to wait patiently while students before them greet the counselor and animal partner in prior in classroom lessons or schoolwide assembly. Practice waiting in a line to have nor more than 1 or 2 students at a time greeting you and your animal partner. • Greet students with a smile and demonstrate a positive interaction
Practice Content:	Implementation guidelines: • Set days for the counselor and animal partner to be a designated spot. • Be consistent in positively interacting with students and the animal partner.
Involve Animal Partner:	• Animal partner is next to counselor • Students and animal partner greet each other (possibly having the animal partner give high fives or shake hands) • Student pets the animal partner
Assess for Animal Welfare:	Assess your partner's comfort and willingness to participate in greeting students. Position you and the animal partner in a safe place where students have room to make a line to greet you. If your animal shows signs of stress and needs a break away from students, take the animal on a break.
Summarize/Close:	During dismissal, greet and say farewell to students, telling them you and your animal partner can't wait to see them soon.

Data Collection Plan	
Participant Data Plan:	
Anticipated number of students:	150–300
Planned length of lesson(s):	20 minutes
ASCA Student Standards Data Plan:	
Pre/Post Assessment Items: 1. Student Surveys 2. Observation	
Outcome Data Plan:	
☐ Academic Achievement: ☐ Attendance: ☒ Behavior: Students will complete feedback forms on what they think about the animal greeting activity.	

Follow-Up Plans

Plans for students who missed lesson: Be at your station regularly so that students can rely on the consistency of seeing you to start the day, as well as knowing they will get to greet the animal partner on the next planned day.

Plan for students who didn't demonstrate mastery: Schedule small group lunch bunches with you and your animal partner.

AASC Lesson Plan 9.2

Lesson Plan Info

AASC Practitioner	Heather Trupia
AASC Animal Partner	Ahsoka
Counseling Theory	Adlerian Therapy
Lesson Plan Title	**Get Caught Being Pawsitive**
Type of Lesson	☒ Schoolwide ☐ Classroom / ☐ Small-Group ☐ Individual Counseling
Target Audience	Grades K - 5
Evidence Base	☒ Best Practice ☐ Action Research / ☐ Evidence-Based ☐ Research-Informed

ASCA Student Standards Targeted / Student Learning Objectives

Identify 1–2 student standards relevant for this targeted group and goal | For each of the selected student standards, write 1–2 learning objectives

M&B#	Mindsets & Behaviors Statement	Student Learning Objectives
M.2	Sense of acceptance, respect, support, and inclusion for self and others in the school environment	Students will act in a way that respects and supports their peers.
B-SS 2	Positive, respectful, and supportive relationships with students who are similar to and different from them	Students will be able to highlight and embrace positive actions of self and others.

Materials:

For Activity:
- Paw print hearts or "Get Caught being Pawsitive" forms
- Posters

For Animal Partner:
- Pictures of your animal partner doing kind things or people doing something kind for them.

Describe how you will:	
Introduce Lesson Topic/Focus:	In order to foster a positive school environment and increase students' sense of belonging and well-being, focusing on catching students being "Pawsitive" is a great twist to "caught being kind." You can focus on year-long challenges or create short-term challenges with various spins or focus throughout the year.
Communicate the Lesson Objective:	• Teachers will focus on catching students being positive or doing kind acts. • Students will focus on catching teachers and other students being positive or doing kind acts. • The overall school climate will increase in positivity and kindness. • Focusing on the positive will foster better academic and student well-being outcomes.
Teach Content:	Read Aloud - a book about kindness. Have class and/or school-wide discussions about what being positive and showing kindness looks like. This is a great time to do reminder training on the correct way to greet and treat your animal partners. Discussion/Processing Questions: • What is something positive that you say to someone? • What is something kind that you can do for someone today? • What is something kind (animal partner) does for our school? • What is something kind you can do for (animal partner)?
Practice Content:	• Begin the challenge by catching students being kind or positive during your lesson or discussion on kindness and positivity. • Think-Pair-Share - 1-2 positive things to say or do, and 1-2 acts of kindness. • Have a mailbox or dropbox where staff and students can place their forms. • Announce students/staff who are "caught" on daily announcements (possibly have them go to you for a pawsitive pin or kindness sticker, etc.) • Hang up forms on a Pawsitive Wall of Fame
Involve Animal Partner:	Your animal partner can be part of the discussions in presence and example. Take photos of your animal partner both giving and receiving kindness.
Assess for Animal Welfare:	Assess your partner's willingness to participate in the activity. Have a centralized comfortable bed for them to lay in if they want to withdraw from walking around and interacting but will still allow students to see them. If they need a break away from students, allow them to do so in their safe place. Have a picture(s) available to use to engage students in discussion instead as needed.
Summarize/ Close:	Think - Pair - Share: What is something kind that you wish someone would do for you?

Data Collection Plan	
Participant Data Plan:	
Anticipated number of students:	15–25
Planned length of lesson(s):	30–45 minutes
ASCA Student Standards Data Plan:	
Pre/Post Assessment Items: 1. Describe something kind that someone has done for you this week. 2. Describe something kind that you did for someone else this week. 3. Describe something positive that you said to someone this week. 4. Describe something positive that someone said to you this week.	
Outcome Data Plan:	
☐ Academic Achievement: ☐ Attendance: ☒ Behavior: Students will create a positive school environment by being caught being kind and positive and catching other being kind and positive.	
Follow-Up Plans	
Plans for students who missed the lesson: Pull students who missed the lesson for a make-up session. Plan for students who didn't demonstrate mastery: Think-Pair-Share: Brainstorm things that you can do or say that are kind and positive. Take and print photos showing examples (speech bubbles can be added to photos). Create a poster with these ideas to hang around the school building.	

AASC Lesson Plan 9.3

Lesson Plan Info	
AASC Practitioner	Heather Trupia
AASC Animal Partner	Ahsoka
Counseling Theory	Cognitive Behavioral Therapy
Lesson Plan Title	**Exploring Identity**
Type of Lesson	☐ Schoolwide ☒ Classroom / ☐ Small-Group ☐ Individual Counseling
Target Audience	Grades K - 5
Evidence Base	☐ Best Practice ☐ Action Research / ☐ Evidence-Based ☒ Research-Informed

ASCA Student Standards Targeted		Student Learning Objectives
Identify 1–2 student standards relevant for this targeted group and goal		For each of the selected student standards, write 1–2 learning objectives
M&B#	**Mindsets & Behaviors Statement**	**Student Learning Objectives**
M.2	Sense of acceptance, respect, support, and inclusion for self and others in the school environment	Students will be able to identify differences in themselves and others and create an inclusive environment. Students will use strategies to learn more about each other.
B-SS 2	Positive, respectful, and supportive relationships with students who are similar to and different from them	Students will be able to support and embrace the differences in themselves and others. Students will look beyond what they see on the surface to get to know others.

Materials:	
For Activity: • Photos of dogs – including your animal partner • Your animal partner • Outline drawing of your animal partner • Outline drawing of a person (or students can draw themselves) • A read-aloud book that is related to identity, being unique, making assumptions when meeting a new student, etc. Examples: *Grandad's Secret Giant* by David Litchfield *Marisol Doesn't Match* by Monica Brown *The Boy Who Grew Flowers* by Jen Wojtowicz *Stand Tall Molly Lou Melon* by Patty Lovell *Big Al* by Andrew Clements *Demo: Story of a Junkyard Dog* by John Bozak & Scott Bruns	For Animal Partner: • Comfortable bed/space • Treat

Describe how you will:	
Introduce Lesson Topic/Focus:	There are many parts to a person's identity. Some are easy to see, and others are more complex and take time to discover. When you first meet them, you can only see a limited view of their identity, such as hair color, height, the color of skin, clothing style, etc. There is much more not visible that we can learn, such as likes & dislikes, personality, opinions, expertise, social identity, etc. This lesson can easily be related to our animal partners.
Communicate the Lesson Objective:	• Students will explore what makes up your animal partner's identity, then relate it to their own identity and the identity of their classmates. • Students will reflect on the importance of getting to know people beyond what we can see on the outside and not making assumptions. • Students will discuss strategies for getting to know people.
Teach Content:	Discussion/Processing Questions: • What can you see about (person or animal)'s identity by just looking at them? • What can't you see or know about their identity by just looking at them? • Has anyone ever made an incorrect assumption about you? How did it make you feel?
	Activities • Have a class discussion on what identity means. • Discuss what you can see about your animal partner just by looking at them • Discuss what you can't see about your animal partner by just looking at them, as if you never met them before (i.e., whether they like people, are cuddly, might hurt someone, etc.) • Think-Pair-Share - 1–2 things about yourself that you can see, and 1–2 things about yourself that you can't see. (can do with one partner, with groups, or with movement to new partners) • Read Aloud - relate questions to identity, making incorrect assumptions, getting to know someone, etc. • Chart size outlines drawing of your pet - as a class, put the things we can see on the outside and the things we need or would like to learn on the inside.
Practice Content:	Discussion/Processing Questions: • How can we ensure that we are not making assumptions about someone? • How do you want someone to get to know you? • What are some ways we can learn about people beyond what we can only see by looking at them? Why do you think it is important to do this? Activity • Give students copies of an outline of a person, or have students create a drawing of themselves. Put the things we can see on the outside of the person and the things we would like people to know about us on the inside of the person. Share and/or hang the drawings.
Involve Animal Partner:	Bring your animal partner into the discussion area or walk around the classroom allowing students to pet or interact with them. Cue your animal partner to do such things as sit, laydown, high-five, or other various tricks.

(Continued)

Describe how you will:	
Assess for Animal Welfare:	Assess your partner's willingness to participate in the activity. Have a centralized comfortable bed for them to lay in if they want to withdraw from walking around and interacting but will still allow students to see them. If they need a break away from students, allow them to do so in their safe place. Have a picture(s) available to use to engage students in discussion instead as needed.
Summarize/ Close:	Think-Pair-Share: • Think of several questions that you can ask your partner to get to know them more. • Pair – take turns asking and answering questions to get to know each other better. • Share with the class something new that you learned about your partner and if you found out something that you have in common with them.

Data Collection Plan

Participant Data Plan:

Anticipated number of students:	15–25
Planned length of lesson(s):	30–45 minutes

ASCA Student Standards Data Plan:

Pre/Post Assessment Items:
1. What is one thing that you know about someone by looking at them?
2. What is one thing that you cannot tell about someone by just looking at them?
3. Describe 3 things about yourself that someone might not be able to see by just looking at you.
4. Describe 3 things about a friend that you cannot tell by just looking at them.

Outcome Data Plan:

☐ Academic Achievement:
☐ Attendance:
☒ Behavior: Students will create a positive environment by accepting each other's differences, and looking past what they see on the surface to get to know others.

Follow-Up Plans

Plans for students who missed the lesson:
Pull students who missed the lesson for a make-up session.
Plan for students who didn't demonstrate mastery:
Partner students up and give them the task of learning about their partner. Have them create a poster that will help the rest of the class get to know them. Have them explain what things they learned that they can see, and what things they learned that they couldn't see. Discuss how they learned about the things they could not see.

AASC Lesson Plan 9.4

Lesson Plan Info

AASC Practitioner	Missy Whitsett
AASC Animal Partner	Gus
Counseling Theory	Cognitive Behavioral Therapy
Lesson Plan Title	**PAWs Down Against Bullying**
Type of Lesson	☒ Schoolwide ☐ Classroom · ☐ Small-Group ☐ Individual Counseling
Target Audience	Grades 6–12
Evidence Base	☐ Best Practice ☐ Action Research · ☐ Evidence-Based ☒ Research-Informed

ASCA Student Standards Targeted / Student Learning Objectives

ASCA Student Standards Targeted		Student Learning Objectives
Identify 1–2 student standards relevant for this targeted group and goal		For each of the selected student standards, write 1–2 learning objectives
M&B#	Mindsets & Behaviors Statement	Student Learning Objectives
M 2	Sense of acceptance, respect, support, and inclusion for self and others in the school environment	Students will learn about bullying, self-acceptance, and social pressure.
B-SS 2	Positive, respectful, and supportive relationships with students who are similar to and different from them	Students will learn about tolerance and acceptance of others with strategies to be positive towards others.

Materials:

For Activity: Paper paw prints, animal talking app for morning announcements, large jar/container of dog treats, form for social pressure game.	For Animal Partner: Nothing extra needed

Describe how you will:	
Introduce Lesson Topic/Focus:	Throughout the week, students will take part in short lessons and interactive activities that seek to expand their knowledge about bullying and ask them to think critically and thoughtfully about themselves and others.
Communicate the Lesson Objective:	Throughout the week, students will gain awareness of what bullying is and how it affects them. They will discuss bullying, self-acceptance, tolerance and acceptance of others, social pressures, and positive ways to interact with others.
Teach Content:	Daily Announcements from Gus: Announcements should be made during a class where teachers can spend a few minutes after letting the class process/discuss the information either as a large class or in small groups. If possible, you can prerecord these with a talking animal app and share the videos with teachers to share. This is a fun way for everyone to interact with the therapy animal! Sample announcements are listed at the end of this document.

Daily Activities:
These should be planned and advertised ahead of time so that everyone has time to prepare. Daily activities are listed at the end of this document.
Daily Announcements and Activities are outlined at the end of this document by day of the week.

PAWs Down Against Bullying Poster Contest: |
| | A couple of weeks to a month before this event, share this event with the student body. Have them create a poster, inspired by your therapy animal that takes a positive stand against bullying and highlights your theme. They can be showcased in a gallery walk, on an online platformplatform, or whatever works for your campus. Invite district staff members to vote for their favorites and announce winners on the last day of the week. They can also be shared on social media platforms for the school and district. |
| Practice Content: | This will be done through daily discussions and activities shared in the morning announcements. |
| Involve Animal Partner: | Announcements: use an animal talking app to record daily messages and share the videos with teachers for them to share or share on a school-wide platform if possible.

Dress Up Days: if the therapy animal enjoys it, they could wear themed costumes, shirts, vests, bandanas, socks, bowties, etc.

Contest winners could be offered special time with the therapy animal if it's logistically possible. |
| Assess for Animal Welfare: | Dress-up (costumes, shirts, or other things) should only be done if the dog enjoys it. |
| Summarize/Close: | Closing will be done with the final daily announcement listed below. |

Data Collection Plan

Participant Data Plan:

Anticipated number of students:	Whole Student Body
Planned length of lesson(s):	1 week

ASCA Student Standards Data Plan:

Pre/Post Assessment Items:
1. I know what bullying is.
2. I know what bullying is not.
3. I know what it means to connect with others.
4. I know what it means to belong to something.
5. I know what individuality is.
6. I know how to make decisions for myself.
7. I know what it means to treat others with kindness.

Outcome Data Plan:

☒ Achievement: Students can define and describe what bullying is and who can be involved. Students can identify what it means to belong and feel connected. Students can understand self-acceptance and individuality.
☐ Attendance:
☐ Behavior:

Follow-Up Plans

Plans for students who missed the lesson: Announcements and activities can be shared by classroom teachers live or in google classrooms for those students who may have been absent.
Plan for students who didn't demonstrate mastery: Students may be monitored and or referred for small group or one-on-one counseling.

Paws Down Against Bullying Weekly Schedule

Monday

Daily Announcement:	Good morning (insert mascot name here) and welcome to the first day of our PAWs Down for Bullying week! Every day, we will share an announcement that will ask you to think about an aspect of bullying. We encourage you to engage in positive discussions. Your teachers have printed paw prints available to you. Throughout the week, please write down positive statements and thoughts as we discuss the different aspects of bullying throughout the week. Turn them in in the front office and we will hang them in the main hallway! Today, we are going to define bullying. The Anti-Bullying Alliance defines bullying as the repetitive, intentional hurting of one person or group by another person or group, where the relationship involves an imbalance of power. Bullying can be physical, verbal, or psychological and can happen face-to-face or online. Within your groups discuss what it means to be bullied, to be a bully, and to be an upstander. Discuss how we can work together to stop bullying within our student body. The counseling and admin team would love to hear your ideas!
Daily Activity:	Paw Print Messages: Print and cut out paw prints for teachers to have students write positive messages, statements, and thoughts about bullying. Paws should be turned into the front office and will be hung in a designated area (e.g., main hallways, foyer, etc.)

Tuesday

Daily Announcement:	Good morning (insert mascot name here)! Welcome to Odd Sock Day! Dr. Suess said, "Today you are you, that is truer than true. There is no one alive who is you-er than you." Today is a great day to think about who you are and who you want to be and then celebrate it! With your groups, discuss individuality. What does that mean to you? Is it easy to be who you are? What stops you? What inspires you? Is there anything others could do to help you?
Daily Activity:	Odd Socks Day: Encourage everyone to wear and show off their odd socks. This is an opportunity to show our unique personalities and celebrate differences.

Wednesday	
Daily Announcement:	Good morning (insert mascot name here)! Today we are going to talk about social pressures and protecting yourself. This is a tough one because it's easy to feel as though you can't say no to things. It may feel easier to go along with someone rather than creating a conflict. But maybe today, you decide it's time to take care of yourself and be your own superhero. You have control over what goes in your body, and what activities you take part in. Your friends or classmates may decide to make choices that could hurt them, but that does not mean you have to join them. Say no to the things that are not good for you or could hurt you. Take care of yourself. Protect yourself. You are the only you on this planet and we need you!!! Your teacher will share today's discussion activity! Good luck!!
Daily Activity:	Social Pressure Game: How many dog treats? (a picture of the dog treat jar will be shared along with the dimensions of the container. The jar will also be displayed all week in the front office) 1. Using the "How Many Dog Treats" form provided, have students do part 1 alone. 2. Once they have completed part 1, have them get into small groups. The goal of the group is to come up with 1 answer for the group. This will be part 2 of the form. 3. Have them go back to being alone to answer part 3 of the form. 4. Collect the forms and keep in a safe place. 5. On Friday, Celebrate the individual(s) with the closest answer and the small group with the closest answer. (Rewards could be a sweet treat, extra credit, lunch with the teacher … anything you like) Superhero Day! The message today talks about being your own superhero. Everyone is encouraged to wear something that represents their favorite superhero.

Thursday	
Daily Announcement:	Good morning (insert mascot name here) and welcome to Belonging and Connection Day! Today is the day we celebrate what it means to belong and be connected. Today, we do this by wearing our _____(name) School colors of _____and_____ . We are all connected to the _____(school name) and _____(district name) family. Belonging comes from being yourself and being seen. That can happen even with people who are totally different from you, even with people who want different things and believe different things. Connecting with others can boost your happiness, reduce stress, build confidence, and even help your physical health! You belong. You matter! Discussion questions: How do you connect with people? What could help you connect with others? What might stop you from connecting with others? How can you be helpful to those who are struggling to connect with others?
Daily Activity:	Everyone should be wearing school colors to show belonging and connection.

Friday	
Daily Announcement:	Good morning (insert mascot name here) and happy Friday!! Today we are celebrating our school and you by sharing the winners of our Door Decorating Contest, Our Gus Inspired Poster Contest, and the Official number of Dog Treats in the jar!!! 1. Announce all winners and prizes. 2. Thanks to all of you for joining us this week in celebration of who we are, how we fit in and contribute to our school, our families, and our communities. I look forward to seeing you all in the halls and classrooms!
Daily Activity:	Wear a shirt that spreads kindness.

How Many Dog Treats?

Name: _____   Class Period: _____

Part 1 (individual)
Do your friends influence you to make decisions? (circle one)

———— Never ———— A little ———— Sometimes ———— A lot ———— Always ————

How many dog treats are in the jar? _____

Part 2 (small group)
How many dog treats are in the jar? (agree on 1 answer for the group) _____

Part 3 (individual)
Do your friends influence you to make decisions? (circle one)

———— Never ———— A little ———— Sometimes ———— A lot ———— Always ————

How many dog treats are in the jar? _____

Paw Print Handout

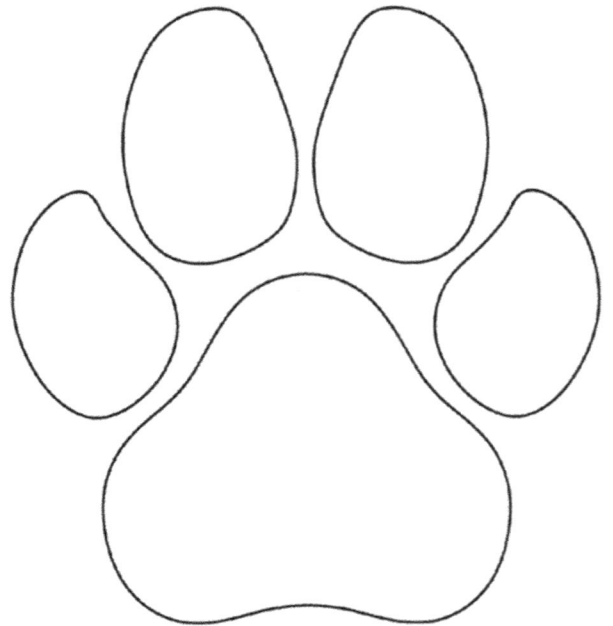

AASC Lesson Plan 9.5

AASC Practitioner	Created by Amy Hutchinson, Adapted by Missy Whitsett	
AASC Animal Partner	Gus	
Counseling Theory	Choice Theory	
Lesson Plan Title	**Personal Space and Needs**	
Type of Lesson	☐ Schoolwide ☒ Classroom	☐ Small-Group ☐ Individual Counseling
Target Audience	Grades 6–12	
Evidence Base	☐ Best Practice ☐ Action Research	☐ Evidence-Based ☒ Research-Informed

ASCA Student Standards Targeted		Student Learning Objectives
Identify 1–2 student standards relevant for this targeted group and goal		For each of the selected student standards, write 1–2 learning objectives
M&B#	Mindsets & Behaviors Statement	Student Learning Objectives
M.1	Belief in development of whole self, including a healthy balance of mental, social/emotional, and physical well-being	Students will be able to identify personal needs
M.2	Sense of acceptance, respect, support, and inclusion for self and others in the school environment	Students will be able to identify personal needs that support themselves and others
B-SMS 9	Personal safety skills	Student will be able to identify the things they need to feel safe
B-SS 8	Advocacy skills for self and others and ability to assert self, when necessary	Students will learn strategies to advocate for the things they need

Materials:	
For Activity: Laminated dog tags, dry erase marker and eraser	For Animal Partner: Hula Hoop, towel, cot, or bed to create a safe and protected space for the animal to "place," Treats if needed

Describe how you will:	
Introduce Lesson Topic/Focus:	Students will explore self-identity, self-confidence, personal needs and wants, personal safety, triggers, and self-care. The students will explore and identify these ideas from the perspective of the animal before comparing and contrasting to themselves.
Communicate the Lesson Objective:	Students will explore and identify things they need to feel safe, secure, nurtured, and challenged. Students will explore and identify things that do harm, set them back, or negatively affect them.
Teach Content:	Lead a discussion on defining personal space, boundaries, and safety.
Practice Content:	Activity guidelines: • Once the animal is in place, ask the students to brainstorm things that belong in the animal's safe and protected space. Write each thing down (or have students write) on one of the laminated dog bones and place them near, around the animal. • Examples of things that may belong inside the safe space: shelter, food/water, treats, love, owner/preferred people, animal friends, belly rubs, toys, fun, safety, collar/leash, veterinary care, etc. • Ask the students to think about the things inside the safe space and compare them to their own personal needs. Is there anything that is different? Anything that should be taken away or added? Next: • Brainstorm things that don't belong in the animal's personal space. Write each thing down (or have students write) on one of the laminated bones and place them outside of the safe space, away from the animal. • Examples of things that may belong outside of the safe space: bad people (mean, abusive, neglectful), bad foods (chocolate, grapes, etc.), loud noises (thunder, hail, gunshots), aggressive animals. Do the same with the things outside of the safe space. What is the same? What could be taken away or added to fit our human needs? Discuss strategies students can utilize to advocate for the things they need and create boundaries for the things they don't need/want.
Involve Animal Partner:	Ask or guide the animal to "place" or rest in the designated area (hula hoop, towel/blanket, cot, etc.)
Assess for Animal Welfare:	The animal should feel comfortable within their safe and protected space. If, at any time they show discomfort, distress, or need to move around, allow space for this. If the animal needs to leave the area, or cannot attend on lesson day, a stuffed animal or picture of your animal can take its place.
Summarize/Close:	Ask for any final thoughts, questions, or connections.

Data Collection Plan	
Participant Data Plan:	
Anticipated number of students:	15–30
Planned length of lesson(s):	45–60 minutes

ASCA Student Standards Data Plan:
Pre/Post Assessment Items: 1. I know what I need to feel safe. 2. I know what makes me feel unsafe. 3. I know what I need to feel connected and supported. 4. I know what makes me feel disconnected and unsupported. 5. I know how to get what I need to feel safe and supported. 6. I know how to say no to things that I don't need or are unsafe. 7. I understand that my wants and needs are different than the wants and needs of others.

Outcome Data Plan:
☒ Achievement: Students can identify positive and negative influences on their personal needs and safety. ☐ Attendance: ☐ Behavior:

Follow-Up Plans
Plans for students who missed the lesson: Students that miss the lesson can attend a make-up lesson. Plan for students who didn't demonstrate mastery: Students who don't engage or fail to demonstrate mastery can be evaluated for small group counseling or one-on-one counseling.

Dog Tag Handout

AASC Lesson Plan 9.6

Lesson Plan Info

AASC Practitioner	Missy Whitsett
AASC Animal Partner	Gus (dog)
Counseling Theory	Cognitive Behavioral Therapy
Lesson Plan Title	**Become a Dog Advocate**
Type of Lesson	☐ Schoolwide ☒ Classroom ☐ Small-Group ☐ Individual Counseling
Target Audience	Grades 6–12
Evidence Base	☒ Best Practice ☐ Action Research ☐ Evidence-Based ☐ Research-Informed

ASCA Student Standards Targeted / Student Learning Objectives

Identify 1–2 student standards relevant for this targeted group and goal		For each of the selected student standards, write 1–2 learning objectives
M&B#	Mindsets & Behaviors Statement	Student Learning Objectives
B LS 1	Critical thinking skills to make informed decisions	Students will learn how to understand canine body language and signals. Students will learn best practice skills to interact with dogs safely and positively.
B-SMS 6	Ability to identify and overcome barriers	Students will discover and identify their fears and triggers in relation to dogs.
B-SMS 7	Effective coping skills	Students will learn strategies to help them feel safer and more confident when interacting with dogs.
B-SMS 9	Personal safety skills	Students will learn best practice skills to help them know when to interact with dogs and when not to interact with dogs.

Materials:

For Activity: Dog Language Posters https://www.doggiedrawings.net/freeposters

Paper and writing/drawing supplies, picture or stuffed animal representing your therapy animal partner, stick or something to treat the animal from a distance

For Animal Partner: Safe and protected space to go to when needed, treats or toys if needed.
It's important to make sure your animal is the right animal for this kind of intervention. If they have a lot of energy, tend to jump or make noise, they may not be a good fit for supporting students with a history of animal trauma.

Describe how you will:	
Introduce Lesson Topic/Focus:	This unit supports students that have a history of adverse animal interactions such as a bite, an attack, or a visually traumatic event. This can also include students who don't have much experience with animals and can also serve as a learning tool for those who do have experience with animals as they learn to support their peers. The lesson is specifically written for a dog but could be adapted to other therapy animals.
Communicate the Lesson Objective:	Students will learn how to read dog body language. Students will learn and practice the proper and safe way to greet a dog. Students will learn and practice the proper and safe way to interact with a dog. Students will explore and identify their fears and triggers. Students will learn and practice strategies that encourage self-discovery, confidence, and self-advocacy. Students will learn how to teach others what they have learned.
Teach Content:	Lesson 1: Journal: This will be an opportunity for students to explore their experiences and feelings as well as keep track of goals and progress. The journal can be used when needed through the activities. Journal Entry 1: Write about your experience with dogs. You may write about positive and negative experiences, fears, anxiousness, excitedness, or any other thoughts you'd like to keep track of. List at least two goals you'd like to set as we become dog advocates. If there is time, encourage students to share out. Lesson 2: Dog Body Language: Go over a dog body language chart (link under Materials.) Have students give examples of personal animals or animals they've seen in similar positions. It's important to also acknowledge exceptions. Ex. Ears back doesn't always mean stress. This can be a great connection to reading human behavior. A chart is linked below. This would also be a great time to create some videos of your animal partner showing signals. If time allows, students could do a game of charades where they pick a behavior, act it out, and try to get other students to guess what they are feeling. Lesson 3: Greeting and interacting: teach and practice how to appropriately interact with a dog. Options: 1. Create a video with your own dog showing someone greeting your dog properly. You can also use one of the free posters linked under Materials. 2. Have a stuffed animal or picture of your dog and have students practice the skills. 3. Divide students into small groups and have them act out greeting a dog. 4. If everyone feels safe, bring in your animal partner and let each student (that wants to) properly greet your dog. 5. It's also important to teach students how to say no to greeting someone's dog, and what do to if a dog comes up to them without their consent.
Practice Content:	Lesson 4: How to teach to others: students can use a poster, video, stuffed animal, or picture to practice teaching others how to properly greet a dog. Option: they could show you a video of them doing this at home with their

(Continued)

	friends or family. Lesson 5: More dog interaction ideas 1. Use an app like My Talking Pet to share videos with students from your dog. They can help you teach concepts, introduce journal entry prompts, send group or personal messages, etc. 2. Take the group to a larger outside space and teach basic brushing skills and play some games like fetch (if space and safety measures allow).
Involve Animal Partner:	The animal partner should be involved whenever the students feel safe enough for them to be there.
Assess for Animal Welfare:	If, at any time they show discomfort, distress, or need to move around, allow space for this. If the animal needs to leave the area, or cannot attend on lesson day, a stuffed animal or picture of your animal can take its place.
Summarize/ Close:	Process with students what they learned. Identify any takeaways from this activity.

Data Collection Plan

Participant Data Plan:

Anticipated number of students:	15–30
Planned length of lesson(s):	4–5 sessions, each 45–60 minutes

ASCA Student Standards Data Plan:

Pre/Post Assessment Items:
1. I know how I feel about dogs.
2. I know what makes me feel unsafe.
3. I know when a dog feels safe.
4. I know when a dog feels unsafe.
5. I know what to do when I feel unsafe around a dog.
6. I know how to properly greet a dog.
7. I know how to properly interact with a dog.
8. I know how to teach others to greet a dog.

Outcome Data Plan:

☒ Achievement: Students can identify canine body signals and react appropriately. Students can demonstrate the appropriate way to greet and interact with a dog and can teach it to others.
☐ Attendance:
☐ Behavior:

Follow-Up Plans

Plans for students who missed lesson: Students will be able to attend a makeup lesson.
Plan for students who didn't demonstrate mastery: Students who don't participate or show a lack of mastery will be evaluated for small group or individual counseling.

AASC Lesson Plan 10.1

Lesson Plan Info		
AASC Practitioner	Crystal Reese	
AASC Animal Partner	Benito	
Counseling Theory	Solution-Focused Therapy	
Lesson Plan Title	**Emotions Hide and Seek**	
Type of Lesson	☐ Schoolwide ☐ Classroom	☒ Small-Group ☒ Individual Counseling
Target Audience	Grades K-3rd	
Evidence Base	☒ Best Practice ☐ Action Research	☐ Evidence-Based ☐ Research-Informed

ASCA Student Standards Targeted		Student Learning Objectives
Identify 1–2 student standards relevant for this targeted group and goal		For each of the selected student standards, write 1–2 learning objectives
M&B#	Mindsets & Behaviors Statement	Student Learning Objectives
M1	Belief in development of whole self, including a healthy balance of mental, social/emotional, and physical well-being	Identify different emotions and behaviors associated with different emotions.
B-SMS 2	Self-discipline and self-control	Identify different coping skills that can be associated with the different emotions.
B-SMS 6	Ability to identify and overcome barriers	

Materials:	
For Activity: Dog Emoji Handout (designed by Vexels)	For Animal Partner: Treats

Describe how you will:	
Introduce Lesson Topic/Focus:	Counselor and student(s) will discuss different emotions and different behaviors that have been difficult to work through as well as the positive emotions and behaviors that the student has been working towards.
Communicate the Lesson Objective:	Student(s) will be able to identity different emotions and behaviors associated with different emotions.
Teach Content:	Share the Dog Emoji handout and discuss the different emotions shown on the handout. Identify different behaviors, positive and negative, that student(s) have when they feel each emotion.
Practice Content:	Have students cut each dog emoji out from the handout. Give each student a dog treat and have them place the treat on one of the emojis – perhaps one that the child has felt recently. Allow the animal to search and find the treat. Together the student(s) and counselor will identify which emotion the animal chose. Discuss when the child has felt that emotion and when the animal partner may have felt that emotion. Key Questions: • When have you felt that emotion? • When do you think the animal partner has felt that emotion? • What do our faces look like when we feel that emotion? • Does your behavior change when you feel that emotion? • Was it a good change or not so good change? • Was this emotion an easy one or a harder one? • How can we act differently when we feel that emotion?
Involve Animal Partner:	Student(s) and counselor will engage the animal to guide the animal to search for treats.
Assess for Animal Welfare:	The animal should have access to water, treats if needed to keep engaged, and a place to take a break. Counselor will assess the animal throughout the activity to make certain the animal is engaged and as well provide a break if needed.
Summarize/ Close:	Process student responses to the key questions.

Data Collection Plan	
Participant Data Plan:	
Anticipated number of students:	1–4 (individual or small group)
Planned length of lesson(s):	30 minutes
ASCA Student Standards Data Plan:	
Pre/Post Assessment Items: 1. Assess number of emotions they can identify before and after activity.	
Outcome Data Plan:	
☐ Academic Achievement: ☐ Attendance: ☒ Behavior: Assess behavior referrals or teacher behavior reports	
Follow-Up Plans	
Plans for students who missed lesson: Individual counseling, if needed. Plan for students who didn't demonstrate mastery: Additional counseling session.	

Dog Emoji Handout

designed by ◈ vexels

AASC Lesson Plan 10.2

Lesson Plan Info		
AASC Practitioner	Kristen Turpin	
AASC Animal Partner	Hank	
Counseling Theory	Cognitive Behavioral Therapy	
Lesson Plan Title	**Many Feelings of Hank**	
Type of Lesson	☐ Schoolwide ☐ Classroom	☐ Small-Group ☒ Individual Counseling
Target Audience	Grades K-3rd	
Evidence Base	☒ Best Practice ☐ Action Research	☐ Evidence-Based ☐ Research-Informed

ASCA Student Standards Targeted		Student Learning Objectives
Identify 1–2 student standards relevant for this targeted group and goal		For each of the selected student standards, write 1–2 learning objectives
M&B#	**Mindsets & Behaviors Statement**	**Student Learning Objectives**
M1	Belief in development of whole self, including a healthy balance of mental, social/emotional, and physical well-being	Identify three different feelings by matching animal partner's feeling to student feelings.
B-SMS 7	Effective coping skills	Describe times when student has those feelings and how student responds behaviorally.

Materials:	
For Activity: Hank's Feelings Chart, sticky notes, paper, pencil	For Animal Partner: Treats

Describe how you will:	
Introduce Lesson Topic/ Focus:	Counselor and student will discuss different feelings associated with the situation that they are working on using the "Hank's Feeling Chart." This chart can be created by taking pictures of the animal partner with 10-15 different expressions (e.g., open mouth, sleeping, yawning, etc.)
Communicate the Lesson Objective:	Student will be able to identify feelings and discuss coping strategies for feelings that may be uncomfortable and discuss strategies to embrace feelings that are uncomfortable.
Teach Content:	Counselor will discuss how students and animals respond in different ways to experiences.
Practice Content:	Student will be given time to look at all the photos and be given sticky notes to put on pictures that they relate to. "Student will be asked to rank each photo (starting with the number 1), rank each photo using a sticky note on the photo you feel the most." After ranking, the student will be given the opportunity to discuss what they would change if they could and what they would like more or less of.
Involve Animal Partner:	Student will also be asked to interpret the feelings Hank is having. Counselor will pick several feelings for Hank and have the student brainstorm how Hank could deal with his feelings.
Assess for Animal Welfare:	The animal should have access to water, treats if needed to keep engaged and a place to "stay." Counselor will assess the animal throughout the activity to make certain the animal is engaged and as well provide a break if needed.
Summarize/ Close:	Lesson extension: Have student draw a human body and an animal body to identify where physically feelings are felt on the human/animal body.

Data Collection Plan	
Participant Data Plan:	
Anticipated number of students:	1 (individual intervention)
Planned length of lesson(s):	30 minutes
ASCA Student Standards Data Plan:	
Pre/Post Assessment Items: 1. Assess number of emotions they can identify before and after activity.	
Outcome Data Plan:	
☐ Academic Achievement: ☐ Attendance: ☒ Behavior: Assess behavior referrals or teacher behavior reports	
Follow-Up Plans	
Plans for students who missed lesson: Individual counseling, if needed. Plan for students who didn't demonstrate mastery: Additional counseling session.	

AASC Lesson Plan 10.3

Lesson Plan Info

AASC Practitioner	Crystal Reese
AASC Animal Partner	Benito
Counseling Theory	Solution-Focused Therapy
Lesson Plan Title	**Paws and Pals**
Type of Lesson	☐ Schoolwide ☐ Classroom	☒ Small-Group ☐ Individual Counseling
Target Audience	Grades 3rd–5th	
Evidence Base	☒ Best Practice ☐ Action Research	☐ Evidence-Based ☐ Research-Informed

ASCA Student Standards Targeted / Student Learning Objectives

ASCA Student Standards Targeted		Student Learning Objectives
Identify 1–2 student standards relevant for this targeted group and goal		For each of the selected student standards, write 1–2 learning objectives
M&B#	Mindsets & Behaviors Statement	Student Learning Objectives
M1	Belief in development of whole self, including a healthy balance of mental, social/emotional, and physical well-being	Students will practice three positive social skills for school, such as sharing and taking turns.
B-SMS 2	Self-discipline and self-control	
B-SMS 6	Ability to identify and overcome barriers	

Materials:

For Activity: Variety of Games – such as Jenga, Connect Four, Tic Tac Toe	For Animal Partner: Water and Treats

Describe how you will:	
Introduce Lesson Topic/Focus:	Review animal, student safety, and group goals.
Communicate the Lesson Objective:	Discuss the lesson objective: Identifying and practicing how to be a positive role model in the school and in the classroom
Teach Content:	• Week 1: Introduction to animal, animal and student safety, goals of the group, and how to greet the animal, (practice greeting animal using a stuffed animal). Show students where the animal likes to be pet, explain how the animal will show if they are happy or not (what signs should you look for). Explain Animal choices and student choices. Set group norms. • Week 2: Activity #1 - How to be a positive role model in the school and in the classroom. What does it look like? What does it look like for the animal partner to show positive behaviors? • Week 3: Activity #2 - Why is it important to practice positive behaviors and why do you think it is important for Hank, our animal partner to practice positive behaviors and what do those look like? How does it help my teacher and school? Let's practice being a good role model- What does this look like in a small group? How can we be positive role models in group, classroom, and in school? • Week 4: Activity #3 - Practicing positive behaviors in small groups: Practice sharing, taking turns, and practicing positive behaviors when hard situations arise like losing. The school counselor may use games to play cooperatively and take turns, i.e., Connect Four, Jenga, or Tic Tac Toe. Use guiding questions during the activity to guide the student; along with that incorporate the animal partner in the activity. Some examples may include, "What does positive behavior look like during lunch time? And how do you think Hank, our canine partner, shows positive behavior during his mealtime?" • Week 5: Activity #4 - Review positive behaviors previously learned in group. Use guiding questions during the activity to guide the student; along with that incorporate the animal partner in the activity. • Week 6: Activity #5 - Review positive behaviors previously learned in group. Assess students: The school counselor should assess students at this point by observing behaviors in group and asking questions (i.e., what are some of the positive behaviors you have learned and what are some of the positive behaviors you have observed here in group from our group members?)
Practice Content:	Practice content such as sharing or taking turns with student and animal partner.
Involve Animal Partner:	Involve the Animal in the games by having the animal take turns in the game and/or involve the animal in to the discussion. Ex: what would it look like if the animal partner did not share.
Assess for Animal Welfare:	Assess animal for welfare and provide breaks if needed.
Summarize/ Close:	Process student responses to the key questions.

Data Collection Plan	
Participant Data Plan:	
Anticipated number of students:	4–6 students
Planned length of lesson(s):	6 weeks
ASCA Student Standards Data Plan:	
Pre/Post Assessment Items: Plan to meet with teachers and/or stakeholders to evaluate the students progress.	
Outcome Data Plan:	
☐ Academic Achievement: ☐ Attendance: ☒ Behavior: Students can list two new positive behaviors they learned in group.	
Follow-Up Plans	
Plans for students who missed lesson: Individual counseling, if needed. Plan for students who didn't demonstrate mastery: Additional counseling session.	

AASC Lesson Plan 10.4

Lesson Plan Info

AASC Practitioner	Elizabeth Kjellstrand Hartwig
AASC Animal Partner	Lilikoi
Counseling Theory	Solution-Focused Therapy
Lesson Plan Title	**Hula Challenge**
Type of Lesson	☐ Schoolwide ☐ Classroom ⫽ ☐ Small-Group ☒ Individual Counseling
Target Audience	Children
Evidence Base	☒ Best Practice ☐ Action Research ⫽ ☐ Evidence-Based ☐ Research-Informed

ASCA Student Standards Targeted / Student Learning Objectives

Identify 1–2 student standards relevant for this targeted group and goal | For each of the selected student standards, write 1–2 learning objectives

M&B#	Mindsets & Behaviors Statement	Student Learning Objectives
M4	Self-confidence in ability to succeed	Explore two alternative solutions to problems.
B-LS 2	Creative approach to learning, tasks, and problem solving	Identify two personal strengths and assets
B-SMS 5	Perseverance to achieve long- and short-term goals	

Materials:

For Activity: hula hoop, strips of construction paper (red, orange & yellow), tape, writing utensil	For Animal Partner: treats

Describe how you will:	
Introduce Lesson Topic/Focus:	Tell the student that the activity will focus on how to overcome challenges by identifying and using personal strengths
Communicate the Lesson Objective:	Discuss how students will be using their problem-solving abilities to help the therapy dog to get through the hoop
Teach Content:	• First, discuss challenges that the animal partner may have (i.e., getting stepped on by people, getting pet when they don't want to be pet). Discuss how the animal partner works through those challenges (i.e., the animal moves out of the way when people look like they might step on the animal). • Next, discuss challenges in the student's life. Write each challenge on a strip of red or orange paper. • After you and the student have come up with several challenges, have the student tape them around the top of a hula hoop. This will make the hula hoop look like a flaming hula hoop.
Practice Content:	• Tell the student that the goal for the activity is to help the animal go through the hoop. Have student problem-solve how to get the animal through the hoop. • Try not to give solutions – let the student work some things out, such as deciding to use treats or having the counselor hold the hoop. • You can say, "Hmm, I wonder what would help the [animal partner] get through the hoop that you haven't tried yet." • You may choose to offer some suggestions if the student has tried, and the animal partner isn't going through the hoop.
Involve Animal Partner:	• If the animal partner chooses to go through the hoop, then give the animal treats and/or positive encouragement. Proceed with the Discussion/Processing Questions. • If the animal partner chooses not to go through the hoop, even with treats and lots of positive encouragement, then that is OK. The animal should not receive any negative feedback or consequence for not going through the hoop. Proceed with the processing questions.
Assess for Animal Welfare:	The AASC practitioner should monitor the animal's behavior for any stress signals throughout the activity. The animal can choose to participate or not in the activity.
Summarize/ Close:	Processing questions: • What was it like to do this activity? • How did you feel when you were trying to help [animal partner]? • How was [animal partner] able to go through the hoop? • What did you do to help [animal partner]? • If the animal partner chose not to go through the hoop, what do you think [animal partner was feeling]? What might be times when we aren't ready for a challenge? • What can you do in your own life to work through challenges? • How could someone else help you work through a challenge?

Data Collection Plan	
Participant Data Plan:	
Anticipated number of students:	1 student (individual counseling)
Planned length of lesson(s):	30 minutes
ASCA Student Standards Data Plan:	
Pre/Post Assessment Items: 1. Student identifies personal strengths before and after activity.	
Outcome Data Plan:	
☐ Academic Achievement: ☐ Attendance: ☒ Behavior: Track behavioral referrals or teacher behavior reports	
Follow-Up Plans	
Plans for students who missed lesson: Reschedule session. Plan for students who didn't demonstrate mastery: Focus on identifying strengths without using the activity	

AASC Lesson Plan 10.5

Lesson Plan Info

AASC Practitioner	Amanda Arriola
AASC Animal Partner	Gracie, the therapy rabbit
Counseling Theory	Cognitive Behavioral Therapy
Lesson Plan Title	**Mindful Moment**
Type of Lesson	☐ Schoolwide ⊠ Small-Group ☐ Classroom ☐ Individual Counseling
Target Audience	Grades 3–5
Evidence Base	⊠ Best Practice ☐ Evidence-Based ☐ Action Research ☐ Research-Informed

ASCA Student Standards Targeted		Student Learning Objectives
Identify 1–2 student standards relevant for this targeted group and goal		For each of the selected student standards, write 1–2 learning objectives
M&B#	Mindsets & Behaviors Statement	Student Learning Objectives
M1	Belief in development of whole self, including a healthy balance of mental, social/emotional, and physical well-being	Develop one mindfulness strategy for reducing anxiety
B-SMS 7	Effective coping skills	

Materials:

For Activity: *I am Peace: A Book of Mindfulness* by Susan Verde	For Animal Partner: treats

Describe how you will:	
Introduce Lesson Topic/Focus:	Write the term "mindfulness" on the board. Allow students to share what they think it means.
Communicate the Lesson Objective:	"Today we are going to practice a mindfulness strategy for reducing feelings of anxiety or stress by using a few of our five senses."
Teach Content:	Define the word "mindfulness" for students. *"Being mindful means to be aware and present in the moment versus focusing on the past or future."* Read the book "I am Peace: A Book of Mindfulness" by Susan Verde.
Practice Content:	• Discuss the strategies that the characters in the book use to relax and practice mindfulness. • Give each student an opportunity to share what helps them to feel relaxed and peaceful during stressful situations.
Involve Animal Partner:	• Ask students to take a few deep breaths and practice paying attention to the present moment and grounding themselves by noticing the therapy rabbit and tracking or naming what the rabbit is doing. The student may notice things like: the rabbit is laying down, the rabbit is twitching its nose, the rabbit's body feels warm, the rabbit's fur is soft, the rabbit is sniffing the carpet. • Have students collaborate to choose a code word or phrase such as "mindful moment." Then whenever the phrase is said, the students will stop what they are doing, take a deep breath, and observe the rabbit for several minutes. • Give students a discussion topic: EX "favorite lunch foods, best vacation spots, preferred subject in school" and prompt them to discuss. • Every so often, the counselor should say the code word or phrase to encourage the students to practice mindfulness. • Allow students to share what they observed. • Repeat 2–3 times by giving a new discussion topic and then saying the code word/phrase again.
Assess for Animal Welfare:	The therapy rabbit should have access to water at all times. The counselor will verbally make note of the animal's body language and demeanor as the activity is unfolding (e.g., "The rabbit's body is relaxed and he/she is sprawled out, he/she is showing us that they are feeling happy").
Summarize/ Close:	Processing questions: • What did it feel like to place all of your attention on the rabbit? • How does your body feel when you focus on the present moment instead of thinking about the past or worrying about the future? -Were you able to bring your attention back to the rabbit when your mind wandered? • What are other things you can notice in your environment at school or at home?

Data Collection Plan	
Participant Data Plan:	
Anticipated number of students:	5–6 students
Planned length of lesson(s):	45 minutes
ASCA Student Standards Data Plan:	

Pre/Post Assessment Items:
1. I understand what it means to be mindful.
2. I know strategies to use when I am feeling anxious or stressed.

Outcome Data Plan:

☒ Academic Achievement: The counselor will compare benchmark test scores for the students before and after participating in eight small group sessions
☐ Attendance:
☐ Behavior:

Follow-Up Plans

Plans for students who missed the lesson: The student will do a make-up session with the counselor prior to the start of the next group session.
Plan for students who didn't demonstrate mastery: The counselor will review the concepts of mindfulness and staying present with students in a follow-up session.

AASC Lesson Plan 11.1

Lesson Plan Info

AASC Practitioner	Jennifer Greene-Rooks
AASC Animal Partner	Conway
Counseling Theory	Adlerian Therapy
Lesson Plan Title	**Our Families**
Type of Lesson	☐ Schoolwide ☒ Classroom ☒ Small-Group ☐ Individual Counseling
Target Audience	Students in grades 6–12
Evidence Base	☒ Best Practice ☐ Action Research ☐ Evidence-Based ☐ Research-Informed

ASCA Student Standards Targeted / Student Learning Objectives

ASCA Student Standards Targeted		Student Learning Objectives
Identify 1–2 student standards relevant for this targeted group and goal		For each of the selected student standards, write 1–2 learning objectives
M&B#	Mindsets & Behaviors Statement	Student Learning Objectives
M2	Sense of acceptance, respect, support, and inclusion for self and others in the school environment	Identify 2 similarities and 2 differences in families.
M4	Self-confidence in ability to succeed	Use 1 affirming response to a peer.

Materials:

For Activity: *The Family Book* by Todd Parr, paper, drawing and coloring materials, magazines, and other pictures representative of varieties of families, scissors, glue	For Animal Partner: N/A

Describe how you will:	
Introduce Lesson Topic/Focus:	School counselor will share that this lesson is about recognizing that families can have similarities and differences. Since people are motivated by a need to belong, families have a big impact on each child.
Communicate the Lesson Objective:	The lesson objectives are to explore similarities and differences with peers and the animal partner, and practice using an affirming response, such as "Your family is unique and special."
Teach Content:	• Read The Family Book by Todd Parr • Discuss all the ways families are different and the same including our 4-legged, furry, winged, and feathered family members • Present the concept of the Crucial Cs
Practice Content:	Family Picture Creation - Students will use materials to create a picture of their family. They can draw and color their family or create a collage. The school counselor will share the animal partner's picture with the group. Students can share who is a part of their family (people and animals) and what makes their family special. Crucial Cs – It's important for children to feel connected, capable, that they count, and that they have courage to feel stable and secure in themselves and in relationships with others. Explore how animals help us incorporate the Crucial Cs. Then discuss how families do or don't support the Crucial Cs and ways to work on building Crucial Cs.
Involve Animal Partner:	We will discuss how we view animals in our family (e.g., outdoor pets or indoor family members). We will explore how pets come to be a part of our family. The school counselor can draw a picture of the animal partner's family, including humans and other pets in the family.
Assess for Animal Welfare:	Students will be taught about how the animal likes to be greeted and pet and about the animal's stress signals. The animal can choose to participate or not in each activity.
Summarize/ Close:	School counselor will facilitate the following processing questions: • What were some of the ways that the families in the book were the same? • In what ways were the families in the book different from each other? • What makes your family special? • What would you like to share about your family? • How does your family support your Crucial Cs?

Data Collection Plan	
Participant Data Plan:	
Anticipated number of students:	6–8 students or classroom
Planned length of lesson(s):	30–45 minutes
ASCA Student Standards Data Plan:	
Pre/Post Assessment Items: 1. I can name two ways in which families are similar and different.	
Outcome Data Plan:	
☐ Academic Achievement: ☐ Attendance: ☒ Behavior: School counselor will use teacher behavior reports to track behavior.	

Follow-Up Plans

Plans for students who missed lesson: Students can miss this lesson and participate in the next lesson,
Plan for students who didn't demonstrate mastery: Students can receive individual counseling sessions, if needed.

AASC Lesson Plan 11.2

Lesson Plan Info			
AASC Practitioner	Jennifer Greene-Rooks		
AASC Animal Partner	Conway		
Counseling Theory	Adlerian Therapy		
Lesson Plan Title	**Affirming Each Other**		
Type of Lesson	☐ Schoolwide ☒ Classroom	☒ Small-Group ☐ Individual Counseling	
Target Audience	Students in grades 6–12		
Evidence Base	☒ Best Practice ☐ Action Research	☐ Evidence-Based ☐ Research-Informed	

ASCA Student Standards Targeted		Student Learning Objectives
Identify 1–2 student standards relevant for this targeted group and goal		For each of the selected student standards, write 1–2 learning objectives
M&B#	**Mindsets & Behaviors Statement**	**Student Learning Objectives**
M2	Sense of acceptance, respect, support, and inclusion for self and others in the school environment	Demonstrate one method for affirming self or a peer related to self-expression.

Materials:	
For Activity: You can use the following picture books: • *The Sissy Duckling* by Harvey Fierstein • *The Paper Bag Princess* by Robert Munsch • *I Am Jazz* by Jessica Herthel and Jazz Jennings • *Julián is a Mermaid* by Jessica Love	For Animal Partner: bandanas, capes, or costumes that represent various ways to express gender.

Describe how you will:	
Introduce Lesson Topic/Focus:	This lesson is designed to affirm the beautiful diversity of all students with a focus on acceptance of those whose gender expression and/or gender identity may be outside the norm.
Communicate the Lesson Objective:	The lesson is to explore different ways to express gender.
Teach Content:	Read one or more books to group or class.
Practice Content:	Dress school counselor's animal partner in various bandanas or outfits that affirm or challenge gendered expectations. Discuss how the books affirm or challenge expectations of gender. Discuss the multiple ways one can express or identify as gendered. Discuss the ways we or people we know challenge gender stereotypes. In this activity, children can explore their strengths and feelings of inferiority related to self-expression. Children will also learn how to develop skills for affirming others and themselves.
Involve Animal Partner:	Animal partner can participate by wearing different bandanas or outfits, depending on their enjoyment of wearing items, to help children explore ideas about gender expression.
Assess for Animal Welfare:	Students will be taught about how the animal likes to be greeted and pet and the animal's stress signals. The animal can choose to participate or not in each activity.
Summarize/ Close:	School counselor will facilitate the following processing questions: • What are some of the ways that we see people behaving or dressing based on gender? • Did the books challenge the way we think about gender? • Did the books or characters affirm how we feel about ourselves or others? • Do the clothes that [animal partner] wears change who they are? Do the clothes change their gender? Does [animal partner] seem happy or content in each outfit? • What clothes do you like to wear, or things do you like to do, that may be different from others (this could be gendered or not)? • How can we make space for and affirm others when their choices may be different from ours? • How can we accept and affirm ourselves?

Data Collection Plan	
Participant Data Plan:	
Anticipated number of students:	4–6 students or classroom
Planned length of lesson(s):	30–45 minutes
ASCA Student Standards Data Plan:	
Pre/Post Assessment Items: 1. I know how to affirm others for how they choose to express themselves.	
Outcome Data Plan:	
☐ Academic Achievement: ☐ Attendance: ☒ Behavior: School counselor will use teacher behavior reports to track behavior.	
Follow-Up Plans	
Plans for students who missed lesson: Students can miss this lesson and participate in the next lesson, Plan for students who didn't demonstrate mastery: Students can receive individual counseling sessions, if needed.	

AASC Lesson Plan 11.3

AASC Practitioner	Wanda Montemayor
AASC Animal Partner	Chango
Counseling Theory	Solution-Focused Therapy
Lesson Plan Title	**Bill of Rights**
Type of Lesson	☐ Schoolwide ☒ Small-Group ☐ Classroom ☐ Individual Counseling
Target Audience	Students in grades 6–12
Evidence Base	☒ Best Practice ☐ Evidence-Based ☐ Action Research ☐ Research-Informed

ASCA Student Standards Targeted		Student Learning Objectives
Identify 1–2 student standards relevant for this targeted group and goal		For each of the selected student standards, write 1–2 learning objectives
M&B#	**Mindsets & Behaviors Statement**	**Student Learning Objectives**
M1	Belief in development of whole self, including a healthy balance of mental, social/emotional, and physical well-being	Become aware of boundaries and be able to articulate one.
		Identify 2 rights that they have at this stage in their life

Materials:	
For Activity: paper, colors, writing utensil	For Animal Partner: animal partner Bill of Rights

Describe how you will:	
Introduce Lesson Topic/Focus:	School counselor will ask group members if they know what the Constitutional Bill of Rights is, and if they know of any other kinds of Bill of Rights.
Communicate the Lesson Objective:	Everybody has rights, as do others, that no one else can take away.
Teach Content:	School counselor will describe the purpose of a Bill of Rights. They will provide examples of Bill of Rights statements: • I have the right to say what I want to say. • I have the right to choose my own friends. • I have the right to say no and set boundaries. • I have the right to love who I want to love. • I have the right to choose my own wardrobe. • I have the right to choose my own food.
Practice Content:	Students will create their own Bill of Rights by writing it out on paper. Students can use colors to draw pictures on their Bill of Rights or just have the statements.
Involve Animal Partner:	School counselor will share an example of the Canine Partners' Bill of Rights. Counselor should have the Canine Partners' Bill of Rights printed and available to compare with what the students created. Discuss why anyone's rights, including animals, would be different from others' rights.
Assess for Animal Welfare:	Students will be taught about how the animal likes to be greeted and pet and about the animal's stress signals. The animal can choose to participate or not in each activity.
Summarize/Close:	School counselor will facilitate a discussion of the similarities and differences among group members' Bill of Rights; allow students to identify statements that are most important to them. Group members can also discuss when it might be easy or challenging to accept or adhere to a person's Bill of Rights.

Data Collection Plan	
Participant Data Plan:	
Anticipated number of students:	6 students
Planned length of lesson(s):	30–45 minutes
ASCA Student Standards Data Plan:	
Pre/Post Assessment Items: 1. I know the purpose of a Bill of Rights.	
Outcome Data Plan:	
☐ Academic Achievement: ☐ Attendance: ☒ Behavior: School counselor will use teacher behavior reports to track behavior.	
Follow-Up Plans	
Plans for students who missed lesson: Students can contribute to Bill of Rights at next session. Plan for students who didn't demonstrate mastery: Students can receive individual counseling sessions, if needed.	

AASC Lesson Plan 11.4

Lesson Plan Info

AASC Practitioner	Wanda Montemayor
AASC Animal Partner	Chango
Counseling Theory	Solution-Focused Therapy
Lesson Plan Title	**True Colors Group**
Type of Lesson	☐ Schoolwide ☒ Small-Group ☐ Classroom ☐ Individual Counseling
Target Audience	Students in grades 6–12
Evidence Base	☒ Best Practice ☐ Evidence-Based ☐ Action Research ☐ Research-Informed

ASCA Student Standards Targeted		Student Learning Objectives
Identify 1–2 student standards relevant for this targeted group and goal		For each of the selected student standards, write 1–2 learning objectives
M&B#	**Mindsets & Behaviors Statement**	**Student Learning Objectives**
M2	Sense of acceptance, respect, support, and inclusion for self and others in the school environment	Identify two ways to create safe space for ourselves and others on campus

Materials:

For Activity: poster paper, magazines, scissors, markers, glue	For Animal Partner: printed image of animal for poster

Describe how you will:	
Introduce Lesson Topic/Focus:	School counselor will start the group by having each member introduce themselves and their pronouns, explain the materials used, and have an example of a completed project.
Communicate the Lesson Objective:	Understand and celebrate diversity and inclusivity, with a focus on safety.
Teach Content:	The five-week lesson plan is provided below.
Practice Content:	• Week 1 – Highs and Lows: introductions with names and pronouns, review how animal partner likes to be pet and stress signals for animal partner, group members share one positive and one negative experience they had over the past week; group sets group norms • Week 2 – What Would An Ally Do: group members will discuss and define what an ally is; students will be given scenarios related to people being unkind to animal partner; students will role play how to be an ally in those situations and advocate for the animal partner; students will then be given scenarios to role play how to be an ally when others are unkind to people who are different • Week 3 – Bully Free Zone: group members will create posters that create awareness about bullying and bully free areas in school; the posters can be from the perspective of the animal partner, such as "Chango says, Stand Up, Stand Strong, and Stand Together!" or "Kind People Are My Kind of People" • Week 4 – Gender Free Group: students play a game in which they practice not using gendered terms in group; student explore how often gender terms are used. • Week 5 – Celebrating Differences: students create a collage of how they are different from their peers; students share their differences and how those differences make them special; students discuss what they have learned from the group and what they will take away from this group experience; animal partner provides each student with a special "pawsitive" note of the strengths and growth they have noticed in each student
Involve Animal Partner:	The animal partner is involved in the activities for all five sessions.
Assess for Animal Welfare:	Students will be taught about how the animal likes to be greeted and pet and also about the animal's stress signals. The animal can choose to participate or not in each activity.
Summarize/ Close:	The Week 5 activity provides guidance on the final group session.

Data Collection Plan	
Participant Data Plan:	
Anticipated number of students:	6 students
Planned length of lesson(s):	5 weeks
ASCA Student Standards Data Plan:	

Pre/Post Assessment Items:
1. I understand what an ally is.
2. I know how to advocate for others.

Outcome Data Plan:

☐ Academic Achievement:
☐ Attendance:
☒ Behavior: School counselor will use teacher behavior reports to track behavior.

Follow-Up Plans

Plans for students who missed lesson: Students can learn what we covered from a peer.
Plan for students who didn't demonstrate mastery: Students can receive individual counseling sessions, if needed.

AASC Lesson Plan 12.1

ASCA Student Standards Targeted		Student Learning Objectives
M&B#	Mindsets & Behaviors Statement	Student Learning Objectives
M4	Self confidence in ability to succeed	Identify three goals for working as a future AASC team
B-SMS 5	Perseverance to achieve long- and short-term goals	

Materials:	
For Activity: 1 sheet of drawing paper, colors (markers, crayons, or oil pastels)	For Animal Partner: dog-safe tempura paint in their favorite color

Describe how you will:	
Introduce Lesson Topic/Focus:	For this activity, we will be exploring your goals for becoming an AASC team.
Communicate the Lesson Objective:	The purpose of this activity is to identify three future goals for working as an AASC team.
Teach Content:	For the first part of this activity, make a list of knowledge, skills, and attitudes that you and your animal partner have for becoming an AASC team. Next, make a list of ways that you would like to make a difference in children's lives as an AASC team.
Practice Content:	For the next part of the activity, draw a picture of you and your animal partner as a future AASC team working together in a school. Add words or symbols to show how you would apply AASC competencies in the school. Write your names at the top of the page.
Involve Animal Partner:	Use the dog-safe paint to add your animal partner's paw print to the picture. Wash their paw with a wet cloth after applying their paw print to the paper.
Assess for Animal Welfare:	If the animal partner does not want paint on their paws, they can choose to not participate.
Summarize/ Close:	Hang your Future AASC Team picture somewhere where you can see it on a regular basis. This could be in your counseling office, classroom, or even at home in your room or kitchen. When you look at this picture, you can think about the steps you can take to achieve this goal.

Data Collection Plan	
Participant Data Plan:	
Anticipated number of students:	1 practitioner (or 10-15 practitioners in an AASC training)
Planned length of lesson(s):	45 minutes

ASCA Student Standards Data Plan:

Pre/Post Assessment Items:
Practitioner identifies AASC competencies before and after the activity.

Outcome Data Plan:

☐ Academic Achievement:
☐ Attendance:
☒ Behavior: Track steps taken to achieve goal of becoming an AASC team.

Follow-Up Plans

Plans for students who missed lesson: Practitioners can complete this activity on their own at any time. Plan for students who didn't demonstrate mastery: Talk to another AASC team and explore ways to get involved in this field.

Index

AASC Animal Health Screening Form 5, 20, 188
AASC Competencies 5–6, 16, 47–60, 64–65, 74, 196–199
AASC Family Survey 85–86, 201
AASC Presentation Slides 5, 22, 189–195
AASC Program Request Form 5, 20, 184–185
AASC Skills Checklist 6, 52, 71, 74–75, 173–174, 200–202
AASC Training Verification Form 5, 20, 186–187
Adlerian therapy: lesson plans 243, 246, 282, 285
American Counseling Association (ACA) 16, 47–48, 50, 83, 116
American School Counselor Association (ASCA) 1–2, 5–6, 14, 98; domains 100–101, 108; national model i, 149–150; position statements 164–165, 168, 171; student standards 102–103, 107–108, 138, 150, 153
Anderson, K. L. 20, 77, 83, 157
animal-assisted activities (AAE) 4, 27, 33
animal-assisted counseling (AAC) 1, 4, 47, 62, 116, 166
animal-assisted education (AAE) 4, 13
animal-assisted interventions (AAI) 1, 4, 47, 119, 174; assessment 102, 106; choosing an animal partner 34, 37; getting school approval 12, 18; training 61–62, 67–68
animal welfare 3, 5, 7, 64, 172–173, 182; AASC Training Verification Form 187; assessment of 103; canine welfare 28; competencies 48, 50–53, 56–59, 62, 196–199; critter welfare 30–36, 40; in schools 15–16, 18, 89, 94, 138–139; training 62–64, 66–67, 73
ASCA Ethical Standards 8, 14–15, 37, 49–52, 84–85, 126–127; assessment 106, 111; interventions 138–139, 154; student-affirming 165, 168, 172; training 64, 78
ASCA Professional Standards and Competencies 8, 14–15, 125, 138, 153–154; assessment 99, 105–106, 108; competencies 48–52, 57–58; preparing school 84–85; student-affirming 165, 167; training 64, 79
assessment 1–9, 83, 98–113, 173, 182; choosing an animal partner 26, 28, 30–31, 37; competencies 48,

52, 54, 59, 196–199; getting school approval 15–16, 20; interventions 153, 157; theoretical applications 125, 131; training 63–64, 66–67, 71–73, 75
attitudes: competencies 5, 16, 47–60, 172, 182, 199; positive 85, 137–138; training 62, 64–66, 73–74, 78–79
Austin–Main, J. 125

Berg, I. K. 120
Berk, M. S. 117, 119
Binfet, J. T. 18, 52, 69, 139, 146
Brelsford, V. L. 112, 161, 174
Bruneau, L. 22, 146

Canine Good Citizen 28, 68–69
caregivers 6, 122, 164, 168, 173, 203; assessment 105, 111, 113; getting school approval 10–11, 15, 17, 19, 21; interventions 149, 152, 155, 158–161; preparing school 83–86, 89, 96; training 68, 74; see also parents
cat 53, 69, 166; choosing an animal partner 5, 26, 30, 34–36, 43, 172
Chandler, C. K. 37, 137, 146, 150–151, 153; cognitive-behavioral therapy 116, 119; getting school approval 12, 15–21; solution-focused therapy 122; training 62–63, 69
child-centered play therapy (CCPT) 123–125; lesson plans 234; see also person–centered therapy
choice theory: lesson plan 260
classroom 5, 7; interventions 67, 109, 135–147, 153, 173, 182; lesson plans: Adlerian 282, 285; choice 260; cognitive-behavioral therapy 223, 225, 249, 264; solution-focused therapy 203, 209; student-affirming 167–170
cognitive-behavioral therapy (CBT) 6, 116–120, 126, 173, 198; cognitive-behavioral play therapy (CBPT) 117, 126; lesson plans: classroom 223, 225, 249, 264; individual 218, 221, 237, 271; schoolwide 225, 253; small–group 279

competencies 3, 5–6, 15–16, 47–60, 83, 182; animal-assisted therapy in counseling 16, 115; attitudes 51, 56, 73, 199; gender–affirming 163; knowledge 50–53, 68, 71, 196–197; skills 51, 53–55, 71, 74, 197–198; training 61, 64–66, 68, 172–173
critter 49, 68, 91, 166; choosing an animal partner 26, 29–31, 38, 40, 42

De Jong, P. 120
dialectical behavior therapy 215
Dimmitt, C. 98–99, 102, 105
district 67, 107, 143–144, 168; getting approval i, 1, 3, 5, 10–25; preparing school 83, 85, 92
diversity 7–8, 146, 182; assessment 111–112; competencies 48, 52–53, 58–59, 197; considerations 22, 41, 96, 130–131, 158–161; lesson plans 285, 291; student-affirming 163, 167–170, 173; training 65, 71–72, 78–79
Drewes, A. A. 117–118, 127

elementary 13, 17, 38–39, 43, 143; assessment 105, 109; lesson plans 203, 206, 212; student-affirming 167–168; training 74–77

Fine, A. H. 48
Flom, B. L. 31, 37–38
Flynn, E. 31, 37–34
Friesen, L. 13–14, 137, 151

Gee, N. R. 138
Grové, C. 31, 40, 137–138, 159
group 4–5, 51, 63, 173, 175; assessment 102, 105, 109, 111; interventions 7, 138, 142, 144, 149–161; lesson plans: Adlerian 282, 285; cognitive-behavioral 279; dialectical behavioral therapy 215; solution-focused 206, 212, 228, 267, 273, 288, 291; preparing school 92, 94; student-affirming 166–170; theoretical applications 116, 125–127; tier 2 2, 136; training 67, 74–75
guinea pig 5, 69, 111, 159, 172; choosing an animal partner 26, 30–31, 33–34, 37, 43; lesson plans 212, 228

Hartwig, E. K.: canine–assisted interventions 18, 52, 69, 146; lesson plans 231, 276, 294; measurable standards 15–16, 37, 48, 63–64, 83; solution-focused play therapy 120–122, 129–130
high school 13, 39–40, 76–77, 102, 157, 168

individual: counseling 7, 94, 102, 108, 149–161, 173; lesson plans: child-centered play therapy 234; cognitive-behavioral 218, 221, 237, 271; solution-focused 212, 231, 240, 267, 276

informed consent 116, 126, 139, 170; AASC Training Verification Form 186–187; competencies 52–54, 196–198; getting school approval 15, 17, 19, 21, 23; preparing school 82, 89, 94, 96; training 63, 66, 71, 73, 79
insurance 19, 85, 96, 179; AASC Training Verification Form 186–187; competencies 52, 198
International Association of Human-Animal Interaction Organizations (IAHAIO) 4, 18, 47

Jalongo, M. R. 17, 23, 37–38, 75
Jones, M. G. 27, 58

Kim, J. S. 120, 122, 131
Kimberly Pruitt, M. 13–14
Knell, S. M. 117–119
knowledge 1, 5–7, 153, 164, 172–174, 182; AASC Program Request Form 184; AASC Training Verification Form 186–187; assessment 100, 111; competencies 47–60, 196–199; getting school approval 16, 20; preparing school 83, 89; theoretical applications 125, 132; training 64–79
Knowles, C. 37–38, 40–42, 112

Landreth, G. L. 72, 79, 116, 123, 125, 131
Lange, A. 120, 146–147, 169
leash 27, 60, 70–71, 91–92, 152
Leos, R. A. 11, 13
lesson plan 102–105, 138, 153, 202–295
LGBTQIA+ see queer
Lick, C. 33–34
Ludy-Dobson, C. R. 41, 78–79

Meints, K. 57, 157, 174
middle school 39, 77, 111, 169, 176–177
Molnár, M. 31–32
multi-tiered system of support (MTSS) 1, 7, 136–137, 150–151

Ng, Z. 12, 18, 63–64, 70, 79

Olson, M. R. 20, 77, 83, 157

parents 100, 107, 159, 163, 169; see also caregivers
Parish-Plass, N. 41, 58–59
Perry, B. D. 41, 78–79
person-centered therapy (PCT) 6, 115, 123–125; see also child-centered play therapy
Pet Partners 16, 35, 69
Pichot, T. 123
play therapy 59, 75, 173; lesson plans 234, 294; theoretical applications 115–121, 123–125, 127
primary–level schools 7–8, 108–109, 127–128, 167–168,

172–173; competencies 56–58; interventions 37–39, 139–142, 153–154; lesson plans 231, 234, 237; training 75–76; *see also* elementary

principal 14, 20, 85, 95–96, 110; signature 185, 187

queer 131, 163–169, 171

rabbit 40, 49, 56, 69, 109–110, 158; choosing an animal partner 5, 26, 30–33; lesson plans 203–204, 223, 279–280

Ray, D. C. 116, 122, 123, 125, 127

Rogers, C. R. 123, 125

Sachser, N. 33–34

schoolwide 92, 102, 150, 160, 173, 182; interventions 2, 5, 7, 67, 135–147; lesson plans 225, 243, 246, 253

Schott, E. 116

secondary–level schools 6–8, 58, 172–173; assessment 101, 107, 109—111; interventions 39–40, 143–146, 156–158; lesson plans 203, 206, 212, 240; theoretical applications 115, 128–129; training 74, 76–77; student-affirming 164, 166, 168–170; Shelby, J. S. 117, 119

Sink, C. A. 2, 99, 112, 136

skills 5–6, 18–19, 137; AASC Skills Checklist 173–174, 200–202; assessment 101, 105–106; Canine Good Citizen 28, 68–69; competencies 83, 47–60, 196–199; coping 37, 108, 116, 135, 150, 155; getting school approval 13, 15; interventions 111, 142, 144, 152–157; relationship-building 141, 151; social 33, 35, 37–42, 83–85; student-affirming 167–170, 172; theoretical applications 119–120; training 16, 61–81

solution-focused therapy 50, 54, 120–123, 126, 173; lesson plans: classroom 203, 209; individual 212, 231, 240, 267, 276; small–group 206, 212, 228, 267, 273, 288, 291; solution-focused play therapy (SFPT) 120, 121

Stewart, L. A. 16, 47, 49–52, 64, 116

Studer, J. R. 98–99, 105, 112

Suba–Bokodi, É. 31–33, 38

superintendent 98

supervision 6–7, 37, 139, 152, 172–174, 182; AASC Program Request Form 184; AASC Training Verification Form 186–187; competencies 47–53, 57–58, 196; getting school approval 14–18, 20–21; preparing school 83; training 61–66, 71–74

Talley, L. P. 125, 136

Taylor, E. R. 120, 122

Tedeschi, P. 42, 58

theory 6, 53, 115–132, 173, 182; assessment 102, 109; biophilia 37; competencies 54, 198, 199; training 65, 71, 73

tier 1 2, 7, 19, 166; interventions 135–147, 150–151

tier 2 2, 7, 18, 166; interventions 149–161; tier 3 2, 19, 151, 166

Tomaszewska, K. 35, 38

training 1–9, 61–80, 172–175, 182; AASC Program Request Form 184–185; AASC Training Verification Form 186–187; assessment 125, 130; choosing an animal partner 27–29, 37, 39–40; competencies 48–50, 52–53, 58, 196; getting school approval 10–11, 14–16, 18–23; interventions 138, 146, 159, 164; preparing school 83, 85–86, 89, 96

transgender 163–164, 166; transgender and gender non-conforming (TGNC) 164

trauma 13, 63, 115

trauma-informed 7–8; considerations for: animal partners 41–42; assessment 111–112; competencies 48, 51, 58–59; interventions 146, 157–158; schools 22, 96; student–affirming services 170–171; theories 130–131; training 78–79

Trevathan-Minnis, M. 47

VonLintel, J. 22, 146

Walsh, F. 14, 150

Webb, L. D. 105, 137

Weinbaum, R. K. 13–14

Zents, C. E. 13–14, 20, 152, 157, 159

For Product Safety Concerns and Information please contact our EU
representative GPSR@taylorandfrancis.com
Taylor & Francis Verlag GmbH, Kaufingerstraße 24, 80331 München, Germany